Ketogenic Diet for Beginners 2020

The Complete 5 Book Compilation Including

Keto Diet for Rapid Weight Loss, Keto Diet After 50, Intermittent Fasting for Women, Vagus Nerve and Autophagy

PUBLISHED BY: Mark Evans & Kate Sinclair
© Copyright 2020 - All rights reserved.

The content contained within this book may not be reproduced, duplicated or transmitted without direct written permission from the author or the publisher.

Under no circumstances will any blame or legal responsibility be held against the publisher, or author, for any damages, reparation, or monetary loss due to the information contained within this book. Either directly or indirectly.

Legal Notice:

This book is copyright protected. This book is only for personal use. You cannot amend, distribute, sell, use, quote or paraphrase any part, or the content within this book, without the consent of the author or publisher.

Disclaimer Notice:

Please note the information contained within this document is for educational and entertainment purposes only. All effort has been executed to present accurate, up to date, and reliable, complete information. No warranties of any kind are declared or implied. Readers acknowledge that the author is not engaging in the rendering of legal, financial, medical or professional advice. The content within this book has been derived from various sources. Please consult a licensed professional before attempting any techniques outlined in this book.

By reading this document, the reader agrees that under no circumstances is the author responsible for any losses, direct or indirect, which are incurred as a result of the use of information contained within this document, including, but not limited to, — errors, omissions, or inaccuracies

Table of contents

Book #1: Ketogenic Diet 1

Introduction 3

Chapter 1: Introducing the Ketogenic Diet 5

Chapter 2: Keto Diet for Weight Loss 7

Chapter 3: Healing with the Keto Diet 11

Chapter 4: Kick Starting Your Ketosis 17

Chapter 5: Keto Diet Meal Plans 21

Chapter 6: Recommended Keto Recipes 33

Chapter 7: Keto Shopping List 200

Closing 202

Book #2: Keto Diet After 50-*Keto for Seniors* 203

Introduction 205

Chapter 1: How the Ketogenic Diet Works 207

Chapter 2: Benefits of Going on a Ketogenic Diet 209

Chapter 3: Ketogenic Diet for People Over 50 212

Chapter 4: Ketogenic Diet FAQs 214

Chapter 5: Primary Keto Guidelines – the Do's and Don'ts of Keto Over 50 216

Chapter 6: Keto Side Effects and How to Solve Them 218

Chapter 7: Additional Things That Can Help 222

Chapter 8: Keto Grocery List 224

Chapter 9: Simple Keto Recipes 229

Chapter 10: 30-Day Ketogenic Diet Meal Plan 312

Conclusion 331

Book #3: Intermittent Fasting for Women 333

Introduction 335

The Basics About Intermittent Fasting 337

The Science on Why Intermittent Fasting IS more than just weight loss 345

Benefits of Intermittent Fasting 354
What Women Need to Watch Out For 370
Addressing Concerns About Intermittent Fasting 374
Individuals That Should Not Do Intermittent Fasting 378
Why Intermittent Fasting Is Better Than Other Diets 379
The Different Methods of Intermittent Fasting and How Each Can Benefit You 381
The Food and Drink Guide for Intermittent Fasting 389
Common Mistakes and How to Fix Them 393
Getting Started with Intermittent Fasting 396
Doing Intermittent Fasting with a Ketogenic Diet 399
Intermittent Fasting Shopping List 401
Intermittent Fasting Recipes and Meal Plans 405
Conclusion 422

Book #4: Autophagy Secrets 425

Introduction 427
Chapter 1: What is Autophagy? 428
Chapter 2: Understanding Its Pros and Cons 431
Chapter 3: Ten Ways to Induce Autophagy 437
Chapter 4: Activating Autophagy through Fasting 445
Chapter 5: Intermittent Fasting 448
Chapter 6: The Different Stages of Fasting 452
Chapter 7: Different Ways to do Intermittent Fasting 456
Chapter 8: Long Term Fasts vs. Short Term Fasts 460
Chapter 9: The Effect of Ketogenic Diets 468
Chapter 10: Keto Meal Plan to Boost Autophagy 475
Chapter 11: The Exercise-Autophagy Connection 483
Chapter 12: Deep Sleep and Autophagy 490
Chapter 13: Time Restricted Feeding 493
Chapter 14: Heat Exposure 497
Chapter 15: Hot and Cold Therapy 502
Conclusion 504

Book #5: Vagus Nerve Unlocked ... 505

Introduction ... 507

PART 1: The Basics ... 509

Chapter 1: The Vagus Nerve: A Tale of Many Cities ... 510

Chapter 2: Fighting the Undefined: The Secret Powers of the Vagus Nerve ... 515

Chapter 3: Is your Vagus Nerve healthy? ... 527

Chapter 4: Jacking up the Vagus Nerve ... 532

PART 2: The Vagus Nerve in your Daily Life ... 542

Chapter 5: Vagus Nerve and Meditation: An Ancient Combination for Modern Life ... 543

Chapter 6: Breathing, the Foundation of Life ... 551

Chapter 7: Breath-Centric Stimulation ... 555

Chapter 8: For that Quick Pick-Me-Up ... 559

PART 3: The Future of Vagus Nerve Stimulation ... 561

Chapter 9: The Vagus Nerve Versus the World ... 562

Chapter 10: New Devices for New Techniques ... 570

CHAPTER 11: Paying It Forward ... 572

Conclusion ... 576

Thank you ... 579

Book #1

Ketogenic Diet

The 30-Day Plan for Healthy Rapid Weight loss, Reverse Diseases, and Boost Brain Function

With Tips on Intermittent Fasting, Autophagy, Keto Meal Prep & Keto Bread Recipes

Introduction

My journey and practice of the ketogenic diet began almost a decade ago when I was much younger. My doctor diagnosed me with type 2 diabetes after one of many other checkups that I have had.

I would have to be honest.

I was young back then (not to mention naïve) and I didn't really have a complete understanding of the gravity of the situation. In short I didn't really know how I should feel about it.

Sure it's diabetes but in my mind it was just another thing that I had to manage. I already had hypertension at such a young age (talk about stress as a young up and coming executive).

On top of that I was overweight also. I guess all of these conditions combined were the perfect recipe for the latest diagnosis that my doctor gave me back then. In my mind I was given a bunch of pills—okay, I can manage that—and then there was this list of foods I shouldn't eat.

Of course the list was largely ignored and I thought the meds were enough to get by. Oh and one more thing, my doctor told me that I may have had diabetes since my late teens—well, I gained some weight back then.

I was overweight but not exactly obese.

So, my doctor suggested that I go on this weight loss regimen and so I went. I worked with a fitness coach to help me lose weight and I thought that I was doing enough to manage my condition.

I was taking my pills and doing these exercises religiously. I should be fine, right?

But I wasn't.

You see, diabetes has a nasty habit of creeping up on you—well, at least according to my experience. The bad news was that I didn't show up for my follow up appointments so I didn't really know if I showed any actual progress or not.

It was about a few months later when I came back. I lost weight and I thought that I had done enough. But lo and behold, after another checkup and the usual blood tests my doctor confirmed that I still had diabetes.

I was totally devastated.

All my hard work in the gym counted for nothing.

Here's what I can tell you. The most common misconception about this kind of medical condition is that it is something that is easy to manage. I realized that in that moment.

I thought I was doing great but I quickly realized that losing weight was only a part of the solution. Sure it helped a bit but there were more factors involved.

Exercising also helped but then again it wasn't the cure all for diabetes. I quickly learned that the combination of exercise routines and meds weren't really enough in my case.

It was at that time when my doctor suggested that I try the keto diet.

Was it easy?

No it wasn't—just like any other diet out there it was never easy at first. But in my mind if this thing can help me overcome this life threatening condition then I will definitely give it a shot.

Two months later I came back for another routine checkup and my doctor was happy to report that my blood sugar levels have improved dramatically. My doctor recommended that I stay on this diet for a few more months.

Six months later my A1C levels went down to 6 percent. By that time I no longer needed insulin. On top of that I was already living a keto lifestyle and have experienced a total body transformation.

I have gone down to two sizes smaller—I still don't have a six pack (I'm still working on it) but I felt great. I didn't wake up with headaches and I felt refreshed every time I woke up in the morning.

The transition was never easy—**but do you want to know what helped me along?**

The secret is this—I was able to find a lot of tasty keto recipes. Some of them were suggested by friends who cared for me. And I found a community of people who were on the keto diet as well who also shared their favorite recipes as well.

In this book I share with you some of the best recipes that I have been using and some of the meal plans that I have personally tried. They have helped me lose weight, get healthier, and reverse the medical conditions that I have suffered from since my teens.

As a bit of a caveat of course—I'm not a doctor. So before you try this diet I highly recommend that you consult with your doctor first. But if you would just like to see how good keto meals really are then I would suggest that you try some of the recipes that I have included in this book.

It's not a restrictive diet actually and if you think that you can live off the food and recipes I have listed here then I can guarantee that you will enjoy eating and living the keto way.

Thank you for purchasing this book and I hope that you enjoy eating the meals that I have concocted in my journey as I live the keto lifestyle.

Chapter 1: Introducing the Ketogenic Diet

The ketogenic diet is one of the most scientific diets today. Dr. Marcelo Campos from Harvard Medical School has dubbed it as the "ultimate low carb diet" [1]. The ketogenic diet or just keto diet for short has become quite popular of late.

However, it should be noted that it isn't something new. In fact this diet is part of a treatment regimen for epilepsy and there are a lot of actual medical studies about it. These studies provide strong evidence about the health benefits that you can get from this diet [2].

I have personally seen how beneficial this diet can be. As I said earlier, it has helped me lose weight and manage my medical conditions such as high blood pressure and Type 2 diabetes.

Some of the benefits cited in these studies include the following [3]:

- Weight loss
- Benefits for diabetics
- Helps in the treatment of cancer
- Big aid in the treatment of epilepsy
- Beneficial for Alzheimer's patients

So, what is the keto diet and why is it a better diet for weight loss and overall healing? We'll go over that and the benefits of this diet in the next section.

Ketogenic Diet Defined

The ketogenic diet is a diet that is low carb, high in healthy fat, and has moderate protein. A lot of health benefits have been associated with this diet and it is used to treat a variety of conditions. Note that it has similarities with the Atkins Diet.

It's called the ketogenic diet because it induces a bodily state called ketosis. Ketosis is that metabolic state where the amount of ketone bodies in your tissues is raised to higher levels.

How Does It Work?

With this diet you will drastically reduce your carbohydrate intake. You will then replace carbs with healthy fats, which becomes your body's primary energy source.

Studies show that doing this is quite beneficial.

When the body switches to fat as its primary source of energy it becomes more efficient at fat burning, which is basically what you want if you're looking to lose weight. Now, this process also has other benefits as well. For instance, when the body converts fat to ketones in the liver, the ketones supply energy to the brain [4].

When applied properly, experts say that the ketogenic diets can result in huge reductions in the body's blood sugar level [5].

Types of Ketogenic Diet

There are actually several types of Ketogenic Diets. They include the following:

1. The Standard Ketogenic Diet – this version of the diet is one that requires really low carb levels. And it typically has high fat levels and a moderate amount of proteins. Your diet will usually consist of 75% fat, carb levels will only be around 5%, and the protein will make up the remaining 20%.

2. Targeted Ketogenic Diet – this version of the keto diet basically follows the same recommended nutrient percentages in the standard keto diet but it will allow you to have carbs on days when you workout or exercise.

3. Cyclical Ketogenic Diet – this version of the keto diet is where there will be days in a week when you will eat a really low carb diet and there will be days when you eat high carb diets. For instance a sample meal plan in this type of diet is where you will have 2 days will be designated as high carb days and the other 5 days will be low carb days.

4. High Protein Keto Diet – this basically takes the same portions as the standard keto diet but it calls for more protein. For example, a diet that has 60% fat, 5% carbs, and 35% protein is considered as a high protein keto diet. As you can see, there are more protein portions in this diet.

It should be noted that only the standard keto diet and the high protein keto diet have been studied extensively. If you're an athlete and especially if you're a body builder then the targeted and cyclical keto diets are better suited for you.

Note that these two latter versions are advanced types of the standard keto diet. They may not be a good fit for you if you are trying the ketogenic diet for the first time.

It is the standard keto diet and the high protein keto diet versions that will be mostly discussed and described in this book. That also applies to the meal plans that we will be presented here.

Note however that since the standard version of the keto diet is the basis for all the other versions, the underlying principles mentioned here may also apply to the more advanced versions as well.

In the next chapter we'll go over the reasons why I think the keto diet is a better option for weight loss compared to other dietary regimens.

Chapter 2: Keto Diet for Weight Loss

In the previous chapter we mentioned that the keto diet is more effective compared to low fat restrictive diets. This is actually only one of the benefits that you will get from this diet.

The Keto Advantage for Weight Loss

There are things occurring on the side as the keto diet helps your body trim down all that excess weight. What happens in the background in the process actually helps lower your risk for certain diseases.

The Production of Ketone Bodies

According to one study conducted by Department of Pediatrics, Gifu University School of Medicine in Japan [6], when you do the keto diet your body switches from using carbs as the main energy source to using fats as the main source of energy. During this transition process your body produces ketone bodies in the liver. The ketone bodies are produced by processing body fat.

When the body starts to produce more ketone bodies it leads to a state called Hyperketonemia. This bodily state is associated with a lot of potential health benefits. Researchers are looking into how this process also lowers elevated circulating insulin levels in the body.

Health Benefits Even in Mild Ketosis

Another study suggests that even if you are only in a mild ketogenic state, you may still enjoy its therapeutic benefits [7]. That means you can still satisfy your sweet tooth on certain days of the week and go back to a ketogenic state to enjoy the health and weight loss benefits of this diet.

It is suggested in another study that a very low carb diet (VLCARB), like the keto diet for instance, is protective from muscle loss [8]. Note that when you undergo calorie restriction (i.e. go on a diet) you tend to lose muscle mass.

Preserves Muscle Mass

Note that when the body undergoes starvation mode (e.g. when you go on a diet) your metabolism slows down. Yes you may begin to lose weight but it may also begin to induce a process called protein catabolism where protein cells in the body (mostly your muscles) are broken down to support the body's needs.

The study compared different diets including low carb diets as well as low fat diets. It was believed that low carb diets tend to induce the catabolism of proteins since the body needed to cover for the reduced amount of carbs. In other words the body needed an alternate source of energy—that is your muscles. And the usual observation is that the body's protein mass gets reduced when the carb intake is reduced.

It is indeed surprising that very low carb diets tend to be more protective of the body's muscles. In other words it prevents protein catabolism especially when there is energy restriction.

However there is a catch—and that is you need to an adequate supply of protein in your diet to combat the natural processing of the body's muscles. And that is where the keto diet shines—well not only is it a very low carb diet, but it is a diet where moderate amounts of protein are prescribed along with high levels of fats.

What this means is that you can go on a keto diet, reduce the amount of carbs you eat, lose weight, and you don't have to worry about losing any muscle mass. In fact, when coupled with an exercise regimen, you may even see proper muscle toning.

Better than Low Fat Diets

The carbs we take in are the things that determine the glucose levels in the body. Simply put, the more carbs we eat the higher our insulin levels go. It has been suggested that the reduced intake of carbs will result in better blood sugar control.

Experts have suggested that lowering carb intakes may help obese patients with Type 2 diabetes, according to a study published by Duke University Medical Center in 2008 [9].

According to that study, a low carb diet (like the keto diet) was able to help 84 obese patients to lose weight. But that wasn't the only benefit that they were able to get from low carb diets.

It also produced better glycemic control—that means they were better able to regulate their insulin levels. The diet was such a success that some of the test subjects no longer had to take their prescribed medication for diabetes.

Experts suggest that low carb diets like the ketogenic diet are also a lifestyle modification tool. They are a mode of intervention that can either improve health conditions of diabetics or even reverse Type 2 diabetes.

Curbing Appetites, Sweet Tooth, and Hunger Pangs

One of the challenges of going on any diet is the fact that you will be haunted by hunger pangs, insatiable appetites, and that good old sweet tooth. These are some of the reasons why we all sneak out and raid the fridge at midnight (or anytime when no one is looking).

According to one study, being in a ketogenic state (aka ketosis) where your body is flooded by ketones will greatly help reduce the enticement of food altogether [10]. It's not really just the ketogenic state that does this.

Being in ketosis will help in the production of hormones and appetite mediating nutrients. Researchers see this as a better alternative compared to re-feeding. In fact, it has been observed that this appetite curbing is better experienced the moment you begin to lose weight and still experience certain levels of ketosis.

Now, you may say that maybe all I have to do is just reduce my carb intake and just take more protein so that I can stop getting hungry all the time. Some diets have this approach believing that since protein takes longer to digest that people will feel hungry a lot less frequently.

However, one study from the Rowett Research Institute in the UK suggests this is not the case [11]. Researchers compared low carb and moderate carb diets – one was a low carb diet with moderate protein intake (i.e. ketogenic) and the other diet was moderate carb with high protein.

The results were quite interesting. Test subjects who were under the keto diet were better able to control hunger issues compared to those who were on a medium carb diet with more protein.

No Need to Track Your Food Intake or Count Calories

I don't know about you but I'm not a fan of counting calories. You may even think that tracking your food intake is a fun idea but it can be laborious after a while.

It can be interesting at first because it's something new. But guess what, you can't keep it up forever.

I bet that after several months of tracking you will have plenty of times when you lose track. The good news is that with a ketogenic diet and a corresponding meal plan, you don't have to count calories or track your food intake.

Some people go into a ketogenic diet by just using keto recipes and meal plans. One study found out that meals on a keto diet were already so filling that people really had very little use for meal tracking and counting calories [12]

Better at Getting Weight Loss Results

Studies also confirm or at least suggest that the keto diet is better at providing weight loss results compared to many other diets. For example, it is suggested in one study [13] that the keto diet can help people lose weight 2.2 times more than low fat diets that are calorie restricted (i.e. the standard weight loss diet). The same study also suggests that the keto diet can also help to improve HDL cholesterol and triglyceride levels.

There was also one study that compared the standard ketogenic diet to the Diabetes UK diet [14]. Study participants who were on the keto diet lost 3 times more weight compared to those who were on the other diet.

Another study points out the fact that when you're on a keto diet your body will experience increased protein intake [15]. Other health benefits such as improved insulin sensitivity, lower blood sugar levels, and increased ketones also play a key role in providing people with benefits as well.

In the next chapter we'll go over how you can heal naturally with the help of the keto diet.

Chapter 3: Healing with the Keto Diet

In the previous chapter we only mentioned the weight loss benefits of going on a ketogenic diet. We also mentioned the advantages of the keto diet over other weight loss schemes as well.

Those are only some of the possible health benefits that you can get from this type of low carb diet. However, research suggests that there are a lot of other benefits that can be gained.

In this chapter we will focus on the healing benefits that people get when they switch over to a keto lifestyle.

Benefits for Headaches and Migraine

I mentioned early on in this book that I suffered frequent headaches. I have observed that after being on a state of ketosis that the headaches got less frequent and in some months I never have headaches at all.

Migraine headaches are some of the worst types of pain that anyone can ever. It can interfere with one's day and may affect your performance at work. It can also reduce one's quality of life.

Migraine is not just a really painful headache. Other symptoms include nausea as well as sensitivity to light.

According to one study, undergoing a ketogenic study may help to ease the symptoms of migraine [16]. According to another study (note that this one is only observational) people with migraine that are on a keto diet see a lower frequency of migraine headaches [17]. This also led to the reduced reliance on pain medication.

In another study, now this one is only a case study, it is suggested that people who go on a cyclical ketogenic diet for losing weight may have all migraine symptoms disappear [18].

However, it should be noted that the two sisters who were involved in the treatment got the symptoms back weeks after they stopped their keto cycles. Note that these aren't the quality of studies that we want to rely on.

However, they do demonstrate the healing potential of undergoing a keto diet. You will see a lot of similar examples in the case studies and other medical reports that we will present here.

Benefits for People with Alzheimer's Disease

Alzheimer's Disease is usually described as a form of progressive dementia. The brain's memory gets impaired for people who suffer from this condition.

Researchers observe that Alzheimer's share some of the same characteristics as type 2 diabetes and epilepsy [19]. These parallel symptoms and features include the following:
- Inflammation
- Inability to use glucose in the brain
- Seizures

According to studies, a ketogenic diet may help with the loss of balance and coordination that are also symptoms of this disease. However, the diet itself doesn't have any effect on the amyloid plaque.

Researchers say that undergoing a keto diet and then supplementing with ketone esters may help reduce Alzheimer's symptoms [20].

There are only a few human studies on the use of ketone esters and the related use of MCT oil. They seem to be promising but there needs to be more conclusive studies before medical experts can come to any conclusion.

Healing Nonalcoholic Fatty Liver Disease

Some people think that obesity and diabetes are the most common diseases in the western world. However, researchers say that it is not—the most common one is nonalcoholic fatty liver disease (NAFLD).

Note however that NAFLD has a strong link to the two aforementioned conditions, which is why it is so prevalent [21]. You see people can still be diabetic even though they may not be obese.

Studies show that it is possible for people with obesity and NAFLD to heal from these conditions [22]. Note that this is only a small study involving a few patients. On top of that they only went through a keto diet for a 12 week period.

But the results were promising. After 12 weeks they significantly lost weight. Their blood pressures also normalized and there was a significant reduction in their liver enzymes.

93% of the test subjects experienced a reduction in the amount of liver fat. 21% of them were healed of their NAFLD completely. More studies need to be conducted to affirm the possibility that a keto diet can help reduce liver fat in people with NAFLD.

Benefits Involving Multiple Sclerosis

Multiple sclerosis or MS is a condition where the protective covering the body's nerves are damaged. This leads to problems of communication between the body and the brain. Its symptoms include problems with memory, vision, movement, and balance.

According to one study, going on a keto diet may reduce the inflammation related to MS. This reduction in inflammation reduces the symptoms of multiple sclerosis which leads to improved physical functions, better learning, and improved memory.

According to medical review, it is believed that undergoing a keto diet can help when it comes to energy production [23]. It improves the capability of cells to use sugar as a source of energy. It is also suggested in the results that a ketogenic diet may help improve cell repair in people with MS.

Again, the current studies show promising results. However, they still lack more human trials in order to make findings more conclusive.

Possible Treatment for Traumatic Brain Injury

Traumatic brain injury or TBI occurs when one receives a blow to the head. These injuries are often caused by car accidents or falls. The nature of the incidents that involved TBI had people's heads striking the ground.

TBI has devastating effects on brain function. It can affect a patient's personality as well as their personality. Researchers observe that the brain recovers very little from such traumatic injury if it recovers at all.

However, it should be noted that researchers observe that TBI also impairs the brain's ability to utilize sugar/glucose as a source of energy. Because of this, researchers believe that a keto diet may help [24].

Some studies involving rats with TBI suggest that undergoing a keto diet right after brain injury may help reduce brain swelling [25]. It also helps the recover better and improves their motor function. However, it should be pointed that these studies were performed on rats and not humans [26].

Help for GLUT1 Deficiency Syndrome

Glucose transporter 1 Deficiency Syndrome or (GLUT1) Deficiency Syndrome is a genetic disorder that is considered to be quite rare. Its symptoms usually appear after the birth of a child and include difficulty with movement, delay in development, and sometimes the symptoms include seizures.

This genetic syndrome involves the deficiency in a special protein. This protein is responsible for moving blood sugar into the brain. Studies suggest that undergoing a keto diet may help ease some of the symptoms [27].

However, it should be noted that the keto diet is not the only low carb diet that has been demonstrated to be able to help with this condition. Another diet that has shown promise is the Modified Atkins Diet or MAD [28]. Researchers found that MAD produced better compliance with fewer side effects.

Treatment for Parkinson's Disease

Parkinson's Disease is a nervous system disorder. One of its marks is the characteristic low levels of dopamine production. This reduced dopamine levels in the brain causes symptoms such as the following:

- Difficulty walking
- Problems with writing
- General stiffness
- Impaired posture
- Tremors

Researchers found that the protective effects of the keto diet on the brain can help people with Parkinson's Disease [29]. Experts are looking into it as a possible accompanying treatment for this disorder [30].

According to one study, 5 out of 7 patients exhibited a 43% improvement in the symptoms of Parkinson's Disease after undergoing a type of keto diet for 4 straight weeks [31].

Of course this is not a controlled study even though it did involve human patients. If the findings are to be conclusive more controlled studies need to be performed. However, the results so far are truly promising.

It May Help Ease Symptoms of Autism Spectrum Disorder

Early research suggests that the ketogenic diet may help ease the symptoms of Autism spectrum disorder (ASD). However, it should be used in tandem with other therapies.

ASD is a condition that is accompanied by problems with social interaction and communication. The features of ASD share the same characteristics as epilepsy with patients also experiencing seizures. Research suggests that a keto diet may help relieve these symptoms [32].

Studies also suggest that the keto diet and other low carb diets can help reduce the over stimulation that occurs in the brain [33]. However, do take note that these studies involved mice and no conclusive human trials have been conducted thus far.

There was a pilot study where 30 children were involved as test subjects. These children underwent the cyclical keto diet for a period of 6 months. 18 out of the 30 children showed improvement [34].

Again, more human trials are required to test whether the keto diet can be very helpful to children with ASD. The recruitment process needs to be randomized as well.

Healing from Certain Cancers

Research suggests that the keto diet may be able to help patients with certain types of cancers. However, the keto dietary treatment should be used in tandem with other therapies as well for it to be effective.

The keto diet is not a one size fits all kind of fix. It should be used as part of an overall and more comprehensive type of treatment.

There are case studies accompanied by patient data that suggest that the keto diet may help with glioblastoma multiforme (GBM) and other forms of brain cancer [35]. Note that GBM is the most aggressive type of brain cancer.

Other studies also point to the possibility that the keto diet can help reduce the progression of certain cancers into other parts of the body [36]. According to another study, it is suggested that the keto diet may help reduce tumor growth [37].

However, it should be pointed out here too that the keto diet doesn't have any significant effect on terminal cancers, which is quite unfortunate [38].

A Big Help for People with Diabetes

Perhaps the biggest benefit that we can get from the ketogenic diet is from its ability to help people who have diabetes. A lot of diabetic patients who have tried the keto diet have shown huge reductions in their blood sugar levels.

It is evident in both types of diabetes—type 1 and type 2. There are plenty of medical studies to support the fact that low carb diets can help control blood sugar levels. A lot of them are even controlled studies [39, 40, 41]

In some of these cases, patients have experienced a return of their blood sugar levels to normal ranges. The keto diet is so effective in some patients that they no longer needed to take any diabetic medication.

Treatment for Polycystic Ovary Syndrome (PCOS)

Polycystic Ovary Syndrome (PCOS) is a condition that results in infertility and irregular periods. Note that this is actually a hormonal dysfunction. One of the distinctive symptoms that people don't immediately notice about this condition is insulin resistance.

That is why a lot of women in the world today who suffer from PCOS are also obese. They also experience a hard time losing weight and due to the increased insulin resistance they are also at risk for Type 2 diabetes [42].

When it comes to PCOS and the ketogenic diet, you will find a lot of anecdotal evidence. That means you will read a lot of testimonies from people who had the condition and tried this diet and succeeded.

There are only a few actual scientific studies on the effects of this diet on women with PCOS. However there are a few actual studies that have been published [43]. Of course anecdotal evidence can't be taken as solid evidence but they do suggest possible positive effects but nothing conclusive.

According to a short study on this condition, a couple of women definitely got pregnant after undergoing a ketogenic diet [44]. The study also reported that their fasting insulin was reduced by 54% and they lost 12% of their weight. They went on the ketogenic diet for 6 months and achieved the aforementioned benefits.

Again, this study is not absolutely conclusive because they are not controlled trials. We can't say that based on this study alone that every woman with PCOS who goes on a keto diet will eventually recover but the results we have seen so far are very promising.

Metabolic Syndrome

You may know this condition by a different name—it's also called pre-diabetes. The characteristic feature of this condition is increased insulin resistance. If you have any three of the symptoms below then you may have this condition:

- Elevated fasting blood sugar
- High blood pressure
- Low HDL cholesterol
- Elevated triglycerides
- Large waistline

The ketogenic diet has been observed to be quite helpful for people who have metabolic syndrome [45]. According to a controlled study, test subjects that were in pre-diabetes went on a keto diet. After 12 weeks test subjects had marked improvements in all the key health markers such as reduced blood sugar, better cholesterol values, and reduced blood pressure [46].

This means that going on a keto diet may improve blood sugar levels, reduce obesity, and provide better health markers for people with metabolic syndrome.

Treatment for Epilepsy

Low carb diets like the keto diet and the Modified Atkins Diet are actually used as treatments for epilepsy. These diets are effective for people who may experience seizures. They are usually the go to treatment approach for patients whose anti-seizure medication isn't tolerated well or have side effects.

There is a lot of scientific evidence backing up the use of the keto diet for people with epilepsy. For example, according to one study, the 4:1 keto diet is quite helpful for patients [47].

This diet does more than just help to control seizures. According to another study 65% of patients who undergo a keto diet have experienced improvements in many different brain patterns [48].

Keto diets can reduce the severity and frequency of seizures in epileptic adults and children especially for those who don't respond that well to drug therapy.

Chapter 4: Kick Starting Your Ketosis

In the previous chapters we have covered what the ketogenic diet is and the different types of this diet. We have also covered the benefits for weight loss and also the other healing benefits of this diet.

At this point you might be wondering how to get started with a keto diet. We'll go over that step by step in this chapter.

Remember that we will be focusing on the standard keto diet in this book. So when we talk about kick starting your keto program we'll just start with the basics. That's the same thing you will see with the meal plans and the keto recipes that follow.

Note however that we will include an intermittent fasting schedule somewhere in the meal plans. We'll cover intermittent fasting in the next chapter. For now let's see what you need to do to get started on ketosis.

Step 1 – Clean Up Your Fridge/Pantry

The first step is to do an inventory of your fridge, cupboards, and pantry. Remember that you will be transitioning to a low carb diet. The first things to go are the carbs. I suggest you donate them to the needy, a soup kitchen, or friends and family who may want to have them.

Any carb or sugar sources must go. All processed carbs must go. Check the label of every can of food in your storage. If it has more than 20 grams of carbs then it must go to charity or to someone else who might need them.

When I did this inventory for the first time I was surprised to find how much carbs and sugar all the food that I have been shopping for. At a later part of this book we will give you a shopping list of keto approved food so don't worry about replenishing your food supplies.

Step 2 – Get Some Coconut Oil

Coconut oil contains medium chain triglycerides or MCTs. MCTs are the kind of fat that gets absorbed rather quickly in the body. They then immediately get processed and converted to ketones thus giving your body a quick boost into ketosis.

This strategy of boosting your keto state by adding coconut oil to your diet is also used for the treatment of Alzheimer's patients [49].

Note that 50% of the MCTs in coconut oil come from lauric acid. Research suggests that people tend to get a more sustained state of ketosis when the fat consumed comes from lauric acid [50]. Note that lauric acid is used in the treatment of epileptic children as well.

Caveat: when you start adding coconut oil to your diet, you should do so moderately. Start with a teaspoon each, increase that to two tablespoons on the third day, and then three tablespoons on the 7th day.

Doing it that way will reduce the digestive side effects of coconut oil. Some people experience diarrhea and stomach cramps when they start consuming coconut oil. So go easy on the stuff when you're doing it for the first time.

Step 3 – Start Working Out

There are studies that provide evidence for supporting ketosis with working out and physical activity. In fact, a growing body of these studies shows that ketosis maybe beneficial to athletes [51].

In short, if you want to get your body into a ketogenic state a lot faster then get started with a workout regimen. It doesn't have to be something complex. You don't even have to sign up for a gym.

If you have been a couch potato for quite a while then start having 30 minute walks 5 days a week. After that you can increase the intensity of your workouts by jogging, and then running, and maybe swimming.

The important thing is that you are doing something that you enjoy. That way your workout is sustainable and you are sure to keep on doing it in the long run.

Caveat: always check with your doctor first before engaging in any exercise program. Even if it is as simple as morning and afternoon walks, if you haven't done any kind of exercise in a long while it would be best to check with your physician first.

Step 4 – Add More Healthy Fat to Your Diet

After a week or two with coconut oil on your diet, it's time to add more healthy fat. In case you can't tolerate coconut oil then you should try other fat sources. Note that consuming more fat when undergoing a keto diet can help speed up ketosis [52].

Now, you should choose healthy and quality fat sources. Examples of which include tallow, lard, butter, coconut oil, avocado oil, and olive oil.

Caveat: if your goal is weight loss then you should make sure to take in enough amounts of fat in your diet. Consuming too much fat can also ruin your diet in this case. Note that the meal plans that we have provided in this book are designed for weight loss, which means that you won't get too much.

Step 5 – Maintain Adequate Protein Intake

It is important that you take adequate amounts of protein to obtain ketosis. Remember that your body needs an alternative source of energy to replace the carbs that you are no longer eating.

Note that some people may advise you to reduce your protein intake so that you will enter ketosis a lot faster. That is actually misplaced advice. Your liver will need the protein for gluconeogenesis.

In other words, your liver makes glucose from the protein that you take in. That is why you still have lots of energy despite not eating carbs. Protein intake should be adequate to maintain muscle mass.

So how much protein should you eat? Experts recommend anywhere from 0.55 to 0.77 grams of protein for each pound of body weight or lean muscle mass [53]. Now, you may want to consult a dietician or your doctor so that you can determine the specific amount of protein that you need each day.

Step 6 – Incorporate Some Fasting

Studies show that incorporating intermittent fasting can help induce ketosis [54]. Now, of course you don't need to fast in order to enter into a ketogenic state. However, if you do fast your body can easily transition into that state a lot faster because it can get used to it.

Note that there is also a lot of research backing up intermittent fasting and its health benefits. For instance, according to one study, there is evidence that intermittent can help to reduce inflammation [55]. Another study provides evidence that it can improve brain function [56]. Another study suggests that it can help control blood sugar [57].

Now, there are different types of intermittent fasting. However, the two most popular types are used in conjunction with a keto diet are the 5:2 method and the 16/8 method.

The 5:2 method is that you will go on a fast for 2 days a week and eat the regular keto diet on the other five days. The 16/8 method on the other hand is that you will only eat within an 8 hour window and then you will not eat in the other 16 hours of that day.

An example of this is when you have dinner at 8 pm and then you go to bed. Your next meal will be at noon to complete the 16 hour fasting period. Breakfast is served at noon.

Note that when your body goes into a fasted state it will begin to process all the carbs that you have taken for that day until all is depleted. Once all the carb stores are gone, your body will then begin to process fats as the main energy source, which parallels the ketogenic process. In other words your body naturally starts to burn fat for its fuel [58].

In this state your insulin levels go down. And then the liver starts to produce ketones. Note that the body needs at least 16 hours of fasting in order to kick start the depletion of glucose stores in the body.

After that the body starts to burn body fat. Another natural body process also gets triggered—autophagy. This is an internal healing process that happens on a cellular level. Once you get used to the fasting cycles you will feel less hungry [59]

Caveat: combining keto and intermittent fasting may not always be the best option for everyone. People with diabetes, heart disease, and other conditions may be at risk of making their blood sugar dropping too low if they incorporate both.

Again, always check with your doctor if it is okay for you to go on a fast while on a keto diet.

Step 7 – Do Ketone Tests to Measure How Well You're Doing

There are 3 types of ketone tests that you can do so you can measure if you're going well into a keto state or not. If the results aren't that good then you can adjust your diet by adjusting your carbohydrate and fat intake.

The 3 tests that you can choose from include:

- **Ketonix Meter** – this is an apparatus that you breathe into and it will indicate how high your ketone levels are.
- **Blood Tests** – blood tests to measure ketone levels make use of a blood ketone meter. This option is the most expensive one of the three.
- **Ketone Urine Strips** – this is by far the cheapest option. You just need to collect your urine either the first thing in the morning or at night after dinner while on a keto diet [60].

  You just dip the strips in your urine. The darker the color of the strip is after dipping the higher is the ketone content of you urine. The strips are rather inexpensive but they're not completely accurate. You should make sure to collect your urine at appropriate times.

Chapter 5: Keto Diet Meal Plans

In this chapter you can choose from 3 different meal plans:

1. Basic 30 Day Keto Plan
2. Keto + Intermittent Fasting Plan
3. Vegan Keto Diet Plan

Choose the meal plan that best suits you. If you're doctor gives you the thumbs up for combining keto with intermittent fasting then use plan number 2. But if you are vegan then choose plan number 3. If you're just starting or you're not going to do any intermittent fasting then choose plan number 1.

Note that the snacks are optional. That is why we haven't included them in any of the schedules in the 3 meal plans. Just check out the snack recipes that we have included in the next chapter.

If you choose to have snacks then you can just eat the snacks anytime in between meals of your choosing.

Please refer to the recipes in the next chapter for each meal that is scheduled in each of the meal plans

Basic 30 Day Keto Plan

Day 1

Breakfast: Keto White Bread

Lunch: Keto Sushi

Dinner: Keto Grilled Chicken with Chorizo Confetti

Day 2

Breakfast: Keto Bread with Chia Seeds

Lunch: Keto Egg and Sausage Sandwich

Dinner: Keto Steak with Ginger- Scallion Sauce

Day 3

Breakfast: Keto Coconut Bread

Lunch: Chicken with Lemon and Herb Mediterranean Salad

Dinner: Keto Salmon with Red Pepper Pesto

Day 4

Breakfast: Keto Coconut Bread

Lunch: Keto Chicken BLT Salad Stuffed Avocados

Dinner: Keto Chicken Stuffed with Goat Cheese

Day 5

Breakfast: Keto Cloud Bread

Lunch: Keto Cheesy Taco Skillet

Dinner: Keto Chicken Sausage with Spinach and Roasted Red Pepper Patties

Day 6

Breakfast: Keto Macadamia Nut Bread

Lunch: Keto Cheesy Taco Skillet

Dinner: Keto Chicken Sausage with Spinach and Roasted Red Pepper Patties

Day 7

Breakfast: Keto Pancakes

Lunch: Keto Caesar Salad

Dinner: Keto Cauliflower Coconut Curry Soup

Day 8

Breakfast: Cauliflower Bread with Poached Eggs, Crispy Bacon, and Avocado

Lunch: Keto Brussels Sprouts with Parmesan Cheese Salad

Dinner: Keto Turkey Sausage, Kale and Butternut Squash Soup

Day 9

Breakfast: Keto Tacos with Guacamole and Bacon

Lunch: Keto Salad in a Jar

Dinner: Keto Chicken Sausage with Spinach and Roasted Red Pepper Patties

Day 10

Breakfast: Keto BLT Salad

Lunch: Keto Egg and Sausage Sandwich

Dinner: Keto Mexican Soup

Day 11

Breakfast: Keto Iced Coffee with Protein Shake

Lunch: Keto Cheesy Taco Skillet

Dinner: Keto Italian Vegetable Soup

Day 12

Breakfast: Keto Tuna with Capers Salad

Lunch: Keto Roasted Salmon with Green Beans

Dinner: Keto Asian Beef Salad

Day 13

Breakfast: Keto Turkey Sausage, Kale and Butternut Squash Soup

Lunch: Keto Chicken Parmesan

Dinner: Keto Chicken Chili

Day 14

Breakfast: Keto Tuna with Capers Salad

Lunch: Keto Zoodles with White Clam Sauce

Dinner: Keto Chicken Chili

Day 15

Breakfast: Keto Tomato Soup with Basil

Lunch: Keto Brussels Sprouts with Parmesan Cheese Salad

Dinner: Keto Seafood Stuffed Mushrooms with Cheese

Day 16

Breakfast: Keto Iced Coffee with Protein Shake

Lunch: Keto Seafood Stuffed Mushrooms with Cheese

Dinner: Keto Tilapia with Lemon Butter

Day 17

Breakfast: Keto Italian Chicken Cacciatore

Lunch: Keto Chicken Caprese Hasselback

Dinner: Keto Chicken with Cream and Poblano Peppers

Day 18

Breakfast: Keto Pancakes

Lunch: Keto Lamb Chops with Tzatziki Sauce

Dinner: Keto Mongolian Beef

Day 19

Breakfast: Keto Asparagus Cream Soup

Lunch: Keto Cabbage and Corned Beef

Dinner: Keto Chopped Buffalo Chicken Salad

Day 20

Breakfast: Keto Blackberry-Filled Lemon Muffins

Lunch: Keto Meatloaf Covered with Bacon

Dinner: Keto Pork Egg Roll in a Bowl

Day 21

Breakfast: Keto Breakfast Bombs

Lunch: Keto Spicy Pork Meatballs

Dinner: Keto Fried Pork Tenderloin

Day 22

Breakfast: Keto Iced Coffee with Protein Shake

Lunch: Keto Prime Rib Roast with Garlic Butter

Dinner: Keto Beef Stew

Day 23

Breakfast: Keto BLT Salad

Lunch: Keto Cauliflower with Ground Beef Lasagna

Dinner: Keto Mongolian Beef

Day 24
Breakfast: Keto Macadamia Nut Bread
Lunch: Keto Cheesy Taco Skillet
Dinner: Keto Chopped Buffalo Chicken Salad

Day 25
Breakfast: Keto Avocado Brownies
Lunch: Keto Shrimp and Cauliflower Rice Salad
Dinner: Keto Lamb Chops with Pesto Sauce

Day 26
Breakfast: Keto Lemon Strawberry Cheesecake
Lunch: Keto Peanut Ginger Zoodle Salad
Dinner: Keto Slow Cooker Lamb Shoulder

Day 27
Breakfast: Keto Pound Cake (Vanilla Flavor)
Lunch: Keto Spicy Pork with Kelp Noodles
Dinner: Keto Lamb Curry

Day 28
Breakfast: Keto Cacao Butter Blondies
Lunch: Keto Peanut Ginger Zoodle Salad
Dinner: Keto Lamb Chops with Tzatziki Sauce

Day 29
Breakfast: Keto Cream Cheese Frosted Carrot Mug Cake
Lunch: Chicken with Lemon and Herb Mediterranean Salad
Dinner: Keto Cauliflower with Ground Beef Lasagna

Day 30
Breakfast: Keto Tacos with Guacamole and Bacon
Lunch: Keto Chicken BLT Salad Stuffed Avocados

Dinner: Keto Chicken Sausage with Spinach and Roasted Red Pepper Patties

Keto Intermittent Fasting Plan

Day 1

Breakfast: Keto Cacao Butter Blondies

Lunch: Keto Peanut Ginger Zoodle Salad

Dinner: Keto Lamb Chops with Tzatziki Sauce

Day 2

Breakfast: Skip Breakfast/No Breakfast

Lunch: Keto Spicy Pork with Kelp Noodles

Dinner: Keto Lamb Curry

Day 3

Breakfast: Keto Lemon Strawberry Cheesecake

Lunch: Keto Peanut Ginger Zoodle Salad

Dinner: Keto Slow Cooker Lamb Shoulder

Day 4

Breakfast: Skip Breakfast/No Breakfast

Lunch: Keto Shrimp and Cauliflower Rice Salad

Dinner: Keto Lamb Chops with Pesto Sauce

Day 5

Breakfast: Keto Macadamia Nut Bread

Lunch: Keto Cheesy Taco Skillet

Dinner: Keto Chopped Buffalo Chicken Salad

Day 6

Breakfast: Keto BLT Salad

Lunch: Keto Cauliflower with Ground Beef Lasagna

Dinner: Keto Mongolian Beef

Day 7

Breakfast: Keto Tacos with Guacamole and Bacon

Lunch: Keto Chicken BLT Salad Stuffed Avocados

Dinner: Keto Chicken Sausage with Spinach and Roasted Red Pepper Patties

Day 8

Breakfast: Keto Iced Coffee with Protein Shake

Lunch: Keto Prime Rib Roast with Garlic Butter

Dinner: Keto Beef Stew

Day 9

Breakfast: Skip Breakfast/No Breakfast

Lunch: Keto Spicy Pork Meatballs

Dinner: Keto Fried Pork Tenderloin

Day 10

Breakfast: Keto Blackberry-Filled Lemon Muffins

Lunch: Keto Meatloaf Covered with Bacon

Dinner: Keto Pork Egg Roll in a Bowl

Day 11

Breakfast: Skip Breakfast/No Breakfast

Lunch: Keto Cabbage and Corned Beef

Dinner: Keto Chopped Buffalo Chicken Salad

Day 12

Breakfast: Keto Pancakes

Lunch: Keto Lamb Chops with Tzatziki Sauce

Dinner: Keto Mongolian Beef

Day 13

Breakfast: Keto Italian Chicken Cacciatore

Lunch: Keto Chicken Caprese Hasselback

Dinner: Keto Chicken with Cream and Poblano Peppers

Day 14

Breakfast: Keto Tomato Soup with Basil

Lunch: Keto Brussels Sprouts with Parmesan Cheese Salad

Dinner: Keto Seafood Stuffed Mushrooms with Cheese

Day 15

Breakfast: Keto Tuna with Capers Salad

Lunch: Keto Zoodles with White Clam Sauce

Dinner: Keto Chicken Chili

Day 16

Breakfast: Skip Breakfast/No Breakfast

Lunch: Keto Chicken Parmesan

Dinner: Keto Chicken Chili

Day 17

Breakfast: Keto Tuna with Capers Salad

Lunch: Keto Roasted Salmon with Green Beans

Dinner: Keto Asian Beef Salad

Day 18

Breakfast: Skip Breakfast/No Breakfast

Lunch: Keto Cheesy Taco Skillet

Dinner: Keto Italian Vegetable Soup

Day 19

Breakfast: Keto Cream Cheese Frosted Carrot Mug Cake

Lunch: Chicken with Lemon and Herb Mediterranean Salad

Dinner: Keto Cauliflower with Ground Beef Lasagna

Day 20

Breakfast: Keto BLT Salad

Lunch: Keto Egg and Sausage Sandwich

Dinner: Keto Mexican Soup

Day 21
Breakfast: Keto BLT Salad
Lunch: Keto Egg and Sausage Sandwich
Dinner: Keto Mexican Soup

Day 22
Breakfast: Cauliflower Bread with Poached Eggs, Crispy Bacon, and Avocado
Lunch: Keto Brussels Sprouts with Parmesan Cheese Salad
Dinner: Keto Turkey Sausage, Kale and Butternut Squash Soup

Day 23
Breakfast: Skip Breakfast/No Breakfast
Lunch: Keto Caesar Salad
Dinner: Keto Cauliflower Coconut Curry Soup

Day 24
Breakfast: Keto Macadamia Nut Bread
Lunch: Keto Cheesy Taco Skillet
Dinner: Keto Chicken Sausage with Spinach and Roasted Red Pepper Patties

Day 25
Breakfast: Keto Cloud Bread
Lunch: Keto Cheesy Taco Skillet
Dinner: Keto Chicken Sausage with Spinach and Roasted Red Pepper Patties

Day 26
Breakfast: Skip Breakfast/No Breakfast
Lunch: Keto Chicken BLT Salad Stuffed Avocados
Dinner: Keto Chicken Stuffed with Goat Cheese

Day 27

Breakfast: Keto Coconut Bread

Lunch: Chicken with Lemon and Herb Mediterranean Salad

Dinner: Keto Salmon with Red Pepper Pesto

Day 28

Breakfast: Keto Bread with Chia Seeds

Lunch: Keto Egg and Sausage Sandwich

Dinner: Keto Steak with Ginger- Scallion Sauce

Day 29

Breakfast: Keto Tuna with Capers Salad

Lunch: Keto Zoodles with White Clam Sauce

Dinner: Keto Chicken Chili

Day 30

Breakfast: Keto Cacao Butter Blondies

Lunch: Keto Peanut Ginger Zoodle Salad

Dinner: Keto Lamb Chops with Tzatziki Sauce

Keto 5 Day Vegan Plan

Day 1
Breakfast: Keto Vegan Creamy Cinnamon Smoothie
Lunch: Keto Vegan Cucumber Tomato Salad
Dinner: Keto Vegan Falafels with Lupini Beans

Day 2
Breakfast: Keto Vegan Granola Bars
Lunch: Keto Vegan Zoodles with Avocado Sauce
Dinner: Keto Vegan Roasted Vegetables

Day 3
Breakfast: Keto Vegan Spaghetti Squash Tots
Lunch: Keto Vegan Triple Green Salad
Dinner: Keto Vegan Mushroom Tacos

Day 4
Breakfast: Keto Vegan Tofu Scramble
Lunch: Keto Vegan Asian Ginger Slaw
Dinner: Keto Vegan Egg Roll in a Bowl

Day 5
Breakfast: Keto Vegan Pancakes
Lunch: Keto Vegan Broccoli Fried Rice
Dinner: Keto Vegan Omega 3 Porridge

Chapter 6: Recommended Keto Recipes

Keto Bread Recipes

Keto White Bread

Yields: 18 slices

Serving size: 1/2 inch thick per slice

Preparation time: 10 minutes

Cooking time: 1 hour 10 minutes

Ingredients:

- 12 pieces large eggs (use the egg whites only, room temperature)
- 1 cup almond flour (blanched)
- 1/4 cup coconut flour
- 1/3 cup butter (melted)
- 1 1/2 tablespoons erythritol
- 2 teaspoons baking powder (gluten-free)
- 1/4 teaspoon xanthan gum
- 1/4 teaspoon sea salt
- 1/4 teaspoon cream of tartar

Directions:

- Pre-heat your oven to 325 degrees Fahrenheit. Prepare a loaf pan measuring 8.5" x 4.5". Line it with parchment paper. Let there be extra parchment paper hanging over the sides to easily remove the loaf when cooked.
- In a food processor, mix well the coconut flour, almond flour, erythritol, baking powder, sea salt, and xanthan gum. Pulse the ingredients until mixed thoroughly.
- Put in the melted butter. Continue to pulse until the mixture becomes crumbly. Scrape down the sides of the food processor when necessary.
- In a mixing bowl, put in the cream of tartar and egg whites. Beat the mixture using a hand mixer. Continue beating until stiff peaks are formed. Make sure to use a very large mixing bowl because the egg whites will expand when beaten.
- Put in 1/2 of the egg white mixture into the food processor. Pulse for a few times to combine the egg white mixture into the flour mixture. Avoid over-mixing it.
- Pour carefully the mixture from the food processor into the remaining egg white mixture in the mixing bowl. Fold gently the mixture until no more chunks are

visible. Never ever stir the mixture. Folding gently will keep the batter mixture to be as fluffy as possible.
- Gently pour the batter into the prepared loaf pan. Spread the batter to cover the surface of the loaf pan. To make a rounded top so that it will look like loaf bread when done, push the batter a little bit towards the center.
- Bake the loaf bread until the top portion turns golden brown (about 40 minutes). Take out the loaf bread from the oven.
- Make a tent on top of the loaf bread using aluminum foil. Put the loaf bread back in the oven. Bake for another 30 to 45 minutes until cooked through. The loaf bread is cooked through when it doesn't make a squishy sound when you press the top down using a finger and the brown top feels firm to the touch. The internal temperature of the loaf bread should reach 200 degrees Fahrenheit.
- Let the loaf bread cool down completely before taking out from the loaf pan. Slice the loaf bread into 18 slices about 1/2 inch thick per slice.

Nutritional info (per serving):

- Calories: 82
- Carbs: 3 g
- Fats: 7 g
- Proteins: 4 g
- Fiber: 2 g

Keto Bread with Chia Seeds

Yields: 12 slices

Serving size: 1 slice

Preparation time: 5 minutes

Cooking time: 30 minutes

Ingredients:

- 1 cup almond flour
- 4 pieces eggs (room temperature)
- 1/2 cup black chia seeds
- 1/4 cup coconut oil
- 1/4 cup unsweetened almond milk
- 1/2 teaspoon salt
- 2 teaspoons baking soda

Directions:

- Pre-heat your oven to 350 degrees Fahrenheit.
- Prepare an 8" x 4" loaf pan and grease it. Set aside.
- In a mixing bowl, combine all the ingredients together. Mix well until there are no more lumps in the batter.
- Transfer the batter into the prepared loaf pan.
- Bake the bread for 30 minutes.
- Take out the bread from the oven. Let it rest in the loaf pan for about 10 minutes.
- Take out the loaf bread from the pan and let it cool completely on a rack.
- Cut into 12 equal slices and serve.

Nutritional info (per serving):

- Calories: 148
- Carbs: 5 g
- Fats: 12 g
- Proteins: 5 g
- Fiber: 3 g

Keto Coconut Bread

Yields: 10 slices

Serving size: 1 slice

Preparation time: 10 minutes

Cooking time: 40 minutes

Ingredients:

- 1/2 cup coconut flour
- ¼ cup coconut oil (melted)
- 1/4 cup almond milk (unsweetened)
- 6 pieces eggs (room temperature)
- 1/4 teaspoon baking soda
- 1/4 teaspoon salt

Directions:

- Pre-heat your oven to 350 degrees Fahrenheit.
- Get a loaf pan (8" x 4") and line it with parchment paper.
- In a mixing bowl, combine well the dry ingredients.
- In another mixing bowl, combine well the wet ingredients.
- Slowly pour the wet mixture into the dry mixture. Combine well until the batter is formed.
- Transfer the batter mixture into the lined loaf pan.
- Bake the loaf bread for 40 minutes or until cooked. If you insert a toothpick in the center of the loaf bread and it comes out clean, then the loaf bread is thoroughly cooked.

Nutritional info (per serving):

- Calories: 108
- Carbs: 3.4 g
- Fats: 8.7 g
- Proteins: 4.2 g
- Fiber: 2.1 g

Keto Cloud Bread

Yields: 10 pieces

Serving size: 1 piece

Preparation time: 15 minutes

Cooking time: 20 minutes

Ingredients:

- 3 tablespoons coconut cream (refrigerate a can of coconut milk (full fat) overnight and spoon out the top part)
- 3 pieces eggs (separated; 1 mixing bowl for the yolks and 1 mixing bowl for the whites)
- 1/2 teaspoon baking powder

Toppings (optional):

- sea salt
- rosemary
- black pepper

Directions:

- Pre-heat your oven to 325 degrees Fahrenheit. Put a rack in the middle part of the oven. Prepare a baking sheet and line it with paper parchment.
- In the mixing bowl with the yolks, put in the coconut cream. Beat them together using a hand mixer for total control. Continue beating until there are no more coconut clumps and the texture is nice and creamy.
- Wash your hand mixer well. Dry them.
- In the mixing bowl with the egg whites, put in the baking powder. Beat them using a hand mixer in medium setting. Continue beating until the mixture becomes firm, thick, and with stiff peaks.
- Moving carefully and quickly, add in the yolk mixture into the white mixture. Fold the mixture using a spatula to combine everything and retain its fluffy texture. Do not stir.
- With the use of a spoon, scoop a spoonful of the batter and drop it on the baking sheet. Do this step as quickly as you can before the mixture starts to melt down.
- Put the baking sheet on the oven's middle rack. Bake the cloud bread for 20 minutes.
- Use a spatula to scoop up the cloud breads from the baking sheet.

Nutritional info (per serving):

- Calories: 36
- Carbs: 0.5 g

- Fats: 3 g
- Proteins: 2 g
- Fiber: 0.1 g

Keto Macadamia Nut Bread

Yields: 10 slices

Serving size: 1 slice

Preparation time: 5 minutes

Cooking time: 30 minutes

Ingredients:

- 5 pieces large eggs
- 5 ounces macadamia nuts
- 1/4 cup coconut flour
- 1/2 teaspoon apple cider vinegar
- 1/2 teaspoon baking soda

Directions:

- Pre-heat your oven to 350 degrees Fahrenheit.
- In a food processor, put in the macadamia nuts. Pulse the nuts until it turns into nut butter.
- Add in the eggs into the nut butter in the food processor. Blend until mixed well. Scrape down the sides of the food processor, if needed, to mix everything well.
- Put in the coconut flour, apple cider vinegar, and baking soda into the nut mixture in the food processor. Pulse the mixture to combine well.
- Oil a standard-sized bread pan using a cooking spray. Pour the batter into the bread pan. Use a spatula to smooth the surface of the batter.
- Place the bread pan on the bottom rack of your oven. Bake the bread until it turns golden brown (about 30 minutes).
- Take out from the oven. Put the pan on a rack to cool down the bread for 20 minutes.
- Take out the bread from the pan. Cut into 10 slices.

Nutritional info (per serving):

- Calories: 151
- Carbs: 4 g
- Fats: 14 g
- Proteins: 5 g
- Fiber: 3 g

Keto Dessert Recipes

Keto Lemon Strawberry Cheesecake

Yields: 2 jars

Serving size: 1 jar

Preparation time: 15 minutes

Cooking time: none

Ingredients:

- 2 pieces large strawberries
- 3 ounces cream cheese (softened)
- 2 teaspoons lemon extract
- 1/3 cup Swerve sweetener
- 3/4 cup heavy whipping cream
- zest of 1 lemon

Directions:

- Prepare two 8-ounce mason jars.
- In a mixing bowl, put in the whipping cream, sweetener, and cream cheese. Beat them on high setting until the texture becomes creamy and smooth.
- Put in the lemon extract. Mix thoroughly.
- Chop one of the strawberries into small pieces. The other strawberry should be sliced into thin heart-shaped slices.
- Fill each mason jar half-way with the cream cheese mixture.
- Make a layer of chopped strawberries on top of the cream cheese mixture in each jar.
- Fill the rest of each jar with the remaining cream cheese mixture.
- Top each jar with the heart-shaped strawberry slices. Arrange the slices to form a flower pattern.
- Sprinkle some lemon zest at the center of each flower.
- Put in the fridge to chill. Serve.

Nutritional info (per serving):

- Calories: 474
- Carbs: 5.7 g
- Fats: 48.2 g
- Proteins: 4.5 g
- Fiber: 0.4 g

Keto Pound Cake (Vanilla Flavor)

Yields: 12 slices

Serving size: 1 slice

Preparation time: 15 minutes

Cooking time: 50 minutes

Ingredients:

- 2 cups almond flour
- 1 cup granular erythritol
- 1 cup sour cream
- 1/2 cup butter (sliced into small squares)
- 2 ounces cream cheese
- 2 teaspoons baking powder
- 1 teaspoon vanilla extract
- 4 pieces large eggs

Directions:

- Pre-heat your oven to 350 degrees Fahrenheit.
- Prepare a 9" bundt cake pan and butter it generously.
- In a mixing bowl, put in the baking powder and almond flour. Mix thoroughly.
- In a microwave safe mixing bowl, put in the sliced butter and cream cheese.
- Microwave them for 30 seconds. Stir the mixture to combine well.
- Put in the sour cream, vanilla extract, and erythritol into the melted cream cheese mixture. Mix well.
- Pour the cheese mixture into the mixing bowl containing the flour mixture. Mix well the batter.
- Put in the eggs into the batter. Mix well.
- Transfer the batter into the prepared bundt cake pan. Bake the cake for 50 minutes. Do the toothpick test to make sure that the cake is cooked thoroughly.
- Take out the cake from the oven. Do not remove it immediately from the bundt pan. It may crumble during the process. Let the cake cool completely in the bundt pan for 2 hours or more, even overnight.
- Take out the cake from the bundt pan. Cut into 12 slices. Serve.

Nutritional info (per serving):

- Calories: 249
- Carbs: 23.23 g
- Fats: 20.67 g
- Proteins: 7.67 g
- Fiber: 2 g

Keto Cacao Butter Blondies

Yields: 20 blondies

Serving size: 1 blondie

Preparation time: 15 minutes

Cooking time: 20 minutes

Ingredients:

- 6 tablespoons cacao butter
- 6 tablespoons erythritol (powdered)
- 2 tablespoons unsalted butter (softened, room temperature)
- 1 teaspoon baking powder
- 2 pieces large eggs (room temperature)
- 1/4 cup almond flour
- 2 1/2 tablespoons coconut flour
- 2 tablespoons coconut cream
- 2 tablespoons walnuts (ground)
- 1/2 ounces dark chocolate (chopped)
- 1 teaspoon vanilla bean seeds
- 1 teaspoon vanilla extract
- 1 pinch stevia extract
- 1 dash salt

Directions:

- Pre-heat your oven to 360 degrees Fahrenheit. Prepare a square baking pan (8") and line it with parchment paper.
- In a microwave-safe mixing bowl, put in the cacao butter. Microwave it for 90 seconds to melt. Stir the melted butter and make sure that there are no more lumps in it. Microwave again to melt the lumps, if needed. Let it cool completely.
- Once the melted cacao butter is cooled, mix in the unsalted butter and stir.
- In another mixing bowl, put in the eggs, vanilla bean seeds, vanilla extract, erythritol, and salt. Mix them well for 2 minutes using a hand electric mixer.
- Put in the coconut cream into the egg mixture. Mix well.
- Put in the cooled melted cacao butter mixture into the egg mixture. Continue mixing until the consistency gets dense.
- In another mixing bowl, sift the almond flour, coconut flour, and baking powder. Mix well.
- Pour the flour mixture into the cream mixture. Mix well.
- Put in the chopped chocolate and ground walnuts. Mix well.

- Transfer the batter into the lined baking pan. Spread out the batter evenly on the baking pan.
- Bake the batter for 20 minutes. Do not over-bake it. Do the toothpick test to know that it is the right time to take the blondies out from the oven.
- Carefully take out the entire batch of blondies from the pan including the parchment paper. Put it on the rack to cool down.
- Once completely cooled, cut into 20 blondie squares. It is recommended to leave the blondies overnight on the counter before serving.

Nutritional info (per serving):

- Calories: 80
- Carbs: 1.6 g
- Fats: 7.3 g
- Proteins: 2.1 g
- Fiber: 0.9 g

Keto Cream Cheese Frosted Carrot Mug Cake

Yields: 2 slices

Serving size: 1 slice

Preparation time: 10 minutes

Cooking time: 2 minutes

Ingredients:

Cake:

- 2 tablespoons almond flour
- 1 tablespoon erythritol
- 1 tablespoon psyllium husk
- 1 tablespoon butter (melted)
- 1 piece large egg (beaten lightly)
- 1 teaspoon cinnamon
- 1/2 teaspoon vanilla extract
- 1/2 teaspoon baking powder
- 1/2 piece small carrot (grated finely)
- 1/4 teaspoon ginger (ground)
- pinch of salt

Frosting:

- 1 tablespoon whipping cream
- 1/4 cup cream cheese (room temperature)
- 1/2 teaspoon vanilla extract
- 1/2 tablespoon erythritol

Directions:

- In a food processor, put in all the ingredients for the cake. Blend to combine everything.
- Pour the blended mixture from the food processor into a microwave-safe mug.
- Microwave it for 90 seconds on high setting.
- Remove the cake from the mug. Set it aside to cool down.
- Cut the cake into two layers. Set aside.
- In a mixing bowl, put in the cream cheese, vanilla extract, and erythritol. Whip them up using an electric hand mixer. Continue whipping until the texture of the mixture becomes soft and creamy.
- Put in the whipping cream into the cream cheese mixture. Mix thoroughly for 5 minutes.

- Get the bottom layer of the cake. Scoop a heaping tablespoon of the cream cheese frosting. Spread the frosting on top of the bottom layer of the cake.
- Get the top layer of the cake. Gently put it on top of the frosted bottom layer of the cake.
- Spread the rest of the cream cheese frosting on top of the cake and on the sides.
- You can chill the cake before serving or you can serve it right away. Cut the cake in half and enjoy.

Nutritional info (per serving):

- Calories: 229
- Carbs: 20 g
- Fats: 17.3 g
- Proteins: 6 g
- Fiber: 15.9 g

Keto Avocado Brownies

Yields: 12 brownies

Serving size: 1 brownie

Preparation time: 10 minutes

Cooking time: 30 minutes

Ingredients:

- 2 pieces large avocadoes (ripe)
- 100 grams Lily's chocolate chips (melted)
- 4 tablespoons cocoa powder
- 3 tablespoons refined coconut oil
- 1/2 teaspoon vanilla
- 2 pieces eggs

Dry Ingredients:

- 90 grams almond flour (blanched)
- 1/4 cup erythritol
- 1 teaspoon baking powder
- 1 teaspoon stevia powder
- 1/4 teaspoon baking soda
- 1/4 teaspoon salt

Directions:

- Pre-heat your oven to 350 degrees Fahrenheit.
- In a mixing bowl, put in all the ingredients listed under dry ingredients. Whisk to combine well. Set aside.
- Cut the avocadoes in half. Scoop out the flesh. Weigh the avocadoes. You will need a total of 250 grams of avocadoes for this recipe.
- Put the avocadoes in a food processor. Process the avocadoes until the texture becomes smooth.
- Put in the rest of the ingredients into the food processor one at a time. Process for a few seconds after each ingredient is added into the avocado mixture.
- Put in the flour mixture into the food processor. Process until everything is well combined.
- Line a baking dish (12" x 8") with parchment paper. Transfer the avocado batter into the baking dish. Spread the batter evenly on the surface of the baking dish.
- Bake the batter for 30 minutes. Do the toothpick test to know if the brownie is done. The top surface of the brownie should be soft to the touch.

- Take the brownie out from the oven. Set it aside to cool down. Cut the brownie into 12 square pieces.

Nutritional info (per serving):

- Calories: 155
- Carbs: 9.78 g
- Fats: 14.05 g
- Proteins: 4.02 g
- Fiber: 6.98 g

Keto Breakfast Recipes

Keto Pancakes

Yields: 10 pancakes

Serving size: 1 pancake

Preparation time: 5 minutes

Cooking time: 15 minutes

Ingredients:

- 1/2 cup almond flour
- 4 pieces large eggs
- 4 ounces cream cheese (softened)
- 1 teaspoon lemon zest
- 1 tablespoon butter (for frying)
- 1 tablespoon butter (for topping)

Directions:

- In a mixing bowl, put in almond flour, eggs, cream cheese, and lemon zest. Whisk until the batter is well combined.
- In a skillet over medium heat, melt the butter for frying.
- Scoop about 3 tablespoons of batter and pour it on the skillet. Cook the pancake for about 2 minutes or until it turns golden.
- Flip the pancake to its other side and cook it for another 2 minutes.
- Transfer the cooked pancake to a plate. Continue cooking the rest of the batter.
- Serve the pancakes topped with butter.

Nutritional info (per serving):

- Calories: 110
- Carbs: 2 g
- Fats: 10 g
- Proteins: 4 g
- Fiber: 1 g

Cauliflower Bread with Poached Eggs, Crispy Bacon, and Avocado

Yields: 2 breads

Serving size: 1 bread

Preparation time: 15 minutes

Cooking time: 45 minutes

Ingredients:

- 2 cups cauliflower (grated)
- 4 pieces eggs
- 1-2 tablespoons coconut flour
- 1/2 – 1 tablespoon psyllium husk
- 1/2 teaspoon garlic powder
- 1/2 teaspoon salt
- 1/4 spring onion (sliced finely)
- 3-4 slices bacon (diced)
- 1 whole avocado

Directions:

- Pre-heat your oven to 350 degrees Fahrenheit. Prepare two baking trays and line them with parchment paper.
- In a mixing bowl, put in the grated cauliflower, 2 pieces of eggs, psyllium husk, salt, 1 tablespoon of coconut flour, and garlic powder. Combine well. You can add another tablespoon of coconut flour to thicken the mixture.
- Equally portion the cauliflower mixture into two. Put each portion on each prepared baking tray. Spread out the mixtures evenly into rectangle-shaped breads. The breads should not be too thick or too thin.
- Bake the breads for 15 minutes.
- Check the breads. Rotate the breads in the oven. Bake the breads for 10 minutes more until they are golden brown.
- Take the breads out from the oven. Spread the bacon on top of the breads. Put the breads back in the oven. Bake for a few minutes until the bacons turn golden brown.
- In a saucepan with water over medium heat, bring the water to a boil. Put in a pinch of salt and a dash of apple cider vinegar.
- Once the water is boiling, crack the remaining 2 eggs into the boiling water to poach them. Cook the eggs for a few minutes until the egg whites are cooked but the egg yolks are still slightly runny.
- Take out the poached eggs from the boiling water using a slotted spoon. Put the poached eggs on some paper towels to absorb the excess water from the eggs.

- Cut the avocado in half and take out the seed.
- Transfer the cauliflower breads on serving plates. Top each bread with a poached egg, half of the avocado, and spring onions.

Nutritional info (per serving):
- Calories: 498
- Carbs: 14 g
- Fats: 38 g
- Proteins: 27 g
- Fiber: 8.5 g

Keto Tacos with Guacamole and Bacon

Yields: 2 tacos

Serving size: 1 taco

Preparation time: 5 minutes

Cooking time: 10 minutes

Ingredients:

- 1/4 cup organic romaine lettuce (chopped)
- 3 tablespoons organic sweet potatoes (diced and cooked)
- 1 tablespoon Brain Octane Oil
- 1 tablespoon ghee (grass-fed)
- 2 pieces eggs (pasture-raised)
- 1 piece medium avocado (organic)
- 2 slices pastured bacon (cooked)
- 1/4 teaspoon Himalayan pink salt
- organic micro cilantro (for garnish)

Directions:

- In a skillet over medium heat, heat up the ghee.
- Get an egg. Crack the egg in the middle of the skillet. Poke the egg yolk.
- Let the egg cook until solid for about 2 minutes per side. Transfer the cooked egg onto a plate lined with paper towels to absorb the excess oil.
- Cook the other egg in a similar way. The 2 cooked eggs will serve as the taco shells.
- In a mixing bowl, put in the avocado, pink salt, and octane oil. Mash the avocado and mix well.
- Equally divide the avocado mixture into 2 portions. Spread each avocado mixture onto each egg taco.
- Arrange the romaine lettuce on top of each taco shell.
- Put a bacon slice on each taco. Top each taco with the cooked sweet potatoes.
- Garnish the tacos with micro cilantro and sprinkle some pink salt for added taste.
- Fold each taco in half. Serve.

Nutritional info (per serving):

- Calories: 387
- Carbs: 9 g
- Fats: 35 g
- Proteins: 11 g
- Fiber: 5 g

Keto BLT Salad

Yields: 6 servings

Serving size: 1/6 of the entire dish

Preparation time: 15 minutes

Cooking time: 30 minutes

Ingredients:

- 6 cups wild rocket (washed and dried)
- 1/2 cup whole-egg mayonnaise
- 250 grams punnet cherry tomatoes
- 2 tablespoons lemon juice
- 2 tablespoons extra virgin olive oil
- 3 pieces bacon rashers (cut crosswise)
- 1 garlic bulb
- 1 bunch chives (chopped coarsely)
- 1 piece avocado (thinly sliced)

Directions:

- Pre-heat your oven to 450 degrees Fahrenheit.
- Arrange the cherry tomatoes on a baking tray. Season the tomatoes with salt and pepper. Drizzle the tomatoes with a couple of teaspoon of oil.
- Roast the tomatoes in the oven for about 8 minutes until they are slightly soft. Take the tomatoes out from the oven. Let them cool down.
- Get the garlic. Wrap it in aluminum foil. Put it in the oven. Cook for about 20 minutes until each clove feels soft. Take out the garlic from the oven. Let them cool down.
- Cut each garlic clove crosswise. Squeeze the pulp into a container. Throw away the skin.
- In a frying pan over medium heat, heat the remaining oil. Put the bacon onto the pan. Cook the bacon for 2 minutes on each side. Put the cooked bacon on a plate with paper towel to absorb the excess grease.
- In a food processor, put in the mayonnaise, squeezed garlic, and lemon juice. Process them until the texture is smooth. Season the dressing with pepper and salt to taste.
- In a salad bowl, put in the sliced avocado, wild rocket, bacon, and tomatoes. Combine well. Sprinkle the chives. Drizzle the dressing on the salad. Serve.

Nutritional info (per serving):

- Calories: 1357

- Carbs: 6 g
- Fats: 30 g
- Proteins: 7 g
- Fiber: 3 g

Keto Iced Coffee with Protein Shake

Yields: 1 glass

Serving size: 1 glass

Preparation time: 5 minutes

Cooking time: 5 minutes

Ingredients:

- 1 1/4 cup almond milk (unsweetened)
- 1/2 cup ice cubes
- 4 ounces Coffee Cold Brew - unsweetened (frozen into cubes)
- 1 scoop Vanilla Collagen Protein
- 1/2 avocado (frozen with skin)
- 1 tablespoon cacao powder
- 1/2 tablespoon Brain Octane Oil
- 1/4 teaspoon Ceylon cinnamon
- Cacao nibs (for garnish)

Directions:

- In a blender, put in all the ingredients excluding the protein powder. Start blending from low speed going up to mix well.
- Put in the protein powder. Blend mixture in low speed to mix the protein powder with the shake.
- Pour the shake into a glass. Garnish with cacao nibs and serve.

Nutritional info (per serving):

- Calories: 288
- Carbs: 15.9 g
- Fats: 19.4 g
- Proteins: 16.5 g
- Fiber: 10.4 g

Keto Snack Recipes

Keto Power Peanut Butter Granola

Yields: 12 servings

Serving size: 1/3 cup

Preparation time: 10 minutes

Cooking time: 30 minutes

Ingredients:

- 1 1/2 cups pecans
- 1 1/2 cups almonds
- 1 cup coconut (shredded)
- 1/3 cup Swerve Sweetener
- 1/3 cup peanut butter
- 1/3 cup vanilla whey protein powder
- 1/4 cup butter
- 1/4 cup sunflower seeds
- 1/4 cup water

Directions:

- Pre-heat your oven to 300 degrees Fahrenheit. Prepare a rimmed baking sheet and line it with parchment paper.
- In a food processor, put in the pecans and almonds. Process them until they look like coarse crumbs.
- In a mixing bowl, put in the shredded coconut, vanilla protein powder, sweetener, sunflower seeds, and processed pecans and almonds. Mix well.
- In a microwave safe container, put in the butter and peanut butter. Microwave them to melt. Keep your eyes on the butter mixture when in the microwave. Make sure that it won't get burn. Stir to mix.
- Pour the melted butter mixture into the nut mixture in the mixing bowl. Stir and toss to combine well.
- Put in the water into the mixture. Stir and let the mixture clump together.
- Transfer the mixture onto the baking sheet. Bake it for 30 minutes. Halfway through the time, take the mixture from the oven. Stir the mixture. Put it back into the oven to continue baking.
- Take out the cooked peanut butter granola from the oven. Let it cool completely. Serve.

Nutritional info (per serving):
- Calories: 338
- Carbs: 9.74 g
- Fats: 30.08 g
- Proteins: 9.36 g
- Fiber: 4.99 g

Keto Apple Cider Donut Bites

Yields: 24 donut bites

Serving size: 2 donut bites

Preparation time: 10 minutes

Cooking time: 20 minutes

Ingredients:

Donut Bites:

- 2 pieces large eggs
- 2 cups almond flour
- 1/3 cup water
- 1/2 cup Swerve Sweetener
- 1/4 cup butter (melted)
- 1/4 cup whey protein powder (unflavored)
- 1 1/2 tablespoons apple cider vinegar
- 2 teaspoons baking powder
- 1 1/2 teaspoons apple extract
- 1/2 teaspoon cinnamon
- 1/2 teaspoon salt

Coating:

- 1/4 cup butter (melted)
- 1/4 cup Swerve Sweetener
- 2 teaspoons cinnamon

Directions:

- Pre-heat your oven to 325 degrees Fahrenheit. Prepare a mini muffin pan with 24 cavities. Grease the pan.
- In a mixing bowl, put in the almond flour, protein powder, cinnamon, salt, baking powder, and sweetener. Whisk them to combine.
- Put into flour mixture the eggs, butter, apple extract, apple cider vinegar, and water. Whisk them very well to combine.
- Pour the batter into the 24 cavities of the greased muffin pan. Bake the donut bites for 15 minutes or until the bites are firm.
- Take out the donut bites from the oven. Let them cool down in the muffin pan for 10 minutes. Take out the bites from the muffin pan. Arrange them on a wire rack. Let them cool completely.
- In a mixing bowl, put in the cinnamon and sweetener for the coating. Mix them well.

- Each donut bite should be dip into the melted butter first. Make sure that the butter coats each bite completely.
- Roll each bite into the mixture of sweetener and cinnamon. Serve.

Nutritional info (per serving):

- Calories: 164
- Carbs: 4.81g
- Fats: 13.71 g
- Proteins: 6.52 g
- Fiber: 2.23 g

Keto Cheesecake Strawberry Popsicles

Yields: 12 popsicles

Serving size: 1 popsicle

Preparation time: 15 minutes

Cooking time: 4 hours

Ingredients:

- 1/3 cup Swerve Sweetener (powdered)
- 2 cups strawberries (chopped)
- 1 cup cream
- 8 ounces cream cheese (softened)
- 1 tablespoon lemon juice
- 1/4 teaspoon stevia extract
- 2 teaspoons lemon zest

Directions:

- Prepare 12 popsicle molds and 12 wooden popsicle sticks.
- In a food processor, put in the cream cheese. Process the cream cheese until the texture is smooth.
- Add in the cream, lemon juice, stevia extract, powdered Swerve, and lemon zest. Continue to process until mixed thoroughly.
- Add in 1 1/2 cups of the chopped strawberries. Continue to process until the mixture is very smooth. Stir into the mixture the rest of the chopped strawberries. Do not process this time around.
- Carefully pour the strawberry mixture into each of the popsicle molds. Push in a popsicle stick about halfway in each of the filled up molds.
- Put the popsicles in the freezer. Freeze them for at least 4 hours. Unmold the popsicles and serve.

Nutritional info (per serving):

- Calories: 122
- Carbs: 3 g
- Fats: 12 g
- Proteins: 2 g
- Fiber: 1 g

Keto Raspberry and White Chocolate Fat Bombs

Yields: 12 fat bombs

Serving size: 1 fat bomb

Preparation time: 5 minutes

Cooking time: 1 hour

Ingredients:

- 1/2 cup raspberries (freeze-dried)
- 1/2 cup coconut oil
- 1/4 cup erythritol sweetener (powdered)
- 2 ounces cacao butter

Directions:

- Prepare a muffin pan with 12 cavities. Line them with paper liners.
- In a saucepan over low heat, heat the cacao butter and coconut oil until they have melted completely. Take away the saucepan from the heat.
- In a food processor, put in the raspberries. Grind them until pulverized.
- Add into the melted butter in the saucepan the sweetener and pulverized berries. Mix until well until the sweetener is dissolve.
- Carefully pour the mixture into each of the muffin cups. You may notice that the pulverized raspberry will settle to the bottom of the saucepan. Keep on stirring the mixture while pouring into the muffin cups so that each of the fat bomb has some raspberry powder in it.
- Put the fat bombs in the fridge for at least 1 hour or until they are firm to the touch. Serve.

Nutritional info (per serving):

- Calories: 153
- Carbs: 1.2 g
- Fats: 16.6 g
- Proteins: 0.2 g
- Fiber: 0.4 g

Keto Raspberry Jam and Peanut Butter Cups

Yields: 12 muffin cups

Serving size: 1 muffin cup

Preparation time: 5 minutes

Cooking time: 10 minutes

Ingredients:

- 3/4 cup creamy peanut butter
- 3/4 cup raspberries
- 3/4 cup coconut oil
- 1/4 cup water
- 1 teaspoon gelatin (grass-fed)
- 6 to 8 tablespoons Swerve Sweetener (powdered)

Directions:

- Prepare a muffin pan with 12 cavities. Line them with paper liners.
- In a saucepan over medium heat, put in the water and raspberries. Let them boil. Lower the heat and simmer the raspberries for about 5 minutes. Using a fork, mash the raspberries.
- While the mashed raspberries are still hot, add in 4 tablespoons of the sweetener. Stir to combine well.
- Add into the raspberry mixture the gelatin. Stir well to combine. Set aside to cool down.
- In a microwave safe mixing bowl, put together the coconut oil and peanut butter. Microwave them for 60 seconds or until they are melted completely.
- Add into the melted peanut butter the rest of the sweetener.
- Divide the peanut butter mixture into two equal parts.
- Pour the first half of the peanut butter mixture equally into the 12 muffin cups.
- Freeze the filled up muffin cups for about 15 minutes until they are firm to the touch.
- Pour the mashed raspberries mixture equally on top of the frozen peanut butter cups.
- Pour the remaining peanut butter mixture equally on top of the mashed raspberries.
- Put back in the fridge. Chill until firm. Serve.

Nutritional info (per serving):

- Calories: 223
- Carbs: 4.52 g
- Fats: 21.77 g
- Proteins: 3.84 g

- Fiber: 1.31 g

Keto Lunch Recipes

Keto Sushi

Yields: 8 pieces

Serving size: 4 pieces

Preparation time: 10 minutes

Cooking time: 10 minutes

Ingredients:

- 1 cup cauliflower (chopped)
- 1 piece nori wrapper
- 1 1/2 ounces cream cheese
- 1/2 avocado (medium)
- 1/4 cup cucumber
- soy sauce (for dipping)
- 1 tablespoon coconut oil

Directions:

- In a food processor, put in the chopped cauliflower. Process until it has the texture of rice.
- In a skillet over medium heat, put in the coconut oil. Heat the oil. Put in the cauliflower rice.
- Cook the cauliflower rice until it becomes slightly brown and cooked (about 5 minutes). Transfer in a bowl. Set aside.
- Slice the cucumber, cream cheese, and avocado as thinly as you can. Put each ingredient in different bowls. Set aside.
- Line a clean and flat surface with a plastic wrap that is larger than the nori wrapper. This is your sushi workspace.
- Spread out the nori wrapper on the surface of the plastic wrap.
- Pour the cauliflower rice on the nori wrapper. Spread the rice evenly on the surface of the nori wrapper. Leave some room on the edges of the nori wrapper.
- Starting from the edge that is closest to you, arrange the avocado slices on top of the cauliflower rice. When the avocado is done, arrange beside the avocado slices the cream cheese slices. Next to the cream cheese slices, arrange the cucumber slices.
- Use the plastic wrap to help you in rolling the sushi securely.
- Lift and hold the edge of the plastic wrap that is closest to you. Make sure that no ingredient will fall off or move places when rolling.

- Carefully roll the nori wrapper around the arranged ingredients with the aid of the plastic wrap.
- After rolling the entire thing, slice it into 8 sushi pieces using a sharp knife. Do not include the plastic wrap when slicing the sushi. Start slicing the sushi in the middle so you will not push the cauliflower rice out of the roll due to knife pressure.

Nutritional info (per serving):

- Calories: 230.75
- Carbs: 8.65 g
- Fats: 22.15 g
- Proteins: 4.45 g
- Fiber: 4.425 g

Keto Egg and Sausage Sandwich

Yields: 1 sandwich

Serving size: 1 sandwich

Preparation time: 5 minutes

Cooking time: 10 minutes

Ingredients:

- 2 pieces large eggs
- 1 tablespoon butter
- 1 tablespoon mayonnaise
- 2 slices sharp cheddar cheese
- 2 sausage patties (2 ounces each patty)
- a few slices of avocado

Directions:

- In a skillet over medium heat, put in the butter. Heat the butter. Carefully put 2 silicone egg molds on the pan.
- Crack an egg into each of the egg mold. Break the yolks using a fork. Whisk the eggs gently. Cover the pan. Cook the eggs until they are thoroughly cooked (about 4 minutes). Take out the eggs from the egg molds.
- Put in the sausage patties in the pan. Cook the patties on each side until they are cooked through. Take out the sausage patties from the pan.
- Put an egg on a plate. Spread half of the mayonnaise on top of the egg. Put a sausage patty on top of the mayonnaise.
- Put a slice of cheese on top of the patty. Put some avocado slices on top of the cheese.
- Put the remaining sausage patty after the avocado. Put on top the remaining slice of cheese.
- Spread the other half of the mayonnaise on the cheese. Finally, top it with the second cooked egg. Enjoy.

Nutritional info (per serving):

- Calories: 880
- Carbs: 8 g
- Fats: 82 g
- Proteins: 32 g
- Fiber: 2 g

Chicken with Lemon and Herb Mediterranean Salad

Yields: 4 servings

Serving size: 1/4 of the entire dish

Preparation time: 10 minutes

Cooking time: 15 minutes

Ingredients:

Dressing:

- 1/4 cup lemon juice (fresh squeezed)
- 2 tablespoons water
- 2 tablespoons olive oil
- 2 tablespoons parsley (fresh chopped)
- 2 tablespoons red wine vinegar
- 2 teaspoons garlic (minced)
- 2 teaspoons basil (dried)
- 1 teaspoon salt
- 1 teaspoon oregano (dried)
- cracked pepper (to taste)

Salad:

- 500 grams chicken breasts (skinless, boneless)
- 4 cups Romaine lettuce leaves (washed and dried)
- 1/3 cup pitted black olives (sliced)
- 2 pieces Roma tomatoes (diced)
- 1 piece large cucumber (diced)
- 1 piece avocado (sliced)
- 1 piece red onion (sliced)
- Some lemon wedges (to serve)

Directions:

- In a mason jar, put all the dressing ingredients. Mix well.
- In a mixing bowl, pour in half of the dressing to be used as a marinade. Put the remaining half of the dressing in the fridge to be used later.
- Put the chicken into the bowl with the dressing. Marinade the chicken for at least 15 minutes.
- In a grill pan over medium heat, put in a tablespoon of oil. Heat the oil. Grill the chicken breasts on each side until they turned brown and thoroughly cooked.
- Let the cooked chicken cool down for a few minutes. Slice the chicken into bite-sizes.

- Prepare 4 personal salad bowls. Equally divide all the salad ingredients into each bowl including the bite-sized chicken.
- Drizzle with the remaining dressing from the fridge each salad in the bowl. Serve each salad bowl with 1 to 2 lemon wedges.

Nutritional info (per serving):

- Calories: 336
- Carbs: 13 g
- Fats: 21 g
- Proteins: 24 g
- Fiber: 6 g

Keto Chicken BLT Salad Stuffed Avocados

Yields: 6 stuffed avocadoes

Serving size: 1 stuffed avocado

Preparation time: 15 minutes

Cooking time: 15 minutes

Ingredients:

- 3 pieces avocados
- 12 slices of turkey bacon
- 2 pieces roma tomatoes
- 1 1/2 cups rotisserie chicken (shredded)
- 1 1/2 cups cottage cheese
- 1 cup romaine lettuce (finely chopped)

Directions:

- Pre-heat your oven to 400 degrees Fahrenheit. Line a baking sheet with aluminum foil.
- Arrange the bacon slices on the baking sheet.
- Bake the bacon slices for 10 minutes. Flip the bacon slices on the other side. Bake them for 5 minutes more. Take them out of the oven. Arrange the bacon slices on paper towel sheets to absorb the excess grease and to cool them down.
- Slice the tomatoes into quarters. Take out the seeds and pulp. Dice the tomatoes into small chunks.
- Crumble the bacon slices into bite sizes.
- In a mixing bowl, put in the crumbled turkey bacon, shredded chicken, tomatoes, romaine lettuce, and cottage cheese. Mix them all together well.
- Season the salad with salt and pepper to taste.
- Cut the avocadoes in half. Take out the pits. Lightly season each half of the avocadoes with pepper and salt.
- Equally divide the salad into 6 portions. Scoop each portion and fill the inside hole of each half avocado. Serve.

Nutritional info (per serving):

- Calories: 291
- Carbs: 13 g
- Fats: 23 g
- Proteins: 25 g
- Fiber: 6 g

Keto Cheesy Taco Skillet

Yields: 6 tacos

Serving size: 1 taco

Preparation time: 5 minutes

Cooking time: 15 minutes

Ingredients:

- 1 pound ground beef (lean)
- 6 pieces taco shells
- 3 cups baby spinach/kale mixture
- 1 can diced tomatoes with green chilis
- 1 1/2 cups jack and cheddar cheese (shredded)
- 2 pieces bell peppers (diced)
- 1 piece large yellow onion (diced)
- taco seasoning
- green onions (to garnish)

Directions:

- In a pan over medium heat, put the ground beef. Crumble it well until the color turns into light brown.
- Remove from the pan the excess fat from the ground beef.
- Add in the peppers and onions with the ground beef. Cook everything until slightly brown.
- Add into the pan with the ground beef the taco seasoning, canned tomatoes, and 1 tablespoon of the liquid from the canned tomatoes. Mix everything very well.
- Add in the greens. Combine with the ground beef mixture until fully wilted.
- Spread the shredded cheese on top of the ground beef mixture. Do not mix. Let the cheese melt.
- Divide equally into 6 portions. Put each portion of the ground beef mixture into a taco shell. Serve.

Nutritional info (per serving):

- Calories: 341
- Carbs: 9 g
- Fats: 20 g
- Proteins: 30 g
- Fiber: 1 g

Keto Dinner Recipes

Keto Grilled Chicken with Chorizo Confetti

Yields: 4 servings

Serving size: 1/4 of the entire dish

Preparation time: 10 minutes

Cooking time: 20 minutes

Ingredients:

- 4 pieces 6-ounce chicken breast halves (skinless, boneless)
- 1/4 cup Mexican pork chorizo (wrappings removed)
- 1/4 cup onion (sliced)
- 1/4 cup red bell pepper (diced)
- 1/4 cup yellow bell pepper (diced)
- 1/4 cup chicken stock (unsalted)
- 2 tablespoons carrot (diced)
- 1 tablespoon fresh cilantro (chopped)
- 2 tablespoons green bell pepper (diced)
- 1/4 teaspoon black pepper (freshly ground)
- 1/2 teaspoon kosher salt (divided into 2)
- Cooking spray

Directions:

- Pre-heat your grill pan on medium setting.
- Season the chicken breasts with pepper and ¼ teaspoon of salt.
- Grease the grill pan using the cooking spray.
- Grill the chicken breasts. Cook each side until done (about 6 minutes per side). Set aside.
- In a skillet over medium heat, put in the chorizo. Crumble the chorizo. Cook for a minute.
- Add in the rest of the salt, carrot, and onion. Cook for 2 minutes. Stir occasionally.
- Add in the bell peppers. Cook for a minute or two until they are tender and crisp.
- Pour in the stock. Simmer for 2 minutes or more until almost all the liquid has evaporated. Scrape the sides and bottom of the pan to loosen the ingredients that are sticking on the pan.
- Remove from heat.

- Put each chicken breast on a plate. Scoop some chorizo mixture (about 3 tablespoons). Put similar amount of the chorizo mixture on top of the chicken breast. Garnish with cilantro. Serve.

Nutritional info (per serving):

- Calories: 254
- Carbs: 3.6 g
- Fats: 8.2 g
- Proteins: 39.2 g
- Fiber: 1.2 g

Keto Steak with Ginger- Scallion Sauce

Yields: 4 steaks

Serving size: 1 steak with toppings

Preparation time: 15 minutes

Cooking time: 15 minutes

Ingredients:
- 2 3/4-inch-thick 10-ounce boneless strip steaks (at room temperature and trimmed)
- 1/4 cup dry sherry
- 2 tablespoons chicken broth (low-sodium)
- 1 tablespoon unsalted butter (still cold and diced)
- 2 scallions (sliced thinly)
- 1 clove garlic (minced)
- 4 teaspoons canola oil
- 2 teaspoons fresh ginger (minced)
- 2 teaspoons oyster sauce
- 2 teaspoons sesame seeds (toasted)
- 1/4 teaspoon black pepper
- 1/4 teaspoon kosher salt

Directions:
- In a skillet over medium heat, put in 2 teaspoons of oil.
- Season the steaks with pepper and salt.
- Put the steaks on the skillet. Cook the steaks for 4 minutes on each side or to how done you want your steaks to be.
- Transfer the steaks on a platter. Tent them with aluminum foil to stay warm.
- In the same skillet, put in the remaining oil. Sautee the ginger and scallions for a minute.
- Put in the garlic. Sautee the garlic for a minute.
- Pour in the broth and sherry. Continue cooking for a minute stirring occasionally. Reduce the liquid to half.
- Put in the oyster sauce. Stir.
- Remove the skillet from the heat. Put in the butter. Swirl until the butter has melted and the sauce has a creamy texture.
- Slice the steaks across the grain producing four equal portions. Put each steak on a plate.

- Top each steak with equal amounts of sesame seeds and scallion mixture. Pour on each steak an equal amount of sauce from the skillet. Serve.

Nutritional info (per serving):

- Calories: 375
- Carbs: 3 g
- Fats: 24 g
- Proteins: 31 g
- Fiber: 1 g

Keto Salmon with Red Pepper Pesto

Yields: 4 servings

Serving size: 1 fillet with pesto

Preparation time: 10 minutes

Cooking time: 10 minutes

Ingredients:

- 7 pieces whole almonds (blanched)
- 4 pieces wild Alaskan salmon fillets (fresh or frozen, 6-ounce per piece)
- 1/3 cup canned roasted red bell peppers (chopped, rinsed and drained)
- 1 tablespoon tomato paste
- 1 teaspoon extra-virgin olive oil
- 3/4 teaspoon kosher salt (divided into 2)
- 1 garlic clove
- Cooking spray

Directions:

- Pre-heat your grill pan to medium setting.
- Season the salmon fillets with 1/2 teaspoon of salt.
- Grease the grill pan using a cooking spray.
- Put the fillets on the grill pan. Cook each side of the fillets for 4 minutes or to your desired doneness.
- Put each grilled salmon fillet on serving plates.
- In a food processor, put in the bell peppers, the remaining salt, and the rest of the ingredients. Process them until they turned into a pesto consistency.
- Top each salmon fillet with equal amount of pesto. Serve.

Nutritional info (per serving):

- Calories: 309
- Carbs: 2.4 g
- Fats: 14.8 g
- Proteins: 39.3 g
- Fiber: 0.6 g

Keto Chicken Stuffed with Goat Cheese

Yields: 4 servings

Serving size: 1 chicken breast

Preparation time: 10 minutes

Cooking time: 10 minutes

Ingredients:

- 4 pieces 6-ounce chicken breasts (skinless and boneless)
- 1 tablespoon olive oil
- 1 tablespoon fresh parsley (minced)
- 2 ounces goat cheese
- 2 teaspoons fresh thyme
- 1/2 teaspoon pepper
- 1/2 teaspoon kosher salt
- 1 garlic clove (grated)

Directions:

- In a mixing bowl, put in the garlic, goat cheese, thyme, and parsley. Mix well to combine everything.
- Make a pocket in each chicken breast by cutting a slit at the middle. Fill the pockets with equal amount of the mixture for stuffing. Season the chicken breasts with pepper and salt.
- In a skillet over medium heat, put in the olive oil. Put in the chicken breasts. Cook the chicken breasts for 6 minutes on each side until thoroughly cooked.
- Transfer the chicken breasts on serving plates. Serve.

Nutritional info (per serving):

- Calories: 274
- Carbs: 1 g
- Fats: 10.9 g
- Proteins: 41 g
- Fiber: 0.0 g

Keto Chicken Sausage with Spinach and Roasted Red Pepper Patties

Yields: 16 patties

Serving size: 2 patties

Preparation time: 15 minutes

Cooking time: 15 minutes

Ingredients:

- 1 1/2 pounds ground chicken
- 1/2 cup bottled roasted red bell peppers (rinsed, drained, and finely chopped)
- 1/2 cup fresh spinach (finely chopped)
- 2 teaspoons olive oil
- 1/2 teaspoon coriander (ground)
- 1/2 teaspoon thyme (dried)
- 1 teaspoon sage (dried)
- 3/4 teaspoon kosher salt
- 3/4 teaspoon red pepper (crushed)

Directions:

- In a mixing bowl, put in the ground chicken, roasted red bell peppers, sage, salt, coriander, spinach, olive oil, crushed red pepper, and thyme. Mix well. Knead to fully combine.
- Shape the ground chicken mixture into 16 patties with 1/2 inch thickness in each patty.
- In a non-stick skillet over medium heat, put in some oil. Cook the patties in batches for 3 minutes each side or until each patty is fully cooked. Serve.

Nutritional info (per serving):

- Calories: 135
- Carbs: 1 g
- Fats: 8.1 g
- Proteins: 15 g
- Fiber: 0.0 g

Keto Soup Recipes

Keto Cauliflower Coconut Curry Soup

Yields: 10 servings

Serving size: 1 cup

Preparation time: 10 minutes

Cooking time: 25 minutes

Ingredients:

- 1 cup coconut milk
- 3 tablespoons yellow curry paste
- 2 tablespoons olive oil
- 2 pieces medium heads cauliflower (cut into florets)
- 1 piece medium onion (chopped finely)
- 1 carton vegetable broth (32 ounces)
- fresh cilantro (minced, for topping)

Directions:

- In a saucepan over medium heat, put in the oil.
- Sautee the onions for 3 minutes until they are softened.
- Put in the curry paste in the saucepan. Cook for 2 minutes until its aromatic.
- Put in the broth and cauliflower. Let the mixture boil. Lower the heat when it is already boiling. Cover the saucepan. Let the curry mixture simmer for 20 minutes.
- Put in the coconut milk. Stir and cook for another minute. Turn off the heat. Let the mixture cool down for a few minutes.
- Pour in the warm mixture into a food processor by batch. Process each batch until it becomes a puree.
- Pour into a bowl. Garnish with cilantro. Serve.

Nutritional info (per serving):

- Calories: 111
- Carbs: 10 g
- Fats: 8 g
- Proteins: 3 g
- Fiber: 3 g

Keto Mexican Soup

Yields: 4 servings

Serving size: 1 1/2 cups

Preparation time: 5 minutes

Cooking time: 20 minutes

Ingredients:

- 1 pound chicken thighs (boneless, skinless and cut into 3/4-inch slices)
- 1 cup salsa
- 1 cup corn (frozen)
- 1 tablespoon taco seasoning (reduced-sodium)
- 2 teaspoons olive oil
- 1 32-ounce carton chicken broth (reduced-sodium)

Directions:

- In a saucepan over medium heat, put in the oil. Put in the chicken. Cook the chicken for 8 minutes or until thoroughly cooked with constant stirring.
- Put in taco seasoning. Stir to mix well.
- Put in the rest of the ingredients. Stir to mix well. Bring the soup to a boil.
- Lower the heat. Let the soup simmer for about 5 minutes.
- Serve while still hot.

Nutritional info (per serving):

- Calories: 254
- Carbs: 14 g
- Fats: 11 g
- Proteins: 25 g
- Fiber: 1 g

Keto Tomato Soup with Basil

Yields: 6 servings

Serving size: 1 cup

Preparation time: 20 minutes

Cooking time: 30 minutes

Ingredients:

- 3 1/2 pounds tomatoes (halved)
- 12 pieces basil leaves (fresh)
- 2 garlic cloves (peeled and halved)
- 1 piece small onion (quartered)
- 2 tablespoons thyme leaves (fresh)
- 2 tablespoons olive oil
- 1/4 teaspoon pepper
- 1 teaspoon salt
- Fresh basil (thinly sliced, for topping)
- Some salad croutons (for topping)

Directions:

- Pre-heat your oven to 400 degrees Fahrenheit. Grease a baking pan (15" x 10" x 1").
- Arrange the tomatoes, garlic, and onions on the greased baking pan.
- Drizzle with olive oil. Sprinkle with pepper, salt, and thyme. Toss carefully to coat everything.
- Put the baking pan into the oven. Roast for 30 minutes stirring only once. Make sure that the tomatoes, garlic, and onions are tender before taking out from the oven.
- Let them cool down enough to be processed in a food processor.
- Put the roasted veggies in the food processor by batch. Add in the basil leaves in each batch. Process until it has a puree consistency.
- Pour all the processed mixture in a saucepan. Heat the soup over medium heat for a few minutes.
- Transfer to 6 serving bowls. Top with sliced basil and croutons. Serve.

Nutritional info (per serving):

- Calories: 107
- Carbs: 15 g
- Fats: 5 g
- Proteins: 3 g
- Fiber: 4 g

Keto Italian Vegetable Soup

Yields: 8 servings

Serving size: 1 1/2 cups

Preparation time: 10 minutes

Cooking time: 20 minutes

Ingredients:

- 1 pound Italian sausage (bulk)
- 1 15-ounce can garbanzo beans (rinsed and drained)
- 1 14.5-ounce can beef broth
- 1 14.5-ounce can diced tomatoes (undrained)
- 2 pieces medium zucchini (1/4-inch slices)
- 1 piece medium onion (sliced)
- 1 1/2 cups water
- 1/2 teaspoon basil (dried)
- Parmesan cheese (grated, for garnish)

Directions:

- In a saucepan over medium heat, put in the sausage and onion. Cook them thoroughly. Drain out any liquid from the mixture.
- Add in the water, basil, beans, zucchini, broth, and tomatoes. Stir to mix.
- Bring the soup to a boil. Lower the heat. Let the soup simmer until the zucchini becomes tender.
- Transfer the soup into serving bowls. Garnish with parmesan cheese. Serve.

Nutritional info (per serving):

- Calories: 173
- Carbs: 14 g
- Fats: 9 g
- Proteins: 10 g
- Fiber: 3 g

Keto Turkey Sausage, Kale and Butternut Squash Soup

Yields: 10 servings

Serving size: 2 cups

Preparation time: 20 minutes

Cooking time: 30 minutes

Ingredients:

- 1 19.5-ounce package Italian turkey sausage (links and wrappings removed)
- 2 32-ounce cartons chicken broth (reduced-sodium)
- 1 piece medium butternut squash (peeled and cubed)
- 1/2 cup parmesan cheese (shaved)
- 1 bunch kale (trimmed and chopped coarsely)

Directions:

- In a soup pot over medium heat, put in the sausages. Cook them for 10 minutes, stirring and breaking the sausages into crumbles.
- Add in the chicken broth and butternut squash. Bring the mixture to a boil.
- Add in the kale by batch. Let each batch wilt slightly before adding in a new batch. Bring the soup to a boil.
- Lower the heat. Let the soup simmer for 20 minutes or until the vegetables have become tender.
- Pour into serving bowls. Top each serving with shaved parmesan cheese. Serve.

Nutritional info (per serving):

- Calories: 163
- Carbs: 20 g
- Fats: 5 g
- Proteins: 13 g
- Fiber: 5 g

Keto Salad Recipes

Keto Caesar Salad

Yields: 2 servings

Serving size: 1/2 of the entire dish

Preparation time: 15 minutes

Cooking time: 30 minutes

Ingredients:

- 2 2/3 pounds chicken breasts
- 3 1/2 ounces parmesan cheese (freshly grated)
- 3 1/2 tablespoons olive oil
- 25 ounces Romaine lettuce
- 10 ounces bacon
- Salt and pepper (to taste)

Dressing:

- 1 3/4 cups mayonnaise
- 7 tablespoons filets of anchovies (finely chopped)
- 3 1/2 tablespoons Dijon mustard
- 1 3/4 ounces parmesan cheese (finely grated)
- 3 1/2 garlic cloves (finely chopped)
- 1 3/4 lemon (juice and zest)
- Salt and pepper (to taste)

Directions:

- Pre-heat your oven to 350 degrees Fahrenheit. Grease a baking dish.
- In a mixing bowl, put in all the dressing ingredients. Whisk to combine them well. Put in the fridge to chill.
- Arrange the chicken breasts on the prepared baking dish.
- Season the chicken breasts with pepper and salt. Drizzle the olive oil on the chicken breasts.
- Bake the chicken breasts until thoroughly cooked, about 20 minutes.
- Let the chicken breasts cool down a bit. Slice into 1/2-inch thick slices.
- In a non-stick skillet over medium heat, put in the bacon. Fry the bacon until they are crispy. Let the bacon cool down a bit. Crumble the bacon into small pieces.
- Chop the lettuce leaves. Arrange the chopped leaves on each of the 2 salad plates. The lettuce leaves will serve as the base for the salad.

- Put on top of the lettuce leaves the chicken slices and the crumbled bacons.
- Pour a generous amount of the dressing onto each salad plate. Top with grated parmesan cheese. Serve.

Nutritional info (per serving):
- Calories: 1018
- Carbs: 4 g
- Fats: 87 g
- Proteins: 51 g
- Fiber: 3 g

Keto Salad in a Jar

Yields: 1 jar

Serving size: 1 jar

Preparation time: 15 minutes

Cooking time: none

Ingredients:

- 4 ounces smoked salmon (cut into bite-sized pieces)
- 1 ounce red bell peppers
- 1 ounce leafy greens
- 1 ounce cherry tomatoes
- 1 piece avocado
- 1 piece carrot
- 1/2 scallion (sliced)
- 1/4 cup mayonnaise

Directions:

- Chop all the vegetables. Layer everything in the jar.
- Arrange at the bottom of the jar the dark leafy vegetables.
- The next layer is the scallion, followed by the carrot, then the avocado, then the bell peppers, and then the tomato.
- The top layer is the smoked salmon.
- Top with the mayonnaise before serving.

Nutritional info (per serving):

- Calories: 1133
- Carbs: 28 g
- Fats: 84 g
- Proteins: 75 g
- Fiber: 17 g

Keto Tuna with Capers Salad

Yields: 4 servings

Serving size: 1/4 of the entire dish

Preparation time: 15 minutes

Cooking time: none

Ingredients:

- 1/2 cup mayonnaise
- 4 ounces tuna flakes in olive oil
- 1/2 teaspoon chili flakes
- 2 tablespoons crème fraîche
- 1/2 leek (finely chopped)
- 1 tablespoon capers
- Salt and pepper (to taste)

Directions:

- Drain the tuna flakes.
- In a mixing bowl, put in all the ingredients. Toss the salad to mix well.
- Scoop the salad into 4 individual salad plates. Serve.

Nutritional info (per serving):

- Calories: 271
- Carbs: 1 g
- Fats: 26 g
- Proteins: 8 g
- Fiber: 0 g

Keto Brussels Sprouts with Parmesan Cheese Salad

Yields: 4 servings

Serving size: 1/4 of the entire dish

Preparation time: 10 minutes

Cooking time: 30 minutes

Ingredients:

- 1 1/2 pounds Brussels sprouts
- 3 ounces parmesan cheese (shaved)
- 1 teaspoon rosemary (dried)
- 3 tablespoons olive oil
- Salt and pepper (to taste)

Directions:

- Pre-heat your oven to 450 degrees Fahrenheit.
- Grease a baking dish.
- Get the Brussels sprouts. Trim them. Cut the Brussels sprouts in half.
- Arrange the Brussels sprouts on the greased baking dish.
- Drizzle them with olive oil. Season with dried rosemary, pepper, and salt.
- Roast the Brussels sprouts until they all turned into a nice color. Take out from the oven.
- Equally divide the roasted Brussels sprouts into portions. Place each portion on a salad plate.
- Top with shaved parmesan cheese. Serve.

Nutritional info (per serving):

- Calories: 245
- Carbs: 9 g
- Fats: 16 g
- Proteins: 13 g
- Fiber: 7 g

Keto Asian Beef Salad

Yields: 2 servings

Serving size: 1/2 of the entire dish

Preparation time: 15 minutes

Cooking time: 10 minutes

Ingredients:

- 2/3 pound ribeye steaks

Sesame mayonnaise:

- 3/4 cup mayonnaise
- 1/2 tablespoon lime juice
- 1 teaspoon sesame oil
- Salt and pepper (to taste)

Beef Marinade:

- 1 tablespoon olive oil
- 1 tablespoon fresh ginger (grated)
- 1 tablespoon fish sauce
- 1 teaspoon chili flakes

Salad:

- 3 ounces cherry tomatoes
- 3 ounces lettuce
- 2 ounces cucumber
- 2 pieces scallions
- 1/2 piece red onion
- 1 teaspoon sesame seeds

Directions:

- In a mixing bowl, put in the sesame mayonnaise ingredients. Mix well to combine. Set aside.
- In another mixing bowl, put in all the ingredients for the marinade. Mix well to combine. Pour the marinade into a resealable plastic bag.
- Put the beef into the resealable plastic bag. Marinade the beef at room temperature for at least 15 minutes.
- Chop all the vegetables for the salad into bite-sized pieces excluding the scallions. Divide the chopped vegetables between two salad plates.
- In a frying pan over medium heat, put in the sesame seeds. Toast the sesame seeds for 2 minutes until they all turned fragrant and lightly browned. Set aside.

- Take the beef out from the marinade. Pat them dry using paper towels.
- In the same frying pan over high heat, sear the marinated beef for a minute on each side.
- Lower the heat to low. Cook the marinated beef until medium rare. Place on a cutting board to cool down a little bit.
- In the same frying pan over medium heat, put in the scallions. Fry them for 1 minute. Set aside.
- Slice the beef into 1/2-inch slices across the grain. Arrange the sliced beef on top of the vegetables. Put a scallion together with the sliced beef on each plate.
- Sprinkle the toasted sesame seeds on top of each salad plate.
- Pour a good amount of sesame mayonnaise on each salad plate. Serve.

Nutritional info (per serving):

- Calories: 1024
- Carbs: 7 g
- Fats: 96 g
- Proteins: 33 g
- Fiber: 3 g

Keto Seafood Recipes

Keto Zoodles with White Clam Sauce

Yields: 4 servings

Serving size: 2 cups

Preparation time: 10 minutes

Cooking time: 10 minutes

Ingredients:

- 2 pounds small clams
- 8 cups zucchini noodles
- 1/2 cup dry white wine
- 1/4 cup butter
- 1/4 cup fresh parsley (chopped)
- 2 tablespoons lemon juice
- 2 tablespoons olive oil
- 1 tablespoon garlic (minced)
- 1 teaspoon kosher salt
- 1 teaspoon lemon zest (grated)
- 1/4 teaspoon black pepper (ground)

Directions:

- In a pan over medium heat, put in the olive oil, butter, pepper, and salt. Stir to melt the butter.
- Put in the garlic. Sautee the garlic until fragrant (about 2 minutes).
- Put in the lemon juice and wine. Cook until the liquid is slightly reduced (about 2 minutes).
- Put in the clams. Cook the clams until they are all opened (about 3 minutes). Discard any clam that doesn't opened after 3 minutes.
- Remove the pan from the heat. Put in the zucchini noodles. Toss the mixture to combine well. Let the zoodles rest for a couple of minutes to soften them.
- Put in the lemon zest and parsley. Stir. Serve.

Nutritional info (per serving):

- Calories: 311
- Carbs: 9 g
- Fats: 19 g
- Proteins: 13 g

- Fiber: 2 g

Keto Roasted Salmon with Green Beans

Yields: 4 servings

Serving size: 1 salmon fillet with green beans

Preparation time: 20 minutes

Cooking time: 25 minutes

Ingredients:

- 4 6-ounce salmon fillets (skinless)
- 1 piece large red bell pepper
- 1 pound fresh green beans
- 2 teaspoons peanut oil
- Salt to taste
- 1 tablespoon black sesame seeds (for garnish)

Glaze:

- 1/3 cup soy sauce
- 2 tablespoons sweetener of your choice
- 2 tablespoons unseasoned rice vinegar
- 1/2 teaspoon garlic powder
- 1 tablespoon Asian sesame oil

Directions:

- Pre-heat your oven to 400 degrees Fahrenheit. Grease a baking sheet using non-stick cooking spray.
- In a mixing bowl, put in the ingredients for the glaze. Whisk them all together to make a glaze.
- Arrange the salmon fillets on a large plate or a cutting board. For thawed salmon fillets, pat them dry with paper towels to absorb excess moisture.
- Brush both sides of each salmon fillet with the glaze. Set aside at room temperature.
- Trim each end of the green beans.
- Remove the stem and seeds of the bell pepper. Slice the bell pepper into long strips just like the size of the green beans.
- Arrange the bell pepper and green beans on the greased baking sheet. Put a space in between each piece of vegetable. Brush the peanut oil on the vegetables. Season with salt to taste.
- Roast the vegetables in the oven for 10 minutes.
- Take out the baking sheet from the oven. Rearrange the vegetables on the baking sheet to make room for the salmon fillets. Brush each salmon fillet again with glaze.

- Reserve some glaze to be used later. Place the salmon fillets on the baking sheet where the vegetables are.
- Put back the baking sheet in the oven. Roast the vegetables and salmon fillets together for 12 minutes until the fish are firm but not hard.
- Take out the baking sheet from the oven. Brush the salmon fillets and vegetables with the rest of the glaze. Garnish with sesame seeds. Serve.

Nutritional info (per serving):

- Calories: 588
- Carbs: 11.1 g
- Fats: 35 g
- Proteins: 55 g
- Fiber: 4 g

Keto Seafood Stuffed Mushrooms with Cheese

Yields: 36 pieces

Serving size: 4 mushrooms

Preparation time: 10 minutes

Cooking time: 50 minutes

Ingredients:

- 36 pieces large white button mushrooms (stems removed and brushed clean)
- 6 ounces cream cheese (room temperature)
- 1 cup shrimp (cooked and finely chopped)
- 1/2 cup sharp cheddar cheese (grated)
- 1/4 cup paleo mayo
- 1/4 cup parmesan cheese (grated)
- 1 4.25-ounce can crab meat (drained)
- 1 tablespoon fresh parsley (chopped)
- 1 teaspoon Dijon mustard
- 1/4 teaspoon garlic powder
- 1/2 teaspoon onion powder

Directions:

- Prepare a baking sheet (13" x 18") and line it with parchment paper.
- In a mixing bowl, put all the ingredients excluding the mushrooms. Mix gently until combined thoroughly.
- Get a mushroom, scoop a spoonful of the seafood mixture, and press the seafood mixture into the cavity of the mushroom. Create a little mound on top of the mushroom but don't overfill the mushroom. Repeat this process until all the mushrooms are stuffed.
- Arrange the stuffed mushrooms on the lined baking sheet. Put in the fridge. Chill the mushrooms for at least 30 minutes.
- Pre-heat your oven to 375 degrees Fahrenheit.
- Put the stuffed mushrooms in the oven. Bake until they are golden brown (about 20 minutes).
- Take out the stuffed mushrooms from the oven. Let them rest to cool down a little bit for about 5 minutes.
- Arrange 4 stuffed mushrooms on each serving plate. Garnish with parsley. Serve.

Nutritional info (per serving):

- Calories: 50
- Carbs: 1 g

- Fats: 4 g
- Proteins: 4 g
- Fiber: 1 g

Keto Tilapia with Lemon Butter

Yields: 4 servings

Serving size: 1 tilapia fillet

Preparation time: 10 minutes

Cooking time: 10 minutes

Ingredients:

- 4 tilapia fillets (6-ounce each fillet)
- 1/4 cup butter (unsalted, melted)
- 2 tablespoons lemon juice (freshly squeezed)
- 2 tablespoons fresh parsley leaves (chopped)
- 3 cloves garlic (minced)
- 1 piece lemon zest
- Kosher salt (to taste)
- Black pepper (freshly ground, to taste)

Directions:

- Pre-heat your oven to 425 degrees Fahrenheit. Lightly grease a baking dish (9" x 13") with non-stick spray.
- In a mixing bowl, put in the lemon juice, garlic, lemon zest, and butter. Whisk them together to combine well. Set aside.
- Season the tilapia fillets with pepper and salt. Arrange the tilapia fillets on the greased baking dish. Drizzle the butter mixture over the tilapia fillets.
- Bake the fillets for about 12 minutes until they flake easily when forked.
- Garnish with parsley. Serve.

Nutritional info (per serving):

- Calories: 276.4
- Carbs: 1.8 g
- Fats: 14.5 g
- Proteins: 35.5 g
- Fiber: 0.3 g

Keto Shrimp and Cauliflower Rice Salad

Yields: 6 servings

Serving size: 1 generous cup

Preparation time: 5 minutes

Cooking time: 5 minutes

Ingredients:

Salad:

- 4 cups riced cauliflower
- 1 cup red cabbage (chopped)
- 2 cups shrimp (cooked, sliced in half lengthwise)
- 1/4 cup fresh basil (chopped)
- 2 tablespoons pink grapefruit zest (grated)

Vinaigrette:

- 1/4 cup pink grapefruit juice (fresh)
- 3 tablespoons erythritol (granulated)
- 3 tablespoons avocado oil
- 2 tablespoons apple cider vinegar
- 1 teaspoon kosher salt
- 1/2 teaspoon black pepper (ground)

Directions:

- In a mixing bowl, put in all the ingredients for the salad. Mix and combine well.
- In a blender, put in all the ingredients for the vinaigrette. Blend them until smooth.
- Pour the blended vinaigrette in the bowl with the salad. Toss to fully coat the salad with the vinaigrette.
- You can serve the salad right away or chill the salad first in the fridge for at least 30 minutes if you want to serve it chilled.

Nutritional info (per serving):

- Calories: 143
- Carbs: 5 g
- Fats: 10 g
- Proteins: 9 g
- Fiber: 2 g

Keto Poultry Recipes

Keto Chicken Parmesan

Yields: 4 servings

Serving size: 1 chicken breast

Preparation time: 10 minutes

Cooking time: 25 minutes

Ingredients:

- 4 pieces large chicken breasts (boneless and skinless breast halves)
- 2 tablespoons olive oil
- Salt and pepper (to taste)

Breading:

- 2 pieces large eggs
- 1 cup pork rinds (crushed)
- 1/2 cup parmesan cheese (grated)
- 1 teaspoon basil (dried)
- 1 teaspoon oregano (dried)
- 1/4 teaspoon onion (granulated)
- 1/4 teaspoon garlic (granulated)
- 1/4 teaspoon pepper
- 1/4 teaspoon salt

Finishing Ingredients:

- 6 ounces mozzarella cheese (fresh)
- 2 cups Marinara Sauce (low carb)
- 1/2 cup Parmesan cheese (grated)

Directions:

- Thaw the chicken breasts completely. After thawing, let the chicken breasts rest at room temperature for at least 30 minutes to take the chill off. Pat the chicken breasts using paper towels to dry.
- Pound each of the chicken breast to the same thickness. Sprinkle with salt and pepper to season.
- Pre-heat your oven to 350 degrees Fahrenheit. Put a rack in the middle of the oven.
- In a mixing bowl, put in all the ingredients for the breading excluding the eggs and parmesan cheese. Mix well.
- In another mixing bowl, crack the eggs into the bowl. Beat the eggs.

- In a cast iron skillet over medium heat, put in the oil. Swirl the oil all over the surface of the skillet.
- Get a chicken breast using a fork. Dip the chicken breast into the beaten egg. Roll the chicken breast on the breading mixture. Make sure to evenly coat the chicken breast on all sides. Put the breaded chicken breast onto the hot skillet to fry. Do this process again for all the remaining chicken breasts.
- Cook the breaded chicken breasts for 3 minutes on each side undisturbed.
- Turn off the heat of the stove. Let the cooked chicken breasts remain on the skillet.
- Add in the parmesan cheese into the remaining breading. Mix well. Sprinkle the mixture on top of the chicken breasts on the skillet.
- Pour a generous amount of marinara sauce over each chicken breast.
- Put the skillet with the chicken breasts in the oven, uncovered. Bake the chicken breasts for 20 minutes.
- Take the skillet out from the oven. Top each chicken breast with the cheeses. Put the skillet back into the oven. Tent the chicken breasts with aluminum foil.
- Bake the chicken breasts for another 5 minutes or until the cheeses have melted.
- Let the chicken breasts rest for 10 minutes or more before serving.

Nutritional info (per serving):

- Calories: 350
- Carbs: 7 g
- Fats: 19 g
- Proteins: 37 g
- Fiber: 1 g

Keto Chicken Chili

Yields: 6 servings

Serving size: 1/6 of the entire dish

Preparation time: 5 minutes

Cooking time: 25 minutes

Ingredients:

- 4 pieces large chicken breasts
- 2 cups chicken broth
- 10 ounces canned tomatoes (diced, undrained)
- 4 ounces cream cheese
- 2 ounces tomato paste
- 1 tablespoon butter
- 1 tablespoon cumin
- 1 tablespoon chili powder
- 1/2 tablespoon garlic powder
- 1 piece jalapeno pepper (chopped)
- 1/2 piece onion (chopped)
- Salt and pepper (to taste)

Directions:

- In a pot over medium heat, put in 4 cups of water. Add in the chicken breasts. Bring to a boil. Boil the chicken breasts for 12 minutes until they are cooked enough to be shred. Take the chicken breasts out from the water. Shred them using two forks.
- In another pot over medium heat, put in the butter. Melt the butter. Put in the onion. Sautee until translucent.
- Add in the chicken broth, shredded chicken, tomato paste, diced tomatoes, cumin, chili powder, jalapeno, and garlic powder. Gently stir the mixture to combine. Bring the mixture to a boil. Lower the heat. Cover the pot. Let it simmer for 10 minutes.
- Slice the cream cheese into 1-inch chunks.
- Uncover the pot. Put in the chunked cream cheese. Stir. Increase the heat to medium. Continue stirring to blend in the cream cheese.
- Take the pot away from the heat. Season the soup with pepper and salt.
- Scoop equal amounts of soup into 6 personal sized bowls. You can garnish it with any topping that you like. Serve.

Nutritional info (per serving):

- Calories: 201
- Carbs: 7 g

- Fats: 11 g
- Proteins: 18 g
- Fiber: 1 g

Keto Italian Chicken Cacciatore

Yields: 6 servings

Serving size: 1/6 of the entire dish

Preparation time: 10 minutes

Cooking time: 20 minutes

Ingredients:

- 2 pounds chicken breasts (boneless and skinless)
- 1 piece large red bell pepper
- 1 piece large green bell pepper
- 1/2 piece medium onion
- 8 ounces mushrooms (sliced)
- 1 cup chicken broth
- 1/3 cup olive oil (divided)
- 1/3 cup sherry
- 1 tablespoon Garlic & Herb Seasoning Blend
- 2 cloves large garlic
- 2 teaspoons water
- 2 teaspoons cornstarch
- 1/4 teaspoon salt

Directions:

- Pat dry the chicken breasts using paper towels. Cut the chicken breasts into strips.
- Get a tablespoon of oil. Pour over the oil on the chicken strips. Mix well.
- Sprinkle the Garlic & Herb Seasoning Blend onto the chicken strips. Mix well to evenly coat the chicken strips.
- In a saucepan over medium heat, put in a couple of tablespoons of oil. Swirl the oil to coat the pan's surface. Cook and brown the chicken strips on the saucepan by batches. Put another couple of tablespoons of oil onto the pan before cooking and browning each batch of chicken strips, if needed.
- Put all the cooked and browned chicken strips on a plate.
- In the same saucepan over medium heat, put in another couple of tablespoons of oil. Cook and brown the mushrooms on each side by batch. Add in a couple of tablespoons of oil in between each batch of mushrooms to be cooked and browned, if needed.
- Put all the cooked and browned mushrooms on a plate.
- Slice the bell peppers, garlic, and onion very thinly. Put all the slices on a plate.

- In the same saucepan over medium heat, put in all the sliced vegetables. Stir and move the vegetables around the pan to soften and scrape the browned bits that are sticking on the surface of the pan.
- Cook the vegetables half-way through.
- Put in the chicken broth followed by the sherry. Stir to mix well with the vegetables.
- Put the mushrooms and chicken strips back into the saucepan. Stir to mix well. Cover loosely the saucepan. Simmer the mixture for a few minutes.
- In a mixing bowl, put in the cornstarch and water. Mix until the texture is slurry.
- Open the saucepan. Pour the cornstarch mixture into the dish. Stir to thicken the sauce. Continue to simmer to another minute.
- Season with pepper and salt. Remove from heat. Scoop equal amounts of the dish into 6 personal sized bowls. Serve.

Nutritional info (per serving):

- Calories: 312
- Carbs: 7 g
- Fats: 14 g
- Proteins: 34 g
- Fiber: 1 g

Keto Chicken Caprese Hasselback

Yields: 4 servings

Serving size: 1 chicken breast

Preparation time: 10 minutes

Cooking time: 25 minutes

Ingredients:

- 4 pieces large chicken breasts (6 ounces per piece)
- 2 pieces medium roma tomatoes (sliced)
- 4 ounces mozzarella cheese (fresh)
- 1/4 cup fresh basil (half is cut into ribbons, the other half is still whole)
- 2 tablespoons balsamic vinegar
- 2 tablespoons olive oil
- Sea salt and pepper (to taste)

Directions:

- Pre-heat your oven to 400 degrees Fahrenheit. Prepare a baking sheet. Line it with parchment paper.
- Cut 6 shallow slits in each chicken breast. Season each chicken breast with pepper and salt. Arrange the chicken breasts on the lined baking sheet.
- Slice the mozzarella cheese into 1/4" thick slices. Cut each slice into pieces that will easily fit into the shallow slits in each chicken breast. Do the same process with the tomatoes.
- Stuff each slit of the chicken breasts with a basil leaf, tomato slices, and mozzarella slices.
- Drizzle over the chicken the balsamic vinegar and olive oil.
- Bake the chicken breasts for 20 minutes or more. Make sure that the chicken breasts are cooked thoroughly.
- Transfer each chicken breast onto a serving plate. Top with basil ribbons. Drizzle with more balsamic vinegar. Serve.

Nutritional info (per serving):

- Calories: 365
- Carbs: 4 g
- Fats: 21 g
- Proteins: 39 g
- Fiber: 1 g

Keto Chicken with Cream and Poblano Peppers

Yields: 4 servings

Serving size: 1 chicken breast

Preparation time: 10 minutes

Cooking time: 20 minutes

Ingredients:

- 4 pieces large chicken breasts (boneless and skinless)
- 3 1/2 ounces medium onion (1/4-inch thick slices)
- 2 pieces medium poblano peppers (roasted, cut into strips)
- 1 large clove garlic (sliced)
- 1 cup heavy cream
- 1/4 cup dry white wine
- 1 tablespoon olive oil (divided)
- 1/8 teaspoon cumin (dried)
- Salt and pepper (to taste)

Directions:

Peppers:

- This is how you roast the poblano peppers. Heat up your grill pan to medium heat. Put the poblano peppers directly on the grill pan. Roast the peppers on all sides until they are blackened.
- Once the peppers are all roasted, put them all in a bowl. Cover the bowl with plastic wrap. Leave the peppers covered for 10 minutes so they can steam off. Peel off the blackened skin of the poblano peppers. Slice the peppers into thin strips. Set aside.

Chicken:

- The chicken breasts should have come to room temperature before cooking them. To do this, leave the chicken breasts on the counter for at least 20 minutes.
- In a non-stick skillet over medium heat, put in 2 teaspoons of oil.
- Pat the chicken with paper towels to dry. Massage the rest of the oil into the chicken breasts. Season the chicken breasts with salt and pepper.
- Cook the chicken breasts on the skillet for 6 minutes on each side. Make sure that the chicken breasts are cooked through. Transfer the cooked chicken breasts on a plate. Tent them with aluminum foil to remain warm.

Sauce:

- In the same skillet over medium heat, sauté the garlic and onions for a minute.

- Take away the skillet from the heat. Put in the wine. Put back the skillet over the heat. Continue cooking and scrape up the brown bits that the chicken breasts have left on the pan until the wine has evaporated almost entirely.
- Put in the poblano peppers, cumin, and cream. Continue cooking until the cream becomes thick to your liking. Adjust the taste with salt and pepper.
- Pour a generous amount of the sauce on each chicken breast. Serve.

Nutritional info (per serving):

- Calories: 484
- Carbs: 6 g
- Fats: 42 g
- Proteins: 20 g
- Fiber: 1 g

Keto Beef Recipes

Keto Cabbage and Corned Beef

Yields: 12 servings

Serving size: 1/3 pound corned beef brisket with vegetables and sauce

Preparation time: 10 minutes

Cooking time: 1 hour and 30 minutes

Ingredients:

Cabbage and Corned Beef:

- 1 pound peeled celery root (sliced into 2-inch pieces)
- 4 pounds corned beef brisket (brined and comes with seasoning packet)
- 2 pieces large onions (peeled and sliced into 6 large slices each)
- 2 cups beef bone broth
- 1 piece large head cabbage (cored and sliced into 12 wedges)
- Black pepper
- Sea salt

Horseradish Sauce:

- 1/2 cup mayonnaise
- 3/4 cup sour cream
- 1/4 cup prepared horseradish
- 1/2 teaspoon garlic powder
- 2 teaspoon lemon juice

Directions:

- Remove the corned beef brisket from its wrapping. Set aside for later use the seasoning packet.
- Wash the corned beef brisket with cold water so it won't be too salty. Pat it dry using paper towels.
- In a pressure cooker, put in the corned beef brisket. The fat side should be up. Open the seasoning packet and pour its contents over the corned beef brisket. Gently pat the brisket to let the seasoning stick.
- Put in the bone broth. Pour the liquid around the brisket and not over the brisket so that the seasoning will not be disturbed.
- Cover the pressure cooker and seal it. Set it to High Pressure. Set the time to 1 hour and 15 minutes. Push the start button.

- When the time is up, push the Quick Release option to let out the pressure. Open the pressure cooker lid if there is no more steam coming out.
- While the corned beef brisket is cooking in the pressure cooker, combine all the ingredients for the horseradish sauce in a mixing bowl. Stir to mix well. Cover the bowl. Put the sauce in the fridge until the corned beef brisket is cooked.
- After the pressure cooker lid is opened, put in the vegetables in this order: onion, celery root, and cabbage. Season lightly with salt and pepper. Do not stir.
- Seal the pressure cooker lid again. Set to High Pressure for 15 minutes only. Release the pressure naturally for 10 minutes. Then, use the Quick Release option.
- Take out the corned beef brisket from the pressure cooker. Slice it to 1/2-inch width slices.
- Transfer the corned beef brisket slices onto 12 serving plates. Put a wedge of cabbage along with celery roots and onions on each serving plate. Drizzle some of the liquid from the pressure cooker on each serving plate. Serve together with the horseradish sauce.

Nutritional info (per serving):

- Calories: 433
- Carbs: 9 g
- Fats: 33 g
- Proteins: 25 g
- Fiber: 3 g

Keto Prime Rib Roast with Garlic Butter

Yields: 20 servings

Serving size: 6.5 ounces of prime rib roast

Preparation time: 5 minutes

Cooking time: 2 hours

Ingredients:

- 1 4-bone standing rib roast
- 2 tablespoons Italian seasoning
- 6 tablespoons butter (melted)
- 1 teaspoon black pepper
- 1 1/2 tablespoons sea salt
- 12 cloves garlic (minced)

Directions:

- Put the prime rib with its fatty side up on a roasting pan with a roasting rack.
- Season the prime rib liberally with pepper and salt.
- Let the prime rib rest at room temperature for about an hour.
- Pre-heat your oven to 450 degrees Fahrenheit.
- In a mixing bowl, put in the minced garlic, Italian seasoning, and melted butter. Carefully pour it over the prime rib. Spread the mixture evenly on the surface of the prime rib with the use of a basting brush.
- Put the prime rib in the oven. Roast it for 30 minutes or until the garlic has turned dark golden brown. Make sure that it is not burnt. Cover the top of the prime rib with aluminum foil like a tent.
- Lower the temperature of the oven to 350 degrees Fahrenheit. Keep roasting the prime rib until it reaches to your desired doneness.
- Take out the prime rib from the oven. Let the meat rest for about 20 minutes so it will continue to cook.
- Carve the roasted prime rib. Serve.

Nutritional info (per serving):

- Calories: 575
- Carbs: 0 g
- Fats: 51 g
- Proteins: 24 g
- Fiber: 0 g

Keto Beef Stew

Yields: 6 servings

Serving size: 1 cup

Preparation time: 10 minutes

Cooking time: 1 hour and 20 minutes

Ingredients:

- 2 pounds beef chuck stew meat (sliced into 1-inch pieces)
- 1 pound peeled celery root (cubed)
- 6 cups beef bone broth
- 2 pieces medium carrots (peeled and cut into 1/4-inch-thick-circles)
- 2 pieces medium bay leaves
- 1 piece medium onion (diced)
- 2 cloves garlic (minced)
- 1 14.5-ounce can diced tomatoes
- 2 tablespoons olive oil (divided)
- 1/2 teaspoon sea salt
- 1 teaspoon Italian seasoning
- 1/4 teaspoon black pepper

Directions:

- Lightly season the beef with pepper and salt.
- In a large Dutch oven over medium heat, put in 1 tablespoon of oil. Arrange the beef in a single layer. You have to work in batches if the beef slices will not fit in a single layer.
- Sear the beef slices for about 5 minutes on each side in each batch until they are well browned. Set aside the seared beef slices on a plate.
- In the same Dutch oven over medium heat, put in another tablespoon of oil. Put in the carrots and onions. Sautee them until they are soft and light brown, about 10 minutes.
- Put in the Italian seasoning and garlic. Sautee for another minute until the garlic releases it fragrance.
- Return the seared beef slices into the Dutch oven. Put in the tomatoes, bay leaves, and broth. Stir to mix well.
- Bring the stew to a boil. Lower the heat. Simmer the stew until the beef slices are tender, about 60 minutes.
- Put in the celery root. Increase the heat and bring the stew to a boil again. Cover the Dutch oven. Simmer the stew for another 15 minutes until the celery root is tender.

- Take out the bay leaves from the stew. Adjust the taste with pepper and salt. Serve.

Nutritional info (per serving):

- Calories: 410
- Carbs: 14 g
- Fats: 22 g
- Proteins: 36 g
- Fiber: 3 g

Keto Cauliflower with Ground Beef Lasagna

Yields: 6 servings

Serving size: 1 cup

Preparation time: 10 minutes

Cooking time: 30 minutes

Ingredients:

- 1 pound ground beef
- 1 cauliflower head (cut into florets)
- 2 cloves garlic (minced)
- 1/2 piece large onion (chopped)
- 1 cup Marinara sauce
- 1 cup mozzarella cheese (shredded)
- 1/2 cup fresh basil (chopped and divided)
- 1 can diced tomatoes (14.5 ounces)
- 1 tablespoon olive oil
- Black pepper (to taste)
- Sea salt (to taste)

Directions:

- Pre-heat your oven to 400 degrees Fahrenheit. Lightly grease a square casserole dish (9" x 9").
- Put the cauliflower florets in the greased casserole dish. Drizzle them with olive oil. Season with pepper and salt. Toss to coat evenly coat the florets with the oil and seasonings.
- Roast the cauliflower florets in the oven for 20 minutes. Stir the florets half-way through the roasting time. Set aside.
- In a skillet over low heat, cook the onions until slightly browned and translucent, about 10 minutes.
- Put in the ground beef. Increase the heat to medium. Cook the ground beef until browned, about 10 minutes. Break apart the ground beef so they will be cooked evenly.
- Put in the marinara sauce, garlic, half of the basil, and diced tomatoes. Lightly season with pepper and salt. Continue cooking for another 2 minutes. Make sure that the sauce is heated through.
- Pour the sauce over the roasted cauliflower in the casserole dish. Top with mozzarella cheese.

- Bake the lasagna for 10 minutes. The mozzarella cheese should have bubbles during this time. Garnish with the rest of the basil leaves. Serve.

Nutritional info (per serving):

- Calories: 386
- Carbs: 13 g
- Fats: 24 g
- Proteins: 28 g
- Fiber: 3 g

Keto Mongolian Beef

Yields: 6 servings

Serving size: 1/4 pound beef

Preparation time: 10 minutes

Cooking time: 2 hours

Ingredients:

- 1 1/2 pounds flank steak
- 1/4 cup coconut aminos
- 1/4 cup erythritol (powdered)
- 4 cloves garlic (minced)
- 2 tablespoons gelatin powder (unflavored)
- 1 tablespoon sesame oil
- 1 tablespoon blackstrap molasses
- 3/4 teaspoon sea salt
- 1/4 teaspoon black pepper
- 1/2 teaspoon ginger (ground)

Directions:

- Cut the flank steak into 1/4-inch slices. The slices should be against the grain.
- In a resealable plastic bag, put in the gelatin powder and the steak slices. Toss so that each steak slice is coated well.
- Arrange the steak slices in the slow cooker.
- In a mixing bowl, put in the coconut aminos, sweetener, sesame oil, salt, garlic, molasses, ginger, and pepper. Whisk them all together to combine well. Pour the mixture over the steak slices in the slow cooker. Stir everything to coat
- Cover the slow cooker. Cook the dish for 3 hours on High setting or 6 hours on Low setting. Make sure that the steak slices are cooked through.
- Transfer the steak slices on the serving plates. Drizzle each beef serving with the liquid from the slow cooker. Serve.

Nutritional info (per serving):

- Calories: 207
- Carbs: 5 g
- Fats: 8 g
- Proteins: 26 g
- Fiber: 0 g

Keto Lamb Recipes

Keto Lamb Chops with Tzatziki Sauce

Yields: 8 lamb chops

Serving size: 2 lamb chops

Preparation time: 10 minutes

Cooking time: 10 minutes

Ingredients:

- 8 pieces lamb chops
- 2 tablespoons olive oil
- 1/4 cup lemon juice
- 1 1/2 teaspoons kosher salt
- 1 clove garlic (grated)
- 1/2 teaspoon pepper

Tzatziki Sauce:

- 2 cups cucumber (diced)
- 2 cups Greek yogurt (plain)
- 1/2 cup fresh dill (minced)
- 2 cloves garlic (grated)
- 1/4 cup lemon juice
- 1/4 teaspoon pepper
- 1/2 teaspoon salt

Directions:

- Arrange the lamb chops on a platter. Pat dry them with paper towels.
- In a resealable plastic bag, put in the salt, pepper, garlic, olive oil, and lemon juice. Mix well.
- Put the lamb chops into the plastic bag. Seal the plastic bag.
- Move the plastic bag and make sure that the lamb chops are coated with the marinade. Put in the fridge. Marinate the lamb chops for at least 30 minutes.
- Take out the marinated lamb chops from the fridge. Let the lamb chops rest at room temperature for about 30 minutes.
- Pre-heat your grill to medium heat.
- Grill the lamb chops for 5 minutes on each side. The temperature inside the meat should be 155 degrees Fahrenheit.
- Transfer the cooked lamb chops on a platter. Let them rest for 10 minutes.

- In a mixing bowl, put in all the ingredients for the Tzatziki sauce. Mix well. Adjust the taste to your liking.
- Serve the lamb chops with the sauce on the side.

Nutritional info (per serving):

- Calories: 336
- Carbs: 8.5 g
- Fats: 15.9 g
- Proteins: 39.2 g
- Fiber: 0.6 g

Keto Lamb Chops with Pesto Sauce

Yields: 4 servings

Serving size: 1/4 of the entire dish

Preparation time: 30 minutes

Cooking time: 15 minutes

Ingredients:

- 1 rack of lamb
- 4 cups basil leaves
- 1/2 cup olive oil
- 1/2 cup pine nuts
- 2 tablespoons ghee
- 1 piece lemon (juiced)
- Pepper (to taste)
- Sea salt (to taste)

Directions:

- Pre-heat your oven to 350 degrees Fahrenheit.
- In an oven safe skillet over medium heat, put in the ghee and melt it.
- Season the rack of lamb with pepper and salt.
- Sear the rack of lamb on the skillet for 1 minute on every side. Press the rack of lamb slightly while searing on all sides.
- Put the skillet with the rack of lamb in the oven. Bake the lamb for 10 minutes until the meat is thoroughly cooked.
- Remove the rack of lamb from the oven. Transfer it on a cutting board. Let the rack of lamb rest for a few minutes before slicing.
- In a food processor, put in the lemon juice, olive oil, pine nuts, basil, pepper, and salt. Pulse to combine everything until the texture becomes smooth. You can add more olive oil, if needed. Also, scrape down the sides of the food processor to fully combine the sauce.
- Slice the rack of lamb between each bone. Arrange the lamb chops on a platter. Pour the pesto sauce on top of each lamb chop. Serve.

Nutritional info (per serving):

- Calories: 603
- Carbs: 2.9 g
- Fats: 51.6 g
- Proteins: 34.9 g
- Fiber: 1 g

Keto Lamb Kebabs with Coconut Curry Sauce

Yields: 12 kebabs

Serving size: 1 kebab

Preparation time: 10 minutes

Cooking time: 15 minutes

Ingredients:

Lamb Kebabs:

- 800 grams ground lamb
- 1 teaspoon coriander (dried)
- 1 teaspoon cumin (dried)
- 1 teaspoon turmeric powder
- 1 piece spring onion (finely sliced)

Coconut Curry Sauce:

- 2 tablespoons curry paste
- 250 ml coconut cream
- 12 pieces bamboo skewers

Directions:

Lamb Kebabs:

- In a mixing bowl, put in all the ingredients for the lamb kebabs. Mix them well using your hands.
- Form the mixture into 12 elongated kebabs.
- Carefully push a skewer into each of the kebab. Press each kebab firmly to stick onto the skewer.
- Heat up your grill to medium heat. Grease the grill.
- Arrange each kebab on the grill. Cook them for 15 minutes until they have turned brown.

Coconut Curry Sauce:

- In another mixing bowl, put in the coconut cream and curry paste. Mix well.
- Drizzle the sauce over the lamb kebabs. You can serve the lamb kebabs with cauliflower rice, if you like.

Nutritional info (per serving):

- Calories: 152
- Carbs: 0.2 g
- Fats: 11.9 g
- Proteins: 11 g

- Fiber: 0.1 g

Keto Slow Cooker Lamb Shoulder

Yields: 4 servings

Serving size: 1/4 of the entire dish

Preparation time: 5 minutes

Cooking time: 5 hours

Ingredients:

- 500 grams lamb shoulder
- 1 tablespoon olive oil
- Salt and pepper (to taste)
- Handful of fresh rosemary

Directions:

- In a slow cooker, put in the olive oil at the bottom. Spread the olive oil all over the surface of the bottom of the slow cooker.
- Season the lam shoulder with salt and pepper. Make sure that all sides are seasoned well.
- Put the lamb shoulder in the slow cooker. Chop the rosemary. Spread the chopped rosemary on the top of the lamb shoulder and around the meat.
- Set the slow cooker to low. Cook the lamb shoulder for 5 hours until the meat is tender.
- Take out the lamb shoulder from the slow cooker. Leave the cooked lamb on a chopping board to rest for about 15 minutes.
- Slice off the cooked lamb meat from the bones. Serve.

Nutritional info (per serving):

- Calories: 134
- Carbs: 0 g
- Fats: 7 g
- Proteins: 15 g
- Fiber: 0 g

Keto Lamb Curry

Yields: 4 servings

Serving size: 1/4 of the entire dish

Preparation time: 15 minutes

Cooking time: 1 hour and 50 minutes

Ingredients:

- 1 piece thumb-sized ginger (sliced into 2, the first half sliced into matchstick sizes, the second half is left as whole)
- 400 grams can tomatoes (chopped)
- 750 grams lamb leg (diced)
- 4 garlic cloves
- 2 pieces onions (quartered)
- 1 small bunch of coriander (leaves roughly chopped and stalks finely chopped)
- 1 piece red chilli (deseeded and sliced)
- 2 tablespoons rapeseed oil
- 1 tablespoon coriander (ground)
- 1 piece cinnamon stick
- 1 teaspoon turmeric (ground)
- 1 teaspoon cumin (ground)
- 1/2 teaspoon fennel seeds
- Mango chutney (to serve)
- Basmati rice (to serve)

Directions:

- In a food processor, put in the whole ginger, onions, garlic, and 300 ml of water. Process until the mixture becomes a puree. Scrape the sides of the food processor using a spoon to combine the mixture well. Make the puree as smooth as possible.
- In a saucepan over low heat, pour the processed mixture. Cover the saucepan. Bring to a boil. Simmer the sauce for 15 minutes.
- Open the saucepan cover. Stir the mixture. Cook for another 5 minutes or until the liquid has completely evaporated. Stir occasionally.
- Put in the rapeseed oil into the saucepan followed by the ginger slices. Increase the heat to medium. Sautee the ginger with the mixture for 5 minutes.
- Put in the cinnamon stick, cumin, coriander, turmeric, fennel seeds, and the diced lamb leg. Stir fry everything until lamb leg has changed its color.
- Put in the tomatoes, 2 cups of water, and red chili. Season with salt and pepper. Cover the saucepan. Let it simmer for an hour.

- Put in the coriander stalks. Stir to mix. Cover the saucepan. Cook for another 30 minutes or until the lamb leg is cooked thoroughly. You can add a cup of water, if needed, so that the dish will not get dry and burnt.
- Put in the coriander leaves. Stir to mix.
- Transfer the dish onto a platter. Serve the lamb leg with basmati rice and mango chutney.

Nutritional info (per serving):

- Calories: 470
- Carbs: 11 g
- Fats: 29 g
- Proteins: 39 g
- Fiber: 3 g

Keto Pork Recipes

Keto Meatloaf Covered with Bacon

Yields: 12 slices

Serving size: 1 slice

Preparation time: 15 minutes

Cooking time: 50 minutes

Ingredients:

- 750 grams ground pork
- 750 grams ground beef
- 100 grams parmesan cheese (grated)
- 6 slices bacon (meatloaf cover)
- 2 slices bacon (diced)
- 2 pieces medium eggs (lightly beaten)
- 1 piece spring onion (sliced)
- 2 tablespoons sun-dried tomatoes (chopped)
- 2 cloves garlic (crushed)
- 2 teaspoon dried oregano
- Handful of fresh basil (chopped)
- Handful of fresh parsley (chopped)
- Pepper (to taste)
- Salt (to taste)
- Vegetables of your choice (diced)

Directions:

- Pre-heat your oven to 350 degrees Fahrenheit. Prepare a baking tray. Line it with parchment paper.
- In a mixing bowl, put in all the ingredients except for the bacon slices for meatloaf cover.
- Mix everything well using your hands. Transfer the mixture onto the lined baking tray. Shape the mixture into a large meatloaf.
- Arrange the bacon slices on top of the meatloaf just like a blanket. You can sprinkle some parmesan cheese on top of the bacon slices, if you like.
- Bake the meatloaf for 50 minutes or more. Make sure that the center of the meatloaf is thoroughly cooked.
- Take out the meatloaf from the oven. Let it rest for a few minutes on the counter.

- Slice the meatloaf into 12 equal slices. Serve.

Nutritional info (per serving):

- Calories: 370
- Carbs: 1.2 g
- Fats: 25 g
- Proteins: 35 g
- Fiber: 0.2 g

Keto Pork Egg Roll in a Bowl

Yields: 6 servings

Serving size: 1/6 of the entire dish

Preparation time: 5 minutes

Cooking time: 25 minutes

Ingredients:

- 1 pound ground pork
- 1/2 cup onion (diced)
- 5 pieces green onions (sliced on a bias, white and green parts separated)
- 3 cloves garlic (minced)
- 3 tablespoons coconut aminos
- 2 tablespoons sesame seeds (toasted)
- 2 tablespoons sesame oil
- 1 tablespoon Sriracha
- 1 tablespoon rice vinegar
- 1/2 teaspoon ginger (ground)
- 14 ounce bag coleslaw mix
- Black pepper (to taste)
- Sea salt (to taste)

Directions:

- In a skillet over medium heat, put in the sesame oil.
- Put in the onion, garlic, and the white parts of the green onions. Sautee them for a minute or two until translucent and fragrant.
- Put in the pork, ginger, pepper, salt, and Sriracha. Cook until the ground pork is thoroughly cooked.
- Put in the coleslaw mix, rice wine vinegar, and coconut aminos. Continue cooking until the coleslaw is cooked.
- Transfer into the serving bowls. Top with sesame seeds and the green parts of the green onions. Serve.

Nutritional info (per serving):

- Calories: 297
- Carbs: 7 g
- Fats: 20 g
- Proteins: 20 g
- Fiber: 1.5 g

Keto Spicy Pork Meatballs

Yields: 12 meatballs

Serving size: 3 meatballs

Preparation time: 10 minutes

Cooking time: 20 minutes

Ingredients:

Meatballs:

- 450 grams ground pork
- 1/4 cup olive oil
- 1 piece egg (whisked)
- 2 tablespoons basil leaves (diced)
- 4 cloves garlic (minced)
- 1 teaspoon chili flakes
- 2 teaspoons hot sauce
- Pepper (to taste)
- Salt (to taste)

Sauce:

- 220 grams tomato sauce
- 2 tablespoons olive oil
- 1 cup basil leaves
- 1 piece medium bell pepper (diced)
- 1/4 piece onion (peeled and diced)
- 1 piece chili pepper (diced)
- Pepper (to taste)
- Salt (to taste)

Directions:

- In a mixing bowl, combine all the ingredients for the meatball except for the olive oil. Mix them well using your hands. Make 12 meatballs out of the entire mixture.
- In a frying pan over medium heat, put in the olive oil. Fry the meatballs until they become golden brown.
- Put in all the ingredients for the sauce except for the basil leaves. Bring to a boil. Lower the heat. Simmer the meatballs for about 10 minutes. Season with pepper and salt.
- Serve the meatballs with zucchini noodles. Top with the basil leaves.

Nutritional info (per serving):

- Calories: 369
- Carbs: 8 g
- Fats: 27 g
- Proteins: 26 g
- Fiber: 2 g

Keto Fried Pork Tenderloin

Yields: 2 servings

Serving size: ½ pound pork tenderloin

Preparation time: 5 minutes

Cooking time: 20 minutes

Ingredients:

- 1 pound pork tenderloin
- 1 tablespoon coconut oil
- Pepper (to taste)
- Salt (to taste)

Directions:

- Slice the pork tenderloin into two equal parts.
- In a frying pan over medium heat, put in the coconut oil. Let the coconut oil melt.
- Put in the pork tenderloin pieces on the frying pan.
- Fry the pork tenderloins on all sides. Continue turning and frying the pork tenderloins until they are cooked through. The internal temperature of the meat should be 145 degrees Fahrenheit.
- Take out the pork tenderloins from the frying pan. Let them rest on a plate for a few minutes.
- Slice the pork tenderloins into 1-inch thick pieces. Serve.

Nutritional info (per serving):

- Calories: 330
- Carbs: 0 g
- Fats: 15 g
- Proteins: 47 g
- Fiber: 0 g

Keto Spicy Pork with Kelp Noodles

Yields: 4 servings

Serving size: 1/4 of the entire dish

Preparation time: 5 minutes

Cooking time: 15 minutes

Ingredients:

- 1 1/2 pounds pork tenderloin (sliced thinly)
- 12 ounces kelp noodles
- 1 piece medium cucumber (sliced)
- 2 cloves garlic (minced)
- 2 tablespoons rice vinegar
- 1 tablespoon olive oil
- 1 teaspoon coconut aminos
- 2 teaspoons sesame oil
- 1/2 teaspoon red pepper flakes
- 1/2 teaspoon ginger (minced)
- Pepper (to taste)
- Salt (to taste)

Directions:

- In a skillet over medium heat, put in the olive oil. Sautee the garlic for a minute or two until fragrant.
- Put in the pork slices. Cook them until they are brown on all sides.
- Put in the cucumber followed by the kelp noodles. Stir to mix.
- Put in the ginger, coconut aminos, sesame oil, vinegar, pepper flakes, pepper, and salt. Stir to mix well.
- Cover the skillet. Continue cooking for another 7 minutes.
- Take out from the heat. Transfer onto a platter. Serve while hot.

Nutritional info (per serving):

- Calories: 223
- Carbs: 4.7 g
- Fats: 7.2 g
- Proteins: 34.1 g
- Fiber: 1.3 g

Keto Meal Prep Recipes

Keto Asparagus Cream Soup

Yields: 4

Serving size: 1/4 of the entire dish

Preparation time: 10 minutes

Cooking time: 20 minutes

Ingredients:

- 8 ounces asparagus (fresh, trimmed and chopped)
- 2 cups chicken broth
- 1 cup coconut cream (scoop only the top part of the coconut milk in a can)
- 1 tablespoon lemon juice (fresh)
- 1 tablespoon avocado oil
- 2 cloves garlic (minced)
- 1 piece green onion (chopped)
- 1 ounce baby spinach (fresh)
- Pepper (to taste)
- Salt (to taste)

Directions:

- In a saucepan over medium heat, put in the oil. Put in the asparagus. Season with pepper and salt. Sautee the asparagus for 4 minutes until they turn into bright green.
- Put in the garlic and green onion. Sautee for a minute until fragrant.
- Put in the broth. Stir to mix well. Bring the soup to a boil. Lower the heat. Le the soup simmer for 12 minutes until the asparagus is cooked.
- Put in the spinach. Stir. Cook the spinach for 2 minutes until wilted.
- Pour the soup into a blender. Blend the soup until smooth in texture. Pour the soup back onto the saucepan over low heat.

- Put in the lemon juice and coconut cream. Stir until mixed well. Adjust the seasoning according to your desired taste. You can serve the soup either hot or cold.
- Divide the soup equally into 4 portions. You can store them in the fridge for up to 2 days.

Nutritional info (per serving):

- Calories: 124

- Carbs: 5.2 g
- Fats: 12.1 g
- Proteins: 4.1 g
- Fiber: 1.5 g

Keto Peanut Ginger Zoodle Salad

Yields: 2 servings

Serving size: ½ of the entire dish

Preparation time: 5 minutes

Cooking time: 5 minutes

Ingredients:

- 200 grams zucchini noodles
- 1/4 cup water
- 1/4 cup peanut butter (unsweetened)
- 1 tablespoon tamari (low-sodium)
- 1 teaspoon fresh ginger (grated)
- 1 clove garlic (crushed)

Garnish (Optional):

- Red pepper flakes
- Chopped peanuts
- Scallions

Directions:

- In a mixing bowl, put in the peanut butter, ginger, garlic, tamari, and water. Whisk them all together until fully combined. You can add a tablespoon of water at a time if the sauce is too thick to your liking. Continue adding stirring in a tablespoon of water until your desired texture of the sauce is achieved.
- Put in the zoodles into the sauce. Toss and mix until all the zoodles are completely coated with the sauce. Garnish as you like.
- Divide the salad equally into 2 portions. You can store them in the fridge for 2 to 3 days.

Nutritional info (per serving):

- Calories: 214
- Carbs: 7.5 g
- Fats: 16.2 g
- Proteins: 10.1 g
- Fiber: 3.8 g

Keto Blackberry-Filled Lemon Muffins

Yields: 12 muffins

Serving size: 1 muffin

Preparation time: 20 minutes

Cooking time: 25 minutes

Ingredients:

Blackberry Filling:

- 1 cup blackberries (fresh)
- 3 tablespoons stevia/erythritol blend (granulated)
- 2 tablespoons water
- 1/4 teaspoon xanthan gum
- 1 tablespoon lemon juice

Muffin Batter:

- 2 1/2 cups almond flour (super fine)
- 1/4 cup almond milk (unsweetened, original flavor)
- 3/4 cup stevia/erythritol blend (granulated)
- 1/4 cup butter (melted)
- 4 pieces large eggs
- 1 teaspoon lemon zest (fresh)
- 1 teaspoon vanilla extract
- 1 teaspoon baking powder (grain-free)
- 1/2 teaspoon sea salt
- 1/2 teaspoon lemon extract

Directions:

Blackberry Filling:

- In a saucepan, put in the xanthan gum and granulated sweetener. Whisk to mix well.
- Put in the lemon juice and water a tablespoon at a time. Whisk the mixture after each addition.
- Put in the blackberries. Mix well. Put the saucepan over low heat. Let the mixture simmer with frequent stirring.
- Keep simmering for about 10 minutes. The blackberries are tender and there is thick syrup just like a jam.
- Turn off the heat. Set aside the blackberry mixture to cool down.

Muffin Batter:

- Pre-heat your oven to 350 degrees Fahrenheit. Line a 12-cavity muffin pan with muffin papers.
- In a mixing bowl, put in the almond flour, baking powder, lemon zest, sea salt, and granulated sweetener. Whisk to mix well.
- In another mixing bowl, put in the almond milk, eggs, lemon extract, and vanilla extract. Whisk to mix well. Gradually put in the butter into the mixture while whisking.
- Gradually pour the wet mixture into the flour mixture as you stir to combine them.
- Pour the batter into the muffin cups filling about 1/3 full. Make a depression at the center of the batter in each muffin cup with a spoon.
- Fill the depression with a spoonful of the blackberry filling.
- Pour a layer of the batter on top of the blackberry filling to cover it until each muffin cup is 2/3 full or higher. Use a spoon to spread the batter to completely cover the filling.
- Bake the muffins for 30 minutes. The tops of the muffin should bounce back when touched lightly.
- Take the muffins out and let them cool down on the counter.
- Put the muffins in a sealed container. You can store them in the fridge for about a week.

Nutritional info (per serving):

- **Calories:** 199
- **Carbs:** 4 g
- **Fats:** 17 g
- **Proteins:** 7 g
- **Fiber:** 3 g

Keto Breakfast Bombs

Yields: 12 breakfast bombs
Serving size: 1 breakfast bomb
Preparation time: 20 minutes
Cooking time: 15 minutes

Ingredients:

- 2 cups almond flour (blanched and finely ground)
- 1/3 cup sour cream
- 1/2 cup cheddar cheese (shredded)
- 1 piece large egg
- 6 pieces large eggs (scrambled)
- 4 tablespoons butter (cold and cubed)
- 2 teaspoons baking powder
- 1/2 teaspoon apple cider vinegar
- 1/4 teaspoon baking soda
- 4 slices bacon (cooked and crumbled)
- 6 ounces breakfast sausage (cooked and crumbled)
- Pinch of salt
- Sugar-free syrup (for topping)

Directions:

- Pre-heat your oven to 350 degrees Fahrenheit.
- In a food processor, put in the almond flour, baking soda, and baking powder. Pulse them a number of times to mix well.
- Put in the butter. Process the mixture for 20 seconds on low setting until it becomes crumbly.
- Put in the egg, sour cream, apple cider vinegar, and salt. Process the biscuit mixture until everything is mixed well.
- Set aside the biscuit mixture to rest for about 5 minutes.
- In a mixing bowl, put in the cheese, bacon, and scrambled egg. Toss to combine.
- Put in the biscuit mixture into the mixing bowl. Combine well using your hands with the rest of the ingredients.
- Grease a muffin pan with 12 cavities. Pour about 1/4 cup of the biscuit mixture into each of the cavity.
- Bake the breakfast bombs for 15 minutes. They should be golden brown in color around their edges. Let the breakfast bombs cool down before serving or storing.

- Put the breakfast bombs in an airtight container. You can store them in the fridge for 4 days.

Nutritional info (per serving):

- Calories: 287
- Carbs: 4.7 g
- Fats: 24.6 g
- Proteins: 11.9 g
- Fiber: 2 g

Keto Chopped Buffalo Chicken Salad

Yields: 3 servings

Serving size: 1/3 of the entire dish

Preparation time: 10 minutes

Cooking time: 20 minutes

Ingredients:

Buffalo Chicken:

- 285 grams chicken (cooked and diced)
- 1/4 cup Sriracha chili sauce
- 3 tablespoons butter (melted)

Salad:

- 4 slices bacon (crisped up and crumbled)
- 4 pieces green onions (thinly sliced)
- 1 piece large romaine lettuce (chopped)
- 1 piece large avocado (diced)
- 1 piece small carrot (diced)
- 1/4 cup green bell peppers
- 1/4 cup blue cheese (crumbled)
- 1/2 cup cherry tomatoes (halved)

Dressing:

- 2 tablespoons blue cheese (crumbled)
- 6 tablespoons ranch dressing
- 1 tablespoon Sriracha chili sauce

Directions:

- In a mixing bowl, put in the ingredients for the buffalo chicken. Toss to mix.
- In another mixing bowl, put in the ingredients for the dressing. Mix well.
- Equally divide the salad ingredients onto 3 salad bowls. Top the salad with the buffalo chicken. Drizzle each salad bowl with the dressing.
- You can store the salad bowls in the fridge for 2 days at the most.

Nutritional info (per serving):

- Calories: 642
- Carbs: 17.2 g
- Fats: 46.4 g
- Proteins: 42.2 g
- Fiber: 8.5 g

Keto Vegan Bread Recipes

Keto Vegan Bread Rolls

Yields: 6 rolls

Serving size: 1 bread roll

Preparation time: 15 minutes

Cooking time: 1 hour

Ingredients:

Flax Egg:

- 3 tablespoons flax seeds (ground)
- 1/2 cup + 1 tablespoon water

Dough:

- 1 1/4 cup almond flour
- 1 1/4 cup water
- 1/2 cup psyllium husk powder
- 1/3 cup flax seeds (ground)
- 1 1/4 teaspoons cream of tartar
- 2 1/2 teaspoons baking soda
- 1 teaspoon salt

Coating:

- 2 teaspoons sesame seeds

Directions:

- Pre-heat your oven to 375 degrees Fahrenheit. Prepare a baking sheet. Line it with parchment paper.
- In a mixing bowl, put in the ingredients for the flax egg. Whisk to combine. Set aside to soak for about 5 minutes or more.
- In another mixing bowl, put in all the ingredients for the dough except for the water. Whisk to combine well. Put in the flax egg. Mix well using an electric mixer.
- In a pot over medium heat, put in the water. Bring the water to a boil.
- Gradually pour the boiling water into the dough mixture while mixing using an electric mixer. Make sure that that all the ingredients are fully incorporated. Set aside the dough to rest for 5 minutes or more.
- Equally divide the dough into 6 portions. Form the portioned dough into rolls.
- In a shallow dish, put in a small quantity of water. In another shallow dish, put in the sesame seeds. Dip the top of each roll in water and then in sesame seeds to coat.

- Arrange the rolls on the lined baking sheet. Bake the rolls for 50 minutes.
- Turn off the oven and slightly open the oven door. Leave the rolls in the oven for 10 minutes more.
- Take out the rolls from the oven. Let them cool down completely. Serve.

Nutritional info (per serving):

- Calories: 229
- Carbs: 23.6 g
- Fats: 14.6 g
- Proteins: 6.5 g
- Fiber: 20.3 g

Keto Vegan Soft Bread

Yields: 16 slices

Serving size: 1 slice

Preparation time: 90 minutes

Cooking time: 50 minutes

Ingredients:

- 1 3/4 cups warm water
- 1 cup coconut flour
- 3/4 cup almond butter
- 40 grams psyllium husks
- 2 1/4 teaspoons active dry yeast
- 1 teaspoon sugar

Directions:

- Prepare a loaf pan. Line it with parchment paper.
- In a mixing bowl, put in the 1/2 cup of warm water, yeast, and sugar. Mix well. Set aside for about 10 minutes to activate the yeast. The mixture will become foamy.
- In another mixing bowl, put in the psyllium husks and coconut flour. Whisk them together to mix well.
- In the mixing bowl with the activated yeast, put in the almond butter and a cup of the warm water. Stir to mix well.
- Put in the flour mixture into the wet mixture. Stir well until there are no more dry bits. Add a tablespoon of warm water at a time to help remove the dry bits. The texture of the dough will not be smooth. Just make sure that all the dry bits are gone.
- Transfer the dough into the lined loaf pan. Spread the dough evenly in the pan.
- Let the dough rise for 90 minutes. The dough should have increased its size to almost double.
- Pre-heat your oven to 350 degrees Fahrenheit.
- Bake the bread for 55 minutes. The crust should be hard.
- Take out the bread from the oven. Remove the bread from the load pan together with the parchment paper. Let the bread cool down completely. Cut into 16 slices. Serve.

Nutritional info (per serving):

- Calories: 90
- Carbs: 8 g
- Fats: 5.4 g

- Proteins: 2.8 g
- Fiber: 6 g

Keto Vegan Pumpkin Bread

Yields: 16 slices

Serving size: 1 slice

Preparation time: 15 minutes

Cooking time: 50 minutes

Ingredients:

- 1 cup pumpkin flour
- 1 cup almond flour
- 1/2 cup coconut flour
- 1/4 cup chia seeds
- 1/3 cup psyllium husk (ground)
- 1 teaspoon salt
- 1 tablespoon baking powder

Liquid Ingredients:

- 2 tablespoons olive oil
- 2 cups lukewarm water
- 1 teaspoon apple cider vinegar

Topping:

- Pumpkin seeds

Directions:

- Pre-heat your oven to fan-bake mode about 400 degrees Fahrenheit.
- Prepare a 9" x 5" loaf pan. Line it with parchment paper. Slightly grease the parchment paper to prevent the bread from sticking to the pan.
- In a mixing bowl, put in all the dry ingredients. Whisk them to mix well, about 30 seconds or less.
- Stir in all the liquid ingredients into the dry mixture. Make sure that the water is lukewarm and not cold or at room temperature.
- Use a spatula first to mix the dough. Knead the dough after with the use of your hands. Kneading should last for about 2 minutes. The dough should come together just like a ball. If it happens that a lot of the dough still sticks to your hands after kneading for 2 minutes, just sprinkle a teaspoon of psyllium husk at a time, knead again, until you should be able to form the dough into a ball without too much dough sticking to your hands.
- Shape the dough into a round cylinder, just like a log, that will fit easily into the loaf pan. Massage the top of the dough to smoothen out any crack. Put the dough in the loaf pan.

- Sprinkle the pumpkin seeds as topping. Press the seeds slightly into the dough so they will stick to the bread when cooked.
- Bake the bread for 50 minutes. Halfway through baking, tent the loaf pan with aluminum foil so that the inside of the bread will get cooked without burning the top.
- The bread is cooked when you insert a toothpick at the center and it will come out clean. If not, then continue baking the bread and check if it is cooked every 10 minutes.
- Leave the bread on the rack on the counter to cool down, about 3 hours. Cut into 16 slices. Serve.

Nutritional info (per serving):

- Calories: 117
- Carbs: 4.3 g
- Fats: 7.8 g
- Proteins: 3.9 g
- Fiber: 2.1 g

Keto Vegan Psyllium and Coconut Flour Flatbread

Yields: 6 flatbreads

Serving size: 1 flatbread

Preparation time: 10 minutes

Cooking time: 15 minutes

Ingredients:

- 1 cup boiling water
- 1/2 cup coconut flour
- 1 1/2 ounces coconut oil
- 2 tablespoons psyllium husk powder
- 1 teaspoon baking powder
- 1/2 teaspoon salt
- Herbs or garlic powder (for flavor)

Directions:

- In a mixing bowl, put in all the dry ingredients. Mix them well.
- Put in the oil. Mix well. The texture is similar to a nut butter.
- Put in the boiling water gradually while mixing. Continue mixing until a dough-like mixture is achieved.
- Equally divide the dough into 6 portions.
- Shape each portion into a ball. Press each ball in between 2 parchment paper sheets to flatten it out.
- In a frying pan over medium heat, dry fry each flatbread for 3 minutes each side. The color of the flatbread should be golden brown. Serve.

Nutritional info (per serving):

- Calories: 119
- Carbs: 10 g
- Fats: 8 g
- Proteins: 2 g
- Fiber: 7 g

Keto Vegan Sandwich Bread

Yields: 12 slices

Serving size: 2 slices

Preparation time: 10 minutes

Cooking time: 90 minutes

Ingredients:

- 300 grams almond flour
- 160 grams chia seeds
- 100 grams psyllium husks
- 100 grams tahini
- 10 grams xanthan gum
- 800 ml warm water
- 2 1/4 teaspoons instant yeast
- 2 teaspoons salt

Directions:

- In a mixing bowl, put in the warm water and tahini. Mix well.
- Put in the yeast and chia seeds. Mix well. Set aside until the chia seeds are ready, about 20 minutes. The mixture is ready when it becomes goopy.
- In another mixing bowl, put in the xanthan gum, salt, and psyllium husks. Mix well.
- Pour the chia seeds mixture into the dry mixture. Mix them well until it becomes doughy. Knead the dough for a few minutes until it comes together.
- Line a loaf pan with parchment paper. Put the dough in the lined loaf pan. Spread the dough across the pan. Set aside the dough to rise for an hour or more.
- Pre-heat your oven to 325 degrees Fahrenheit.
- Bake the bread for 90 minutes. The cooked bread has an internal temperature of 200 degrees Fahrenheit.
- Take out the bread from the oven. Let the bread cool down completely. Cut into 12 slices. Serve.

Nutritional info (per serving):

- Calories: 287.9
- Carbs: 19.5 g
- Fats: 21.2 g
- Proteins: 9.1 g
- Fiber: 15.2 g

Keto Vegan Dessert Recipes

Keto Vegan Blueberry Cake

Yields: 12 slices

Serving size: 1 slice

Preparation time: 10 minutes

Cooking time: 35 minutes

Ingredients:

- 2 cups rolled oats (gluten free and grounded into a flour)
- 1 cup milk of choice
- 1/2 cup coconut palm sugar
- 1/4 - 1/2 cup blueberries
- 6 tablespoons almond butter (smooth)
- 1 tablespoon baking powder
- 1 teaspoon vanilla extract
- 1 flax egg
- Pinch of sea salt

Directions:

- Pre-heat your oven to 350 degrees Fahrenheit. Prepare a loaf pan. Line it with parchment paper.
- In a high-speed blender, put in all the ingredients. Blend for a few minutes until the batter becomes smooth.
- Pour the batter into the lined loaf pan.
- Bake the blueberry cake for 40 minutes. Insert a toothpick in the middle of the cake. If the toothpick comes out clean, then the blueberry cake is cooked through.
- Take out the blueberry cake from the oven. Leave the cake in the loaf pan on the counter for 10 minutes to cool down.
- Take out the cake from the loaf pan. Leave the cake on a cooling rack to cool completely.
- Cut to 12 slices. Serve.

Nutritional info (per serving):

- Calories: 135
- Carbs: 7 g
- Fats: 11 g
- Proteins: 8 g

- Fiber: 4 g

Keto Vegan Flourless Chocolate Muffins

Yields: 12 muffins

Serving size: 1 muffin

Preparation time: 5 minutes

Cooking time: 25 minutes

Ingredients:

- 1 cup pumpkin puree
- 1 cup sunflower seed butter
- 1/2 cup cocoa powder
- 1/2 cup monk fruit sweetener
- 1/4 cup mini chocolate chips
- 1/4 cup granulated sweetener
- 1/4 cup dark chocolate morsels
- 1 teaspoon baking powder

Directions:

- Pre-heat your oven to 350 degrees Fahrenheit. Prepare a 12-cavity muffin pan. Line it with muffin liners.
- In a mixing bowl, put in all the ingredients excluding the chocolate chips. Mix well to fully incorporate everything.
- Put in the chocolate chips into the batter. Stir. Reserve some of the chocolate chips to use as toppings later.
- Pour the batter into each of the muffin cup. Top each muffin with the remaining chocolate chips.
- Bake the muffins for 30 minutes.
- Take out the muffins from the oven. Let them cool completely on a cooling rack. Serve.

Nutritional info (per serving):

- Calories: 150
- Carbs: 8 g
- Fats: 12 g
- Proteins: 6 g
- Fiber: 5 g

Keto Vegan Coconut Pineapple Bars

Yields: 20 bars

Serving size: 1 bar

Preparation time: 1 minute

Cooking time: 4 minutes

Ingredients:

- 3 cups shredded coconut (unsweetened)
- 3 tablespoons sticky sweetener
- 1 1/2 cups coconut oil (melted)
- 1 - 2 tablespoons dried pineapple (unsweetened)
- 1/2 teaspoon pineapple extract

Directions:

- Prepare a deep pan (8" x 8"). Line it with parchment paper.
- In a microwave-safe mixing bowl, put in the coconut oil, shredded coconut, and sweetener. Microwave the mixture until it has melted. The shredded coconut should have softened.
- Let the melted mixture cool down a little bit. Put in the dried pineapple and pineapple extract. Mix well.
- Transfer the batter into the prepared deep pan. Spread the batter in the pan and press it firmly to stay in place.
- Put the batter in the fridge until it feels firm to the touch.
- Take out the batter from the fridge. Let it thaw for a few minutes. Cut the batter into 20 bars. Serve.

Nutritional info (per serving):

- Calories: 108
- Carbs: 3 g
- Fats: 11 g
- Proteins: 2 g
- Fiber: 2 g

Keto Vegan Fudgy Pumpkin Brownies

Yields: 14 brownies

Serving size: 1 brownie

Preparation time: 5 minutes

Cooking time: 40 minutes

Ingredients:

- 4 chia eggs
- 2 cups cocoa powder
- 1 cup avocado (mashed)
- 1 cup pumpkin puree
- 1 cup coconut milk (unsweetened)
- 2/3 cup sticky sweetener
- 1/2 cup chocolate chips
- 6 tablespoons coconut flour
- 1 tablespoon baking soda

Directions:

- Pre-heat your oven to 350 degrees Fahrenheit. Prepare a baking pan (8" x 8"). Line it with parchment paper.
- To make a chia egg, you need to do this step. In a mixing bowl, put in 12 tablespoons of water and 1/4 cup of chia seeds. Mix well. Set the mixture aside to let it form into a gel. It would usually take about 15 minutes for the gel to form. One chia gel is equivalent to 1 chia egg. This recipe needs 4 chia eggs. You have to simultaneously make chia eggs in 4 separate bowls.
- In a high-speed blender, put in all the listed ingredients excluding the chocolate chips and coconut milk. Blend the ingredients until mixed thoroughly.
- Put in half of the coconut milk. Blend again. Do not put in the remaining half of the coconut milk if the batter is already pourable and smooth. However, if the batter is very thick, put in the remaining half of the coconut milk and blend.
- Pour the brownie batter into the prepared baking pan. Stir in the chocolate chips in the batter. Reserve some of the chocolate chips for topping later.
- Bake the brownies in the oven for 35 minutes until cooked through.
- Let the brownies cool down in the baking pan on the counter.
- Allow brownies to cool completely in pan, before slicing into bars. Cut into 14 brownie bars.

Nutritional info (per serving):

- Calories: 99

- Carbs: 17 g
- Fats: 5 g
- Proteins: 4 g
- Fiber: 12 g

Keto Vegan Chocolate Cookies

Yields: 20 cookies

Serving size: 1 cookie

Preparation time: 4 minutes

Cooking time: 10 minutes

Ingredients:

- 1 cup almond flour
- 1 cup chocolate nut
- 1/4 cup chocolate chips
- 2 tablespoon chocolate protein powder
- 4 tablespoons chia seeds (ground)

Directions:

- Pre-heat your oven to 350 degrees Fahrenheit. Prepare a baking tray. Line it with parchment paper.
- In a mixing bowl, put in all the ingredients. Mix very well.
- Form 20 balls out of the cookie dough.
- Arrange the cookie balls on the lined baking tray.
- Press each cookie ball lightly using your hands to flatten it.
- Bake the cookies for 12 minutes. Take out the baking tray from the oven. Let the cookies coon down while still on the baking tray for about 20 minutes. Transfer the cookies on a wire rack to cool down totally. Serve.

Nutritional info (per serving):

- Calories: 105
- Carbs: 3 g
- Fats: 8 g
- Proteins: 5 g
- Fiber: 2 g

Keto Vegan Breakfast Recipes

Keto Vegan Creamy Cinnamon Smoothie

Yields: 1 jar

Serving size: 1 jar

Preparation time: 5 minutes

Cooking time: none

Ingredients:

- 1/2 cup coconut milk
- 1/4 cup vanilla whey protein powder
- 1/2 cup water
- Some ice cubes
- 1 tablespoon MCT oil
- 1 tablespoon chia seeds (ground)
- 1/2 teaspoon cinnamon

Directions:

- In a blender, put in the chia seeds, cinnamon, protein powder, and coconut milk.
- Put in next the MCT oil, water, and some ice cubes. You can put some drops of stevia if you want your smoothie to be a little bit sweeter.
- Blend everything until smooth. Pour the smoothie in a mason jar. Serve.

Nutritional info (per serving):

- Calories: 467
- Carbs: 8.2 g
- Fats: 40.3 g
- Proteins: 23.6 g
- Fiber: 3.5 g

Keto Vegan Granola Bars

Yields: 15 servings

Serving size: 1/2 cup

Preparation time: 10 minutes

Cooking time: 20 minutes

Ingredients:

- 250 grams coconut chips (desiccated)
- 100 grams pumpkin seeds
- 100 grams sunflower seeds
- 70 grams walnuts (chopped)
- 60 grams flaxseeds
- 50 grams coconut oil (melted)
- 1 teaspoon ginger (ground)
- 1 teaspoon cinnamon (ground)

Directions:

- Pre-heat your oven to 350 degrees Fahrenheit.
- In a baking dish with sides, put in the nuts, seeds, and coconut chips.
- Put in next the coconut oil, ginger, and cinnamon.
- Mix everything well.
- Bake the granola mix for 20 minutes.
- You should stir the mixture every 3 minutes because they will burn easily when left unmoved in the oven.
- Let the cooked granola coo down completely before storing in air tight containers.

Nutritional info (per serving):

- Calories: 317
- Carbs: 9.4 g
- Fats: 29.1 g
- Proteins: 6.2 g
- Fiber: 5.3 g

Keto Vegan Spaghetti Squash Tots

Yields: 24 tots

Serving size: 4 tots

Preparation time: 10 minutes

Cooking time: 20 minutes

Ingredients:

- 1 piece medium green onion (separate the white and green parts, thinly sliced)
- 1 piece medium spaghetti squash
- 1/4 teaspoon black pepper
- 1/2 teaspoon salt

Directions:

- Pre-heat your oven to 425 degrees Fahrenheit. Grease a mini muffin tin with 24 cavities with olive oil.
- Prick the squash a number of times using a fork. Put the squash on a microwave safe platter.
- Microwave the squash on high setting for 8 minutes. The squash should be a little bit soft when pinched. Let the squash cool down.
- Cut the squash in half lengthwise. Scrape out all of the seeds. Take out the spaghetti strands of the squash using a fork. Throw away the skins.
- Put the spaghetti strands on some clean paper towels. Wrap the paper towels on the strands. Wring out the strands and let the paper towels absorb as much moisture as possible from the strands.
- Transfer the squash in a mixing bowl. Cut the strands into smaller pieces using a sharp knife.
- Put in the rest of the ingredients with the spaghetti squash. Mix them very well.
- Fill the mini muffin cups about half full with the spaghetti squash mixture. Flatten the top of each tot using your fingers.
- Spray with olive oil the surface of the tots. Bake the tots for 10 minutes. They should all turn into golden brown.
- Take out the tots from the oven. Flip over each tot very carefully because they can crumble easily.
- Spray with olive oil the surface of the tots. Bake the tots again for another 10 minutes. The tots are cooked thoroughly when both sides have become golden brown in color.
- Let the tots cool down on a cooling rack for at least 5 minutes. Invert the muffin tin to release the tots. Sprinkle with Kosher salt. Serve while still warm.

Nutritional info (per serving):
- Calories: 50
- Carbs: 11.36 g
- Fats: 0.92 g
- Proteins: 1.08 g
- Fiber: 2.48 g

Keto Vegan Tofu Scramble

Yields: 2 servings

Serving size: 1/2 of the entire dish

Preparation time: 10 minutes

Cooking time: 15 minutes

Ingredients:

- 1 block firm organic tofu (drained)
- 1 package of mushrooms (chopped)
- 1 1/2 cups spinach (fresh)
- 1 tablespoon olive oil
- 1 piece red pepper (chopped)
- 1/2 piece onion (chopped)
- 1/2 teaspoon turmeric
- 1/4 teaspoon garlic powder
- Pepper (to taste)
- Salt (to taste)
- Pinch of paprika (optional)
- A bit of veggie broth

Directions:

- In a skillet over medium heat, put in the olive oil. Sautee the onions, pepper, and mushrooms for 8 minutes.
- Crumple the tofu while putting in on the skillet. Put in the spices and veggie broth so that the tofu will not stick on the bottom of the skillet. Stir. Cook for 5 minutes.
- The tofu should have heated through. Put in the spinach. Stir. Cook until wilted.
- Transfer the scramble to a platter. Serve.

Nutritional info (per serving):

- Calories: 315
- Carbs: 14 g
- Fats: 20 g
- Proteins: 29 g
- Fiber: 4.5 g

Keto Vegan Pancakes

Yields: 1 serving

Serving size: 1 batch of pancakes

Preparation time: 10 minutes

Cooking time: 15 minutes

Ingredients:

- 1/4 cup almond milk (unsweetened)
- 2 tablespoons almond butter (unsweetened)
- 1 tablespoon coconut flour
- 1 tablespoon flax (ground)
- 1/2 teaspoon baking powder

Directions:

- In a mixing bowl, put in the almond milk and almond butter. Mix well.
- In another mixing bowl, put in the rest of the ingredients. Mix well.
- Put the milk mixture into the flour mixture. Mix well. Set aside the batter for about 5 minutes. Give some time for the coconut flour and flax to absorb the milk mixture.
- In a cast iron skillet over low heat, use a cooking spray to lightly oil the skillet. Heat up the oil for a few minutes.
- Scoop some batter and put it on the skillet. Spread the batter gently to shape into a pancake.
- Cook the pancake for 5 minutes. Flip the pancake and cook the other side for another 3 minutes.
- Continue cooking the rest of the batter.
- Top the pancakes with any vegan pancake topping that you want. Serve.

Nutritional info (per serving):

- Calories: 260
- Carbs: 13.9 g
- Fats: 20.8 g
- Proteins: 9.6 g
- Fiber: 8.8 g

Keto Vegan Snack Recipes

Keto Vegan Energy Balls

Yields: 40 balls

Serving size: 1 ball

Preparation time: 5 minutes

Cooking time: 5 minutes

Ingredients:

- 2 cups smooth tahini
- 3/4 cup coconut flour
- 1/2 cup sticky syrup

Directions:

- In a mixing bowl, put in the tahini. The texture of the tahini should be mixable and smooth. If ever the tahini has a slightly firm or stiff texture, you can heat the tahini in the microwave for a minute or until the texture becomes smooth and easy to stir.
- Put in the sticky syrup in the bowl with the tahini. Mix well.
- Put in the coconut flour into the mixture. Mix well until everything is fully incorporated. If ever the result dough is thin, you can add a small amount of coconut flour at a time until the dough becomes thick.
- Get a plate. Line it with parchment paper. Make 40 balls out of the dough. Arrange the balls on the lined plate.
- Refrigerate the balls until they are firm to touch. Serve.

Nutritional info (per serving):

- Calories: 57
- Carbs: 3 g
- Fats: 4 g
- Proteins: 2 g
- Fiber: 1.5 g

Keto Vegan Protein Bars

Yields: 20 muffin cups

Serving size: 1 muffin cup

Preparation time: 4 minutes

Cooking time: 1 minute

Ingredients:

- 2 cups almond butter (smooth)
- 2 cups chocolate chips
- 3/4 cup coconut flour
- 1/2 cup sticky sweetener
- 2 tablespoons almond flour

Directions:

- Prepare a mini muffin tin with 20 cavities. Line it with muffin liners.
- In a mixing bowl, put in all the ingredients except for the chocolate chips. Mix the mixture well until it becomes a thick batter. In the instance that the batter becomes crumbly, put in some liquid like milk or water a little at a time to form the batter.
- Pour the batter into each of the muffin cup up to 3/4 full. Refrigerate the protein bars until they are firm to the touch.
- Melt the chocolate chips. Pour the melted chocolate over the protein bars to serve as frosting. Chill for a few minutes to harden the chocolate. Serve.

Nutritional info (per serving):

- Calories: 139
- Carbs: 5 g
- Fats: 10 g
- Proteins: 9 g
- Fiber: 3 g

Keto Vegan Chocolate Cookies

Yields: 20 cookies

Serving size: 1 cookie

Preparation time: 2 minutes

Cooking time: 3 minutes

Ingredients:

- 2 cups Low Carb Nutella
- 3/4 cup coconut flour
- 1/2 cup sticky sweetener

Directions:

- Prepare a plate. Line it with parchment paper.
- In a mixing bowl, put in all of the ingredients together. Mix very well. Make sure that the dough is thick.
- Shape 20 small balls out of the dough. Arrange the balls on the lined plate.
- Press each ball to flatten and will look just like a cookie. Refrigerate the cookies until they are firm to touch. Serve.

Nutritional info (per serving):

- Calories: 98
- Carbs: 5 g
- Fats: 8 g
- Proteins: 4 g
- Fiber: 3 g

Keto Vegan Peanut Butter Chocolate Balls

Yields: 40 balls

Serving size: 1 ball

Preparation time: 5 minutes

Cooking time: 5 minutes

Ingredients:

- 2 cups peanut butter (smooth)
- 2 cups chocolate chips (sugar-free)
- 1/2 cup sticky sweetener
- 3/4 cup coconut flour

Directions:

- Prepare a baking tray. Line it with parchment paper.
- In a mixing bowl, put in all the ingredients excluding the chocolate chips. Mix well until everything is combined. You can add a small amount of liquid like milk or water at a time if the batter is crumbly until it becomes a thick and formable batter.
- Form 40 small balls out of the thick batter. Arrange the balls on the lined baking tray.
- Put the balls in the refrigerator for about 10 minutes to make them firm.
- In a microwave safe bowl, put in the chocolate chips. Microwave them for a minute or until they have melted.
- Coat each peanut butter ball with the melted chocolate with the help of two forks.
- Put back each coated peanut butter ball on the lined baking tray.
- Put the balls back in the refrigerator for about 20 minutes until the chocolate coating has hardened. Serve.

Nutritional info (per serving):

- Calories: 54
- Carbs: 3 g
- Fats: 4 g
- Proteins: 2 g
- Fiber: 1.5 g

Keto Vegan Hazelnut Chocolate Bars

Yields: 20 bars

Serving size: 1 bar

Preparation time: 5 minutes

Cooking time: 5 minutes

Ingredients:

- 2 cups homemade Nutella
- 1 - 2 cups chocolate chips
- 1/2 cup hazelnuts (crushed)
- 3/4 cup coconut flour
- 1/2 cup sticky sweetener
- 1 tablespoon water

Directions:

- Prepare a baking pan (10" x 10"). Line it with parchment paper.
- In a mixing bowl, put in all the ingredients except for the chocolate chips. Mix very well until you have formed a thick dough. You can add small amounts of water if the dough is too crumbly until it becomes a smooth but thick dough.
- Transfer the dough into the baking pan. Spread the dough over the surface of the pan. Press the dough firmly in place. Put the baking tray in the fridge until the dough is firm.
- Cut the dough into 20 bars.
- In a microwave safe bowl, put in the chocolate chips. Microwave the chocolate chips for a minute until all have melted.
- Dip each hazelnut bar into the melted chocolate. Make sure that each bar is coated evenly with chocolate.
- Put the bars in the fridge until the chocolate coating hardens. Serve.

Nutritional info (per serving):

- Calories: 103
- Carbs: 4.5 g
- Fats: 7.5 g
- Proteins: 4.5 g
- Fiber: 7.5 g

Keto Vegan Lunch Recipes

Keto Vegan Cucumber Tomato Salad

Yields: 4 servings

Serving size: 1/4 of the entire dish

Preparation time: 10 minutes

Cooking time: none

Ingredients:

- 1 1/2 cups cherry tomatoes (quartered)
- 1/8 - 1/4 cup avocado oil
- 1 - 2 pieces ripe avocados
- 1 piece English cucumber
- 1 piece green bell pepper
- 1 piece lemon (juiced)
- 2 tablespoons cilantro (fresh)
- 1 tablespoon red wine vinegar
- Salt (to taste)
- Pepper (to taste)

Directions:

- Chop all the vegetables into bite-size pieces. Remove the skin, stems, and seeds, if necessary.
- For the English cucumber, just keep the skin and seeds on.
- In a mixing bowl, put in all the chopped vegetables.
- In another mixing bowl, put in all the rest of the ingredients. Whisk everything together. Pour the mixture over the chopped vegetables.
- Toss the salad mixture to combine well. Serve.

Nutritional info (per serving):

- Calories: 176
- Carbs: 13 g
- Fats: 14 g
- Proteins: 2 g
- Fiber: 5 g

Keto Vegan Zoodles with Avocado Sauce

Yields: 2 servings

Serving size: 1/2 of the entire dish

Preparation time: 10 minutes

Cooking time: none

Ingredients:

- 12 pieces cherry tomatoes (sliced)
- 1 piece zucchini
- 1 piece avocado
- 1/3 cup water
- 1 1/4 cup basil
- 2 tablespoons lemon juice
- 4 tablespoons pine nuts

Directions:

- Using a Spiralizer, make the zoodles from the zucchini.
- In a blender, make the avocado sauce. Put in all the listed ingredients in the blender except for the tomatoes and zoodles. Blend everything until the texture is smooth.
- In a mixing bowl, put in the zoodles, sauce, and tomatoes. Toss to coat everything with the sauce. Serve.

Nutritional info (per serving):

- Calories: 313
- Carbs: 18.7 g
- Fats: 26.8 g
- Proteins: 6.8 g
- Fiber: 9.7 g

Keto Vegan Triple Green Salad

Yields: 4 servings

Serving size: 1/4 of the entire dish

Preparation time: 14 minutes

Cooking time: 1 minute

Ingredients:

Part 1:

- 8-10 ounces Tuscan kale
- 2 teaspoons extra virgin olive oil
- 2 teaspoons toasted sesame oil
- 1 teaspoon fresh ginger (grated)
- 2 small garlic cloves (crushed)
- Pinch of coarse sea salt

Part 2:

- Large handful of snow peas (chopped)
- Small handful of scallions (chopped)
- 2 teaspoons aged balsamic vinegar
- 2 teaspoons coconut aminos
- Orange zest
- 1 piece ripe avocado (sliced)
- Hemp seeds (for toppings, as much as you like)

Directions:

- Carefully and meticulously wash the kale. Pat them with paper towels to dry. Cut each kale leaf from the center stem using a paring knife. Make sure that all the stems are removed from the leaves.
- Stack a layer of 5 kale leaves on a chopping board. Roll up the layer of leaves together. Chop the rolled leaves into small pieces.
- In a mixing bowl, put in all the ingredients listed under Part 1. Gently mix and massage the kale leaves with the rest of the ingredients for a few seconds using your hands.
- Put in the ingredients listed under Part 2 into the mixing bowl. Toss everything to combine well. Serve.

Nutritional info (per serving):

- Calories: 135
- Carbs: 10 g

- Fats: 10 g
- Proteins: 3 g
- Fiber: 3 g

Keto Vegan Asian Ginger Slaw

Yields: 8 servings

Serving size: 1 cup

Preparation time: 15 minutes

Cooking time: none

Ingredients:

Coleslaw:

- 6 cups red cabbage (thinly sliced)
- 6 cups green cabbage (thinly sliced)
- 2 cups carrots (shredded)
- 3/4 cup green onions (sliced)
- 1 cup cilantro (chopped roughly)

Asian Dressing:

- 2 tablespoons almond butter
- 2 tablespoons tamari
- 1 tablespoon maple syrup
- 1 tablespoon olive oil
- 1 tablespoon rice wine vinegar
- 1 tablespoon apple cider vinegar
- 1 teaspoon sesame oil
- 1/4 teaspoon cayenne pepper
- 1 clove garlic (minced)
- 1 1/2 inch piece ginger (grated)
- 1 piece medium lime (zest and juice)
- Sea salt (to taste)
- Pepper (to taste)

Directions:

- In a blender, put in all the ingredients for the dressing. Blend everything until the texture becomes smooth.
- In a mixing bowl, put in all the ingredients for the coleslaw. Pour over the dressing onto the coleslaw. Toss everything to mix well.
- Refrigerate the coleslaw for at least an hour to let the flavors set in. Serve.

Nutritional info (per serving):

- Calories: 144
- Carbs: 19 g

- Fats: 6 g
- Proteins: 4 g
- Fiber: 5 g

Keto Vegan Broccoli Fried Rice

Yields: 4 servings

Serving size: 1 cup

Preparation time: 5 minutes

Cooking time: 3 minutes

Ingredients:

- 2 heads of broccoli florets (chopped)
- 4 tablespoons cilantro (chopped)
- 1 tablespoon garlic (finely chopped)
- 1 tablespoon avocado oil
- 1 tablespoon coconut aminos
- 1 1/2 teaspoon toasted sesame oil
- 1/4 – 1/2 teaspoon frozen ginger (grated)
- 1/4 – 1/2 teaspoon coarse salt (to taste)
- 2 bulbs scallions (chopped)
- Quarter of 1 piece of lime (juiced)
- Almonds (sliced, for garnish)

Directions:

- In a food processor, put in the broccoli. Pulse the florets until they become rice grain in texture. Scrape the sides of the processor to make sure that all are rice grain sized.
- In a skillet over medium heat, put in the avocado oil.
- Put in the garlic. Sautee for a minute.
- Put in the broccoli rice. Sautee for another minute.
- Season with sesame oil, coconut aminos, and salt. Sautee for 2 minutes more until the broccoli rice has turned bright green in color and should not be mushy.
- Turn the heat off. Put in the ginger and lime juice. Stir to mix well.
- Garnish with almonds, cilantro, and scallions. Serve.

Nutritional info (per serving):

- Calories: 87
- Carbs: 7 g
- Fats: 5 g
- Proteins: 2 g
- Fiber: 2 g

Keto Vegan Dinner Recipes

Keto Vegan Falafels with Lupini Beans

Yields: 5 servings

Serving size: 3 falafels

Preparation time: 10 minutes

Cooking time: 30 minutes

Ingredients:

- 1 bag Sea Salt Brami Lupini Beans
- 3 tablespoons Manitoba Harvest Hemp Hearts
- 1/2 bag Garlic & Herb Brami Lupini Beans
- 3 tablespoons olive oil
- 3 tablespoons fresh parsley (chopped)
- 3 - 4 tablespoons water
- 2 teaspoons garlic powder
- 2 teaspoons onion powder
- 1/2 teaspoon baking powder
- 2 teaspoons hot sauce
- 1/2 teaspoon coriander (ground)
- 1/4 teaspoon paprika
- 1/2 teaspoon cumin
- 1/4 teaspoon pepper
- 1/4 teaspoons salt

Directions:

- Pre-heat your oven to 400 degrees Fahrenheit. Line a cookie sheet with parchment paper.
- In a food processor, put in all the lupini beans. Pulse the beans until they are chopped roughly.
- Put in the hemp hearts, parsley, olive oil, hot sauce, garlic powder, and onion powder into the food processor. Blend well. Gradually put the water into the mixture while blending. The mixture should have a smooth texture.
- Pour the blended beans into a mixing bowl. Add in the rest of the ingredients. Mix well.
- Make 15 falafel balls out of the mixture. Use a cookie scooper to make the balls.
- Arrange the falafel balls on the lined cookie sheet.

- Bake the falafel balls for 19 minutes until they are golden brown in color.
- Let the balls cool down for 10 minutes. Serve.

Nutritional info (per serving):

- Calories: 181.3
- Carbs: 8.5 g
- Fats: 20 g
- Proteins: 8.8 g
- Fiber: 7.2 g

Keto Vegan Roasted Vegetables

Yields: 4 servings

Serving size: 1/4 of the entire dish

Preparation time: 10 minutes

Cooking time: 20 minutes

Ingredients:

Vegetables:

- 8 ounces cauliflower (chopped)
- 4 ounces whole mushrooms (quartered)
- 6 ounces green beans (sliced)

Masala:

- 1/2 cup tomato puree
- 2 teaspoons fresh ginger (minced)
- 2 tablespoons olive oil
- 1 clove garlic (minced)
- 1/4 teaspoon garam masala
- 1/2 teaspoon chili powder
- 1/4 teaspoon turmeric
- Pepper (to taste)
- Salt (to taste)

Garnish:

- Cilantro (chopped)
- Green onion (sliced)
- Siracha

Directions:

- Pre-heat your oven to 400 degrees Fahrenheit. Position a rack in the middle of the oven. Line a baking pan with parchment paper.
- In a mixing bowl, put in the ginger, garlic, spices, and tomato puree. Mix well.
- Put in the olive oil. Stir.
- Put in the vegetables. Stir well to coat the vegetables.
- Pour the mixture onto the lined baking pan. Spread the vegetables all over the surface of the pan. Season with pepper and salt.
- Roast the vegetables for 20 minutes. Cook the vegetables to your desired doneness. Serve.

Nutritional info (per serving):

- Calories: 105
- Carbs: 10 g
- Fats: 7 g
- Proteins: 3 g
- Fiber: 4 g

Keto Vegan Mushroom Tacos

Yields: 6 tacos

Serving size: 1 taco

Preparation time: 15 minutes

Cooking time: 25 minutes

Ingredients:

- 12 – 14 ounces tofu Italian "sausage" – either sweet or spicy (sliced lengthwise, then sliced crosswise)
- 24 ounces baby bella mushrooms (thinly sliced)
- 1 bunch scallions (thinly sliced, separate the white parts from the dark green and the light green parts)
- 6 pieces flour tortillas (warmed)
- 1/2 small head green cabbage (cored and thinly sliced)
- 4 large cloves garlic (minced)
- 1/3 cup + 2 tablespoons water
- 1/4 cup dry roasted unsalted peanuts (finely chopped)
- 3 tablespoons hoisin sauce
- 3 tablespoons seasoned rice vinegar
- 2 tablespoons extra-virgin olive oil (divided)
- 2 tablespoons + 2 teaspoons soy sauce (low-sodium)
- 1 tablespoon fresh ginger (minced)
- 1 – 2 teaspoons sriracha

Directions:

- In a wok over medium heat, heat a tablespoon of oil. Put in the tofu sausage. Cook the sausage for 6 minutes until all sides are browned. Transfer to a plate.
- In the same wok over medium heat, put in the rest of the olive oil. Put in the mushrooms, cabbage, and water (1/3 cup). Cook for 15 minutes, stirring often. The mushrooms should have given up their liquid and are browned and soft. The cabbage should be tender. You can a small amount of water if ever the mixture is too dry and starts to stick on the bottom of the wok to prevent burns.
- Put in the onions (light green and white parts), ginger, and garlic. Cook for a minute with constant stirring.
- Put in the chili paste, remaining water (2 tablespoons), soy sauce, hoisin, rice vinegar, and sautéed tofu sausage. Cook with constant stirring until well combined and heated through.
- Adjust the taste, if needed.

- Put in the peanuts and stir to mix.
- Turn off the heat. Sprinkle the dark green parts of the onions.
- Scoop the fillings onto the warm tortillas. Serve.

Nutritional info (per serving):

- Calories: 327
- Carbs: 24 g
- Fats: 16 g
- Proteins: 25 g
- Fiber: 4 g

Keto Vegan Egg Roll in a Bowl

Yields: 2

Serving size: 1/2 of the entire dish

Preparation time: 5 minutes

Cooking time: 15 minutes

Ingredients:

- 2 pieces celery stalks (chopped)
- 2 pieces carrots (shredded)
- 1/2 piece red onion (thinly sliced)
- 4 cups cabbage (shredded)
- 1 cup mushrooms (sliced)
- 2 tablespoons tamari
- 1 tablespoon olive oil
- 1 teaspoon toasted sesame oil
- 1/4 teaspoon fine sea salt
- Black pepper (freshly ground, to taste)
- Sesame seeds (for garnish)
- Green onions (chopped, for garnish)

Directions:

- In a deep skillet over medium heat, put in the olive oil.
- Sautee the onion, celery, and carrots for 5 minutes. They should have started to soften.
- Put in the mushrooms, cabbage, tamari, pepper, and salt. Stir to mix. You can add a splash of water to stop the ingredients from sticking onto the bottom of the skillet.
- Cover the skillet. Reduce the heat. Cook for 15 minutes until the vegetables are tender.
- Right after the vegetables are tender, put in the sesame oil. Stir.
- Garnish with sesame seeds and green onions. Serve while warm.

Nutritional info (per serving):

- Calories: 178
- Carbs: 20 g
- Fats: 9 g
- Proteins: 6 g
- Fiber: 6 g

Keto Vegan Omega 3 Porridge

Yields: 1 serving

Serving size: entire dish

Preparation time: 5 minutes

Cooking time: 3 minutes

Ingredients:

- 1/4 cup almond milk
- 1/4 cup coconut cream (room temperature)
- 2 ounces hemp hearts
- 6 pieces walnut (halves and chopped)
- 1 tablespoon pumpkin seeds (whole and raw)
- 1 teaspoon powdered stevia
- 1/2 teaspoon chia seeds
- 1/2 teaspoon ground Ceylon cinnamon (divided)
- 1/8 teaspoon fine sea salt
- 1 teaspoon coconut (shredded)
- 4 drops liquid stevia

Directions:

- In a mixing bowl, put in the chia seeds, pumpkin seeds, hemp hearts, salt, half of the cinnamon. Mix well.
- In another mixing bowl, put in the almond milk and coconut cream. Whisk to mix.
- Put the seed mixture into the cream mixture. Mix well to combine. Put the mixture in the fridge overnight to chill.
- Transfer the mixture in a microwave safe bowl. Heat up the chilled porridge in the microwave for a minute. Stir.
- Put in the liquid stevia, powdered stevia, and the rest of the cinnamon. Mix well. Adjust the taste.
- Top with walnuts and coconut. Serve.

Nutritional info (per serving):

- Calories: 570
- Carbs: 22 g
- Fats: 47 g
- Proteins: 23 g
- Fiber: 8 g

Keto Vegan Soup Recipes

Keto Vegan Butternut Squash Soup

Yields: 8 cups

Serving size: 1 cup

Preparation time: 10 minutes

Cooking time: 1 hour

Ingredients:

- 1 piece 2-pound butternut squash (cut in half, seeds removed)
- 1 13.5-ounce can coconut milk
- 4 cups vegetable broth
- 6 cloves garlic (minced)
- 2 tablespoons avocado oil (divided)
- 2 tablespoons fresh thyme
- 1/8 teaspoon nutmeg
- 1/2 teaspoon cinnamon
- Black pepper
- Sea salt

Directions:

- Pre-heat your oven to 400 degrees Fahrenheit. Prepare a baking sheet. Line it with parchment paper.
- Put the butternut squash on the baking sheet with the open side up. Drizzle the top of the butternut squash with half of the avocado oil. Season with pepper and salt. Turn over the butternut squash. The open side is now facing down.
- Roast the butternut squash for 55 minutes until tender.
- While the butternut squash is roasting halfway through, prepare a large pot. Put the pot on medium heat. Heat the rest of the avocado oil. Put in the garlic, nutmeg, cinnamon, and thyme. Sautee them until fragrant, about 1 minute.
- Put in the coconut milk and broth. Bring to a boil. Reduce the heat. Simmer the mixture for 20 minutes.
- Take the butternut squash out from the oven. Scoop the flesh out of the shells.
- In a mixing bowl, put the butternut squash and the simmered mixture together. Blend everything using an immersion blade until it looks like a puree. Serve.

Nutritional info (per serving):

- Calories: 183

- Carbs: 12 g
- Fats: 12 g
- Proteins: 6 g
- Fiber: 2 g

Keto Vegan Vegetable Soup

Yields: 12 servings

Serving size: 2 cups

Preparation time: 10 minutes

Cooking time: 1 hour and 40 minutes

Ingredients:

- 1 pound green beans (fresh or frozen)
- 1 pound spinach leaves (chopped)
- 64 ounces vegetable broth
- 15 ounces pumpkin puree
- 6 stalks celery (chopped)
- 1 piece small onion (chopped)
- 1 piece large turnip (cubed)
- 1 piece medium carrot (chopped)
- 2 cups water
- Salt (to taste)
- 1/4 teaspoon thyme leaves
- 1 tablespoon fresh basil (chopped)
- 1/8 teaspoon rubbed sage

Directions:

- In a pot over medium heat, put in all the ingredients excluding the spinach. Bring the mixture to a boil.
- Lower the heat. Cover the pot. Simmer the soup for 90 minutes. Make sure that the vegetables are tender.
- Turn off the heat. Put in the spinach. Stir. Cover the pot to let the spinach leaves wilt. Serve.

Nutritional info (per serving):

- Calories: 51
- Carbs: 10 g
- Fats: 0 g
- Proteins: 3 g
- Fiber: 3 g

Keto Vegan Mushroom Soup

Yields: 4 servings

Serving size: 1/4 of the entire dish

Preparation time: 3 minutes

Cooking time: 2 minutes

Ingredients:

- 500 grams mushrooms
- 250 ml coconut milk
- 250 ml vegetable stock
- 1 tablespoon parsley
- 1 teaspoon thyme
- Salt (to taste)
- Pepper (to taste)

Directions:

- In an Instant Pot, put in the vegetable stock at the bottom.
- Put the trivet on the bottom of the inner pot.
- Arrange the mushrooms on the trivet. Seal the lid of the Instant Pot.
- Cook the mushrooms for 2 minutes on manual pressure.
- Release the pressure manually (QPR) of the Instant Pot.
- In a blender, put in the mushrooms and what's left of the stock. Put in the rest of the ingredients except for the coconut milk. Blend.
- Put in the coconut milk into the mixture in the blender. Continue to blend until the texture becomes creamy. Serve.

Nutritional info (per serving):

- Calories: 31
- Carbs: 4.7 g
- Fats: 0.4 g
- Proteins: 4.2 g
- Fiber: 1.6 g

Keto Vegan Creamy Zucchini and Cauliflower Soup

Yields: 8 servings

Serving size: 1 1/4 cups

Preparation time: 20 minutes

Cooking time: 25 minutes

Ingredients:

- 500 grams zucchini (chopped)
- 700 grams cauliflower (chopped)
- 2 cups water
- 2 cups vegetable stock
- 1 cup coconut milk
- 1 clove garlic (chopped finely)
- 2 celery stalks (chopped)
- 1 piece small brown onion (chopped)
- 4 tablespoons extra virgin olive oil
- 2 tablespoons olive oil
- 1/2 teaspoon onion powder
- 1 teaspoon fresh thyme (chopped)
- Pepper (to taste)
- Sea salt (to taste)

Directions:

- In a saucepan over medium heat, put in the olive oil. Sautee the garlic and onion until they are fragrant and translucent.
- Put in the zucchini, celery, cauliflower, seasonings, water and broth. Stir to mix. Bring the mixture to a boil.
- Cover the saucepan. Lower the heat. Simmer the mixture for 15 minutes until the vegetables are soft.
- Turn off the heat. Using an immersion mixer, blend the mixture in the saucepan until it becomes a puree.
- Put in the coconut milk. Stir. Turn on the heat to medium. Heat up the soup mixture.
- Pour the soup into individual serving bowls. Garnish with thyme. Drizzle with extra virgin olive oil. Serve.

Nutritional info (per serving):

- Calories: 258
- Carbs: 8.3 g

- Fats: 23.6 g
- Proteins: 4.4 g
- Fiber: 2.7 g

Keto Vegan Cauliflower and Turmeric Soup

Yields: 6 servings

Serving size: 1/6 of the entire dish

Preparation time: 5 minutes

Cooking time: 25 minutes

Ingredients:

- 1 cup coconut milk
- 1 large cauliflower head (sliced into 8 large chunks)
- 1 piece ginger (thumb size and sliced into 4 pieces)
- 1/2 large carrot (peeled and sliced into 4 pieces)
- 2 tablespoons turmeric
- 2 teaspoons salt
- 1 teaspoon black pepper

Tofu Croutons:

- 454 grams tofu (extra firm)
- 1 tablespoon soy sauce
- 1 tablespoon olive oil
- 1 teaspoon smoked paprika
- 1 teaspoon lemon juice
- 1/2 teaspoon cumin

Garnishing:

- 1 cup full fat coconut milk
- Black pepper (freshly ground)
- Dried dill

Directions:

- Pre-heat your oven to 400 degrees Fahrenheit. Line a cookie sheet with parchment paper.
- In a pot over medium heat, put in 8 cups of water. Bring the water to a boil.
- Put in the carrots, ginger, and cauliflower. Cook for 20 minutes. The vegetables should be very soft and cooked through.
- While the vegetable soup is cooking, make the tofu croutons. Slice the tofu block into 32 cubes.
- In a mixing bowl, put in all the ingredients for the tofu croutons. Mix well to coat each tofu cube with the seasonings.
- Transfer the tofu cubes on the lined cookie sheet. Spread the cubes evenly on the surface of the cookie sheet.

- Bake the tofu cubes for 20 minutes. They should be browned and crispy.
- Turn off the heat on the vegetable soup. Let the vegetable soup cool down completely. Blend the soup in the pot using an immersion blender until it becomes like a puree.
- Put back the pureed soup on the stovetop over medium heat. Put in the coconut milk, black pepper, turmeric, and salt. Stir to mix. Cook for 5 minutes more.
- Turn off the heat. Let the soup cool down for a few minutes.
- Top each serving with tofu croutons, and the garnishing.

Nutritional info (per serving):

- Calories: 471
- Carbs: 9.5 g
- Fats: 34 g
- Proteins: 32.7 g
- Fiber: 3.9 g

Keto Vegan Salad Recipes

Keto Vegan Avocado, Blueberry, and Almond Salad

Yields: 1 serving

Serving size: entire dish

Preparation time: 5 minutes

Cooking time: none

Ingredients:

- 15 grams almonds (sliced)
- 1 cup arugula mix
- 1 ounce blueberries
- 1/2 cup cruciferous crunch
- 1 - 2 tablespoons green goddess dressing
- 1/2 piece ripe avocado
- 1 tablespoon MCT oil

Directions:

- In a mixing bowl, put in all the ingredients. Toss the salad. Serve.

Nutritional info (per serving):

- Calories: 256.4
- Carbs: 16.5 g
- Fats: 20.2 g
- Proteins: 6.2 g
- Fiber: 8.6 g

Keto Vegan Cucumber and Cabbage Salad

Yields: 8 servings

Serving size: 1/8 of the entire dish

Preparation time: 20 minutes

Cooking time: none

Ingredients:

- 2 pieces Persian cucumbers (sliced)
- 1/2 head white cabbage (chopped, discard core)
- 1/2 piece lemon (juiced)
- 3 tablespoons avocado oil
- 2 tablespoons green onions (chopped)
- 2 tablespoons fresh dill (chopped)
- 2 teaspoon unrefined salt (divided)
- Pepper (to taste)
- Additional salt (to taste)

Directions:

- In a mixing bowl, put in the cabbage and a teaspoon of salt. Mix them well. Use your hands to press the cabbage so it will release its natural juice. Set aside for 5 minutes.
- Put in the cucumbers, green onions, and dill. Mix well.
- Put in the lemon juice, pepper, salt, and avocado oil. Mix well. Adjust the taste. Serve.

Nutritional info (per serving):

- Calories: 70
- Carbs: 5 g
- Fats: 5 g
- Proteins: 1 g
- Fiber: 1 g

Keto Vegan Curried Coconut Cabbage Salad

Yields: 2 servings

Serving size: 1/2 of the entire dish

Preparation time: 1 hour and 5 minutes

Cooking time: none

Ingredients:

- 1/3 cup desiccated coconut (unsweetened)
- 1/4 cup Tamari sauce
- 1/4 cup coconut oil
- 1/2 head white cabbage (shredded)
- 1 piece lemon (juiced)
- 3 teaspoons sesame seeds
- 1/2 teaspoon curry powder
- 1/2 teaspoon ginger (dried)
- 1/2 teaspoon cumin

Directions:

- In a mixing bowl, put in all the ingredients. Toss to mix well.
- Refrigerate the salad for 1 hour or more. Serve.

Nutritional info (per serving):

- Calories: 309
- Carbs: 12 g
- Fats: 29 g
- Proteins: 5 g
- Fiber: 6 g

Keto Vegan Asian Noodle with Peanut Sauce Salad

Yields: 4 servings

Serving size: 1 1/2 cups

Preparation time: 10 minutes

Cooking time: none

Ingredients:

Salad:

- 4 cups shiritake noodles (rinsed and drained)
- 1 cup green cabbage (shredded)
- 1 cup red cabbage (shredded)
- 1/4 cup cilantro (chopped)
- 1/4 cup scallions (chopped)
- 1/4 cup peanuts (chopped)

Dressing:

- 1/2 cup filtered water
- 1/4 cup peanut butter (sugar free)
- 2 tablespoons ginger (minced)
- 1 tablespoon lime juice
- 1 tablespoon erythritol sweetener (granulated)
- 1 tablespoon toasted sesame oil
- 1 tablespoon coconut aminos
- 1 tablespoon soy sauce (wheat-free)
- 1 teaspoon garlic (minced)
- 1/2 teaspoon kosher salt
- 1/4 teaspoon cayenne pepper

Directions:

- In a mixing bowl, put in all the ingredients for the salad. Mix well.
- In a blender, put in all the ingredients for the dressing. Blend until the texture is smooth.
- Pour the dressing into the bowl of salad. Toss the salad to coat well. Serve.

Nutritional info (per serving):

- Calories: 212
- Carbs: 9 g
- Fats: 16 g
- Proteins: 7 g

- Fiber: 3 g

Keto Vegan Thai Cucumber Salad

Yields: 4 servings

Serving size: 1 cup

Preparation time: 10 minutes

Cooking time: none

Ingredients:

Dressing:

- 6 pieces bird's eye chilies (crushed)
- 1 clove garlic (minced)
- 2 tablespoons fresh lime juice
- 1 tablespoon soy sauce
- 1 1/2 tablespoons coconut aminos
- 1 tablespoon apple cider vinegar
- 2 teaspoons sesame oil
- 1/4 teaspoon black pepper
- 1/4 teaspoon salt

Salad:

- 1/2 cup fresh cilantro leaves (chopped)
- 2 pieces large cucumbers
- 1/4 cup sesame seeds (toasted)

Directions:

- In a mixing bowl, put in all the ingredients for the dressing. Whisk them very well. Set aside.
- Using a spiralizer, slice the cucumbers thinly. Put the sliced cucumbers into the mixing bowl with dressing. Toss to coat very well.
- Top with cilantro and sesame seeds. Serve.

Nutritional info (per serving):

- Calories: 127
- Carbs: 8.3 g
- Fats: 8.3 g
- Proteins: 4 g
- Fiber: 2.9 g

Keto Vegan Meal Prep Recipes

Keto Vegan Buddha Bowl

Yields: 1 serving

Serving size: entire dish

Preparation time: 10 minutes

Cooking time: 35 minutes

Ingredients:

- 1 cup Brussels sprouts
- 1 1/2 cups broccoli florets
- 2 tablespoons pumpkin seeds
- 2 tablespoons tahini
- 10 pieces Kalamata olives
- 1/2 teaspoon oil
- Sesame seeds (for topping)
- 1/2 piece avocado (for serving)
- Pinch of salt

Directions:

- Pre-heat your oven to 425 degrees Fahrenheit. Line a baking pan with parchment paper.
- Put on the lined baking pan the pumpkin seeds, Brussels sprouts, and broccoli. Season them with salt, tahini, and oil. Toss to combine.
- Roast the vegetables for 35 minutes.
- Take out the roasted vegetables from the oven. Put in the Kalamata olives onto the baking pan. Toss to mix well with the roasted vegetables.
- Top with avocado slices and sesame seeds. Serve.

Meal Prep:

- In an airtight container, put together the pumpkin seeds and vegetables. Put in the fridge.
- When it is time to cook it, just follow the cooking directions above.

Nutritional info (per serving):

- Calories: 641
- Carbs: 33 g
- Fats: 50 g
- Proteins: 23 g

- Fiber: 20 g

Keto Vegan Easy Fat Bombs

Yields: 12 fat bombs

Serving size: 3 fat bombs

Preparation time: 10 minutes

Cooking time: 2 hours

Ingredients:

- 1/4 cup coconut oil (at room temperature)
- 3/4 cup macadamia nut butter

Directions:

- Prepare a 12-cavity silicone mold.
- In a microwave safe mixing bowl, put in the macadamia nut butter. Microwave the butter until warmed.
- Put in the coconut oil. Mix well.
- Equally portion the mixture into the 12 molds.
- Freeze the fat bombs for at least an hour to set.
- Remove the fat bombs from the silicone molds.
- Put the fat bombs in an airtight container. You can store them for 3 to 5 days or more in the freezer.

Nutritional info (per serving):

- Calories: 320
- Carbs: 5 g
- Fats: 35 g
- Proteins: 3 g
- Fiber: 3 g

Keto Vegan Curried Tofu Scramble

Yields: 4 servings

Serving size: 1 cup

Preparation time: 10 minutes

Cooking time: 20 minutes

Ingredients:

Tofu Scramble:

- 2 - 3 cups greens - arugula, spinach, kale, and dandelion (roughly chopped)
- 6 ounces mushrooms (sliced)
- 2 - 3 tablespoons vegetable broth (low-sodium)
- 1 piece large red pepper (diced)
- 1/2 piece medium onion (diced)
- 1 block extra firm organic tofu (pressed and drained)

Curry Seasoning:

- 1 tablespoon water
- 1/2 teaspoon curry powder
- 1/2 teaspoon cumin
- 1/2 teaspoon garlic powder
- 1/4 teaspoon paprika
- 1/4 teaspoon coriander
- 1/4 teaspoon garam masala
- 1/4 teaspoon turmeric
- 1/4 teaspoon black salt

Directions:

- In a pan over medium heat, put in the vegetable broth. Sautee the onions for 5 minutes.
- Put in the red peppers and mushrooms. Cook them for about 10 minutes.
- Push aside the cooked vegetables to one side of the pan. Put the block of pressed tofu onto the pan. Break up the tofu into chunks using a spatula. Sautee the crumbled tofu until heated through for 3 minutes.
- In a small mixing bowl, put in all the ingredients for the curry seasoning. Whisk them well. Pour the seasoning over the crumbled tofu on the pan. Stir to coat the tofu with the seasoning.
- Mix together the tofu and cooked vegetables. Put in the chopped greens. Stir to mix. Cover the pan. Continue cooking until the greens are wilted.

- Equally divide the dish into 4 servings. Put each serving in separate airtight containers. You can store them in the fridge for 3 – 4 days.

Nutritional info (per serving):

- Calories: 119
- Carbs: 9 g
- Fats: 5 g
- Proteins: 11 g
- Fiber: 3 g

Keto Vegan Maple Oatmeal

Yields: 4 servings

Serving size: 1/4 of the entire dish

Preparation time: 5 minutes

Cooking time: 20 minutes

Ingredients:

- 60 grams pecans
- 60 grams walnuts
- 15 grams coconut flakes
- 40 grams sunflower seeds
- 1000 ml almond milk (unsweetened)
- 4 tablespoons chia seeds
- 1/2 teaspoon cinnamon
- 3/8 teaspoon stevia powder
- 1 teaspoon maple flavoring

Directions:

- In a food processor, put in the sunflower seeds, pecans, and walnuts. Pulse them for a few seconds until they are crumbly.
- In a pot over low heat, put in all of the ingredients. Let the mixture simmer for 30 minutes with frequent stirring to prevent the oatmeal from sticking on the bottom of the pot. Let the chia seeds absorb almost all of the liquid.
- Turn off the heat when the oatmeal has already thickened. Serve.
- Let the oatmeal cool down completely before putting it in the fridge. Leftover servings are good to eat up to 2 days in the fridge.

Nutritional info (per serving):

- Calories: 374
- Carbs: 12.37 g
- Fats: 34.59 g
- Proteins: 9.25 g
- Fiber: 9.1 g

Keto Vegan Tofu Cauliflower Tacos

Yields: 8 tacos

Serving size: 1 taco

Preparation time: 10 minutes

Cooking time: 30 minutes

Ingredients:

Roasted Vegetables:

- 1/2 pound cremini mushrooms (sliced)
- 1 medium cauliflower head (florets removed)
- 2 pieces medium bell pepper (sliced)
- 1 teaspoon cumin
- 1 teaspoon chili powder
- 1 teaspoon onion powder
- 1 teaspoon smoked paprika
- 1 teaspoon garlic powder
- 1 tablespoon olive oil
- Pepper (to taste)
- Sea salt (to taste)

Crumbled Tofu:

- 1 piece medium red onion (diced)
- 1 pack extra-firm tofu (pressed and drained)
- 3 garlic cloves (minced)
- 1 tablespoon olive oil
- 1 tablespoon vegan Worcestershire sauce
- 1 tablespoon tomato paste
- 1 teaspoon smoked paprika
- 1 tablespoon chili powder
- 1/4 teaspoon sea salt
- 1 teaspoon cumin
- 1/8 teaspoon black pepper

Taco Toppings and Wraps:

- Butter lettuce
- 8 pieces low-carb tortillas
- Hot sauce
- 1 piece avocado (sliced)

Directions:

Roasted Vegetables:

- Pre-heat your oven to 400 degrees Fahrenheit. Prepare 2 baking trays. Line them with silicone mat.
- Arrange the mushrooms, bell pepper, and cauliflower florets on the lined baking trays.
- Season the vegetables with black pepper, sea salt, garlic powder, smoked paprika, onion powder, cumin, chili powder, and olive oil. Toss to evenly coat the vegetables with the seasoning.
- Bake the vegetables for 30 minutes until they are tender and lightly browned especially the florets.

Crumbled Tofu:

- In a skillet over medium heat, put in the olive oil. Sautee the red onion for 10 minutes until translucent.
- Put in the garlic, Worcestershire sauce, and tomato paste. Cook for 2 more minutes.
- Push them to the one side of the skillet. Put the pressed tofu on the cleared surface of the skillet. Break apart the tofu to crumbles like that of grounded meat.
- Put in the pepper, salt, cumin, smoked paprika, and chili powder on the tofu. Stir to coat the tofu crumbles with the seasoning.
- Mix the tofu with everything on the skillet. Lower the heat. Cook the mixture for 10 minutes more with occasional stirring.
- It is now time to build your tacos. Lay a tortilla wrap on a plate. Layer on it a butter lettuce, tofu crumbles, roasted veggies, avocado slices, and hot sauce. Fold the tortilla wrap on the fillings just like a taco.
- Store the roasted veggies and tofu crumbles in different airtight containers. Put them in the fridge and they are good for up to 5 days.

Nutritional info (per serving):

- Calories: 166
- Carbs: 14 g
- Fats: 4 g
- Proteins: 8 g
- Fiber: 5 g

Chapter 7: Keto Shopping List

The following is a short shopping list that you can use as a guide. Remember the goal is to base the majority of your meals around these ingredients.

Meat
- Turkey
- Chicken
- Bacon
- Sausage
- Ham
- Steak
- Red meat

Eggs
- Omega 3 whole eggs
- Pastured eggs

Fatty Fish
- Mackerel
- Tuna
- Trout
- Salmon

Cream/Butter
- Preferably from grass fed sources

Nuts and Seeds
- Chia seeds
- Pumpkin seeds
- Flax seeds
- Walnuts
- Almonds

Cheese
- Mozzarella
- Blue cheese
- Cream cheese
- Goat cheese
- Cheddar cheese
- Other unprocessed cheese

Condiments

- Pepper
- Salt
- Healthy herbs
- Garden fresh spices

Veggies

- Peppers
- Onions
- Tomatoes
- Green veggies

Oils

- Avocado oil
- Coconut oil
- Olive oil

Closing

I hope this book was able to help you to get started on the keto diet. A lot of the things that I have mentioned here are based on my personal experience and extensive research. The recipes that are included here are some of my favorites and I hope you enjoyed them well.

The meal plans that I have presented here are the simplest ones that I have tried. They have helped me get started on the keto diet and I hope that they have helped you a lot as well.

The next step is to make an inventory of your fridge and take out any food items that aren't keto. After that you should shop for keto based food and ingredients. Please make use of a keto shopping list. You can follow the list of foods that I have used here and of course you can alter it as needed to suit your own specific needs.

Don't rush and be forgiving of yourself.

If you find that your levels haven't really gone that high as you hoped after the first month, then just keep going. Modify your meal plan and make an inventory of the recipes that you have used.

During that inventory you may find a recipe or two that you may have to modify or replace. There are plenty of recipes out there that you can try other than the ones that are listed here in this book.

Make sure to regularly measure your ketone levels so that you can determine your progress. I suggest that you skip intermittent fasting during the first 3 months—unless of course you have already tried some form of fasting before and you're already comfortable with it.

After four weeks into the keto diet, you may want to try implementing an intermittent fasting plan. Be sure to check with your doctor before you start any fasting regimen.

Remember to be more forgiving of yourself. The keto diet may be easy but there will be times when it is going to be quite challenging. Carbs can be very enticing sometimes.

When you do give in, learn to forgive yourself. And then recommit yourself to the keto diet and continue following the meal plans provided here in this book.

It's a truly rewarding path to follow. I wish you the best of luck!

Book #2
Keto Diet After 50

Keto for Seniors

The Complete Guide to Burn Fat, Lose Weight, and Prevent Diseases - With Simple 30 Minute Keto Recipes and a 30-Day Meal Plan

Introduction

Face it – we all struggled with weight problems at some point in our life. In fact, some people still struggle with weight loss and would happily lose a few more pounds, if given the chance. I definitely did. As I found out, the ability to lose the excess fat became more difficult as I got older. Metabolism slows down and physical activity starts to decrease so all those calories stack up and lodge themselves everywhere – belly, thighs, arms, neck, chin, and so on. Even if I wanted to exercise and lose all those excess fat – it isn't really possible because, well, exercise makes me feel constant chronic pain. I try to take a relaxing 3 minute walk and feel my legs and thighs throbbing for the rest of the day.

So what did I do? I did my research and found out that adopting a good diet for weight loss is usually the best solution. In fact, studies show that what you eat is more important than exercise when it comes to maintaining a healthy weight. The question here is – what kind of diet should I follow if I'm approaching my later years?

I tried winging it first – not following a specific diet but just making consciously healthy decisions. When that didn't work, I tried several diet types like the Paleo Diet, the Vegetarian route, and I even tried going Vegan. Finally, I decided to go to my doctor (which I should have done in the first place) and he told me to try the Ketogenic Diet, given my diabetic background. Since this was recommended by my doctor, I decided to be a wee bit more dedicated to the diet – and I started losing the excess weight! Before starting the Ketogenic Diet, I weighed 220 pounds, which for my height of 6 feet, puts me in the overweight category. In fact, if I went one pound over, I'd be obese.

Now, I'm at a healthy 190 pounds, and all credit goes to the Ketogenic Diet lifestyle. I want to share this discovery with everyone by introducing this new diet dubbed as the Ketogenic Diet.

It's not exactly brand new – but it is definitely one of the most effective methods of losing weight and gaining better health nowadays. Since I started the Ketogenic Diet, I managed to lose 30 pounds, have better clarity, experience less foggy days, and even wake up in the morning feeling completely refreshed. If you're like me – then chances are you've woken up in the morning and you feel just as tired as you did the night before.

I want you to know that this is not a fly by night creation. I personally went through this and it is NOT easy. However, the results are so wonderfully satisfying that I felt it my duty to share this information with the world.

Don't believe me? Do your research the same way I did. Many medical publications today talk about the advantages of going on the Ketogenic Diet. These studies consider many factors related to the dietary plan such as how it compares with a low-carbohydrate approach or a low-calorie approach.

In this book, I've made every effort to communicate what I know and have learned after years of enjoying the benefits of the Ketogenic Diet. If you've read Keto books before and became frustrated about the in-depth and complicated explanations – don't worry anymore! I've made sure that this book is as simple and as straightforward, giving you only what is considered essential in order to make the most out of the Ketogenic Diet.

But that's enough talking – read on and find out exactly what you can enjoy even as you enter your older years!

Chapter 1: How the Ketogenic Diet Works

What Is the Ketogenic Diet?

The Ketogenic Diet actually follows a fairly simple principle: keep your food consumption low-carb and high-fat. So basically, being on the diet means eating less carbohydrates and adding more fats in your daily meals. Don't be confused. When we say "fat" we're not talking about the literal kind that's attached to your body. Fat has gotten a bad reputation nowadays, but "fat" the nutrient is actually very different from the "fat" that makes your clothes fit tight.

Good fats are the kind you get from avocado, nuts, and fish. For example, there are the omega-3 and omega-6 fatty acids that actually help you lose weight, get better heart health, and have excellent hair and nails.

What Happens to Your Body When You Eat Keto?

Even before we talk about how to do keto – it's important to first consider why this particular diet works. What actually happens to your body to make you lose weight?

As you probably know, the body uses food as an energy source. Everything you eat is turned into energy, so that you can get up and do whatever you need to accomplish for the day. The main energy source is sugar so what happens is that you eat something, the body breaks it down into sugar, and the sugar is processed into energy. Typically, the "sugar" is taken directly from the food you eat so if you eat just the right amount of food, then your body is fueled for the whole day. If you eat too much, then the sugar is stored in your body – hence the accumulation of fat.

But what happens if you eat less food? This is where the Ketogenic Diet comes in. You see, the process of creating sugar from food is usually faster if the food happens to be rich in carbohydrates. Bread, rice, grain, pasta – all of these are carbohydrates and they're the easiest food types to turn into energy.

So the Ketogenic Diet is all about reducing the amount of carbohydrates you eat. Does this mean you won't get the kind of energy you need for the day? Of course not! It only means that now, your body has to find other possible sources of energy. Do you know where they will be getting that energy? Your stored body fat!

So here's the situation – you are eating less carbohydrates every day. To keep you energetic, the body breaks down the stored fat and turns them into molecules called ketone bodies. The process of turning the fat into ketone bodies is called "Ketosis" and obviously – this is where the name of the Ketogenic Diet comes from. The ketone bodies take the place of glucose in keeping you energetic. As long as you keep your carbohydrates reduced, the body will keep getting its energy from your body fat.

Sounds Simple, Right?

The Ketogenic Diet is often praised for its simplicity and when you look at it properly, the process is really straightforward. The Science behind the effectivity of the diet is also well-documented, and has been proven multiple times by different medical fields. For example, an article on Diet Review by Harvard provided a lengthy discussion on how the Ketogenic Diet works and why it is so effective for those who choose to use this diet.

But Fat Is the Enemy…Or Is It?

No – fat is NOT the enemy. Unfortunately, years of bad science told us that fat is something you have to avoid – but it's actually a very helpful thing for weight loss! Even before we move forward with this book, we'll have to discuss exactly what "healthy fats" are, and why they're actually the good guys. To do this, we need to make a distinction between the different kinds of fat. You've probably heard of them before and it is a little bit confusing at first. We'll try to go through them as simply as possible:

Saturated fat. This is the kind you want to avoid. They're also called "solid fat" because each molecule is packed with hydrogen atoms. Simply put, it's the kind of fat that can easily cause a blockage in your body. It can raise cholesterol levels and lead to heart problems or a stroke. Saturated fat is something you can find in meat, dairy products, and other processed food items. Now, you're probably wondering: isn't the Ketogenic Diet packed with saturated fat? The answer is: not necessarily. You'll find later in the recipes given that the Ketogenic Diet promotes primarily unsaturated fat or healthy fat. While there are definitely many meat recipes in the list, most of these recipes contain healthy fat sources.

Unsaturated Fat. These are the ones dubbed as healthy fat. They're the kind of fat you find in avocado, nuts, and other ingredients you usually find in Keto-friendly recipes. They're known to lower blood cholesterol and actually come in two types: polyunsaturated and monounsaturated. Both are good for your body but the benefits slightly vary, depending on what you're consuming.

Polyunsaturated fat. These are perhaps the best in the list. You know about omega-3 fatty acids right? They're often suggested for people who have heart problems and are recognized as the "healthy" kind of fat. Well, they fall under the category of polyunsaturated fat and are known for reducing risks of heart disease by as much as 19 percent. This is according to a study titled: Effects on coronary heart diseases of increased poly-unsaturated fat in lieu of saturated fat: systematic review & meta-analysis of randomized controlled tests. So where do you get these polyunsaturated fats? You can get them mostly from vegetable and seed oils. These are ingredients you can almost always find in Ketogenic Recipes such as olive oil, coconut oil, and more. If you need more convincing, you should also know that omega-3 fatty acids are actually a kind of polyunsaturated fats and you will find them in deep sea fish like tuna, herring, and salmon.

Chapter 2: Benefits of Going on a Ketogenic Diet

So what exactly can you look forward to once you go on a Ketogenic Diet? There are tons of benefits! Here are some of the pros of this brand new diet:

Efficient Way to Lose Weight

Let's forget calories for a few minutes and just concentrate on the kind of nutrients you have in your food. A study published in PubMed which allows for a *meta-analysis of randomized controlled trial between a very-low carbohydrate ketogenic diet versus a low-fat diet for long term weight loss* shows that the low-carb option provides for better long-term results. It can even help reduce risk factors of cardiovascular problems, which simply means that you'll have less chances of suffering from heart problems or high blood pressure.

The science behind this isn't that complicated. The fact is that the body finds it easier to turn sugar into energy – which is why when given the choice, your body will always choose to run on sugar. Fat is also a possible source of energy – but it takes more work, which is why you lose weight more consistently with a Ketogenic Diet.

Reduces the Risk of Acne

You'd think a person in their 50's wouldn't have acne – and you'd probably be right. Note though that a large part of what you eat affects skin health, even if you're already in your 50s. In fact, people in their 50s need to be extra careful with skin health because this is when growths, blackheads, pore blockages, and more become persistent. Studies show that rapid changes in blood sugar have an effect on skin health as discussed in a study titled: *Nutrition and acne – therapeutic potential of ketogenic diets.*

May Help Reduce Cancer Risks

Switching to the Ketogenic Diet may help reduce the risk of cancer, especially as the risk of it increases upon reaching the age of 50. Although that's just a small percentage, it's definitely worth noting – especially if you happen to have a history of cancer in the family. It's also interesting to note that the Ketogenic Diet is usually prescribed as a complement to chemotherapy. A study titled *"Ketogenic diets as an adjuvant cancer therapy: history and potential mechanism"* concluded that the deprivation of sugar causes more stress to the cancer cells. This simply means that cancer cells depend more on the glucose you have on your body and once their energy source is cut-off, they're more likely to die off.

Reduces Risk of Heart Problems

Healthy fat found in avocado, nuts, and other food items promoted by the Ketogenic Diet can help reduce the possibility of heart problems. In a study titled: The long-term effects of a ketogenic diet in obese patients, it was seen that going on a Keto Diet significantly increases HDL and lowers LDL. HDL is known as the "good cholesterol" while LDL is the "bad cholesterol" known for increasing the likelihood of heart problems. So does this mean that all fat is healthy? No. Remember, we're only talking about the good fat here as previously discussed. The bad type are still discouraged and are not part of the Ketogenic Diet.

Protects Brain Function

Have you ever found yourself trying to remember simple things – like what things to buy from the store or what day to pay the power bill? Forgetfulness becomes more common as you grow older – but it doesn't have to be! In a study titled: The effects of Ketogenic Diet on behavior and cognition, it was revealed that children following the diet have better cognitive functioning and alertness. It's also theorized that the diet has neurological protective benefits – which basically means that it can help prevent problems that affect brain function. For example, you'll have slightly lower risks of Parkinson's, Alzheimer's, and other forms of dementia.

Bone Health

Osteoporosis becomes more likely as a person advances in age. This is especially true if you weren't able to introduce appropriate amounts of calcium in your body. As you probably known, osteoporosis makes the bone brittle and fragile. This means that your likelihood of having serious injury from seemingly small accidents increases. A simple slip and bones can fracture or hips may become dislocated. Persistent inflammation of the joints could become an everyday problem. The Ketogenic Diet is a good way of preventing these from happening because the diet naturally involves the intake of healthy dairy or milk products. More importantly, the Ketogenic Diet promotes the intake of low-toxin food products. Hence, your body absorbs food nutrients better, ensuring that all the minerals you need is distributed evenly throughout the body.

But I'm Over 50!

I understand that you have several concerns when using the Ketogenic Diet. Sure, the benefits are definitely great – but many of these benefits are experienced by those who are in their 40s or younger. This means that aside from the excess weight, they don't really have any other health problems to contend with. But what if you're already in your 50s or more? From what I see, most people in their 50s already have several health issues. Usually, these are health problems that occur simply because of age – so don't feel too bad about yourself!

For example, high blood pressure, heart problems, and diabetes are common problems for people in their 50s. If you happen to be this situation – it's important to first consult your doctor before going on the Ketogenic Diet – or any other diet for that matter. Since we're doing our best to cover all areas of Ketogenic Diet for people over 50, this book will also talk about some of the downsides if you have existing health problems. As someone who has done extensive research and have a ton of personal experiences from working with clients, I want you to know that there is absolutely NOTHING to be afraid of when switching to this brand new dietary plan.

Check out the next Chapter and find out what else to expect with this new diet!

Chapter 3: Ketogenic Diet for People Over 50

I've encountered instances where a person wants to go on a Ketogenic Diet but hesitated because they have pre-existing health problems. As mentioned, if you're in your 50s, you likely have several health problems and even if you don't, you still have to be extra careful with any new lifestyle choice. Even when exercising, older individuals have to choose workouts that don't put too much strain on the bones and muscles!

In this Chapter therefore, we're going to consider the use of Ketogenic Diet if you've been diagnosed with health problems or at a risk for it or if you're just 50 years old or above.

Keto for People with Diabetes

We've already mentioned this – Keto is good for people with diabetes. In fact, this is the primary reason why the Ketogenic Diet was recommended to me by my doctor. The science behind this is fairly straightforward – people with diabetes usually have high levels of sugar in their body. As mentioned, what food type is the quickest source of sugar for the body? Carbohydrates! Simply put, people with diabetes eat lots of carbohydrates, causing their blood sugar to rise and over time, it develops into diabetes. Note though, we're talking about Type 2 Diabetes here which occurs due to diet. Type 1 Diabetes has something to do with the hormones and is usually controlled through medication.

With the Ketogenic Diet, you're basically swapping the carbohydrates for a healthier and more sustainable option. This doesn't just sound good in theory though – there have been studies done on this and it was proven multiple times by the scientific community. In fact, you might find that some doctors recommend the Ketogenic Diet to the diabetic patients (like me). In a study published in Nutrition and Metabolism titled *"The effect of a low-carb diet, ketogenic diet vs. low-glycemic index diet on blood sugar control in Type 2 Diabetics"*, it was concluded that the Ketogenic Diet actually led to improvements on sugar control.

It's also important to note that diabetes is a problem that increases the risk of other health issues. Basically, this means that if you have diabetes, then there's a good chance that you'll also develop other health problems in the future – like high blood pressure and heart problems.

Note that even people with diabetes can have a low blood sugar. In fact, if you have diabetes and go on a Keto diet, there's a good chance that the blood sugar *will* dip to levels that are no longer healthy. Again, this is why we encourage diabetics to go to the doctor first before doing any kind of diet.

The Calorie and Nutrient Balance

Do you know why else the Ketogenic Diet is good for you specifically, as someone who just hit 50 years of age? What you should keep in mind is that as a person advances in age, their calorie needs decrease. For example, instead of 2,000 calories per day – you'll need only 1,800 calories per day. Why is that? Well, when we start to age –our physical activity significantly decreases. Hence, we don't need as much energy in our system. However, that doesn't mean our nutrient needs also go down. We still need the same amount of vitamins and minerals.

The Ketogenic Diet manages to hit a balance between these two needs. You get high nutrition for every calorie you get – which means that you'll maintain a decent amount of weight without really feeling less energetic for day to day activities.

Chapter 4: Ketogenic Diet FAQs

Why are you here?

OK – first things first – why are you here? I mean, why are you reading this book? Do you want to lose weight or do you want to just have a healthier lifestyle? This is an important question to ask and in all honesty, I feel like this is a question that we should have addressed in the first stage of the book.

If you'll notice, the book talks about how you can burn fat, lose weight, and prevent diseases with the Ketogenic Diet. Following this dietary plan will give you all three of these results – but finding out your ultimate goal will help you better plan your diet to achieve those goals. For example, if you're already happy with your weight and only want to have a healthier lifestyle, then you don't have to adhere so strictly to the carbohydrate requirement.

This is why I always encourage going to your primary physician first to find out what your dietary limits are. This was the first mistake I made when I decided to follow a weight loss regiment. Keep in mind – we're trying to improve the quality of your life and not make it worse.

Is there such a thing as too much fat?

Everything in moderation. If you consume too much of one thing, it doesn't matter even if its water – it will be too bad for you. So yes, you can eat too much fat – even if it's healthy fat as already discussed. Remember how we talked about the importance of calories? Well, you have to understand that of all the nutrients found today, fat is perhaps the most compact type. This means that each gram of fat has more calories than any other nutrients you can find today.

What does this mean? This means that if you eat too much fat, there's a good chance that you'll go beyond your calorie requirements. If your goal is weight loss or maintaining a healthy weight, then this is a bad route to take because you won't be experiencing a calorie deficit. Simply put – you'd actually gain weight instead of losing it. I want you to understand this because I don't want you eating more than you should in the mistaken belief that its "healthy" for you.

How much weight can you lose?

The amount of weight you can lose on the Ketogenic Diet depends primarily on how well you stick to the plan. The healthy rate is 2 pounds per week and I strongly recommend that you don't speed it up too much. As mentioned, I lost 30 pounds on the diet – but this took years of hard work and personal research on my part!

Should I be counting calories?

Generally, counting calories is the go-to for people who want to lose weight. You will find however that this is not a problem when you're on a Keto Diet. That doesn't mean you should forget calories altogether – it only means that it's not that big of an issue in the grand scheme of things.

So the question is – how many calories should you be eating if you're on a Ketogenic Diet? Well, this depends from one person to the next. You will find that there are calculators that can help you get the proper amount of calories you want to maintain while on Keto. A good online calculator is known as the Mifflin St. Jeor calculator which allows for a calorie suggestion based on your height, weight, and age.

Of course, if you want to be challenged, here's the typical formula.

For males: 10 multiplied by weight in kilograms + 6.25 x height in centimeters less 5 multiplied by age + 5

For females: 10 multiplied by weight in kilograms + 6.25 x height in centimeters less 5 multiplied by age – 161

Once you get the results, you'll have to multiply it using the following situations:
- Sedentary: x 1.2, if you have minimal physical activities such as having a desk job
- Lightly active: x 1.375 light jogging at least once a week
- Moderately active: x 1.55 moderate activity, at least 6 times a week
- Very active: x 1.725 hard exercise daily or hard exercise twice a week

So it's a little tough – but the online calculator should make the whole thing easier. Generally however, you'd want to maintain a calorie count of 1500 calories per day for weight loss. For health maintenance without the need to lose weight, you can hit 1800 to 2000 calories – depending on the level of activity you experience every day.

Here's the most important question however: do you have to be strict about it? The short answer is: YES. Just because you're on the Ketogenic Diet doesn't mean you can eat all the meat you want. This is not a free pass – you still have to be mindful of what you eat.

The good news is that if you follow the Ketogenic Diet strictly, you'll find that the period of satiation is longer. Simply put, you won't feel hungry so quickly on the diet. There will be no mid-afternoon cravings for a snack as you feel full all through the hours between lunch and dinner. Even if you *do* feel hungry, there are a bunch of Keto-friendly snacks you can reach for.

Chapter 5: Primary Keto Guidelines – the Do's and Don'ts of Keto Over 50

The Ketogenic Diet isn't as complicated as you would think. The general guidelines are simple and straightforward. Even for someone already in their 50s, the Keto Principle works just as well. Sure, there might be a need to make a few tweaks here and there to guarantee compatibility – but for the most part, everything one needs is easy to access.

What do we mean by that? Well, think about it – a person in their 50s is likely to have several maintenance medicines to help with their health. I know I've been taking several medications to help with problems like blood pressure, blood sugar, and so on. Once I made the decision to start a Ketogenic Diet, all of these medicines have to be taken into consideration. Like, is it OK to limit my food if I'm taking XXX medicine?

Of course, that's actually just one of the things I had to keep in mind. Here are other things you definitely have to consider when starting this brand new dietary lifestyle.

Do Consult Your Doctor Beforehand

I can't stress this enough – especially for people who fall into a certain age group. Your general practitioner will know your medical history better, your current health status, and whether going on a Ketogenic Diet would be a good idea. It's important to remember that any diet has an impact on things like your mental health and psychological health. The change from a regular carb-full diet to a carb-free one can create pressure on yourself, not just physically and mentally. Simply put, this means that if you're under any sort of stress – the dietary change can do more harm than good. Your general doctor would be able to consider all these factors and give good guidance. At the very least, they can make slight changes to the Ketogenic Diet Principles to meet your health needs.

Do Eat Less Than 50 Grams of Carbohydrates

The whole point of going on a Ketogenic Diet is to force the body to enter that state of Ketosis. To do that, one has to eat less than 50 grams of carbohydrates in a day. To put that in perspective, you should know that a single slice of white bread contains 49 grams of carbohydrates! Hence, people who are used to eating sandwiches for their meals are already eating way beyond the required limit. To let you better understand the low-carbohydrate principle, you should also note that the typical American eats around 225 to 325 grams of carbohydrates every day. For a healthy person with a normal weight, eating carbohydrates of around 225 to 325 is not a problem. For people trying to lose weight however, this amount should definitely be reduced.

Do Increase Your Fat Intake

When we say fat, we're talking about the healthy kind of fat. We already talked about this in a previous Chapter so I won't explain it so exhaustively this time. Try to stay away from products that are labeled as "fat free" because this is often packed with starchy ingredients.

Do Eat the Good Kind of Meat

Here's the good news for those following the Ketogenic Diet – meat is your friend. However, meat is you friendly only if it's the basic kind. What does this mean? Well, anything processed is not a good idea. You'd want to buy something that's as close to the real thing as possible. Sausages, hotdogs, and other meat products that went through a curing or preservation process are discouraged. If you can buy one directly from the farm, then that would be perfect.

Do Avoid Excessive Exercise

Especially during the first few weeks of keto, try not to exercise or do anything strenuous. I want you to focus on the diet to help yourself better stay faithful to the meal plan. This is because if you push yourself to exercise AND follow the Ketogenic Diet, there's a good chance that you'll fail in both. Pour all your willpower into keeping with the meal plans, even if you only do very little exercise during the week. You will find that even with this approach, you can still lose a significant amount of weight.

The End Goal: Achieving Ketosis

The end goal for the Ketogenic Diet is the same for everyone: achieving that state of Ketosis. That's the time when your body is getting energy from the stored fat instead of the readily-available sugar you eat on a daily basis – but you know about that already.

The real question here is – how do you know you're *there?* Because weight loss in the Ketogenic Diet may be quick, but it's not *that* quick! You will be able to observe other changes even before the weight loss begins.

Chapter 6: Keto Side Effects and How to Solve Them

It would be very irresponsible of me if I only tell you all the good things about the Ketogenic Diet and ignore the side effects. The truth is that there are negative effects that could happen once you start the Ketogenic Diet – but that's actually true for all of them! All types of diet have negative effects to start with because your body has gotten used to the bad habits. Once you make the shift to a more positive way of eating, the body sort of goes on a rebellious phase so it feels like everything is going wrong. For example, a person who used to eat lots of sugar in a day can have severe headaches once they start to avoid the sugar. This is a withdrawal symptom and tells you that your diet is actually making positive changes to the body – albeit it takes a little bit of pain on your part.

So what can one expect when they make that change towards a healthy Ketogenic Diet? Here are some of the things to expect and of course – how to troubleshoot these problems.

Long Term Side Effects

A study titled *"Metabolic Effects of the Very Low Carbohydrate Diets: Misunderstood Villains of Human Metabolism"* shows that for short-term purposes, the Ketogenic Diet is very effective. It lets you burn all those excess fat quickly but in a healthy way. If you do this for a long period of time however, there will be side effects. For example, there can be muscle loss, dizziness, kidney problems, acidosis, and problems with focus. Does that mean you shouldn't go on a Ketogenic Diet at all? Of course not! This only means that you'll have to be careful when using this diet. Don't push it too hard and you will be able to get all the positive results with none of the downsides!

Do you know why a low carbohydrate diet is bad if done for a long time? Well, balance is important in anything you do and the Ketogenic Diet doesn't really support balance. If you get rid of an entire food group for a long period of time, your body will rebel against you. Remember – the Ketogenic Diet relies on stored fat in your body. If there are no more stored fat, it really won't work anymore so you will have to increase your carbohydrates. To solve this problem, I recommend going on a 30-day Ketogenic Diet first and assessing your health before moving forward. Asking your doctor what to do "next" after the 30-day plan or after hitting your weight goal is also a good idea. Personally, I decided to increase my carbohydrate intake slightly after hitting my goal weight.

Keto Flu

The Keto Flu is the most prominent problem you'll encounter when starting the diet. It's a perfectly normal reaction by the body that may seem alarming because, well, the symptoms don't really feel good. You have to understand, your body has been running on a specific type of gasoline for years. It's been taking fuel from sugar and with the Ketogenic

Diet, it's like you're changing your fuel source to a cleaner and more sustainable type. It makes sense that the engine growls a little in protest – but after that, you'll be able to run beautifully without the guilt.

The Keto Flu has the following symptoms:
- Headaches
- Fatigue
- Irritability
- Brain fog or difficulty focusing
- Motivational problems
- Sugar cravings
- Dizziness
- Nausea
- Muscle cramps
- Frequent urination

These symptoms are all heavily dependent on the kind of person doing the Keto Diet. Since you're already in our 50s, the symptoms may be more prominent, especially if you rely heavily on carbohydrates in your diet. If you eat mostly low-carb food however, these effects may not be as obvious.

But how do you solve them? Here are some of the best way to get rid of the Keto Flu as quickly as possible!

First, increase your water and salt consumption. This happens a lot once you start a Ketogenic Diet. You may not notice it, but a lot of the salt you consume is through carbohydrates like bread, pasta, rice, and so on. Salt tends to make you thirsty so if you eat little salt, you're also less likely to look for water during the day. So what happens now? Every time you feel dizzy or tired or nauseous while on a Keto Diet, just dissolve salt in water and gulp it down. Now, this is not going to taste good - but I promise that it will help you feel better. You can always try consuming the salt and water separately – whatever you find most convenient. Beef stock, bone broth, or chicken stock are also great alternatives and tastier too! I provided recipes for those in a later Chapter. As for water, try to hit a target of 3 liters of water every day. The good news is that this doesn't have to be plain water – your smoothies, coffee, and tea drinks are also counted.

Add more fat in your diet. Because of all the wrong information circulating today, a lot of people are afraid of fat. We've discussed this before but it bears repeating – fat is not your enemy. During the Ketogenic Diet, it makes sense to eat lots of fats especially if your carbohydrate intake dips to an all-time low. If you lower the carbohydrate consumption without an equal fat increase, then you will always feel hungry and tired.

Don't be impatient – go slower. Remember what we said about the body changing fuels when you're switching to the Ketogenic Diet? Well, the changing process doesn't have to be overnight. Choose to convert one meal at a time to a Keto-friendly set instead of changing all of them on your first day. Of course, it's recommended that you only do this if the salt water method doesn't for you. Just remember – the Keto Flu *will* pass so the first few days of discomfort should not discourage you in the slightest. If you want to minimize the trouble, try starting your Ketogenic Diet on a low-stress period – like a holiday. So basically, instead of eating less than 50 grams of carbohydrates a day, you can have a target of 50 to 70.

Do NOT count calories or restrict your food consumption. When it comes to the Ketogenic Diet – you don't have to calorie count. Again, you don't want to just stuff yourself with food just because you don't have to count calories, but the truth is calories do not matter so much when your body is at a state of Ketosis. It doesn't matter so much how many you're getting – your body will *always* break down the fat deposits and there will be weight loss. Stressing about the calorie intake or depriving yourself of food because of the calories can actually worsen the symptoms of Keto Flu and will make it more difficult for you to stick to the diet. The bottom line is this: as long as you're eating the allowed food items in allowed portions, then you're OK.

Limit your physical activity. That's the good news with the Ketogenic Diet – you don't have to exercise. Sure, you may not be running marathons or going to the gym on a weekly basis, but if you're health-conscious, then chances are you do light walks on a routine basis. That's perfectly OK – as long as you don't over-exert yourself. Now, there will be days when you will actually feel too good. Like you can go out and exercise because you have all this extra energy. When this happens, resist the temptation to do too much too soon. Your body is already burning as much fat as it can – don't push it too hard or you might get sick. If you're restless, try doing yoga, light walking, or just stretching.

Take some supplements. People using the Ketogenic Diet for a long time may also have vitamin and mineral deficiency. It's not easily obvious but it could happen so you'll have to be prepared. The usual vitamins and minerals lacking in a Ketogenic Diet include calcium, zinc, selenium, and vitamin D – so try taking a multivitamin during your diet. Again, I can't stress this enough: always consult your doctor before taking any sort of medication. This is especially true if you have pre-existing health problems and are also taking medication for maintenance.

Constipation or Diarrhea

These problems are fairly common because, well, you're changing your diet! Your body will react one way or another and in both cases, the solution is practically the same – water and fiber. Make sure you get enough fluids in your system and take fiber supplements which is available through many stores. You can also try taking laxatives that are made especially without carbohydrates.

If alarming symptoms occurs while you're on the Ketogenic Diet, I want you to consult your doctor ASAP! Again, reactions may vary from one person to the next and I don't want you shrugging off certain symptoms as if they're just "part" of the diet. Stay motivated but also be mindful of what is happening to your body. Remember – we want you to be healthy!

Chapter 7: Additional Things That Can Help

The Ketogenic Diet isn't as hard as it used to be thanks to the sudden popularity of the diet. For example, this book alone gives you dozens of ingredients to keep you satisfied even if you eat less carbohydrates. Aside from the basic Keto guidelines, here are additional sources of help to keep you going:

Keto Calculators

Not sure about the carbohydrate content of what you're eating? The good news is that there are Ketogenic Calculators today that should help you with the whole process! Thanks to the internet, you can go on your phone and search for the carb content of whatever you happen to be eating. The recipes provided in this book will also give you nutritional information and of course, there are some apps today that will give you Keto-friendly recipes complete with their nutritional content. Modern technology is a wonderful thing and can help you achieve ketosis!

Meal Plan Applications

The mobile phone is your friend. If you're having a tough time following a set meal plan or routine using the Ketogenic Diet, you will find several online apps that can help. They're often free and will give you basic insight on how to proceed. While they're not ideal for the long haul, it can help you gain enough leverage to pursue this brand new lifestyle.

Ketone Test Strips

There are also these things called ketone test strips which are basically like pregnancy test kits or diabetes strips. They can be used to find out if you're already in that state of "ketosis" which means that your body is using the stored fat as fuel. Now, there are two types of ketone tests in the market today. The first one uses blood and the other uses urine.

Which one is more accurate? The blood of course! It works just like a diabetes indicator where you lance your finger, put some blood on the strip and insert it in a ketone meter. The meter will tell you if you're in a state of ketosis. This is the perfect measuring tool if you want to stick to ketosis for a long period of time.

Now, if you're perfectly new to the Ketogenic Diet, then the urine strips would be the better and more convenient option. It's not as accurate, but at least it doesn't require you to lance yourself. The only drawback of using urine strips is that they only work for the first few weeks of the Ketogenic Diet. Why is that? Because during the first few weeks of the Ketogenic Diet, your body still isn't used to using the ketones. Hence, there's a high chance that your body will be disposing the ketones through urine. A high concentration of ketones in your urine tells you the diet is working. If you stick to the diet all through the

3rd and 4th week, the body becomes more used to using ketones. Hence, the ketone count during the 3rd and 4th week will be lower, so you'll actually have a faulty reading.

So to sum it up: urine ketone test strips are best used during your first and second weeks. After that, you can switch to blood strips or maybe just trust on the effectiveness of the diet and wait for the results!

List It Down

I want to encourage you to have some form of recording system. What does this mean? Simply put – I want you to have some kind of notebook or video or picture blog that can help you keep track of where you've been and where you're going. If you prefer the old-fashioned way of doing things, then you should thrive well with a notebook and a pen. Tracking your weight and writing down what you feel during a particular day will give you some insight on how the diet is doing for you. Plus, it can be an excellent source of motivation if you find yourself losing the drive to continue.

Chapter 8: Keto Grocery List

I've had people complain about the difficulty of switching their grocery list to one that's Ketogenic-friendly. The fact is that food is expensive – and most of the food you have in your fridge are probably packed full with carbohydrates. This is why if you're committing to a Ketogenic Diet, you need to do a clean sweep. That's right – everything that's packed with carbohydrates should be identified and set aside to make sure you're not eating more than you should. You can donate them to a charity before going out and buying your new Keto-friendly shopping list.

But what should be included in that list? The list really depends on what you want to eat. Fortunately, I have a wide range of Keto-friendly recipes in a later Chapter. Generally though, these are the food products you want to include in your cart:

Seafood

Seafood means fish like sardines, mackerel, and wild salmon. It's also a good idea to add some shrimp, tuna, mussels, and crab into your diet. This is going to be a tad expensive but definitely worth it in the long run. What's the common denominator in all these food items? The secret is omega-3 fatty acids which is credited for lots of health benefits. You want to add food rich in omega-3 fatty acids in your diet.

Low-carb Vegetables

Not all vegetables are good for you when it comes to the Ketogenic Diet. The vegetable choices should be limited to those with low carbohydrate counts. Pack up your cart with items like spinach, eggplant, arugula, broccoli, and cauliflower. You can also put in bell peppers, cabbage, celery, kale, Brussels sprouts, mushrooms, zucchini, and fennel.

So what's in them? Well, aside from the fact that they're low-carb, these vegetable also contain loads of fiber which makes digestion easier. Of course, there's also the presence of vitamins, minerals, antioxidants, and various other nutrients that you need for day to day life. Which ones should you avoid? Steer clear of the starch-packed vegetables like carrots, turnips, and beets. As a rule, you go for the vegetables that are green and leafy.

Fruits Low in Sugar

During an episode of sugar-craving, it's usually a good idea to pick low-sugar fruit items. Believe it or not, there are lots of those in the market! Just make sure to stock up on any of these: avocado, blackberries, raspberries, strawberries, blueberries, lime, lemon, and coconut. Also note that tomatoes are fruits too so feel free to make side dishes or dips with loads of tomatoes! Keep in mind that these fruits should be eaten fresh and not out of a can. If you do eat them fresh off the can however, take a good look at the nutritional information at the back of the packaging. Avocadoes are particularly popular for those practicing the Ketogenic Diet because they contains LOTS of the good kind of fat.

Meat and Eggs

While some diets will tell you to skip the meat, the Ketogenic Diet actually encourages its consumption. Meat is packed with protein that will feed your muscles and give you a consistent source of energy through the day. It's a slow but sure burn when you eat protein as opposed to carbohydrates which are burned faster and therefore stored faster if you don't use them immediately.

But what kind of meat should you be eating? There's chicken, beef, pork, venison, turkey, and lamb. Keep in mind that quality plays a huge role here – you should be eating grass-fed organic beef or organic poultry if you want to make the most out of this food variety. The organic option lets you limit the possibility of ingesting toxins in your body due to the production process of these products. Plus, the preservation process also means there are added salt or sugar in the meat, which can throw off the whole diet.

Nuts and Seeds

Nuts and seeds you should definitely add in your cart include: chia seeds, brazil nuts, macadamia nuts, flaxseed, walnuts, hemp seeds, pecans, sesame seeds, almonds, hazelnut, and pumpkin seeds. They also contain lots of protein and very little sugar so they're great if you have the munchies. They're the ideal snack because they're quick, easy, and will keep you full. They're high in calories though, which is why lots of people steer clear of them. As I mentioned earlier though – the Ketogenic Diet has nothing to do with calories and everything to do with the nutrient you're eating. So don't pay too much attention on the calorie count and just remember that they're a good source of fats and protein.

Dairy Products

OK – some people in their 50s already have a hard time processing dairy products, but for those who don't – you can happily add many of these to your diet. Make sure to consume sufficient amounts of cheese, plain Greek yogurt, cream butter, and cottage cheese. These dairy products are packed with calcium, protein, and the healthy kind of fat.

Oils

Nope, we're not talking about essentials oils but rather, MCT oil, coconut oil, avocado oil, nut oils, and even extra-virgin olive oil. You can start using those for your frying needs to create healthier food options. The beauty of these oils is that they add flavor to the food, making sure you don't get bored quickly with the recipes. Try picking up different types of Keto-friendly oils to add some variety to your cooking.

Coffee and Tea

The good news is that you don't have to skip coffee if you're going on a Ketogenic Diet. The bad news is that you can't go to Starbucks anymore and order their blended coffee choices. Instead, beverages would be limited to unsweetened tea or unsweetened coffee in order to keep the sugar consumption low. Opt for organic coffee and tea products to make the most out of these powerful antioxidants.

Dark Chocolate

Yes – chocolate is still on the menu, but it is limited to just dark chocolate. Technically, this means eating chocolate that is 70 percent cacao, which would make the taste a bit bitter.

Sugar Substitutes

Later in the recipes part of this book, you might be surprised at some of the ingredients required in the list. This is because while sweeteners are an important part of food preparation, you can't just use any kind of sugar in your recipe. Remember: the typical sugar is pure carbohydrate. Even if you're not eating carbohydrates, if you're dumping lots of sugar in your food – you're not really following the Ketogenic Diet principles.

So what do you do? You find sugar substitutes. The good news is that there are LOTS of those in the market. You can get rid of the old sugar and use any of these as a good substitute.

Stevia. This is perhaps the most familiar one in this list. It's a natural sweetener derived from plants and contains very few calories. Unlike your typical sugar, stevia may actually help lower the sugar levels instead of causing it to spike. Note though that it's sweeter than actual sugar so when cooking with stevia, you'll need to lower the amount used. Typically, the ratio is 200 grams of sugar per 1 teaspoon of powdered stevia.

Sucralose. It contains zero calories and zero carbohydrates. It's actually an artificial sweetener and does not metabolize – hence the complete lack of carbohydrates. Splenda is actually a sweetener derived from sucralose. Note though that you don't want to use this as a baking substitute for sugar. Its best use is for coffee, yogurt, and oatmeal sweetening. Note though that like stevia, it's also very sweet – in fact, it's actually 600 times sweeter than the typical sugar. Use sparingly.

Erythritol. It's a naturally occurring compound that interacts with the tongue's sweet taste receptors. Hence, it mimics the taste of sugar without actually being sugar. It does contain calories, but only about 5% of the calories you'll find in the typical sugar. Note though that it doesn't dissolve very well so anything prepared with this sweetener will have a gritty feeling. This can be problematic if you're using the product for baking. As for sweetness, the typical ratio is 1 1/3 cup for 1 cup of sugar.

Xylitol. Like erythritol, xylitol is a type of sugar alcohol that's commonly used in sugar-free gum. While it still contains calories, the calories are just 3 per gram. It's a sweetener that's good for diabetic patients because it doesn't raise the sugar levels or insulin in the body. The great thing about this is that you don't have to do any computations when using it for baking, cooking, or fixing a drink. The ratio of it with sugar is 1 to 1 so you can quickly make the substitution in the recipe.

What About Condiments?

Condiments are still on the table, but they won't be as tasty as you're used to. Your options include mustard, olive oil mayonnaise, oil-based salad dressings, and unsweetened ketchup. Of all these condiments, ketchup is the one with the most sugar, so make a point of looking for one with reduced sugar content. Or maybe avoid ketchup altogether and stick to mustard?

What About Snacks?

The good news is that there are packed snacks for those who don't have the time to make it themselves. Sugarless nut butters, dried seaweeds, nuts, and sugar-free jerky are all available in stores. The nuts and seeds discussed in a previous paragraph all make for excellent snack options.

What About Labels?

Let's not fool ourselves into thinking that we can cook food every single day. The fact is that there will be days when there will be purchases for the sake of convenience. There are also instances when you'll have problems finding the right ingredients for a given recipe. Hence, you'll need to find substitutes for certain ingredients without losing the "Keto friendly" vibe of the product.

So what should be done? Well, you need to learn how to read labels. Food doesn't have to be specially made to be keto-friendly, you just have to make sure that it doesn't contain any of the unfriendly nutrients or that the carbohydrate content is low enough.

Here's a step by step procedure on how to make a decision based on the labels:
1. First, take a good look at the ingredient list. You can usually find this at the bottom portion of the label and properly designated as "Ingredients".
2. The first step is to look at the sugar ingredient. If it's listed as one of the first five ingredients, then that already means there's too much sugar in the product to be keto friendly. Note though that sugar comes with many names. The words: glucose,

fructose, maltose, lactose, dextrose, corn syrup and more, are all indicative of sugar content. You'd want to make sure they're not listed within the first 5 ingredients of the food product you're buying. That's one of the best things about the food industry – they're required to list ingredients in the order of quantity so that the first ones listed have more volume in the product.
3. If the food passes the "sugar" test, you should next look at the carbohydrate content.
4. You'll notice that carbohydrates are often broken down into groups. Hence, labels may indicate that total carbohydrates are 5grams and then right below that, you can see Dietary Fiber at 1gram and Sugar at 1gram. The important thing to note here is that the dietary fiber and the sugar are part of the total carbohydrates.
5. Why is this important? Well, most people count the total carbohydrates when computing their carbohydrate consumption for the day. Hence, if your goal is to eat less than 50grams of carbohydrates during the day, then you'll be computing using the 5gram amount.
6. Some people however make use of the "net carbohydrates" when computing their consumption. Net carbohydrates are what you get when you subtract the other carbohydrate sources from the total carbohydrates. Hence, 5 grams less 1 gram for the fiber and another gram for sugar mean that you'll have 3 grams of net carbohydrates.
7. Again – why is this important? The main distinction occurs for people who have diabetes. It's all about the insulin levels. At the end of the day however, it's all about the 50 grams of carbohydrates limitation in your diet. If you want to stay on the safe side however, then counting the total carbohydrates is usually the best option.
8. Look at the serving size. Most people think that the nutrition information in the packet refers to all the food items in the pack – but that's not the case at all. The nutritional information is per serving so you'd want to make sure that the carbohydrate content you picture in your head is equal to the food you usually eat in one sitting. For example, a packet of nuts contains 5 serving in total, each serving containing around 5 grams of carbohydrates. If you eat 2 servings in one sitting, then you'll have to remember that you're consuming 10 grams instead of just 5.

Once you've figured this out, you can quickly make calculations in your head about carbohydrate content of what you're eating based on the labels. You will find that this can be easily adjusted to your eating habits so that you always know what you're consuming even if you're not following a set recipe.

Chapter 9: Simple Keto Recipes

The beauty of the Ketogenic Diet is that there are numerous recipes available today to help you get started. In this Chapter, I'll walk you through some of the more popular Keto recipes available today and the nutritional information each one has to help guide you through the process.

Keto Breakfast Recipes

Banana Waffles

Cooking Time: 30 minutes

Servings: 4 servings

Ingredient List:

- 4 eggs
- 1 ripe banana
- ¾ cup coconut milk
- ¾ cup almond flour
- 1 pinch of salt
- 1 tbsp. of ground psyllium husk powder
- ½ tsp. vanilla extract
- 1 tsp. baking powder
- 1 tsp. of ground cinnamon
- Butter or coconut oil for frying

Instructions:

1. Mash the banana thoroughly until you get a mashed potato consistency.
2. Add all the other ingredients in and whisk thoroughly to evenly distribute the dry and wet ingredients. You should be able to get a pancake-like consistency
3. Fry the waffles in a pan or use a waffle maker.
4. You can serve it with hazelnut spread and fresh berries. Enjoy!

Nutrition Facts: each waffle contains 4g of carbohydrates, 13g fat, 5g protein, and 155 kcalories

Keto Cinnamon Coffee

Cooking Time: 5 minutes

Servings: 1 serving

Ingredient List:

- 2 tbsp. ground coffee
- 1/3 cup heavy whipping cream
- 1 tsp. ground cinnamon
- 2 cups water

Instructions:

1. Start by mixing the cinnamon with the ground coffee.
2. Pour in hot water and do what you usually do when brewing.
3. Use a mixer or whisk to whip the cream 'til you get stiff peaks
4. Serve in a tall mug and put the whipped cream on the surface. Sprinkle with some cinnamon and enjoy.

Nutrition Facts: 1 gram net carbs, 1 gram fiber, 14 grams fat, 1 gram protein, 136kcalories

Keto Waffles and Blueberries

Cooking Time: 10 to 15 minutes

Servings: 8

Ingredient List:

- 8 eggs
- 5 oz. melted butter
- 1 tsp. vanilla extract
- 2 tsp. baking powder
- 1/3 cup coconut flour
- 3 oz. butter (topping)
- 1 oz. fresh blueberries (topping)

Instructions:

1. Start by mixing the butter and eggs first until you get a smooth batter. Put in the remaining ingredients except those that we'll be using as topping.
2. Heat your waffle iron to medium temperature and start pouring in the batter for cooking
3. In a separate bowl, mix the butter and blueberries using a hand mixer. Use this to top off your freshly cooked waffles

Nutrition Facts: 3g net carbs, 5g fiber, 56g fat, 14g protein, and 575 kcalories

Baked Avocado Eggs

Cooking Time: 30 minutes maximum

Servings: 4 servings

Ingredient List:

- 2 avocados
- 4 eggs
- ½ cup bacon bits, around 55 grams
- 2 tbsp. fresh chives, chopped
- 1 sprig of chopped fresh basil, chopped
- 1 cherry tomato, quartered
- Salt and pepper to taste
- Shredded cheddar cheese

Instructions:

1. Start by preheating the oven to 400 degrees Fahrenheit
2. Slice the avocado and remove the pits. Put them on a baking sheet and crack some eggs onto the center hole of the avocado. If it's too small, just scoop out more of the flesh to make room. Salt and pepper to taste.
3. Top with bacon bits and bake for 15 minutes.
4. Remove and sprinkle with herbs. Enjoy!

Nutrition Facts: Contains around 271 calories, 21g of fat, 7g fat, 5g fiber, 13g protein, and 7g carbohydrates

Mushroom Omelet

Cooking Time: 5 minutes

Servings: 1 serving

Ingredient List:

- 3 eggs, medium
- 1 oz. shredded cheese
- 1 oz. butter used for frying
- ¼ yellow onion, chopped
- 4 large sliced mushrooms
- Your favorite vegetables, optional
- Salt and pepper to taste

Instructions:

1. Crack and whisk the eggs in a bowl. Add some salt and pepper to taste.
2. Melt the butter in a pan using low heat. Put in the mushroom and onion, cooking the two until you get that amazing smell.
3. Pour the egg mix into the pan and allow it to cook on medium heat.
4. Allow the bottom part to cook before sprinkling the cheese on top of the still-raw portion of the egg.
5. Carefully pry the edges of the omelet and fold it in half. Allow it to cook for a few more seconds before removing the pan from the heat and sliding it directly onto your plate.

Nutrition Facts: 5 grams of carbohydrates. 1 gram of fiber, 44 grams of fat, 26 grams of protein, and 520 kcalories

Soft Boiled Keto Eggs

Cooking Time: 15 minutes

Servings: 1 serving

Ingredient List:

- 3 large eggs
- 1 tbsp. of unsalted butter
- ¼ tsp. thyme leaves
- Freshly ground black pepper
- Salt to taste

Instructions:

1. Grab a saucepan and fill it halfway with water, apply high heat until the water boils.
2. When boiling, gently place the eggs in the water. Set a timer for 6 minutes.
3. Take on tablespoon of butter and put it in the microwave for around 20 seconds or until it melts.
4. Remove the eggs from the saucepan, carefully pouring the hot water in the sink. This is great because the hot water can also help remove clogs from your pipes!
5. Carefully take a bowl and fill it with cold water. Put the eggs inside so it can cool off. Once done, peel the egg and place it in your bowl of melted butter.
6. Add salt and pepper to taste and thyme for garnishing. Make sure to eat it while fresh!

Nutrition Facts: 340 kcalories,

French Omelet

Cooking Time: 20 to 25 minutes

Servings: 2 servings

Ingredient List:

- 2 large eggs
- 4 large egg whites
- ¼ cup fat-free milk
- ¼ cup cubed ham, cooked
- ¼ cup cheddar cheese, shredded
- 1/8 tsp. salt
- 1/8 tsp. pepper
- 1 tbsp. onion, chopped
- 1 tbsp. green pepper, chopped

Instructions:

1. Whisk together the eggs and egg whites until blended.
2. Add the salt, pepper, and milk, mixing them together until fully blended.
3. Using medium heat, coat your skillet with cooking spray and pour the egg mixture in when the surface is hot and ready.
4. As it cooks, push it around the edges so the uncooked portion flows around until there are no runny liquid on top.
5. When it's already around ¾ cooked, put all the remaining ingredients on top and continue cooking until done.

Nutrition Facts: Per serving there's around 186 calories, 9 grams of fat, 4 grams carbohydrate, 22 grams protein, 648 mg of sodium and 207 mg of cholesterol.

Apple Chicken Sausage

Cooking Time: 25 to 30 minutes

Servings: 8 patties

Ingredient List:

- 1 large tart apple, diced
- 1 pound ground chicken
- ¼ tsp. pepper
- 1 tsp. salt
- 2 tsp. poultry seasoning

Instructions:

1. Grab a large bowl and combine all the ingredients except the ground chicken
2. Combine the chicken in the mix and blend well. Create a total of 8 patties of similar sizes which should be around 3 inches in diameter each.
3. Cook them up using medium heat. Make sure each side gets around 5 to 6 minutes of cooking time.

Nutrition Facts: each sausage patty contains 92 calories, 5 grams of fat, 9 grams of protein, 4 grams of carbohydrates, 1 gram of fiber, 38 mg of cholesterol, and 328 mg of sodium.

Keto Cereal

Cooking Time: 1 hour and 15 minutes

Servings: 12 servings

Ingredient List:

- 1 cup shredded coconut, unsweetened
- 1 cup flaked coconut, unsweetened
- ½ cup flaxseeds
- ½ cup flaked almonds
- 1/3 cup Pepitas
- 1/3 cup sunflower seeds
- 1/3 cup chia seeds
- 1/3 cup erythritol
- 1/3 cup melted coconut oil
- 1 tbsp. ground cinnamon
- 1 tsp. vanilla extract

Instructions:

- Preheat your over to 150 degrees Celsius or 300 degrees Fahrenheit
- Mix all the ingredients together in one convenient bowl.
- Once they're combined, spread them over a pan on top of a lined cookie sheet
- Bake them for 25 to 35 minutes. You might have to take them out every five minutes and stir up the mix to prevent burning.
- The goal is to create an even golden brown or have them reach that lightly toasted color. Once you've got that, remove them from the oven.
- Allow to cool and break them up and store in an airtight container.

Nutrition Facts: each serving should contain 244 kcalories, 9 grams of carbohydrates, 4 grams of protein, 22 grams of fat, 8 mg of sodium, 195 mg of potassium, 6 grams of fiber, 1 gram of sugar.

Keto Breakfast Burrito

Cooking Time: 10 minutes

Servings: 1 serving

Ingredient List:

- 1 tbsp butter
- 2 eggs medium
- 2 tbsp full fat cream
- choice of herbs or spices
- salt and pepper to taste

Instructions:

1. Grab a bowl and whisk the eggs and cream together. Add your choice of herbs and spices, depending on personal preferences.
2. Melt the butter in a frying pan using low to medium heat.
3. Pour the egg mixture into the pan.
4. Cook and swirl to create a thin layer of egg burrito.
5. Gently lift the egg burrito from the frying pan. Put the fillings you want inside and roll it up. Enjoy!

Nutrition Facts: 331 calories, 30g fat, 1g carbohydrates, and 11g protein.

Keto Lunch Recipes

Low Carb Keto Meatloaf

Cooking Time: 60 minutes

Servings: 6 servings

Ingredient List:

- 2 lbs 85% lean grass fed ground beef
- 2 large eggs
- 4 cloves garlic
- 1/2 tbsp fine salt
- 2 tbsp avocado oil
- 1 tbsp lemon zest
- 1 tsp black pepper
- 1/4 cup nutritional yeast
- 1/4 cup chopped parsley
- 1/4 cup chopped fresh oregano

Instructions:

1. Preheat oven to 400 degrees Fahrenheit
2. Grab a bowl and put in the beef, salt, nutritional yeast, and black pepper
3. In a separate bowl, mix the eggs, herbs, garlic, and oil. Blend them together until you get a really frothy mixture. It's best to use a blender for this so that the other ingredients come out minced and fully mixed.
4. Combine the egg blend and beef.
5. Put the beef mixture in a loaf pan. Smoothen it out.
6. Place on the middle rack and bake for 60 minutes.
7. Remove and allow it to drain. Let cool for the next 10 minutes
8. Served best with fresh lemon.

Nutrition Facts: contains 344 calories, 29g fat, 2g fiber, 33g protein, and 4g carbohydrates.

Grilled Cedar Plan Salmon Burgers

Cooking Time: 30 minutes
Servings: 4 servings
Ingredient List:

- 1 stalk celery, diced
- 1 ½ lbs wild caught salmon fillets
- 1 ½ tbsp mayonnaise
- 1 ½ tbsp mustard
- 2 tbsp fresh dill
- 2 cloves garlic, minced
- 2 tsp salt
- 1 tsp black pepper
- ½ small red onion, diced
- Fresh lemon juice, to taste

Instructions:

1. Soak the cedar planks for 2 hours in water.
2. Preheat the grill to 350 degrees Fahrenheit
3. Remove the skin and bones from the salmon. Cut it up into smaller pieces and put in the food processor.
4. Add mayo, mustard, pepper, salt, and garlic in the processor and pulse several times until you get a smooth paste.
5. Scrap the paste and put it in a mixing bowl. Put the onion and celery and mix thoroughly.
6. Put the planks on the grill and let them preheat.
7. While waiting, form the salmon mixture into patties.
8. Grill the patties on the plan for 30 minutes each side or until you're satisfied that it's cooked all the way through.
9. Serve with squeezed lemon top

Nutrition Facts: contains 360 calories, 16.76g fat, 1.7g net carbohydrates, and 47g protein

Keto Egg Salad

Cooking Time: 30 minutes

Servings: 2 servings

Ingredient List:

- 1 avocado
- 6 eggs
- 1/3 cup mayonnaise
- 1 tsp Dijon mustard
- Splash of lemon juice to prevent avocado from browning
- Salt & pepper to taste

Instructions:

1. Put water in a saucepan and bring to boil. Put the eggs inside it and turn off the heat. The hot water will cook the egg for the next 10 to 15 minutes.
2. Put the egg in cold water. Allow it to cool before peeling the shells.
3. Chop the eggs and sprinkle with salt & pepper to taste. Set it aside.
4. Mash the avocado and season it with salt & pepper as well.
5. Grab a bowl and mix the eggs, mashed avocado, and mayonnaise together. Put in the lemon juice, mustard, and the herbs you want.
6. Chill and serve.

Nutrition Facts: 575 calories, 51g fat, 7g carbohydrates, 5g fiber, and 2g protein.

Keto Chicken Bacon Cheese Wraps

Cooking Time: 7 minutes

Servings: 2 servings

Ingredient List:

- 6 mozzarella cheese slices
- 2 cheddar cheese slices
- 1 tbsp ranch
- 2 tbsp Guacamole
- ½ cup cooked chicken
- ¼ cup Lettuce
- 4 cooked bacon

Instructions:

1. Start by preheating the oven to 375 degrees Fahrenheit. Prepare your baking pan with parchment paper.
2. Spread the 6 slices of cheese on the pan with the edges touching each other.
3. Bake the cheese for 4 to 5 minutes or until the edges turn brown. This will give you cheese tortilla
4. Let it cool down before placing the guacamole on the edges of the cheese wrap. Spread the lettuce on the guacamole.
5. Cover the guacamole with the cooked bacon and chicken. Cover it all with the cheddar slices.
6. Spread the dressing on the other end of the wrap. This will be like the glue of the wrap as you tightly roll it around.

Nutrition Facts: each wrap is worth 2 servings, each serving containing 450 calories, 30.6g fat, 1.9g carbohydrates, 42.5g protein, and 0.8g fiber

Stuffed Peppers

Cooking Time: 30 minutes

Servings: 6 servings

Ingredient List:

- 1½ cups marinara sauce
- 6 bell peppers
- 1 lb 4 oz ground beef
- 1 tsp paprika
- ½ tsp dried oregano
- ½ tsp ground mustard
- 1 sweet onion, minced
- 2 garlic cloves, minced
- ¾ cup cooked rice
- ¼ cup chopped fresh parsley
- ½ cup shredded Jack cheese
- Salt and freshly ground black pepper

Instructions:

1. Start by preheating the oven to 375 degrees Fahrenheit.
2. Prepare the oven-safe skillet by pouring marinara sauce on the base.
3. Cut off the top of the pepper and remove the ribs and seeds, leaving it completely empty.
4. Grab a bowl and mix the onion, rice, paprika, garlic, oregano, mustard, and beef together. Stir thoroughly before adding the parsley, salt, and pepper to taste. Combine thoroughly to properly distribute the flavor.
5. Stuff the meat mixture into each pepper all the way up to the rim.
6. Put the peppers in the skillet, making sure they're standing up on the rack.
7. Garnish with 1 ½ tbsp of cheese on top.
8. Bake for 25 minutes or until the pepper becomes tender.
9. Serve with sauce as soon as its cooked. This doesn't keep for long so try to eat it as soon as it's done.

Nutrition Facts: each serving contains 166 calories, 23g carbohydrates, 6g protein, and 5g fat

Keto Chicken Casserole

Cooking Time: 20 to 30 minutes

Servings: 1 serving

Ingredient List:

- 2 tbsp. heavy whipping cream
- 1/10 cup cream cheese
- 1/10 lemon juice
- ½ tbsp. green pesto
- ¼ oz. butter
- 1/3 lb. skinless, boneless chicken cut into small pieces
- 1/6 leek, chopped
- 1/6 lb. cauliflower, cut
- Salt & pepper to taste
- 2/3 oz cherry tomatoes, halved
- 1 ¼ oz. shredded cheese

Instructions:

1. Start by preheating the oven to 400 degrees Fahrenheit
2. Mix the cream and cream cheese together with the lemon juice and pesto. Use the salt & pepper to taste. Set aside.
3. Using medium heat, melt the butter in a large pan. Put in the seasoned chicken and fry until you get that nice golden brown color.
4. Once done, put the greased chicken in a baking dish and place the creamy mixture on the chicken.
5. Top off the chicken with the tomatoes, leek, and cauliflower. Sprinkle some cheese on top and bake it for 30 minutes.
6. Remove and enjoy!

Nutrition Facts: contains 739 kcalories, 37g protein, 2g fiber, 62g fat, and 7g net carbohydrates

Lasagna Stuffed Portobello's

Cooking Time: 1 hour to 1 hour and 30 minutes

Servings: 4 servings

Ingredient List:

- 4 portobello mushrooms, large
- 12 oz. of ground meat of your choice
- 1 cup sugar free marinara sauce
- 1 cup whole milk shredded mozzarella cheese
- 1 cup whole milk ricotta cheese
- Chopped parsley for garnishing

Instructions:

1. Preheat your oven to 375 degrees Fahrenheit
2. Start cleaning the mushrooms by removing stems as well as scraping brown portions along the ribs.
3. Stuff the meat inside the mushrooms until well packed.
4. Pack in around ¼ cup of ricotta into the mushroom cup and press, leaving just enough room in the center where the sauce will be placed
5. Spoon in the ¼ cup of marinara on the top. Finally, sprinkle some mozzarella cheese on top of the mushroom
6. Bake for 40 minutes. Garnish with parsley after removing from the oven. Enjoy!

Nutrition Facts: each portobello is one serving with a total of 482 calories, 36 grams of fat, around 6.5 grams of carbohydrates, and 28 grams of protein.

Keto Baked Salmon with Lemon Butter

Cooking Time: 25 to 30 minutes

Servings: 6 servings

Ingredient List:

- 1 lemon, thinly sliced
- 1 tbsp. olive oil
- 2 lbs. salmon
- 1 tsp. sea salt
- 7 oz. butter, thinly sliced
- Ground black pepper

Instructions:

1. Preheat the oven to 400 degrees Fahrenheit
2. Grease the baking dish with olive oil and put the salmon on the surface. Make sure to put it skin-side down. Season with salt & pepper to taste.
3. Place the thinly sliced lemons on the salmon and cover it with the butter.
4. Place in the middle rack and back for 30 minutes or until the salmon turns flaky.
5. Grab some more butter and heat it in a sauce pan. Put some lemon juice in the mix and serve beside the tuna. Enjoy!

Nutrition Facts: contains 1g of carbohydrates, 49g fat, 573 kcalories, and 31g protein

Keto Chicken and Cabbage Plate

Cooking Time: 5 to 10 minutes

Servings: 2 servings

Ingredient List:

- 7 oz. fresh green cabbage, shredded
- 1 lb. rotisserie chicken
- ½ red onion
- ½ cup mayonnaise
- 1 tbsp. olive oil
- Salt & pepper

Instructions:

1. Thinly slice the onions and combine it with the shredded cabbage in a plate.
2. Add the rotisserie chicken in the plate and put a tablespoon of mayonnaise on the side
3. Drizzle some olive oil, salt, and pepper to taste. Enjoy!

Nutrition Facts: Contains 1041kcalories, 48g protein, 7g net carbohydrates, 91g fat, and 3g fiber

Keto Chicken Recipe

Cooking Time: 30 minutes

Servings: 4 servings

Ingredient List:

- 8 medium sized uncooked chicken breast tenders
- 24-oz pickle jar
- 2 scoops of 100% whey protein powder, unflavored
- ¼ cup grated parmesan
- 2 tbsp avocado oil
- 1 tsp paprika
- 2 large eggs
- Salt & pepper to taste

Instructions:

1. Put chicken in a plastic bag and pour the pickles inside. Put a lid on it and allow the chicken to marinate in the pickle.
2. In the meantime, mix together the protein powder, salt, pepper, paprika, and grated parmesan.
3. Crack the eggs in a separate bowl and beat thoroughly.
4. Preheat the skillet. Put the avocado oil on the pan.
5. While heating up the oil, dip the chicken tender in the egg. When done, coat it with the bread mixture.
6. Fry the chicken until golden brown and fully cooked.

Nutrition Facts: 342.53 calories, 14.8g fats, 1.68g net carbohydrates and 47.6g protein.

Ginger Mackerel Lunch Bowl

Cooking Time: 30 to 45 minutes

Servings: 2 servings

Ingredient List:

- 1 tbsp grated ginger (marinade)
- 1 tbsp lemon juice (marinade)
- 3 tbsp olive oil (marinade)
- 1 tbsp coconut aminos (marinade)
- Salt & pepper, to taste (marinade)
- 8 oz boneless mackerel fillets (lunch bowl)
- 1 oz almonds (lunch bowl)
- 1 ½ cups broccoli (lunch bowl)
- 1 tbsp butter (lunch bowl)
- ½ small yellow onion (lunch bowl)
- 1/3 cup diced red bell pepper (lunch bowl)
- 2 small sun-dried tomatoes, chopped (lunch bowl)
- 4 tbsp mashed avocado (lunch bowl)

Instructions:

1. Preheat the oven to 400 degrees Fahrenheit.
2. In a bowl, combine the grated ginger, olive oil, lemon juice, coconut aminos, salt & pepper. Rub half of the marinade on the mackerel fillets.
3. Line the baking tray with parchment paper. Place the mackerel fillets with the skin side facing upwards.
4. Roast it for 12 to 15 minutes until it gets crispy
5. On a separate baking sheet, roast the almonds for 5 minutes until they turn brown. Allow them to cool down before chopping it up. Set aside.
6. Steam the broccoli to soften it up before chopping.
7. Preheat the pan using medium heat. Melt the butter and fry the onions and pepper until they become soft.
8. Put the sun dried tomatoes and broccoli and cook.
9. When done, turn the heat off and the roasted almonds and the rest of the dressing.
10. Serve it with avocado.

Nutrition Facts: 649.55 calories, 53 fats, 9g net carbohydrates, and 28g protein

Keto Baking Recipes

Keto Chocolate Chip Cookies

Cooking Time: 50 minutes

Servings: 12 cookies

Ingredient List:

- 1 egg
- 3.5 oz salted butter
- 4.5 oz erythritol
- 3 oz sugar free chocolate chips
- 6 oz almond flour
- 1 tsp vanilla extract
- 1/2 tsp baking powder
- 1/4 tsp salt

Instructions:

- Start by preheating the oven to 355 degrees Fahrenheit
- Microwave the butter for 30 seconds to melt.
- Combine the melted butter with the erythritol and beat thoroughly.
- Add the egg and vanilla. Mix it again for 15 seconds.
- Put in the baking powder, almond flour, salt, and xantham gum. Beat until fully combined.
- Press the dough together and knead. Add the chocolate chips.
- Divide into 12 balls and arrange it on the baking tray. Bake for 10 minutes.
- Let it cool before serving. Enjoy!

Nutrition Facts: contains 168kcalories, 17.3g fat, 2.3g carbohydrates, 4g protein.

Basic Keto Bread

Cooking Time: 55 minutes

Servings: 16 slices

Ingredient List:

- 7 eggs
- 1 tsp baking powder
- 1/2 tsp xantham gum
- 1/2 tsp salt
- 3.5 oz melted butter
- 1 oz coconut oil
- 7 oz almond flour

Instructions:

1. Preheat the oven to 355 degrees Fahrenheit
2. Crack and beat the eggs for 2 minutes or until foamy.
3. Put in the melted butter, xantham gum, salt, and baking powder. Beat it until the mixture becomes thick
4. Put it in a loaf pan prepped with baking paper. Bake for 45 minutes
5. Slice into 16 thin slices. Store this in an airtight container in the fridge. It should last for up to 7 days.

Nutrition Facts: 165kcalories per slice, 15g fat, 4.8g saturated fat, 3g carbohydrates, 6g protein, and 1.5g fiber

Keto Lemon Bars

Cooking Time: 60 minutes

Servings: 8 servings

Ingredient List:

- 3 lemons
- 3 eggs
- 1/2 cup melted butter
- 1 3/4 cups almond flour, divided
- 1 cup powdered erythritol, divided

Instructions:

1. Preheat the oven to 350 degrees Fahrenheit
2. Mix the butter, a pinch of salt, 1 cup almond flour, and ¼ cup erythritol in a bowl.
3. Put the resulting mixture into a prepared baking dish.
4. Cook for 20 minutes. Let it cool for 20 minutes.
5. While cooling, juice all the lemons in a bowl and zest one of them. Add the eggs, ¾ cup almond flour, ¾ cup erythritol, and just a pinch of salt. Combine it thoroughly. This will be your filling.
6. Pour the filling on the crust and bake for 25 more minutes
7. Serve with a sprinkle of erythritol on top. Enjoy!

Nutrition Facts: per bar contains about 272 calories, 26g fat, 46 carbohydrates, 8g protein

Easy Keto Butter Cake Recipe

Cooking Time: 2 hours 40 minutes

Servings: 10 slices

Ingredient List:

- 2 large eggs
- 3 tbsp coconut flour
- 1 tsp baking powder
- 8 tbsp butter
- 1/4 cup powdered erythritol
- 1/2 tsp vanilla extract
- 8 tbsp butter, room temperature (top layer)
- 8 oz cream cheese, room temperature (top layer)
- 1/4 cup powdered erythritol (top layer)
- 1/2 tsp vanilla extract (top layer)
- 50 drops liquid stevia (top layer)
- 2 large eggs, room temperature (top layer)

Instructions:

1. Start by preheating your oven to 350 degrees. While waiting, grease an 8-inch springform pan sprayed with coconut oil.
2. We're starting with the bottom layer first. Combine the butter, eggs, and vanilla extract in a mixing bowl and whisk them all together thoroughly.
3. Put in the erythritol, coconut flour, and baking powder. Blend and set aside.
4. We'll start with the bottom layer next. Put together the cream, cream cheese, and butter. Mix it together in a large mixing bowl.
5. Put in the vanilla, erythritol, eggs, and stevia. Combine until smooth.
6. Put in the bottom layer mixture into the springform pan. This will be the cake's crust.
7. Next, pour the top layer slowly. Make sure to tap the pan a few times to prevent bubbles from forming.
8. Bake for 30 to 35 minutes.
9. When the sides are browning, take it out of the oven and allow it to cool. This should take 15 to 20 minutes.

Nutrition Facts: 1 slice will have 295 calories, 30g total fat, 9g cholesterol, 2g carbohydrates, 1g sugar, 5g protein.

Low Carb Keto Cupcake Recipe

Cooking Time: 35 minutes

Servings: 12 cupcakes

Ingredient List:

- 4 eggs
- 1/3 cup coconut flour
- ½ cup unsweetened cocoa powder
- ¼ cup powdered erythritol
- 1 tsp. baking powder
- ½ tsp baking soda
- ¼ tsp. salt
- 1 tsp. vanilla extract
- 4 tbsp. extra light olive oil
- ½ cup unsweetened almond milk

Instructions:

1. Start by preheating oven the 350 degrees Fahrenheit. Grab the muffin tin and grease is up or put the cupcake liners while waiting.
2. Grab a bowl and combine the cocoa powder, coconut flour, baking powder, baking soda, salt, and erythritol. Whisk all the ingredients thoroughly.
3. Add the eggs, vanilla extract, almond oil, and olive oil. Mix completely until they're well combined. Allow it to sit for 5 minutes. Check to see if the mixture has the desired thickness. If not, you can add water until gets the thickness you want. Make sure to add one tablespoon at a time to help control the amount.
4. Put around 2 tablespoons of the batter into the muffin tin.
5. Bake for 20 minutes or until a toothpick comes out clean after inserting it in the center of the muffin.

Nutrition Facts: contains 66 kcalories, 45g fat, 16g saturated fat, 1mg cholesterol, 88mg potassium, 2g fiber, and 1g protein.

Chocolate Keto Cake

Cooking Time: 15 to 20 minutes

Servings: 8 servings

Ingredient List:

- 3 eggs
- 2 tbsp. Dutch cocoa
- 1 ½ tsp. pure vanilla extract
- 1 ½ cups fine almond flour
- ¼ cup cocoa powder
- 1/3 cup water or milk
- 1/3 cup regular sugar
- 2 ¼ tsp. baking powder
- ½ tsp. salt

Instructions:

1. Preheat the oven to 350 degrees Fahrenheit. While waiting, grease an 8-inch pan.
2. Combine the ingredients and stir well before putting it in the pan. Smooth the top surface and jiggle the pan a little to get rid of any possible air pockets inside.
3. Put the pan on the center rack and bake for 14 minutes. Make sure it's completely cooked before you put frosting.

Nutrition Facts: Contains 130 calories, 2.7g of net carbohydrates, 9g of fat, 175mg of sodium, and 3.3g of dietary fiber.

Keto Avocado Brownies

Cooking Time: 45 to 60 minutes

Servings: 16 servings

Ingredient List:

- 4 large eggs
- 2 ripe avocado
- ½ cup melted butter
- 6 tbsp. unsweetened peanut butter
- 2 tsp. baking soda
- 2 tsp. pure vanilla extract
- ½ tsp. kosher salt
- 2/3 cup granulated sugar, preferably keto-friendly
- 2/3 cup cocoa powder, unsweetened

Instructions:

1. Start by preheating the oven to 350 degrees.
2. Grab a square pan and line it with parchment paper.
3. Take a blender and just dump all the ingredients inside it. Blend until smooth. If you have a food processor, you can use that too.
4. Transfer the batter onto the pan, smoothing out the surface with a spatula
5. Bake the brownies for 25 to 30 minutes or until the brownies are soft and firm. Allow to cool before serving

Nutrition Facts: 260 calories per serving, with 7 grams of protein, 11 grams carbohydrates, 5 grams fiber, 1 gram sugar, 23 grams fat, 9 grams saturated fat, and around 570mg of sodium.

Keto Fudge

Cooking Time: 15 to 20 minutes

Serving Size: 12

Ingredient List

- 1 cup coconut oil, soft but still sold
- ¼ cup full fat coconut milk
- ¼ cup Swerve confectioners
- ¼ cup organic cocoa powder
- 1 tsp. vanilla extract
- ½ tsp. Celtic sea salt
- ½ tsp. almond extract

Instructions:

1. Combine the coconut oil and coconut milk in a bowl and mix them together for 6 minutes or until you get that glossy well-mixed texture.
2. Put in all the remaining ingredients and stir, going slow first and then slowly increasing it so that the cocoa doesn't wind up all over the kitchen counter.
3. Taste the resulting mixture and just add in ingredients depending on your favored sweetness.
4. Pour them all in small molds or put them in a pan lined with wax paper. Store them in the freezer for just 15 minutes to solidify the whole thing up.
5. Cut them up and put them in a container ready to be served. Remember, you'll have to store them in the fridge or the mix will liquefy.

Nutrition Facts: contains 170 Calories, 19 grams Fat, 1 gram Protein, 1 gram fiber,

Keto Cookies

Cooking Time: 45 minutes to 1 hour

Servings: 15 cookies

Ingredient List:

- 4 egg yolks, large
- 3 tbsp. of butter
- ½ tsp. kosher salt
- 1 cup coconut flakes
- 1 cup sugar free dark chocolate chips
- ¼ cup of coconut oil
- ¾ cup walnuts, chopped
- 3 tbsp. of granulated Swerve sweetener

Instructions:

1. Start by preheating your oven to 350 degrees. Prepare your baking sheet by lining it with parchment paper.
2. Grab a large bowl and put in the coconut oil, sweetener, salt, butter, and egg yolks. Mix them all together until you get a creamy consistency. Add the chocolate chips, coconut, and walnuts and mix it some more.
3. Drop the resulting mix onto the baking sheet, one spoonful glob at a time.
4. Bake them for 15 minutes or until golden. Enjoy!

Nutrition Facts: 130 calories per serving, 2 grams of protein, 1 gram of fiber, 13 grams of fat, 8 grams of saturated fat, 25 mg of sodium, and 2 grams of carbohydrates.

Keto Vanilla Pound Cake

Cooking Time: 1 hour 5 minutes

Servings: 12 servings

Ingredient List:

- 4 large eggs
- Top of Form
- Bottom of Form
- 2 cups almond flour
- 1 cup erythritol
- 1 cup sour cream
- 1/2 cup butter
- 2 tsp baking powder
- 1 tsp vanilla extract
- 2 ounces cream cheese

Instructions:

1. Start by preheating the oven to 350 degrees Fahrenheit
2. Butter a 9 inch pan for the baking
3. Grab a large bowl and put the flour and baking powder inside.
4. Cut the butter into squares and add cream cheese. Microwave it for 30 seconds to melt both. Stir until they're well combined
5. Add the erythritol sweetener, sour cream, and vanilla extract to the mix of butter and cream cheese.
6. Combine the wet ingredients with the dry ingredients.
7. Crack the eggs open and beat thoroughly. Add them to the other ingredients and stir complete.
8. Pour the batter into the pan and bake for 50 minutes. Make sure the cake cools for 2 hours before serving.

Nutrition Facts: Each serving contains 249 calories, 20.67g fat, 5.2g carbohydrates, and 7.67 protein

Keto Dinner Recipes

Keto Sloppy Joes

Cooking Time: 30 to 45 minutes

Servings: 1 serving

Ingredient List:

- 1 ¼ cup almond flour (for the bread)
- 5 tbsp. ground psyllium husk powder (for the bread)
- 1 tsp. sea salt (for the bread)
- 2 tsp. baking powder (for the bread)
- 2 tsp. cider vinegar (for the bread)
- 1 ¼ cups boiling water (for the bread)
- 3 egg whites (for the bread)
- 2 tbsp. olive oil (for the meat sauce)
- 1 ½ lbs. ground beef (for the meat sauce)
- 1 yellow onion (for the meat sauce)
- 4 garlic clover (for the meat sauce)
- 14 oz. crushed tomatoes (for the meat sauce)
- 1 tbsp. chili powder (for the meat sauce)
- 1 tbsp. Dijon powder (for the meat sauce)
- 1 tbsp. red wine vinegar (for the meat sauce)
- 4 tbsp. tomato paste (for the meat sauce)
- 2 tsp. salt (for the meat sauce)
- ¼ tsp ground black pepper (for the meat sauce)
- ½ cup mayonnaise as toppings
- 6 oz. shredded cheese as toppings

Instructions:

- We're going to start by cooking the bread. First, preheat the 350 degrees Fahrenheit and then mix all the dry ingredients in a bowl.
- Add some vinegar, egg whites, and boiling water in the bowl. Whisk thoroughly for 30 seconds or use a hand mixer to speed up the process. You'd want a consistency that's a lot like play-doh
- Form the dough into 5 or 8 pieces of bread. Layer then on the lowest oven rack and cook for 55 to 60 minutes.
- In the meantime, you'll be cooking the meat sauce. Grab a pan and cook the onion and garlic until you get that fragrant smell.

- Add the ground beef and cook the meat thoroughly. Once done, add the other ingredients and cook
- Allow it to simmer for 10 minutes in low heat. Add other seasonings to taste.

Nutrition Facts: per serving, you'd get around 57g of protein, 1070 kcalories, 83g fat, 12g fiber, and 15g net carbohydrates

Low Carb Crack Slaw Egg Roll in a Bowl Recipe

Cooking Time: 15 minutes

Servings:

Ingredient List:

- 1 lb. ground beef
- 4 cups shredded coleslaw mix
- 1 tbsp. avocado oil
- 1 tsp. sea salt
- ¼ tsp. black pepper
- 4 cloves garlic, minced
- 3 tbsp. fresh ginger, grated
- ¼ cup coconut aminos
- 2 tsp. toasted sesame oil
- ¼ cup green onions

Instructions:

1. Start by heating the avocado oil in a large pan using a medium-high heat. Put in the garlic and cook for a little bit until you get that fragrant smell.
2. Add the ground beef and cook until it gets brownish. This should take about 10 minutes to finish. Season with salt and black pepper.
3. Once cooked, you can lower the heat and add the coleslaw mix and the coconut aminos. Stir to cook for 5 minutes or until the coleslaw gets tender.
4. Remove and put in the green onions and the toasted sesame oil.

Nutrition Facts: 457 kcalories for 1.5 cups of the dish. Contains 7g carbohydrates, 33g protein, 2g fiber, 2g sugar, and 33g protein.

Low Carb Beef Stir Fry

Cooking Time: 20 minutes

Servings: 2 servings

Ingredient List:

- ½ cup zucchini, spiral them into noodles about 6-inches each
- ¼ cup organic broccoli florets
- 1 bunch baby bok choy, stem chopped
- 2 tbsp. avocado oil
- 2 tsp. coconut aminos
- 1 small know of ginger, peeled and cut
- 8 oz. skirt steak, thinly sliced into strips

Instructions:

1. Heat the pan and add 1 tablespoon of oil. Sear the steak on it on high heat. This should only take around 2 minutes per side.
2. Reduce the heat to medium and put in the broccoli, ginger, ghee, and coconut aminos. Cook for a minute, stirring as often as possible.
3. Add in the bok choy and cook for another minute
4. Finally, put the zucchini into the mix and cook. Note that zucchini noodles cook quickly so you'd want to pay close attention to this.

Nutrition Facts: contains 582 calories, 55g protein, 2g fiber, 36g fat, and 14g carbohydrates.

One Pan Pesto Chicken and Veggies

Cooking Time: 30 minutes

Servings: 4 servings

Ingredient List:

- 2 tbsp. olive oil
- 1 cup cherry diced tomatoes
- ¼ cup basil pesto
- 1/3 cup sun-dried tomatoes, chopped and drained
- 1 pound chicken thigh, bones and skinless, sliced into strips
- 1 pound asparagus, cut in half with the ends trimmed

Instructions:

1. Start by heating up a large skillet. Put two tablespoons of olive oil and sliced chicken on medium heat. Season with salt and add ½ cup of the sun-dried tomatoes.
2. Cook for a few minutes until the chicken is cooked thoroughly. Spoon out the chicken and tomatoes and put them in a separate container.
3. Don't wash the skillet just yet. You'll be using the oil there later.
4. Next, put the asparagus in the skillet and pour in the pesto. Turn the heat on medium and add the remaining sun-dried tomatoes. Cook the asparagus for 5 to 10 minutes. Put it on a separate plate when done.
5. Put the chicken back in the skillet and pour in pesto. Stir under medium heat for 2 minutes. You only need to reheat the chicken during this so when done, you can serve it together with the asparagus.

Nutrition Facts: 423 kcalories, 32g fat, 112mg cholesterol, 261mg sodium, 12g total carbohydrates, and 856mg potassium

Crispy Peanut Tofu and Cauliflower Rice Stir-Fry

Cooking Time: 1 hour and 30 minutes

Servings: 2 servings

Ingredient List:

- 12 oz. tofu, extra-firm
- 1 tbsp. toasted sesame oil
- 2 cloves minced garlic
- 1 small cauliflower head
- 1 ½ tbsp. toasted sesame oil (sauce)
- ½ tsp. chili garlic sauce (sauce)
- 2 ½ tbsp. peanut butter (sauce)
- ¼ cup low sodium soy sauce (sauce)
- ½ cup light brown sugar (sauce)

Instructions:

1. Start by draining the tofu for 90 minutes before getting the meal ready. You can dry the tofu quickly by rolling it on an absorbent towel and putting something heavy on top. This will create a gentle pressure on the tofu to drain out the water.
2. Preheat the oven to 400 degrees Fahrenheit. While the oven heats up, cube the tofu and prepare your baking sheet.
3. Bake for 25 minutes and allow it to cool.
4. Combine the sauce ingredients and whisk it thoroughly until you get that well-blended texture. You can add more ingredients, depending on your personal preferences with taste.
5. Put the tofu in the sauce and stir it quickly to coat the tofu thoroughly. Leave it there for 15 minutes or more for a thorough marinate.
6. While the tofu marinates, shred the cauliflower into rice- size bits. You can also try buying cauliflower rice from the store to save yourself this step. If you're doing this manually, use a fine grater or a food processor.
7. Grab a skillet and put it on medium heat. Start cooking the veggies on a bit of sesame oil and just a little bit of soy sauce. Set it aside.
8. Grab the tofu and put it on the pan. Stir the tofu frequently until it gets that nice golden brown color. Don't worry if some of the tofu sticks to the pan – it will do that sometimes. Set aside.
9. Steam your cauliflower rice for 5 to 8 minutes. Add some sauce and stir thoroughly.
10. Now it's time to add up the ingredients together. Put the cauliflower rice with the veggies and tofu. Serve and enjoy. You can reheat this if there are leftovers, but try not to leave it in the fridge for long.

Nutrition Facts: each serving will have around 524 calories, 34g of fat, 38.5g of carbohydrates, 7g of fiber, 24.5g of protein and 1400mg of sodium

Simple Keto Fried Chicken

Cooking Time: 30 minutes

Servings: 4 servings

Ingredient List:

- 4 boneless and skinless chicken thighs
- Frying oil
- 2 large eggs
- 2 tbsp. heavy whipping cream
- 2/3 cup grated parmesan cheese (breading)
- 2/3 cup blanched almond flour (breading)
- 1 tsp. salt (breading)
- ½ tsp. black pepper (breading)
- ½ tsp. cayenne (breading)
- ½ tsp. paprika (breading)

Instructions:

1. Grab a bowl and put together the eggs and heavy cream. Beat them together until perfectly mixed.
2. Grab another bowl, this time combining all the breading ingredients and mix well. Set it aside for now.
3. Cut the chicken thigh into 3 even pieces. Make sure they're not wet by patting the moist area with a paper towel. This will help prevent the oil splashes when you start frying them.
4. So now you have the chicken and 2 bowls. One bowl contains the egg wash and the other contains the breading. Dip the chicken in the bread first before dipping it in the egg wash and then finally, dipping it in the breading again. Make sure it's completely covered.
5. Put 2 inches worth of oil in a pot and heat it up until it reaches around 350 degrees Fahrenheit or when it starts to become steamy. When this happens, try to gradually lower the heat so you can maintain that temperature. This is important since a perfectly heated oil will help create really crunchy chicken.
6. Put the coated chicken in your hot oil. Do this gently with a pair of tongs, making sure there are no splashes of any kind. Frying time should take around 5 minutes or until the coating becomes deep brown in color.
7. Prepare some paper towels and put the cooked chicken on it. This will help remove any excess oil.
8. Try not to overcrowd the pan so all of them will cook beautifully. Serve while still crispy for best results.

Nutrition Facts: 380 calories, 2.5g net carbs per serving, 26g of fat, 920mg of sodium, 218mg of cholesterol, 5g total carbohydrates, and 34g of protein.

Keto Butter Chicken

Cooking Time: 30 minutes

Servings: 2 to 4 servings

Ingredient List:

- 1.5 lb. chicken breast
- 1 tbsp. coconut oil
- 2 tbsp. garam masala
- 3 tsp. grated fresh ginger
- 3 tsp. minced garlic
- 4 oz. plain yogurt
- 2 tbsp. butter (for sauce)
- 1 tbsp. ground coriander (for sauce)
- ½ cup heavy cream (for sauce)
- ½ tbsp. garam masala (for sauce)
- 2 tsp. fresh ginger, grated (for sauce)
- 2 tsp. minced garlic (for sauce)
- 2 tsp. cumin (for sauce)
- 1 tsp. chili powder (for sauce)
- 1 onion (for sauce)
- 14.5 oz. crushed tomatoes (for sauce)
- Salt to taste (for sauce)

Instructions:

1. Start by cutting the chicken into pieces measuring around 2 inches each. Place it in a large bowl and add 2 tablespoons of garam masala, 1 teaspoon of minced garlic, and 1 teaspoon of grated ginger. Stir slowly and add the yogurt. Make sure that mix is evenly distributed before putting a lid on the container and chilling it in the fridge for 30 minutes.
2. For the sauce, grab a blender and put in the ginger, garlic, onion, tomatoes, and spices. Blend until smooth.
3. Leave the blended sauce aside and grab a skillet. Using medium heat, remove the chicken from the fridge and cook, allowing it to brown on both sides.
4. Once cooked, pour in the sauce and allow it to simmer for 5 more minutes
5. Finally, put in the cream and ghee, still using medium heat. Add some salt for taste and serve!

Nutrition Facts: contains around 293 calories, 17g of fat, 7g net carbs, and 6g of protein.

Keto Shrimp Scampi Recipe

Cooking Time: 30 minutes

Servings: 2 servings

Ingredient List:

- 2 summer squash
- 1 pound shrimp, deveined
- 2 tbsp. butter unsalted
- 2 tbsp. lemon juice
- 2 tbsp. chopped parsley
- ¼ cup chicken broth
- 1/8 tsp. red chili flakes
- 1 clove minced garlic
- Salt and pepper to taste

Instructions:

- Start by cutting the summer squash into noodle-like shapes. You can use a spiralizer to get this done or perhaps use a fork to scrap the surface.
- Spread the noodles on top of paper towards and sprinkle them with salt. Set aside for 30 minutes.
- Blot the excess water with a paper towel.
- In a frying pan, melt butter over medium heat and fry the garlic until you get that fragrant smell. Add some chicken broth, red chili flakes, and lemon juice.
- Once it boils, add the shrimp and allow it to cook. Reduce the heat once the shrimp turns pink.
- Add more salt and pepper to taste before adding the summer squash noodles and parsley to the mix. Make sure all the ingredients are well-coated by the sauce. Serve.

Nutrition Facts: 332 kcalories, 8.49g carbohydrates, 48.4g protein, 13.1g fat, 352mg of sodium, 2.3g of fiber, and 187mg of calcium.

Keto Lasagna

Cooking Time: 1 hour and 30 minutes

Servings: 8 servings

Ingredient List:

- 8 oz. block of cream cheese
- 3 large eggs
- Kosher salt
- Ground black pepper
- 2 cups of shredded mozzarella
- ½ cup of freshly grated parmesan
- Pinch crushed red pepper flakes
- Chopped parsley for garnish
- ¾ cup marinara (for the sauce)
- 1 tbsp. tomato paste (for the sauce)
- 1 lb. ground beef (for the sauce)
- ½ cup of freshly grated parmesan (for the sauce)
- 1.5 cup of shredded mozzarella (for the sauce)
- 1 tbsp. of extra virgin olive oil (for the sauce)
- 1 tsp. dried oregano (for the sauce)
- 3 cloves minced garlic (for the sauce)
- ½ cup chopped onion (for the sauce)
- 16 oz. ricotta (for the sauce)

Instructions:

1. Start by preheating the oven to 350 degrees and preparing the baking tray by lining it with parchment and cooking spray.
2. Grab a microwave-safe bowl and throw in the cream cheese, mozzarella, and parmesan, melting them together for a few seconds in the microwave. Mix them in thoroughly before adding the eggs and blending the whole thing together. Add a pinch of salt and pepper for seasoning.
3. Spread the mixture on a baking sheet and bake for 15 to 20 minutes.
4. While baking, grab a skillet and using medium heat, coat the surface with oil. Put in the onion and allow them to cook for 5 minutes before adding the garlic. Once you get that fragrant smell, wait 60 more seconds before adding the tomato paste onto the mixture. Make sure to stir all the items around until the onion and garlic are well-coated.
5. Add the ground beef in the skillet and cook the mixture, breaking up the meat until it's no longer pink in appearance. Add salt and pepper to taste. Cook it for a few more minutes before setting it aside and allowing it to cool. There should be a bit of

fluid remaining in the skillet – try to drain that out of the meat before proceeding with the next step.
6. Turn on the stove again, keeping the medium heat constant. Add some marinara sauce and season with pepper, red pepper flakes, and ground pepper. Stir around to evenly distribute the flavor.
7. By this time, your noodles should be ready from the oven. Take them out and start cutting them in half width-wise and then cut them again into 3 pieces.
8. Start layering! Use an 8 inch baking pan for this, placing 2 noodles at the bottom of the dish first and layer as you wish. Alternate the parmesan and mozzarella shreds depending on your personal preferences.
9. Bake until the cheese melts and the sauce bubbles out. Should take about 30 minutes.
10. Garnish and serve.

Nutrition Facts: 308 calories, 21.7 grams of fat, 852 grams of sodium, 0.5 grams of dietary fiber, 2.2 grams of carbohydrates, and 23.3 grams of protein.

Creamy Tuscan Garlic Chicken

Cooking Time: 20 to 25 minutes

Servings: 6 servings

Ingredient List:

- 1.5 pounds boneless and skinless chicken breast, thinly sliced
- ½ cup chicken broth
- ½ cup parmesan cheese
- ½ cup sun dried tomatoes
- 1 cup heavy cream
- 1 cup chopped spinach
- 2 tbsp. olive oil
- 1 tsp. garlic powder
- 1 tsp. Italian seasoning

Instructions:

1. Grab a large skillet and cook the chicken using olive oil using medium heat. Do this for 5 minutes for each side or until they're thoroughly cooked. Set it aside in a plate.
2. Using the same skillet, combine the heavy cream, garlic powder, Italian seasoning, parmesan cheese, and chicken broth. Expose it to medium heat and just whisk away until the mixture thickens.
3. Add the sundried tomatoes and spinach and let it simmer until the spinach wilts.
4. Add the chicken back and serve.

Nutrition Facts: per serving, you have 368 calories from fat which amounts to 25 grams of fat, 133 mg of cholesterol, 379mg of sodium, 7g of carbohydrates, 1g of fiber, 4g sugar, and 30g protein.

Keto Snack Recipes

Parmesan Cheese Strips

Cooking Time: 30 minutes

Servings: 12 servings

Ingredient List:
- 1 cup shredded parmesan cheese
- 1 tsp dried basil

Instructions:
1. Preheat the oven to 350 degrees Fahrenheit. Prepare the baking sheet by lining it with parchment paper.
2. Form small piles of the parmesan cheese on the baking sheet. Flatten it out evenly and then sprinkle dried basil on top of the cheese.
3. Bake for 5 to 7 minutes or until you get a gold brown color with crispy edges. Take it out, serve, and enjoy!

Nutrition Facts: contains 31 calories, 2g fat, and 2g protein

Peanut Butter Power Granola

Cooking Time: 40 minutes

Servings: 12 servings

Ingredient List:

- 1 cup shredded coconut or almond flour
- 1 1/2 cups almonds
- 1 1/2 cups pecans
- 1/3 cup swerve sweetener
- 1/3 cup vanilla whey protein powder
- 1/3 cup peanut butter
- 1/4 cup sunflower seeds
- 1/4 cup butter
- 1/4 cup water

Instructions:

1. Preheat the oven to 300 degrees Fahrenheit and prepare a baking sheet with parchment paper
2. Place the almonds and pecans in a food processor. Put them all in a large bowl and add the sunflower seeds, shredded coconut, vanilla, sweetener, and protein powder.
3. Melt the peanut butter and butter together in the microwave.
4. Mix the melted butter in the nut mixture and stir it thoroughly until the nuts are well-distributed.
5. Put in the water to create a lumpy mixture.
6. Scoop out small amounts of the mixture and place it on the baking sheet.
7. Bake for 30 minutes. Enjoy!

Nutrition Facts: 338kcalories, 30g fat, 5g carbohydrates, 9.6g protein, and 5g fiber

Homemade Graham Crackers

Cooking Time: 1 hour 10 minutes

Servings: 10 servings

Ingredient List:

- 1 egg, large
- 2 cups almond flour
- 1/3 cup swerve brown
- 2 tsp cinnamon
- 1 tsp baking powder
- 2 tbsp melted butter
- 1 tsp vanilla extract
- salt

Instructions:

1. Preheat the oven to 300 degrees Fahrenheit
2. Grab a bowl and whisk the almond flour, cinnamon, sweetener, baking powder, and salt. Stir all the ingredients together.
3. Put in the egg, molasses, melted butter, and vanilla extract. Stir until you get a dough-like consistency.
4. Roll out the dough evenly, making sure that you don't go beyond ¼ of an inch thick. Cut the dough into the shapes you want for cooking. Transfer it on the baking tray
5. Bake for 20 to 30 minutes until it firms up. Let it cool for 30 minutes outside of the oven and then put them back in for another 30 minutes. Make sure that for the second time putting the biscuit, the temperature is not higher than 200 degrees Fahrenheit. This last step will make the biscuit crispy.

Nutrition Facts: 156 kcalories, 13.35g fat, 6.21g carbohydrates, 5.21g protein, and 2.68g fiber.

Keto No Bake Cookies

Cooking Time: 10 minutes

Servings: 18 cook

Ingredient List:

- 2/3 cup of all natural peanut butter
- 1 cup of all natural shredded coconut, unsweetened
- 2 tbsp real butter
- 4 drops of vanilla lakanto

Instructions:

1. Melt the butter in the microwave.
2. Take it out and put in the peanut butter. Stir thoroughly.
3. Add the sweetener and coconut. Mix.
4. Spoon it onto a pan lined with parchment paper
5. Freeze for 10 minutes
6. Cut into preferred slices. Store in an airtight container in the fridge and enjoy whenever.

Nutrition Facts: 80 calories per serving.

Swiss Cheese Crunchy Nachos

Cooking Time: 20 minutes

Servings: 2 servings

Ingredient List:

- ½ cup shredded Swiss cheese
- ½ cup shredded cheddar cheese
- 1/8 cup cooked bacon pieces

Instructions:

- Preheat the oven to 300 degrees Fahrenheit and prepare the baking sheet by lining it with parchment paper.
- Start by spreading the Swiss cheese on the parchment. Sprinkle it with bacon and then top it off again with the cheese.
- Bake until the cheese has melted. This should take around 10 minutes or less.
- Allow the cheese to cool before cutting them into triangle strips.
- Grab another baking sheet and place the triangle cheese strips on top. Broil them for 2 to 3 minutes so they'll get chunky.

Nutrition Facts: 280 calories per serving, 21.8 fat, 18.6g protein, and 2.44g net carbohydrates

Homemade Thin Mints

Cooking Time: 60 minutes

Servings: 20 servings

Ingredient List:

- 1 egg slightly beaten
- 1 3/4 cups almond flour
- 1/3 cup cocoa powder
- 1/3 cup swerve sweetener
- 2 tbsp butter melted
- 1 tsp baking powder
- 1/2 tsp vanilla extract
- 1/4 tsp salt
- 1 tbsp coconut oil (coating)
- 7 oz sugar free dark chocolate (coating)
- 1 tsp peppermint extract (coating)

Instructions:

1. Preheat the oven to 300 degrees Fahrenheit. Prepare the baking sheet by lining it with parchment paper.
2. Grab a large bowl and combine the cacao powder, sweetener, almond flour, salt, and baking powder. Mix thoroughly before adding the already beaten egg, vanilla extract and butter.
3. Knead the dough and roll it on the parchment paper. Make sure it doesn't go beyond a thickness of ¼ inch.
4. Cut the cookie into your desired shapes. Combine and reroll, cut it up and again and repeat until nothing is left.
5. Bake the cookies for 20 to 30 minutes.
6. For the coating, melt the oil and chocolate in a bowl and stir until it's completely smooth. Use a microwave to do this or make sure of a pan placed in boiling water.
7. Once melted, stir in the peppermint extract.
8. Take the cookies and dip them in the coating, depending on your personal preferences. Allow it to dry on the surface and then refrigerate to keep it fresh.

Nutrition Facts: 116kcalories per 2 calories, 10.41g fat, 6.99g carbohydrates, 8g protein, 5mg cholesterol

Mozzarella Cheese Pockets

Cooking Time:
Servings: 8 servings
Ingredient List:

- 1 large egg
- 8 pcs of mozzarella cheese sticks, whole
- 1 ¾ cup mozzarella cheese
- ¾ cup almond flour
- 1 oz. cream cheese
- ½ cup of crushed pork rinds

Instructions:

1. Start by grating the mozzarella cheese.
2. In a bowl, mix together the almond flour, mozzarella, and the cream cheese. Microwave them for 30 seconds until you get that delicious gooey mixture.
3. Put in a large egg and mix the whole thing together. You should get a nice thick batch of dough.
4. Put the dough in between two wax papers and roll it around until you get a semi-rectangular shape
5. Cut them into smaller rectangle pieces and wrap them around the cheese sticks. Mold it depending on the shape you want.
6. Roll the stick onto crushed pork rinds.
7. Bake for 20 to 25 minutes at 400 degrees Fahrenheit. You can also try deep frying them if you have Keto-friendly oil options.
8. You can store them in the fridge if you don't want to cook them just yet. When serving, try using Keto-friendly ketchup or just some marinara sauce.

Nutrition Facts: 272 calories, 22g fat, 2.4g net carbohydrates, and 17g protein. Note that the dipping you use is a different nutrition count.

No Bake Coconut Cookies

Cooking Time: 10 minutes

Servings: 8 servings

Ingredient List:

- 3 cups of unsweetened shredded coconut
- ½ cup sweetener
- 3/8 cup coconut oil
- 3/8 tsp. salt or to taste
- 2 tsp. vanilla
- Optional toppings: coconut shreds or finely-chopped nuts

Instructions:

1. Put all the ingredients in a food processor without the optional toppings. You can also use the blender but try not to turn it too high because you'll end with a liquefied mix which won't produce the cookies in this recipe.
2. Remove and start forming them into the shape you want. Decorate as you want with the toppings.
3. Leave them to firm up for as long as necessary. This shouldn't take more than a few hours.
4. Store in the fridge to lengthen its shelf life.

Nutrition Facts: 329 kcalories, 4.1g carbohydrates, 2.1g protein, 30g fat, 122mg sodium, 2.3g sugar, 25.7g saturated fat, and .39g polyunsaturated fat.

Cheesy Cauliflower Breadsticks

Cooking Time: 45 minutes to 1 hour

Servings: each serving should be around 99 grams

Ingredient List:

- 4 eggs
- 4 cups of cauliflower riced
- 2 cups mozzarella cheese
- 4 cloves minced garlic
- 3 tsp. oregano
- Salt and pepper to taste

Instructions:

1. Start by preheating your oven to 425 degrees Fahrenheit.
2. Prepare the baking sheet by lining it with parchment paper.
3. Put cauliflower in a food processor or blender until finely chopped or when it resembles rice.
4. Put it in a covered bowl and microwave for just 10 minutes. Allow it to cool and if it's a little wet, make sure to drain it first before adding eggs, oregano, garlic, salt, pepper, and mozzarella. Mix them well.
5. Start separating the mixture into individual sticks – or really, just about any form you want.
6. Bake the crust for 25 minutes or until it gets that nice golden color. Take it out of the oven and sprinkle some more mozzarella on top while still hot. Put it back in the oven for just 5 minutes so that the cheese melts.
7. Bonus! You can also use the same recipe as a pizza crust.

Nutrition Facts: each 99 gram stick contains kcalories, 4 grams carbohydrates, 13 grams protein, 11 grams fat, 114 mg cholesterol, 310 mg sodium, 1 gram fiber, 232 mg potassium, and 1 gram sugar.

Easy Peanut Butter Cups

Cooking Time: 1 hour 35 minutes

Servings: 12 servings

Ingredient List:

- 1/2 cup peanut butter
- 1/4 cup butter
- 3 oz. cacao butter, chopped
- 1/3 cup powdered swerve sweetener
- 1/2 tsp vanilla extract
- 4 oz. sugar free dark chocolate

Instructions:

1. Line a muffin tin with parchment paper or cupcake liners.
2. Using low heat, melt the peanut butter, butter, and cacao butter in a saucepan. Stir them until completely combined.
3. Add the vanilla and sweetener until there are no more lumps.
4. Carefully place the mixture in the muffin cups.
5. Refrigerate it until firm
6. Put chocolate in a bowl and set the bowl in boiling water. This is done to avoid direct contact with the heat. Stir the chocolate until completely melted.
7. Take the muffin out of the fridge and drizzle in the chocolate on top. Put it back again in the fridge to firm it up. This should take 15 minutes to finish.
8. Store and serve when needed.

Nutrition Facts: 200kcalories, 19g fat, 6g carbohydrates, 2.9g protein and 3.6g fiber

Keto Dessert Recipes

Keto Cheesecake with Blueberries

Cooking Time: 1 hour 30 minutes

Servings: 12 servings

Ingredient List:

- 1¼ cups almond flour (crust)
- 2 tbsp erythritol (crust)
- ½ tsp of vanilla extract (crust)
- 2 oz. butter (crust)
- 20 oz. cream cheese (filling)
- 2 eggs (filling)
- 1 egg yolk (filling)
- ½ cup of crème fraîche or heavy whipping cream (filling)
- 1 tsp lemon zest (filling)
- ½ tsp of vanilla extract (filling)
- 2 oz. fresh blueberries (optional)

Instructions:

1. Preheat the oven to 350 degrees Fahrenheit. While waiting, prepare a springform pan by lining it with butter or putting in parchment paper.
2. Melt the butter until you smell that nutty scent. This will help create a toffee flavor for the crust.
3. Remove the pan from the heat and add almond flour, vanilla, and the sweetener. Mix the ingredients until you get a dough-like consistency.
4. Press it into the pan and bake for 8 minutes until you get a slightly golden crust. Set aside to cool.
5. Now we're going to work on the filling. Mix all the filling ingredients together and beat it heavily. Pour the mixture on the crust.
6. Increase the oven's heat to 400 degrees Fahrenheit and bake for the next 15 minutes
7. Once done, lower it to 230 degrees Fahrenheit and bake again for 45 to 60 minutes
8. Turn the heat off and leave it inside in the oven to cool.
9. Remove after it has cooled completely. You can store it in the fridge and served with fresh blueberries on top.

Nutrition Facts: each slice contains 4g net carbohydrates, 33g fat, 7g protein, and 335 kcalories

Keto Lemon Ice Cream

Cooking Time: 1 hour 30 minutes

Servings: 6 servings

Ingredient List:

- 3 eggs
- 1 lemon, zest and juice
- ⅓ cup erythritol
- 1¾ cups heavy whipping cream

Instructions:

1. Grate the lemon to get the zest and then squeeze out the juice. Set it aside in the meantime.
2. Separate the eggs. Using a hand mixer beat the eggs until they become stiff. Afterwards, beat the egg yolks and sweetener until it becomes light and fluffy.
3. Add the lemon juice in the egg yolks. Beat it before carefully folding the egg whites into the yolk.
4. In a separate bowl, whip the cream until you get soft peak. Gently fold the egg mix into the cream
5. Pour the whole thing into an ice cream maker and use it according to instructions of the manufacturer.
6. For those who don't have an ice cream maker, you can just put the bowl in the freezer. You'll have to take it out every 30 minutes to stir it. This should be done for the next two hours until you get the consistency you want.

Nutrition Facts: contains 27g fat, 5g protein, 3g net carbohydrates, and 269 kcalories

Peanut Butter Balls

Cooking Time: 20 minutes

Servings: 18 servings

Ingredient List:

- 1 cup of salted peanuts chopped finely (not peanut flour)
- 1 cup of peanut butter
- 1 cup of sweetener
- 8 oz of sugar free chocolate chips

Instructions:

1. Mix the peanut butter, sweetener, and chopped peanuts together. You'll get a dough-light substance by doing this.
2. Knead until smooth and then divide the dough into 18 pieces. Shape them into balls.
3. Place the dough on a baking sheet lined with wax paper before putting them in the fridge to harden.
4. In the meantime, melt the chocolate chips in a microwave.
5. Take out the peanut butter balls and dip them in the melted chocolate. Put them back in the fridge to set. Enjoy!

Nutrition Facts: 194 kcalories, 17g total fat, 7g carbohydrates, 1g sugar, and 7g protein.

Keto Cake Donuts

Cooking Time: 30 minutes

Servings: 8 servings

Ingredient List:

- 6 eggs
- ½ cup coconut flour
- ¼ tsp sea salt
- ¼ tsp baking soda
- 1 tsp vanilla extract
- ¼ tsp almond extract
- ½ cup butter or coconut oil
- ½ cup erythritol
- ½ tsp of vanilla extract (frosting)
- ¼ cup melted butter or coconut oil (frosting)
- ¼ cup cream cheese, softened (frosting)
- ¼ cup powdered erythritol (frosting)
- 3 tbsp melted butter (chocolate drizzle)
- 2 tbsp powdered erythritol (chocolate drizzle)
- 1 tbsp cocoa powder, unsweetened (chocolate drizzle)

Instructions:

1. Start by preheating the oven to 350 degrees Celsius Fahrenheit
2. Grab a large bowl and out in the donut ingredients.
3. Take a greased donut pan and will it with batter around 2/3 of the way
4. Bake for 20 minutes.
5. While waiting, start making the frosting. Do this by putting all the frosting ingredients in a bowl and stir completely with a hand mixer. Add sugar to taste.
6. Dip the now cool donuts in the frosting and set it on the parchment to cool.
7. For the chocolate drizzle, put all the ingredients in a small bowl and stir. Drizzle with the liquid as desired.

Nutrition Facts: contains 294 kcalories, 2g net carbohydrates 4g fiber, 28g fat, and 6g protein

Chocolate Coconut Candies

Cooking Time: 20 minutes

Servings: 20 mini cups

Ingredient List:

- 1/2 cup coconut butter
- 1/2 cup Kelapo coconut oil
- 1/2 cup unsweetened shredded coconut
- 3 tbsp powdered swerve sweetener powdered swerve sweeter
- 1 ½ oz. cocoa butter (topping)
- 1 oz. unsweetened chocolate (topping)
- ½ cup cocoa powder (topping)
- 1/4 cup powdered swerve sweetener (topping)
- 4 tsp vanilla extract (topping)

Instructions:

1. Start by lining the mini muffin with paper liners.
2. Put the coconut oil and coconut butter in a saucepan and melt it using low heat. Stir completely before adding the shredded coconut and sweetener into the mix.
3. Divide the mixture onto the mini muffin cups. Set them aside so they'll become firm.
4. In a separate pan, put cocoa butter and unsweetened chocolate together. Melt them by setting the container in a pan of boiling water. This is done to avoid directly heat on the pan containing the chocolate.
5. Put the powdered sweetener and cocoa powder slowly until it smoothens into a thick consistency.
6. Remove it from the heat and put the vanilla extract. Blend carefully.
7. Spoon the chocolate topping on the firm coconut candies. Wait 15 to 20 minutes for it to set.

Nutrition Facts: 240kcalories, 5g carbohydrates, 4g of fiber, 25g fat, 2g protein, 6mg sodium

Flourless Chocolate Cake

Cooking Time: 1 hour

Servings: 12 servings

Ingredient List:

- 4 large eggs
- 1/3 cup water
- 1/2 sugar substitute
- 12 ounces unsweetened baking chocolate
- 2/3 cup butter or ghee, cut into tablespoon size pieces
- 1/4 teaspoon salt
- Boiling water

Instructions:

1. Start by preparing the springform pan for cooking by lining it with parchment paper.
2. Grab a small pot and apply medium heat. Put in the water, salt, and sweetener until fully dissolved.
3. Using a microwave, melt the baking chocolate.
4. Mix the melted chocolate and the butter using an electric mixer
5. Add it in the hot water mixture and beat thoroughly until well blended.
6. Beat the eggs in a separate container and slowly add into the mixture. Combine it thoroughly
7. Pour the resulting mixture in the pan and wrap the exterior with foil.
8. Now put the pan in a larger cake pan. Put boiling water outside of the pan, keeping the depth at just 1 inch.
9. Bake the cake in the water for 45 minutes at 350 degrees Fahrenheit. Chill it in the fridge overnight before serving.

Nutrition Facts: Contains 295kcalories, 8g carbohydrates, 6g protein, 1g polyunsaturated fat, 16g saturated fat, and 5g fiber.

No Bake Low Carb Lemon Strawberry Cheesecake

Cooking Time: 15 to 20 minutes

Servings: 2 servings

Ingredient List:

- 3 oz. cream cheese, softened
- ¾ cup heavy whipping cream
- 1/3 cup sweetener
- 2 tsps. Lemon extract
- 2 large strawberries, chopped
- Lemon zest

Instructions:

1. Grab a mixing bowl and put in the cream cheese, whipping cream, and sweetener. Beat all three on high until you get that smooth and creamy consistency.
2. Put in the lemon extract and mix again. Grate in the lemon zest if you want that additional lemony flavor, otherwise you won't need it at all.
3. Put the cream cheese mixture into your containers. Sprinkle some of the strawberries in between just to add some layer into the mix. Completely fill your container and then sprinkle some more of the strawberries on top. If you have some more lemon zest, you can sprinkle those on top too.
4. Refrigerate until you're ready to eat.

Nutrition Facts: contains 474 calories, 5.7g carbs, 0.4g fiber, 48.2g fat, and 4.5g protein.

Keto Fudge Recipe

Cooking Time: 1 hour

Servings: 12 servings

Ingredient List:

- 1 cup solid coconut oil
- 1 tsp. vanilla extract
- 1/8 tsp. sea salt
- ¼ cup powdered erythritol, to taste
- ¼ cup cocoa powder

Instructions:

1. Start by lining a rectangular glass container with parchment paper.
2. Keeping it at low speed, use a hand mixer to beat the coconut oil together with the sweetener until fully combined.
3. Add in the cocoa powder, vanilla, and sea salt to taste. Add some of the sweetener according to your personal preferences. Beat further with a hand mixer
4. Transfer the mix to the container. Smoothen out the surface.
5. Refrigerate for 45 to 60 minutes or until fully solid. Sprinkle the top portion with sea salt flakes or any other topping you might want.

Nutrition Facts: 161 kcalories per cube, 18 grams of fat, 0.6 grams fiber.

Low Carbohydrate Brownie

Cooking Time: 3 minutes

Servings: 1 serving

Ingredient List:

- 1 whole egg
- 32 grams or 1 scoop of chocolate protein powder
- 1 tbsp. coconut flour
- 1 tbsp. granulates sweetener (optional)
- 1 tbsp. cocoa powder
- 1 tbsp. chocolate chunks (optional)
- ½ tsp. baking powder
- ¼ cup milk

Instructions:

1. Start by mixing all the dry ingredients first and combining them thoroughly.
2. Add the wet ingredients next until you get a nice and thick batter. The thickness depends on your personal preference so if you think it's too much, you can try adding spoonful's of milk until you're happy with the results.
3. Grease a microwave safe bowl and pour in the resulting mix. Cooking it via the microwave should take around 55 to 60 seconds. Feel free to take it out every now and then until you get the texture you want.
4. Some people use an oven for this. If you do, try cooking at a temperature of 350 degrees Fahrenheit for 12 to 15 minutes.

Nutrition Facts: 100kcalories

Keto Friendly Ice Cream

Cooking Time: 30 to 40 minutes exclusive of the freezing process

Servings: ½ cup

Ingredient List:

- 3 tbsp. butter
- 3 cups heavy cream, separated
- 1/3 cup powdered erythritol
- ¼ cup MCT oil or MCT oil powder
- 1 tsp. vanilla extract
- 1 medium vanilla bean, scraped

Instructions:

- Start by melting the butter over medium heat. Add around 2 cups of heavy cream and erythritol together and allow it to boil before reducing the heat. Let it simmer for the next 30 to 45 minutes. Stir it occasionally to check the consistency of the mixture. There should be an obvious decrease of volume when you heat it up. The cream should thoroughly coat the back of a spoon if you try to take some out.
- Once done, pour the concoction into a large bowl and let it cool. Put in the vanilla extract and vanilla seeds afterwards. Add the MCT oil or oil powder and whisk.
- Pour in the last cup of heavy cream and whisk again until you get the beautiful smooth consistency.
- Now, once you're done with this, you have two options: you can make ice cream with an ice cream maker or you can just use your freezer.
- If you're using an ice cream maker, just churn the mixture according to the instructions of the ice cream maker. Store in the fridge and enjoy!
- If you don't have an ice cream maker, you can still have ice cream! It's important though that you added the MCT oil or oil powder – otherwise you might not get the results you want. To use the freezer, just line the ice cream container with parchment paper and put it all inside. Freeze the whole mix for 5 to 6 hours, making sure to stir the ice cream every 30 minutes during the first 2 hours. After that, you can stir it every 60 minutes.
- Once done, serve!

Nutrition Facts: 347 kcalories, 36g of fat, 2g protein, 3g total carbohydrates, and 2g of sugar.

Keto Vegan Recipes

Before I start talking about Keto Vegan recipes, it's important to first talk about these two different concepts. Of course, we already talked about the Ketogenic Diet, but what about Veganism? The first thing you should remember is that Vegan is different from Vegetarian. A vegetarian is fairly obvious – it's a diet that refuses animal meat. Veganism however refuses everything produced by animals. Hence, a vegetarian will eat eggs and milk because it's not animal meat. A vegan however will not drink milk or eat eggs because they came from animal, even if you didn't have to kill anything to get them.

So now that we've made that explanation, here are some popular Ketogenic Vegan recipes.

Chocolate Sea Salt Smoothie

Cooking Time: 5 minutes

Servings: 2 servings

Ingredient List:

- 1 avocado (frozen or not)
- 2 cups almond milk
- 1 tbsp tahini
- ¼ cup cocoa powder
- 1 scoop perfect Keto chocolate base

Instructions:

1. Combine all the ingredients in a high speed blender and mix until you get a soft smoothie.
2. Add ice and enjoy!

Nutrition Facts: contains 235 calories, 20g fat, 11.25 carbohydrates, 8g fiber, and 5.5g protein

8 Ingredient Zucchini Lasagna

Cooking Time: 1 hour 20 minutes

Servings: 9 servings

Ingredient List:

- 3 cups raw macadamia nuts or soaked blanched almonds (for ricotta)
- 2 tbsp nutritional yeast (for ricotta)
- 2 tsp dried oregano (for ricotta)
- 1 tsp sea salt (for ricotta)
- 1/2 cup water or more as needed (for ricotta)
- 1/4 cup vegan parmesan cheese (for ricotta)
- 1/2 cup fresh basil, chopped (for ricotta)
- 1 medium lemon, juiced (for ricotta)
- Black pepper to taste (for ricotta)
- 1 28-oz jar favorite marinara sauce
- 3 medium zucchini squash thinly sliced with a mandolin

Instructions:

1. Preheat the oven to 375 degrees Fahrenheit
2. Put macadamia nuts to a food processor.
3. Add the remaining ingredients and continue to puree the mixture. You want to create a fine paste.
4. Taste and adjust the seasonings depending on your personal preferences.
5. Pour 1 cup of marinara sauce in a baking dish.
6. Start creating the lasagna layers using thinly sliced zucchini
7. Scoop small amounts of ricotta mixture on the zucchini and spread it into a thin layer. Continue the layering until you've run out of zucchini or space for it.
8. Sprinkle parmesan cheese on the topmost layer.
9. Cover the pan with foil and bake for 45 minutes.
10. Remove the foil and bake for 15 minutes more.
11. Allow it to cool for 15 minutes before serving. Serve immediately.
12. The lasagna will keep for 3 days in the fridge.

Nutrition Facts: Contains 338 calories, 34g fat, 10g carbohydrates, 5g fiber, 4.7g protein.

Vegan Keto Scramble

Cooking Time: 10 to 15 minutes

Servings: 1 serving

Ingredient List:

- 14 oz. firm tofu
- 3 tbsp. avocado oil
- 2 tbsp. yellow onion, diced
- 1.5 tbsp. nutritional yeast
- ½ tsp. turmeric
- ½ tsp. garlic powder
- ½ tsp. salt
- 1 cup baby spinach
- 3 grape tomatoes
- 3 oz. vegan cheddar cheese

Instructions:

1. Start by squeezing the water out of the tofu block using a clean cloth or a paper towel.
2. Grab a skillet and put it on medium heat. Sauté the chopped onion in a small amount of avocado oil until it starts to caramelize
3. Using a potato masher, crumble the tofu on the skillet. Do this thoroughly until the tofu looks a lot like scrambled eggs.
4. Drizzle some more of the avocado oil onto the mix together with the dry seasonings. Stir thoroughly and evenly distribute the flavor.
5. Cook under medium heat, occasionally stirring to avoid burning of the tofu. You'd want most of the liquid to evaporate until you get a nice chunk of scrambled tofu.
6. Fold the baby spinach, cheese, and diced tomato. Cook for a few more minutes until the cheese melted. Serve and enjoy!

Nutrition Facts: 212 calories, 17.5g of fat, 4.74g of net carbohydrates, and 10g of protein

Keto Soup Recipes

Low Carb Vegetarian Ramen

Cooking Time: 30 minutes

Servings: 4 servings

Ingredient List:

- 4 cups filtered water
- 4 pastured eggs
- 1 tbsp sugar-free red curry paste
- 1 tbsp coconut oil
- 2 tsp ground ginger
- 1 tsp ground turmeric
- 1 tsp garlic powder
- 2 cups full-fat canned coconut milk
- 1 cup of purple cabbage, chopped
- 1 cup of large-sized shredded rainbow carrots
- 1 cup Brussels sprouts, halved
- 2 large zucchinis, spiralized
- Salt and pepper to taste

Instructions:

1. Grab a large pot and pour the water inside it, bringing it to a boil.
2. When boiling, add the coconut milk and spices. Reduce the heat to medium-low.
3. Put in the cabbage, brussel sprouts, and carrots. Stir in a while before adding the curry paste and coconut oil.
4. Cook until the vegetables are soft and tender. This should take about 20 minutes
5. While waiting, soft boil the eggs. This should take about 6 minutes. Take it out of the pot and put in cold water.
6. When the vegetables are soft, put in the zucchini and allow it to cook for 4 minutes.
7. Your vegetarian ramen is ready. Serve it with the peeled and halved eggs.
8. Put in some lime juice and cilantro.

Nutrition Facts: 237 calories, 15g fat, 15g total carbohydrates, 4g fiber, 7g sugar and 10g protein.

Low Carb Smoked Salmon Chowder

Cooking Time: 20 minutes

Servings: 6 servings

Ingredient List:

- 1 stalk celery chopped
- 1 clove garlic minced
- 2 tbsp salted butter
- 2 tbsp capers
- 2 tbsp chopped red onion
- 1 tbsp tomato paste
- ½ tsp salt
- ¼ cup chopped onion
- 1½ cups chicken broth
- 1½ cups heavy whipping cream
- 4 oz cream cheese
- 6 oz smoked salmon hot smoked, chopped

Instructions:

1. Grab a large saucepan and melt butter in it using medium heat.
2. Put onion, celery, and sprinkle some salt onto the pan.
3. Sauté until the vegetables are tender.
4. Put in the onion until fragrant.
5. Add the chicken broth and tomato paste.
6. Allow the mix to simmer, constantly stirring until you get a smooth concoction.
7. In the meantime, put the cream cheese in a blender and put some of the broth mixture inside it. Blend until smooth. You can do this slowly if this will make it easier.
8. Put the broth back in the saucepan and add the salmon, capers, and cream.
9. Allow it to simmer again for a few minutes. The soup is ready now. Before serving, try sprinkling some chopped red onion on top.

Nutrition Facts: 373 kcalories, 31.84g carbohydrates, 0.5g fiber, and 12.9g protein.

Keto Bone Broth

Cooking Time: 24 hours

Servings: 12 servings

Ingredient List:

- 3 Pastured Chicken Carcasses
- 10 cups of filtered water
- 2 tbsp. peppercorns
- 3 tsp turmeric
- 1 tsp salt
- 2 tbsp apple cider vinegar
- 1 lemon
- 3 bay leaves

Instructions:

1. Preheat the oven to 400 degrees Fahrenheit.
2. Put the bones on a sheet pan and slightly sprinkle with salt. Roast the chicken for 45 minutes.
3. Transfer the cooked chicken to the slow cooker bowl. Put in the peppercorns, apple cider vinegar, water, and bay leaves
4. Cook on low heat for 23 hours.
5. When done, strain the bowl using a fine mesh sieve.
6. Discard the solid ingredients.
7. Divide the broth in mason jars, about 2 cups each container.
8. Put in 1 tsp of turmeric for each day and 2 slices of lemon.
9. If you're putting it in a large container, just make sure to maintain the ration. Hence, if the large container has 4 cups worth of broth, you should put 2 teaspoons of turmeric and 4 slices of lemon inside.
10. Heat slowly and serve when needed

Nutrition Facts: contains 70 calories, 4g of fat, 1g carbohydrates, and 6g protein

Note: This is a base recipe, which means you can use it for making other soup recipes provided in this Chapter. Feel free to alter it slightly, depending on your personal preferences.

Slow Cooker Vegetable Beef Soup

Cooking Time: 6 hours 30 minutes

Servings: 12 servings

Ingredient List:

- 4 slices bacon sliced into 1/2 inch pieces
- 2 pounds stew meat cut into 1" cubes, patted dry
- 1 small celeriac diced
- 2 tbsp red wine vinegar
- 2 tbsp tomato paste
- 1/2 tsp dried rosemary
- 1/2 tsp dried thyme
- 1/2 tsp ground black pepper
- 1 tsp sea salt
- 1/4 cup green beans cut into 1 inch pieces
- 1/4 cup carrots diced
- 1 28 oz can diced tomatoes
- 2 cloves garlic crushed
- 32 oz beef broth low-sodium
- 1 medium yellow onion chopped

Instructions:

1. Put a large skillet on medium high heat. Cook bacon until crispy and store it in the fridge for later.
2. Remove most of the bacon grease, keeping only a small amount enough to cook the beef cubes in small batches. Season them with salt and pepper.
3. Cook until the beef cubes are browned. You don't have to cook the meat thoroughly, just sear it a little at the side.
4. When brown, place the beef in a slow cooker crock.
5. Once all the beef cubes are in the slow cooker, turn your attention to the skillet. Lower the heat to medium and add vinegar to the skillet.
6. Stir the vinegar around until you get a thicker consistency.
7. Pour ¼ cup of the broth in the skillet.
8. When done, pour the liquid in the slow cooker.
9. Remember, we only transferred ¼ cup of the broth to the skillet. The remaining broth will now be cooked in the pan. This time, you'll beading the celeriac, carrots, diced tomatoes, tomato paste, onion, green beans, rosemary, thyme, and salt to the mixture. Put some pepper as well depending on the taste.
10. Cook for 5 minutes before transferring the whole thin to the slow cooker as well.
11. Stir constantly for 5 minutes.

12.   Cover the slow cooker and set it to run for 7 hours. Taste every 2 hours and adjust as needed. Garnish with the bacon bits when serving.

Nutrition Facts: contains 212 calories per serving, 13g of fat, 6g of carbohydrates, 1g of fiber, 17g of protein, and 5g of net carbohydrates.

Beef Cabbage Soup

Cooking Time: 35 minutes

Servings: 8 people

Ingredient List:

- 1 pound scotch fillet steak, cut into 1-inch pieces
- 1 large onion, chopped
- 1 stalk celery, chopped
- 2 large carrots, diced
- 1 small green cabbage chopped into bite-sized pieces
- 4 cloves garlic minced
- 6 cups beef stock or broth
- 3 tbsp fresh chopped parsley plus more to serve
- 2 tbsp olive oil
- 2 tsp dried thyme
- 2 tsp dried rosemary
- 2 tsp onion or garlic powder
- Salt and freshly-cracked black pepper to taste

Instructions:

1. Put oil in a large pot and apply medium heat.
2. Sear the beef on all sides until brown. They don't have to be cooked as they will be cooked later.
3. Put in the onions and cook them for 3 minutes
4. Put the celery and carrots. Cook them while constantly stirring for 4 minutes
5. Put in the cabbage and continue cooking until the cabbage softens up. Put in the garlic until you get that very fragrant flavor.
6. Add the stock or broth. Follow it up with the dried herbs, parsley, and the onion or garlic powder. Remember that you're using low to medium heat all this time.
7. Mix well and bring it to a simmer. Cover the pot with a lid and leave it like that for 15 minutes.
8. Constantly check to see if the carrots are already cooked as these will take the longest. When they're already soft, season the soup with salt and pepper to taste.
9. Serve hot and enjoy! You can keep this in the fridge for up to 3 days or even 2 months if you freeze them.

Nutrition Facts: contains 177kcalories per serving, 4g carbohydrates, 12g protein, 11g fat, 2g sugar, and 34mg cholesterol

Keto Chicken Soup

Cooking Time: 40 minutes

Servings: 4 servings

Ingredient List:

- 2 tbsp avocado oil
- 2 stalks celery, chopped
- 4 cups chicken broth
- 2 cups riced cauliflower
- 1/2 tsp dried thyme leaves
- 1/2 tsp paprika
- 1/4 cup chopped onions
- 2 cloves garlic, minced
- 1 lb of skinless, boneless chicken thighs, cubed
- salt & pepper, to taste

Instructions:

1. Start by grabbing a large saucepan and heating the oil over medium heat.
2. Put in the onion and celery. Season it with salt and pepper before cooking.
3. Wait until the vegetable becomes soft before adding the garlic, paprika, and thyme. You should be able to get a fragrant smell
4. Put in the broth and stir for a few minutes.
5. Add the riced cauliflower and the chicken. Allow it to boil before reducing it to simmer. This should take about 12 minutes or until the chicken is cooked all the way to the center.
6. Add salt & pepper to taste

Nutrition Facts: contains 196 calories, 10.4g fat, 1.8g fiber, 5.8g carbohydrates, and 26.4g protein

Another Low Carb Keto Chicken Soup

Cooking Time: 30 minutes

Servings: 4 servings

Ingredient List:

- 1 1/4 small yellow onion finely diced
- 2 medium carrots peeled and chopped
- 1 small leek chopped
- 3 medium stalks celery chopped
- 1.5 liters chicken stock
- 1 cup chopped kale
- 1/4 tsp black pepper or to taste
- 1 tbsp butter or extra virgin olive oil
- 1 tbsp thyme leaves chopped
- 300 g cooked chicken
- 2 bay leaves
- 8 g fresh parsley
- 1 garlic clove minced
- Salt to taste
- Squeeze of lemon juice (for serving)
- 1 tbsp olive oil (for serving)
- 1 tsp fresh parsley (for serving)

Instructions:

1. Grab a soup pot and put 1 tablespoon of butter or olive oil. Cook it over medium heat and sauté the onion, celery, leek, carrots, and thyme in the pan. Wait until they start to soften.
2. Put in the stock and bay leaves. Season and raise the heat so that the soup will start to boil.
3. Reduce the heat to a simmer and allow it to cook for 15 minutes or so.
4. Add in the chicken.
5. Optional: remove half of the mixture and pulse it for a few seconds using a stick blender. This is a great way to thicken the soup and promote flavor. Put the soup back afterwards. However, if you don't have a stick blender, you can skip this step entirely.
6. Mix the olive oil with lemon juice and put it in the soup. Place the fresh parsley and season the soup according to your taste.

Nutrition Facts: 286kcalories, 7.6g net carbohydrates, 10.2g carbohydrates, 29g protein, 2.7g fiber, and 395mg sodium

Keto Low Carb Vegetable Soup Recipe

Cooking Time: 35 minutes

Servings: 12 servings

Ingredient List:

- 2 tbsp olive oil
- 1 tbsp Italian seasoning
- 2 cups Green beans trimmed, cut into 1-inch pieces
- 8 cups chicken broth
- 1 large onion, diced
- 2 large Bell peppers diced
- 4 cloves Garlic minced
- 1 medium head Cauliflower cut into 1-inch florets
- 2 14.5-oz cans diced tomatoes
- Salt and pepper to taste

Instructions:

1. Heat olive oil over medium heat using a pot.
2. Put in the bell pepper and onions. Cook for 10 minutes or until the onions become browned.
3. Put in the garlic and cook until fragrant.
4. Place the 8 cups of chicken broth.
5. Add the green beans, cauliflower, broth, diced tomatoes, and Italian seasoning. Add salt and pepper to taste
6. Increase the heat and have the soup boiling before reducing it to a simmer and putting a lid on top. The soup is ready when the green beans are already soft and ready for consumption.
7. Enjoy!

Nutrition Facts: contains 79kcalories, 2g fat, 2g protein, 11g total carbohydrates, 3g fiber, and 5g sugar

Egg Drop Soup

Cooking Time: 20 minutes

Servings: 6 servings

Ingredient List:

- 4 large eggs
- 2 quarts chicken or vegetable stock
- 1 tbsp grated turmeric
- 1 tbsp grated ginger
- 6 tbsp extra virgin olive oil
- 2 tbsp coconut aminos
- 2 tbsp freshly chopped cilantro
- 1 tsp salt or to taste
- 2 cloves garlic, minced
- 2 cups sliced brown mushrooms
- 4 cups chopped Swiss chard/spinach
- 1 small chili pepper, sliced
- 2 medium spring onions, sliced
- freshly ground black pepper to taste

Instructions:

1. Put the chicken stock in a large pot. Apply medium heat until it starts to simmer
2. Put the turmeric, ginger, chili pepper, mushroom, coconut aminos, and char stalks into the pot. Allow it to simmer for 5 more minutes.
3. Include the sliced chard leaves and allow it to cook for another minute
4. In a separate bowl, whisk the eggs and then pour them carefully into the soup. Stir constantly until the egg is cooked
5. Add the chopped cilantro and spring onions to the pot.
6. Add salt and pepper to taste.
7. Serve with a drizzle of extra virgin olive oil. You can store this for five days in an airtight container in the fridge.

Nutrition Facts: 255kcalories, 10.8g protein, 2.9g net carbohydrates, and 22.4g fat

Instant Pot Chili Verde

Cooking Time: 40 minutes

Servings: 4 servings

Ingredient List:

- 2 lbs boneless skinless chicken thighs
- 12 oz tomatillos, husked and quartered
- 8 oz poblano peppers stemmed, seeded, and chopped
- 4 oz jalapeño peppers stemmed, seeded, and chopped
- 4 oz onions chopped
- 1/4 cup water
- 1 1/2 tsp salt
- 2 tsp ground cumin
- 5 cloves garlic
- ¼ oz chopped cilantro leaves (for finishing)
- 1 tbsp fresh lime juice (for finishing)

Instructions:

1. Put the poblanos, jalapenos, onions, and tomatillos in a pressure cooker. Add the water and sprinkle the cumin, salt, and garlic on top.
2. Put the chicken inside and seal the lid.
3. Turn the pressure on high for 15 minutes.
4. Release the pressure and uncover the lid. Put the chicken on a cutting board and cut it into small pieces. Set it aside.
5. Add cilantro and lime juice to the pressure cooker.
6. Choose the sauté mode on the pressure cooker.
7. Put the chicken back to the mixture and boil for the next 10 minutes to cause the chicken sauce to thicken. Stir it occasionally.
8. Serve and garnish with more cilantro if you want.

Nutrition Facts: 310 calories, 15g total fat, 10g total carbohydrates, 37g protein

Keto Salad Recipes

Keto Cobb Salad

Cooking Time: 5 minutes

Servings: 1 serving

Ingredient List:

- 4 cherry tomatoes, diced
- 1 avocado, sliced
- 1 hardboiled egg, sliced
- 2 oz. chicken breast, shredded
- 1 oz. feta cheese, crumbled
- ¼ cup cooked bacon, crumbled
- 2 cups mixed green salad

Instructions:

1. Mix the green salad in a large bowl. Add the chicken breast, feta cheese, and the crumbled bacon.
2. Put the tomatoes, avocado, egg, chicken, bacon, and feta cheese on top of the greens.
3. Enjoy! You can also try adding some ranch dressing but be aware that this adds to the total fat and calorie content of your salad.

Nutrition Facts: contains 412 calories, 23.6g of fat, 264.3mg of cholesterol, 6g of fiber, and 38.4g of protein.

5 Ingredient Keto Salad

Cooking Time: 10 to 15 minutes

Servings: 2 servings

Ingredient List:

- 2 boneless chicken breasts with skin
- 1 large avocado, sliced
- 3 slices of bacon
- 4 cups mixed leafy greens of choice
- 2 tbsp. dairy-free ranch dressing
- Salt and pepper to taste
- Duck fat for greasing

Instructions:

1. Start by preheating the oven to 200 degrees Celsius or 400 degrees Fahrenheit.
2. Season the chicken with salt and pepper. Grab a skillet and grease it with duck fat before cooking the chicken on the hot pan.
3. Keep the heat on high until you get a golden brown skin surface. This should take around 5 minutes per side.
4. Once done, you can cook the chicken in the oven for 10 to 15 minutes. You can also put the bacon in with the chicken to save on the cooking time. You can also fry it in a pan, depending your personal preferences.
5. After cooking, let the chicken rest for a few minutes.
6. Slice the avocado and the cooked chicken.
7. Start assembling your salad, adding together the leafy greens, crispy bacon, sliced chicken, and avocado.
8. Use 2 tablespoons of ranch dressing. Mix together until all ingredients are thoroughly coated. Enjoy!

Nutrition Facts: 3.1g carbs, 38.7g protein, 43.8g fat, and 581 kcalories

Vegetarian Keto Cobb

Cooking Time:

Servings: 3 servings

Ingredient List:

- 3 large hard boiled eggs, sliced
- 4 ounces cheddar cheese, cubed
- 2 tbsp. sour cream
- 2 tbsp. mayonnaise
- ½ tsp. garlic powder
- ½ tsp. onion powder
- 1 tsp. dried parsley
- 1 tbsp. milk
- 1 tbsp. Dijon mustard
- 3 cups romaine lettuce, torn
- 1 cup cucumber, diced
- ½ cup cherry tomatoes, halved

Instructions:

1. The dressing is a combination of the source cream, mayonnaise, and dried herbs. Mix them well together until full combined.
2. Add one tablespoon of milk into the mix until you get the thickness you want.
3. Layer in the salad, adding all the ingredients that's not part of the dressing recipe. Put the mustard on the center of the salad.
4. Drizzle with your dressing and enjoy! Each serving should have just 2 tablespoons of dressing to meet the nutritional information given below.

Nutrition Facts: 330 calories, 26.32g fat, 16.82g protein, and 4.83g net carbohydrates

Keto Chicken Salad w/ Avocado

Cooking Time: 20 minutes

Servings: 2 servings

Ingredient List:

- 2 pcs. of boneless chicken thigh fillets
- 2 tbsp. olive oil
- ¼ cup water
- 1 tsp. salt
- 1 tsp. sweet chili powder
- 1 tsp. dried thyme
- ½ tsp. ground black pepper
- 4 cloves garlic
- Handful of cherry tomatoes (salad)
- 2 cups arugula (salad)
- 1 cup purslane leaves (salad)
- ½ cup fresh dill (salad)
- 1 tbsp. olives (salad)
- 1 tsp. sesame seeds (salad)
- 1 tsp. nigella seeds (salad)
- ½ tbsp. olive oil (salad)
- 2 tbsp. avocado dressing (salad)
- 1 avocado, sliced (salad)
- Basil leaves (salad)

Instructions:

1. Pour ¼ cup of water on a skillet and cook the chicken fillets over medium heat, keeping the lid covered until the water drains completely.
2. Drizzle 2 tbsp. of olive oil on the chicken. Add some garlic cloves and then season it with salt and pepper. Add some thyme and sweet chili powder. Cook them again until golden, making sure you flip the chicken every now and again to even out the sides.
3. Put all the salad ingredients in a bowl. Put in some nigella seeds and sesame seeds with some olive oil and avocado dressing. Mix and enjoy!

Nutrition Facts: contains 1093 calories, 17g of sugar, 81g of fat, 68g protein, and 34g of carbohydrates.

Keto Chicken Salad

Cooking Time: 20 to 25 minutes

Servings: 4 servings

Ingredient List:

- 2 cups cooked chicken, shredded
- 2 boiled eggs, chopped
- ¼ cup pecans, chopped
- ¼ cup dill pickles, chopped
- ½ cup mayonnaise
- ¼ cup minced yellow onion
- 1 tsp. yellow mustard
- 1 tsp. white distilled vinegar
- 1 tsp. fresh dill
- Salt and pepper to taste

Instructions:

1. Except for the chicken, add everything together in a mixing bowl and stir together until thoroughly combined.
2. Add the chicken and stir well, making sure that all of the chicken are well coated.
3. Add salt and pepper to taste.
4. Chill in the fridge for one hour before serving. You can keep it stored in the fridge for 3 to 5 days.

Nutrition Facts: Each serving contains 394 calories, 33g saturated fat, 6g trans fat, 25g cholesterol, 3g carbohydrates, 1g sugar, and 21g protein.

Tuna Fish Salad – Quick and Easy!

Cooking Time: 10 minutes maximum

Servings: 1 serving

Ingredient List:

- 10 kalamata olives, pitted
- 1 small zucchini sliced lengthwise
- ½ diced avocado
- 2 cups of mixed greens
- 1 large diced tomato
- 1 sliced green onion
- 1 can chunk light tuna in water, drained
- ¼ cup fresh parsley, chopped
- ½ cup fresh mint, chopped
- 1 tbsp. extra virgin olive oil
- 1 tbsp. balsamic vinegar
- ¼ tsp. fine sea salt
- ¾ tsp. black pepper, cracked

Instructions:

1. Grill the zucchini slices on both sides for a few minutes or as desired. Once cooked, cut it into bite-size pieces.
2. Grab a large bowl and just put all the ingredients together in the container, mixing them together until the liquid ingredients are evenly distributed.
3. Serve while still fresh. This salad would taste best if eaten immediately so try not to have any leftovers.

Nutrition Facts: contains 563 calories, 30.9g total fat, 37.5g carbohydrates, 15.7g dietary fiber, and 41.8g protein.

Chapter 10: 30-Day Ketogenic Diet Meal Plan

Okay, so you we're given recipes above to help start your journey towards a Keto-friendly diet. I understand however that many of those recipes are a bit more complicated than most – especially if you're a complete beginner. Chances are you're having a hard time with the groceries and the unknown food items that are suddenly included in your grocery list.

While you're strongly encouraged to do some shopping and try out many of the recipes I gave above, I understand how this healthier lifestyle is a bit new to you. This is why in this Chapter, I'm introducing a 30-day diet plan that would be perfect if you're brand new to the lifestyle. The goal of this 30-day diet is to help you blend easily into the Ketogenic Diet without breaking the bank. Many of these recipes will have 8 or less ingredients and should take less than 30 minutes to make.

Preparations: What to Do

Week 1 is the start of the Ketogenic Diet, but that doesn't mean that you start preparing on that same week. Ideally, the preparation process begins a day before the first day of the diet. Why? Well, before the first day, I want you to have everything you need easily within reach.

Step 1: Take a good look at your fridge and figure out what food products do not go with your new Keto-friendly lifestyle. I want you to get rid of those items without throwing them in trash. Maybe donate them to the nearest charity store?

Step 2: Figure out what you want to eat for breakfast, lunch, and dinner on your first week of the Ketogenic Diet. For this, I want you to refer to the chapter on recipes for the simplest and easiest ones to make. If you don't cook often or prefer to make your own dishes, then here's a rough guideline of what you should and should not eat.

Eat: meat including fish, eggs, beef, lamb and poultry; high-fat dairy like cheese, butter, and cream; low-carb vegetables like spinach, broccoli, and kale; avocado and berries; coconut oil, high-fat salad dressing, and substitute sweeteners. This has been explained thoroughly in a previous Chapter and should give you a good jump off point.

In contrast, avoid eating the following: all types of grains, fruits, potato, yams, and sugar like honey and maple syrup.

Step 4: Write down your meals for the entire week. Grab a notebook or any other note-taking tool you have and start planning what you will eat for the next 7 days. While you're perfectly free to choose any day of the week for this, I strongly encourage that you choose a non-busy day. Perhaps the weekend to help you better works in the meals to your plan. Starting on a relaxing day will make it easier for you when changing something important in your lifestyle.

Step 5: Go to the grocery store and start buying what you need based on the meals you've decided to prepare. I want you to understand that you don't have to be overly complicated on this. Even egg fried on butter complies with the Ketogenic Diet so if you're not big on cooking – there's nothing wrong with that!

Step 6: You will basically be repeating all the steps given here on a weekly basis. While you're perfectly welcome to formulate a 30-day meal plan for yourself, it's usually a better idea to take it one week at a time. This will help you get used to the idea and make each week feel easier than the last. Plus, you can make adjustments your routine depending on how the last week turned out.

Week 1: What to Expect

During the first week of your 30-day diet, expect to experience many of the signs of Ketogenic Flu as discussed in a previous Chapter. So you're likely going to feel tired some days and energetic on other days. You'll have headaches, feel thirsty, have days of lightheadedness days, and days when you feel like you can conquer the world.

If you've enjoy a carbohydrate rich diet before jumping into the Ketogenic Diet, then chances are you'll also have some cravings throughout the first few days of the diet. What do you do? You power through it of course! The first 7 days are the toughest so these are actually the days when you want to establish a solid meal plan. Precision is important from your breakfast, lunch, dinner, and snacks.

Why is that? This is because I want you to remove the possibility of bargaining. Your first 7 days in the diet will be tough and you're probably going to tell yourself "I don't have to quit carbohydrates completely – I can just eat 2 Keto-friendly meals and 1 carbohydrate-rich one and still be on the Ketogenic Diet.

I don't want you going through this kind of self-bargaining process because you'll only be fooling yourself. Having a set meal plan during the first 7 days will remove the possibility of you talking yourself out of the situation.

So what happens now? Here, our goal is to keep things simple and leftover friendly. This is important since your first week of dieting shouldn't be so difficult. One of the top reasons why people quit their diet is because it's too hard to follow so we'll try to make sure this isn't an ordeal for you.

So let's do this:

Breakfast Suggestion: Bacon and Eggs

Cooking Time: 5 to 10 minutes

Servings: 4 servings

Ingredient List

- 8 eggs, medium sized
- 5 oz. sliced bacon
- Fresh parsley optional
- Cherry tomatoes optional

Instructions:

- Fry the bacon on medium heat using keto-approved oil and put it aside when crispy.
- Using the same pan, fry the eggs in the remaining bacon grease and oil.
- When the eggs are just about cooked, cut up the tomatoes and put them in with the eggs.
- Remove the eggs from the pan and put parsley on top as wished. Used salt and pepper to taste.

Nutrition Facts:

- 1 gram carbohydrates
- 22 grams fat
- 15 grams protein
- 0 grams fiber
- 272 kcal

Note: We're starting breakfast quick and easy with ingredients that you probably already have. Note though, this makes 4 servings so if you're only eating for yourself, try reducing the ingredients significantly.

Breakfast Suggestion: Low Carb Oatmeal

Cooking Time: 20 minutes

Servings: 1 serving

Ingredient List:

- 1 cup of unsweetened almond milk
- 1/2 cup of hemp hearts
- 1 tsp of flax meal
- 1 tsp of chia seeds
- 1 tsp of coconut flakes
- 1 tsp of cinnamon
- 1 scoop of vanilla MCT oil powder

Instructions:

1. Combine all the ingredients in a large sauce pot. Stir thoroughly.
2. Bring it to a simmer until it gets thick enough to your liking.
3. Garnish with berries and enjoy!

Nutrition Facts: contains 44 grams of fat, 584 calories, 16g fiber, 31g protein, and 17g carbohydrates

Lunch Suggestion: Cauliflower Mac and Cheese

Cooking Time: 30 minutes

Servings: 3 servings

Ingredient List:

- 1 tsp salt
- 1/2 tsp black pepper
- 1 1/4 tsp paprika
- 8 oz heavy cream
- 4 oz sharp cheddar, shredded
- 4 oz fontina, shredded
- 2 oz cream cheese
- 1 large head of cauliflower

Instructions:

1. Start by preheating the oven to 375 degrees Fahrenheit. Grab a baking dish and butter the sides while waiting for the desired temperature.
2. Cut the cauliflower into small pieces, about 1 inch each
3. Steam the cauliflower for 5 minutes until it becomes slightly tender. Drain.
4. In a pot, combine the cheese, cream cheese, salt, pepper, heavy cream, and paprika.
5. Add cauliflower to the cheese mixture. Toss it around to coat everything
6. Pour into the baking dish and bake for 30 minutes.

Nutrition Facts: each serving contains 393 calories, 33g fat, 10f carbohydrates, 14g protein and 4g fiber

Lunch Suggestion: Bacon, Egg, and Spinach Salad

Cooking Time: 10 to 15 minutes

Servings: 2 servings

Ingredient List:

- 3.5 ounces of cooked bacon, crumbled
- 4 cups of baby spinach
- ½ tsp. of Dijon mustard
- 1 ½ tbsp. of red wine vinegar
- 3 tbsp. of extra virgin olive oil
- Salt and pepper to taste

Instructions:

1. Start by boiling the eggs in the saucepan. At the same time, you can cook the bacon in the stovetop using olive oil as your main medium.
2. Set aside the eggs and bacon after cooking.
3. Grab a bowl and whisk the red wine vinegar, olive oil, and mustard together.
4. Add the bacon, eggs, and spinach in the bowl. Toss and serve

Nutrition Facts: each serving contains 397 calories, 21 grams of protein, 33 grams of fat, 1 gram of fiber, and 7 grams of carbohydrates

Note: If you have some leftovers for breakfast, then feel free to eat that instead of this recipe! Remember, we're trying to keep things simple for you.

Dinner: Keto Tuna Plate

Cooking Time:
Servings: 2 servings
Ingredient List:

- 4 eggs
- 2 oz. baby spinach
- 10 oz. tuna in olive oil
- 1 avocado
- ½ cup mayonnaise
- Salt and pepper to taste
- ¼ lemon (optional)

Instructions:

1. Start by boiling the eggs for 4 to 8 minutes, depending on whether you like them soft boiled or hard boiled. Set aside to cool without removing the shell just yet.
2. Put together the spinach and tuna in one place. Put some mayonnaise on the side and if you want lemon, put a wedge on the edge of the plate.
3. Remove the eggshell and add it onto the plate.
4. Add some salt and pepper to taste

Nutrition Facts: each serving contains 3g of net carbohydrates, 7g of fiber, 931 kcalories, 76g of fat, and 52g of protein.

Week 2: What to Expect

You'll notice that there are no dessert recipes for Week 1 – and that's because we're trying to keep the sugar count low. Dessert is OK for the 3rd and 4th week, but unfortunately, the first 2 weeks would be dessert-free. Hence, this week's recipes will be just as simple. Fortunately, you can still snack in between meals if you want.

I really hope you stuck to your dietary routine during the first week. You should be proud of yourself if you stuck to the diet despite the occurrence of the Keto Flu symptoms. You're probably wondering: will it still be present during the second week?

The answer really depends on your personal situation. If you have a lot of weight to lose or if you've been on a carbohydrate-rich diet for years, then the Keto Flu can extend as far as the second week. Again: power through it!

Other things you might expect during the second week are constipation. Increase your water and fiber intake during these days. On the upside, you'll experience better sleep and on some days, you'll enjoy a mental clarity unlike any other. Of course, there will be days of frustration and cravings – but I want you to power through it still! Eat keto-friendly snacks like nuts and avocado to help stave off the cravings. The good news is that you won't be hungry as fat keeps you feeling full for longer periods of time. Cravings however are another matter entirely, but you got this far and you can go further still.

Breakfast Suggestion: Keto Coffee

Cooking Time: 2 minutes

Servings: 16 ounces

Ingredient List:

- 2 cups of hot coffee, freshly brewed
- 2 tbsp grass fed butter
- 1 scoop of Perfect Keto MCT powder
- 1 tsp Ceylon cinnamon

Instructions:

1. Combine all ingredients in a blender
2. Use a frother and blend the mix for 30 seconds or until you get that beautiful frothy consistency.
3. Serve and enjoy!

Nutrition Facts: 280 calories, 31g fat, carbohydrates 2.8g, protein 1g, and 2.2g fiber.

Breakfast Suggestion: Keto Pancakes

Cooking Time: 10 to 15 minutes

Servings: 4 servings

Ingredient List:

- 4 eggs
- 7 oz. of cottage cheese
- 2 oz. butter for cooking
- 1 tbsp. ground psyllium husk powder
- 2 oz. fresh raspberries or blueberries or strawberries
- butter as topping

Instructions:

1. Start by combining the cottage cheese, eggs, and psyllium husk and mixing them together. Leave it there for around 5 to 10 minutes to thicken up.
2. Melt the butter in a non-stick skillet using medium heat. Carefully fry the pancake batter, keeping each pancake small so you'd be able to flip them easily.
3. Serve with berries and butter on top. Some people like to use whipped cream as topping and this is also OK as long as you opt for a low-sugar option.

Nutrition Facts: 4 grams of carbohydrates per serving, 3 grams of fiber, 39 grams of fat, 13 grams of protein, and 424 kcalories

Lunch Suggestion: Keto Caesar Salad

Cooking Time: 15 to 20 minutes
Servings: 4 servings
Ingredient List:

- ¾ lb. chicken breasts
- 1 tbsp. olive oil
- 3 oz. bacon
- 7 oz. romaine lettuce, chopped
- 1 oz. parmesan cheese, grated
- Salt and pepper to taste
- ½ cup mayonnaise (for dressing)
- 1 tbsp. Dijon mustard (for dressing)
- ½ lemon zest and juice (for dressing)
- ½ oz. parmesan cheese, grated (for dressing)
- 2 tbsp. anchovies, finely chopped (for dressing)
- 1 garlic clove (for dressing)
- Salt and pepper to taste (for dressing)

Instructions:

1. Preheat the oven to 350 degrees Fahrenheit
2. Mix all the ingredients for the dressing and whisk them into a fine and smooth blend. Set it aside in the fridge.
3. Grab the chicken and season it with salt, pepper, and olive oil. Bake for 20 minutes or until you get the crispiness that you want. Remove and slice according to your personal preferences.
4. Fry the bacon until crispy.
5. Take the chopped lettuce and put it on the plate. Top with chicken and bacon, layering it on the surface for as much as you want.
6. Take the dressing out of the fridge and finish it all off with a small dollop on the side. Grate some parmesan cheese on top and enjoy!

Nutrition Facts: contains 1019 kcalories, 51g protein, 87g fat, and 3g fiber.

Dinner Suggestion: Keto Chicken Burges with Tomato

Cooking Time: 30 minutes

Servings: 4 servings

Ingredient List:

- 1 egg
- 2 oz. butter for frying (for patties)
- 1 ½ lbs. ground chicken (for patties)
- 1 tsp. ground sea salt (for patties)
- ½ yellow onion, grated (for patties)
- ½ tsp. ground black pepper (for patties)
- 1 tsp. dried thyme (for patties)
- 1 ½ lbs. green cabbage
- 3 oz. butter
- 1 tsp. salt
- ½ tsp. ground black pepper
- 4 oz. butter (sauce)
- 1 tbsp. tomato paste (sauce)
- Salt and pepper to taste (sauce)

Instructions:

1. Start by preheating the oven to 220 degrees Fahrenheit
2. Combine all patty ingredients and whisk thoroughly until you achieve a smooth concoction.
3. Shape and fry the patties in butter until cooked. Set them aside. Ideally, you should keep them in the oven so they'll remain warm.
4. Shred the cabbage and fry them on the same skillet where you fried the chicken patties. Season with salt and pepper.
5. Next, you'll be making the tomato butter. Combine all the ingredients for the sauce and whisk them with a handheld mixer.
6. Take the chicken patties back and serve on a plate. The friend cabbage and the tomato butter will be your side dishes and dips. Enjoy!

Nutrition Facts: contains 771 kcalories, 8g of carbohydrates, 5g fiber, 67g fat, and 34g protein.

Week 3: What to Expect

Congratulations for reaching the third week! Around the third week of your diet, you're probably already struggling a little with this whole thing. If you're using Keto Strips, then the reading should wind down by the end of the third week. This means that you'll be positive for Ketosis during the first and 2nd week, but this might not longer be positive on the 3rd week.

For the 3rd week – we're going to do a slight change on your diet. Instead of cooking your breakfast, you'll be drinking your breakfast. Why are we doing this? Well, the third week is the introduction of a very slight fast. Slightly depriving your body of food during the 3rd week can help speed up the fat burning process of the body.

Of course, I want to stress out that the fast is only a good idea if you're actually trying to lose weight. If you're only doing this to keep your health up – then fasting during the 3rd week is NOT advisable. Instead, I want you to take a good look at the recipes already mentioned in the previous Chapter and try those out. Or maybe try out some of the breakfasts you made in the first and second weeks.

Breakfast Suggestion: Strawberry Avocado Keto Smoothie

Cooking Time: 2 minutes

Servings: 1 serving

Ingredient List:

- 1 lb. frozen strawberries
- 1 large avocado
- 1 ½ cup unsweetened almond milk
- ¼ cup erythritol or any other sweetener of your choice

Instructions:

- Puree all the ingredients in a blender. Add with ice and enjoy.

Nutrition Facts: 106 kcalories

Lunch Suggestion: Keto Cheeseburger

Cooking Time: 15 to 20 minutes

Servings: 4 servings

Ingredient List:

- 2 tomatoes (salsa)
- 2 scallions (salsa)
- 1 avocado (salsa)
- Salt (salsa)
- Fresh cilantro to taste (salsa)
- 1 tbsp. olive oil (salsa)
- 1 ½ lbs. ground beef (burger)
- 7 oz. shredded cheese – divided (burger)
- 2 tsp. onion powder (burger)
- 2 tsp. garlic powder (burger)
- 2 tsp. paprika powder (burger)
- 2 tbsp. fresh oregano, chopped (burger)
- 2 oz. butter for frying (burger)
- 5 oz. lettuce
- ¾ cup mayonnaise
- 4 tbsp. Dijon mustard
- 5 oz. crumbled cooked bacon
- 4 tbsp. pickled jalapenos, chopped
- 2 ½ dill pickles, sliced

Instructions:

1. Start by chopping up all the ingredients meant for the salsa. Add them together in a bowl and set aside.
2. Now focus on the meat. Mix all the seasoning and half of the cheese into a bowl. Mix your raw burger meat thoroughly to distribute the flavor evenly.
3. Divide the meat into 4 patties, forming them into even circles for frying.
4. Once cooked, sprinkle the remaining cheese on top of the patty.
5. Serve with the lettuce, bacon, mayonnaise, jalapeños, mustar, and dill pickle. Make sure to choose your bread properly because bread is packed with carbohydrates. You can try following any of the bread recipes provided in this book or you can purchase a keto-friendly bread option. You can also choose not to have any bread with your patty.

Nutrition Facts: per serving you get 8g of net carbohydrates, 104g fat, 53g protein, 6g fiber, and 1194 kcalories

Dinner Suggestion: Chicken Drumsticks

Cooking Time: 30 minutes to 1 hour

Servings: 1 serving

Ingredient List:

- ½ tbsp. light olive oil
- ½ tbsp. lime juice
- ½ tsp. salt
- 1/8 tsp. cayenne pepper
- ¼ tbsp. smoked paprika powder
- ¼ tbsp. garlic powder
- ¾ lb. chicken drumsticks

Instructions:

1. Start by preheating the oven to 400 degrees Fahrenheit
2. Grab a large bowl and whisk together all the ingredients for the chicken. Once done, marinade the chicken thighs overnight until the juice really seeps into the chicken. Make sure the chicken is completely coated by the liquid.
3. Once done with the chicken, put the drumsticks on a wire rack and bake for 30 minutes. Remove and enjoy!

Nutrition Facts: Includes 11g of net carbohydrates, 4g of fiber, 77g fat, 64g protein, and 1016 kcalories

Note: The beauty of this recipe is that you can keep the uncooked chicken in the fridge for long periods of time. Every time you want dinner, you can take them out of the fridge and pop them in the oven for a quick meal.

Week 4: What to Expect

You're now at the fourth week of your 30-day Ketogenic Meal Plan! I'm really proud of how far you've gone and I want you to know that even if you stumbled along the way, you can still push forward with the Ketogenic Diet.

By the fourth week, your health status should be more good than bad. The signs of the Keto Flu should have subsided so that you're only enjoying the positive effects of the diet.

Breakfast: Cauliflower Hash Browns

Cooking Time: 15 minutes

Servings: 4 servings

Ingredient List:

- 1 lb. cauliflower
- 3 eggs
- 1 tsp. salt
- 2 pinches pepper
- ½ yellow onion, grated
- 4 oz. butter for frying

Instructions:

1. Start by grating the cauliflower or putting it in food processors until you get a rice-like texture.
2. Put the grated cauliflower in a bowl and add all the other ingredients except for the butter, of course. Whisk them all together until you get a nice mixture.
3. Fry the cauliflower the butter. Keep the heat on low to make sure the cauliflower cooks thoroughly without any burnt edges. This should take about 3 to 4 inches per side.

Nutrition Facts: contains 282 kcalories, 5g of carbohydrates, 3g of fiber, 26g of fat, and 7g protein.

Lunch: Low Carb Bakes Eggs

Cooking Time: 5 to 10 minutes

Servings: 1 serving

Ingredient List:

- 3 oz. ground beef
- 2 eggs
- 2 oz. shredded cheese

Instructions:

1. Start by preheating the oven to 400 degrees Fahrenheit
2. Place the ground beef in a baking dish. Press it into the baking dish and create two holes with a spoon. It should be large enough that you can crack the eggs into the hole.
3. Once cracked, sprinkle some of the cheese on top.
4. Bake the whole thing in the oven for 15 minutes
5. Let it cool before serving. Enjoy!

Nutrition Facts: 2g net carbohydrates, 35g fat, 41g protein, and 498 k calories

Dinner: Strawberry and Spinach Salad

Cooking Time: 10 minutes

Servings: 4 servings

Ingredient List:

- 4 cups cut spinach
- 2 cups sliced strawberries
- ½ cup goat cheese, crumbled
- ¼ cup almonds
- ½ cup mayonnaise (for dressing)
- 1 tbsp. olive oil (for dressing)
- 1 tbsp. white vinegar (for dressing)
- 1 tbsp. poppy seeds (for dressing)
- 2 tbsp. sweetener, hone or maple (for dressing)
- ¼ tsp. sea salt

Instructions:

1. Just add the entire salad ingredients together in one bowl.
2. In a separate bowl, whisk together the dressing ingredients until properly combined. You can thin it out with some water or more oil if you want. Adjust seasoning to taste.
3. Drizzle on your salad and enjoy

Nutrition Facts: contains about 247k calories, 23g fat, 5g carbohydrates, 2g fiber, and just 2g sugar.

Fast Way of life

As much as it pains me to put this in here, I have to consider the likelihood that not everyone has the luxury of time. You may have a demanding career or schedule that makes it difficult for you to prepare your meals every single time. The good news is that there are recipes you can prepare by bulk. For example, the chicken broth recipes can be made in large quantities and just reheated for a meal.

However, what if even that becomes difficult to do? While I strongly DISCOURAGE resorting to fast food or restaurant meals as this would make it difficult to monitor what you eat, I have to consider that there will be days when you have no choice. If or when this happens, here are food items you can order:

- Bunless Burgers – you can order the burgers and just don't eat the buns to significantly lower the carbohydrate content of the food. The good news is that you can do this with practically any burger product, whether it's being served by McDonalds, Burger King or Wendy's. McDonalds also has a nutrition calculator which should help you better choose what food to order when you're out. Their Artisan Grilled Chicken Sandwich without the bun and ketchup only has 2 grams worth of carbohydrates and Wendy's version of the same sandwich also has the same 2g carb count. The Whopper Jr. with no buns and plainly made has ZERO calories.
- Salads – not all salads are created equal. The rule is that you want to avoid the sweet dressings on your salad – no matter how packed it is with fresh greens. Skip the fruits as well or stick to berries instead of the sugary fruit treats. The Chipotle Salad Bowl with steak, romaine cheese, and sour cream has only 7 grams of carbohydrates, 30 grams of protein and 405 calories. Arby's Roast Turkey Farmhouse Salad with buttermilk rank dressing only contains 10 grams of carbohydrates, 22 grams of protein, 35 grams of fat, and 440 calories.
- Burrito Bowls – yes, you can still enjoy some burrito! The Taco Bell Cantina PowerSteak Bowl w/ extra guacamole without the rice & beans only has 8 grams of carbohydrates, 23 grams of fat, 310 calories, and 20 grams of protein. Chipotle's Steak Burrito with the salsa, sour cream, lettuce, and cheese only has 6 grams of carbohydrates while their Chicken Burrito has 10 grams of carbohydrates.
- Egg Breakfasts – Panera Bread's Power Breakfast Bowl of eggs, avocado, tomato, and steak contain all of 5 grams of carbohydrates, 230 calories, and 20 grams of protein. There's also McDonald's Big Breakfast without the hash browns and biscuit which should add up to just 2 grams of carbohydrates, 29 grams of fat, and 19 grams of protein.

Conclusion

Congratulations for making it this far! By now, I trust you already have a good understanding of the Ketogenic Diet and how it applies to you as you enjoy your 50s. Obviously, our goal here is to provide a Keto Diet guideline that works for *you*, taking into account your unique situation so that the best and most effective results can be enjoyed.

So what did we cover in this book? We talked about the Ketogenic Diet, how it works, and how to tackle the problems you might encounter because of this brand new diet change. We also talked about the different recipes you can try out for the Ketogenic Diet and of course, the 30-day meal plan to get you started on this new healthy lifestyle choice.

We also talked about how the Ketogenic Diet applies to your unique situation. Unfortunately, at the age of 50 and above, not all food is good food. That's why we had to talk about how to adjust the Ketogenic Diet in such a way that it works with your unique situation. This is important because I want you to stay healthy even while losing weight.

But I think the most important thing I want you to learn from this book is this: it's never too late to make that change! It's never too late to try something new for self-improvement! Don't get set in your ways, especially if your old ways don't do much for your overall health. I want you to know that you have what it takes to be better not just physically, but also mentally and psychologically. Of course, the mere fact that you purchased and read this book is a good start. I know you can do it – all you have to do is take that first important step.

So what should you do next now? I want you to go to the kitchen and take a long good look at the refrigerator. I want you to start evaluating its contents and make a distinction between what's good for you, and which aren't based on the Ketogenic Diet we just discussed. I want you to take that very important first step of deciding on a Keto-friendly breakfast, lunch, and dinner for tomorrow. Choose from any of the recipes mentioned above or choose any method you deem best!

Book #3

Intermittent Fasting for Women

Lose Weight, Balance Your Hormones, and Boost Anti-Aging with the Power of Autophagy – 16/8, One Meal a Day, 5:2 Diet, and More!

Introduction

Intermittent fasting has gained popularity in recent years. Hundreds of books and articles have already been written about it. No one can blame these authors since it is a revolutionary way of achieving weight loss. There is no diet. All you have to do is time when you eat and do not eat. Unfortunately, a lot of the information written were created with a male audience or men and women, in general, in mind.

This is where the problem becomes evident. What is written for men rarely applies to women. The body of a man works different to that of a woman and vice versa. Therefore, it is only natural for women to react differently to intermittent fasting. And, as you would find out, this is actually the case.

Moreover, given that there's a difference with how it affects men and women, the methods, tips, and solutions written for men might not actually be effective for women. Women might actually be placing their health at risk by following advice meant for the opposite sex.

It is for this reason that this book was written. This book aims to look at intermittent fasting and see how it can specifically affect women. It looks into the effects and benefits for their health. It would also look into how women can do intermittent fasting in a way that suits them best.

Aside from this, this book would delve deeper into the aspects of intermittent fasting. There a lot of talk about its effects on weight and fat loss. But, it is rarely discussed that intermittent fasting can do so much more than just helping people lose weight. In fact, with its potential benefits for your health, it can be said that everyone should actually do intermittent fasting using one of the methods available.

Why?

Intermittent fasting triggers a reaction in your body that is essential to its survival, longevity, and overall health. From a book wherein its audience would probably expect to talk only about fat loss, this book goes so much deeper that it delves into disease prevention, mental enhancement, and potential degenerative disease treatment. Of course, proper research was done to ensure that what is provided in this book can be applied to your life.

Furthermore, this book will provide you with the tools to implement the strategy that will help you have an easier time achieving your goal. It will also clarify some misunderstandings about it and fix some misconceptions about intermittent fasting, weight loss, and diet. It will also provide information on what you need to get started and why you need them.

After reading this book, you will have a better understanding of intermittent fasting, its mechanics, and its actual method. You will also have an idea on how you can do intermittent fasting in a way that works best for your physiology, health condition, preferences, and lifestyle. You will even be given a guide on how to make intermittent fasting easier or, at the very least, more manageable for you. You will also be equipped on how to go about when changing your goals.

From all of these, you will know everything you need to know to get started with intermittent fasting immediately. The only thing missing is for you to start and take action.

The Basics About Intermittent Fasting

Fasting is nothing new. You probably have heard of various cultures and religions with practices that willingly restrain or reduce their consumption of all or certain types of drink, food, or both, for a given amount of time. You might have also experienced, or know someone who has, fasting as a way to prepare for a surgery or a medical test.

What is not common is willingly fasting on a regular basis for weight loss. Such practices are often compared to alternative medicine practices that have a reputation for having no scientific basis. In some cases, it is even viewed as unhealthy.

However, this is not the case for intermittent fasting. Although it would trigger a fasted state, your body would still get the macro and micronutrients it needs to maintain its health and functions. This results in weight loss that does not come with negative health effects for you.

What Is Intermittent Fasting?

Intermittent fasting is different from the usual diet plan that focuses on the caloric content or macronutrient type of your food choices. It focuses more on when you can eat to create the effects that it can cause to your body. Instead, intermittent fasting would have you follow a dieting pattern involving alternating phases of fasting and eating.

During the fasting phase, you are restricted from eating anything that contains calories. It is only during the eating phase that you can consume food or drink containing calories.

Contrary to popular belief, intermittent fasting alone does not directly cause weight loss. It is still caused by the caloric deficit, which is brought about by the fewer meals that arise from the limited time you have for eating. However, unlike diets that solely rely on caloric deficit, it is more sustainable in the long term, more satisfying, and more flexible.

This focus on when you eat your food instead of what you eat gives intermittent fasting its simplicity. You do not have to count calories for every meal. You do not have to restrict your food choices. And, you do not have to follow a meal plan with stringent macronutrient portions.

The Different Ways You Can Do Intermittent Fasting

16/8 method

This is the most popular approach to intermittent fasting. It involves a fasting phase of 16 hours and an eating phase of 8 hours within a single day. This means, if you start your eating phase at 11 in the morning, you will stop eating and start fasting at 7 in the evening. The said fasting phase would then end at 11AM on the next day.

You are free to set the time for your eating and fasting phase. This makes it easy for you to tailor your own intermittent fasting plan to a schedule that would work best for your lifestyle.

The lean gains method falls under this approach. It has the same 16 hours of fasting and 8 hours of eating. However, it was designed for those with a highly active lifestyle such as athletes, weight trainers, and fitness enthusiasts.

The lean gains method places an importance on caloric intake for better fat loss and, at the same time, muscle gain. It also has recommendations on which macronutrient and how much caloric intake work best for the first meal after fasting, pre-workout meals, or rest day meals.

Eat-stop-eat method

The eat-stop-eat method involves a fasting phase that lasts for 24 hours. This 24-hour fasting phase would be done twice per week.

The key to this method is that there should be a meal at least once every day. This means that you should have had eaten a meal before starting a 24-hour fasting phase that starts, for example, at 9 in the morning.

Like the 16/8 method, you can set the start of your fasting phase whenever you want. But, most people following this method choose to set their fasting period from 6PM until 6PM of the next day. This way they do not sleep hungry, which would often be the case for those just starting intermittent fasting.

5:2 method

The 5:2 method derives its name from the five days of normal eating and the two days of fasting involved for a single week. Unlike the other methods, this method does not involve a complete restriction from food during the fasting phases. Instead, the fasting phases come in the form of restricting food intake to 25 percent of a person's daily calorie intake.

These calorie-restricted days can be scheduled whichever day that you want. However, there should always be at least a single day of normal eating between the fasting days.

There is no restriction on one's food choices during the fasting days. There is also no limit on the number of meals in it as long as the total calories does not exceed the limit. Like the modified approach to alternate day fasting, you can spread out the calories for the day to two to three meals.

The common practice for this method is to schedule the fasted days during the weekdays. In this way, they would not be missing out on social events where food is likely involved.

Alternate day fasting (ADF)

The alternate day fasting, or ADF, involves a full day of fasting every other day. This method could be done by a fast that starts the moment you wake up until the time you wake up the next day, or by starting to fast in the evening and ending it after 24 hours. Unlike the eat stop eat method, you will be fasting every other day.

With this method, you are encouraged to drink as much calorie-free beverage that you can. This would include water, and unsweetened tea and coffee. Some would argue that the tea and coffee should have no dairy as well since these contain sugars that your body converts to calories.

You can modify this method so it does not involve a complete restriction from food during the fasting phase. Instead, you can limit your total caloric limit to 25 to 30 percent of your daily calories spread out to two to three meals within the day. In this way, you can stave off the feeling of hunger but still remain on a fasted state. Unlike the two day low calorie fasts of the 5:2 method, you will eat a low amount of calories on alternating days of the week.

The Warrior Diet

The Warrior Diet is called such due to the belief that it was how ancient Paleolithic humans ate at the time. This diet involves a fasting phase of little to no food during the day and an eating phase of consuming as much food as desired.

The fasting phase starts from the moment of waking up during the day. It would last for 20 hours wherein it is encouraged to consume dairy products, raw fruits and vegetables, eggs, and non-caloric beverages in small amounts.

Once the 20-hour fasting phase ends, you are free to "feast" as much as you desire. This eating phase is said to be patterned after how the Spartan and Roman warriors would feast at night after a hard day's work.

As the name implies, the Warrior Diet goes beyond the simple eating and fasting schedule of the other intermittent fasting methods. It involves an actual diet that aims to improve the body's utilization of fat for its metabolism.

Also, it is encouraged for the one following it to take daily multivitamins, probiotics, and amino acids. It is also said to work best while doing a workout plan for increasing strength and speed to lose as much fat as possible during the diet's duration.

One Meal a Day (OMAD)

The One Meal a Day method utilizes a 23-hour fasting phase and a 1-hour eating phase. This would be just enough for you to have a single meal each day. It is a more advanced method compared to the Warrior Diet. You would also be more likely eating less calories in it since you only have an hour to eat.

How Intermittent Fasting Affects Your Body

Intermittent fasting gained its popularity for its simplicity. You just have to follow a schedule on when you can eat and when you cannot. What's great about this simplicity is that it works.

Furthermore, the effects of intermittent fasting goes beyond weight loss. It also has positive effects to the hormones and cells that play a role in your overall and long-term health.

Here are some of the hormones, organs, and cells that intermittent fasting affects that, in turn, contribute to your overall health.

Decreased insulin levels and resistance

Insulin is a hormone produced by the pancreas. It is released when your blood sugar rises. Once released, it triggers the cells to absorb blood sugar. The cells would then use them for energy or, in the case of fat cells, store them for later use.

Insulin is a crucial hormone in the body's moderation of its blood sugar levels. It prompts the liver if there is too much of it to prevent complications arising from hyperglycemia like cardiovascular disease, and damage on the nerves and kidneys.

Unfortunately, we often experience high blood sugar because of the carbohydrate-rich nature of today's diet. This causes frequent spikes in insulin levels that eventually lead to the body developing insulin resistance. This increased resistance results to the body requiring higher levels of insulin to regulate its' blood sugar levels.

This high insulin resistance would eventually manifest in a variety of symptoms such as fatigue, increased belly fat, elevated fasting blood sugar, high blood pressure, and carbohydrate cravings. For women, it could even cause acquired polycystic ovarian syndrome and hair loss.

This body's abnormal resistance to the hormone can be broken through fasting. This is due to the practice of increasing the production of proteins that improve insulin sensitivity.

This was observed from a group of Muslims fasting during the season of Ramadan. The good news is that you do not need to follow their practice of fasting from dawn to sunset for 30 days. You can replicate the same results through the easier and shorter fasting regimen that intermittent fasting can provide.

Increased human growth hormone production

Human growth hormone plays a role in inducing growth during childhood, and reaches its peak production during one's teenage years. This slowly declines with age, but it still plays a role in the body's tissue repair, energy, metabolism, brain function and muscle growth. It is produced by your pituitary gland, the pea-sized gland found at the lower part of your brain.

The body increases the production of growth hormone during fasted states while asleep or awake. This increase is caused by the decline in the released insulin six hours after eating a meal. Growth hormone levels start to increase after 6 more hours and reach the highest amounts around 18 to 20 hours into the fast. This increase can go up to as much as 2000% as one's average levels and can last for up to 48 hours.

Improved cellular repair

Fasting is among the ways to trigger autophagy in the body. Autophagy is the self-cleaning process done by cells to break down and recycle its damaged organelles and molecules. Although it is a constant process, autophagy increases dramatically when the body's insulin level drops during a fasted state.

The increased cell repair during a fasted state is believed to be the cause of the increased longevity among humans and other organisms that consume a low caloric diet. It arises from how stem cells can regain their regenerative ability through cellular repair. This results to stem cells being able to recover the damage to tissue at a rate that was only possible at a younger age.

Improved resistance from oxidative damage

Free radicals occur naturally in the body because of the various metabolic processes in it or the exposure from external sources. The antioxidants produced by your body and obtained from your diet neutralize these to prevent damage to the molecules that make up your cells.

Unfortunately, there will be cases wherein the body has an excess amount of free radicals. This could even be the norm for those who have a poor diet or lifestyle that both contribute to low levels of antioxidants. In such cases, the cells suffer from chronic oxidative stress that leads to damage to their structures. If left unchecked, it could trigger conditions such as heart disease, diabetes, chronic inflammation, neurodegenerative diseases, and cancer.

Fasting can address this and even improve the body's resistance to oxidative damage. This is thanks to the increased production of the gene SIRT. This gene helps prevent the production of free radicals and improve the processes that reverse the damage done on the cells and its organelles.

Improved heart health

The increased insulin levels brought about by chronically high blood sugar and insulin resistance increases the risk for developing cardiovascular disease. This risk further increases when combined with the complications brought about by the same conditions – obesity and high cholesterol levels.

As previously mentioned, a fasted state will dramatically decrease one's insulin levels. If done consistently through an intermittent fasting schedule, it can eventually bring one's insulin sensitivity back to normal levels. With the improved insulin sensitivity, one can reach a healthier weight, lower their body fat composition, and reduce their blood cholesterol levels. Since these markers have improved, there is a lower chance for heart disease as well.

Better brain function

The improved moderation of blood sugar levels, and reduced oxidative stress and inflammation brought about by intermittent fasting can also improve your brain function. This is due to the neurons switching from cell growth and reproduction to resource conservation and stress resistance. When this happens, the cells remove damaged molecules and dysfunctional organelles. This results to cells with better quality. These neurons would then reproduce when they shift back to growing and reproducing once you eat after fasting.

Also, fasting increases the levels of a hormone known as brain-derived neurotrophic factor (BDNF). This hormone is a critical component in the brain for learning, memory storage and recall, and neuron generation. Also, it helps brain cells to be resistant to stress caused by free radicals, fatigue, and your environment.

Possible prevention of chronic diseases related to cell health

The wastes, damaged molecules, and dysfunctional organelles, especially the mitochondria, increase the risk for diseases such as cancer, Alzheimer's and Parkinson's. With fasting triggering autophagy, these unwanted elements in your cells are flushed out. This could possibly be the reason why fasting has been observed to provide nerves with protection from mechanisms that cause Alzheimer's disease. In addition, it has been observed that short-term fasting can improve the effects of cancer treatment while improving the patient's tolerance against chemotherapy.

Better gene expression

Gene expression is the process of converting instructions found in our DNA into a useable product. This is what gives our cells the capability to respond to the different changes that happen in our environment. The responses often result in the form of proteins that would then trigger functions within the cell. Examples of these functions include immune response to a bacterial infection, protective response to a detected disease, and hormonal response to changes inside or outside the body.

The numerous gene expressions that happen in our different cells can degrade due to inflammation, oxidative stress, aging, and toxins. This degradation can sometimes lead to the onset of age-related and chronic illnesses and symptoms.

Intermittent fasting has been found to induce changes in the gene expressions. These changes have been noticed to improve the malformed gene expressions that increase the risk for chronic illnesses like heart disease, ischemic stroke, and metabolic disorders.

Less hunger and more satiety for certain individuals

Your body feels hunger and satiety due to the hormones released by your body. The one that makes you feel hungry is known as ghrelin while the hormone that makes you feel full is leptin. These hormones are produced from your stomach and fat cells when certain conditions are met.

Women experience an increase in the production of appetite suppressing hormones while going through a schedule of long-term fasting. However, this decrease is not observed among men with healthy body compositions. In fact, leptin decreases after undergoing a schedule of intermittent fasting.

Moreover, women are more likely to maintain their weight after returning to their regular eating schedule. This is attributed to the higher levels of the hormone suppressing the appetite that resulted from intermittent fasting.

Before You Get Started

It may seem that you can immediately start to intermittently fast after reading the first chapter of this book. After all, it only involves knowing when to stop and start eating during the day. How hard can it be, right?

This thought is where most people start to do more harm than good to themselves in doing intermittent fasting.

Individuals will have varying experiences while doing an intermittent fast. Because of this, it is easy to miss important information, especially if you are only depending on other people's experiences and advice. Their experiences are dependent on their unique situation and more often, yours are different from theirs.

This is evident with how a woman's reproductive system responds to certain forms of fasting. Women will experience disruptions in their menstrual cycle and a decrease in their fertility with certain types of fasts. According to research, this is due to the increased production of the stress hormone cortisol, and the disruption of sleeping patterns.

These effects can be properly addressed with adequate caloric and nutritional intake from meals. But, for those uninformed about this, they could be disheartened by the experience, especially if they are trying to get pregnant while doing this. Furthermore, it could lead to complications if they already have existing health issues.

This is why it is important to get all the facts straight before starting an intermittent fasting schedule. It is also crucial to seek the advice of your doctor before proceeding with any fasting schedule written in this book. A doctor's expert opinion is even more important for those with existing eating disorders, since fasting will cause changes with the hormones related to their appetite.

The Science on Why Intermittent Fasting IS more than just weight loss

The body is in a growth state as long as it is well-fed. Through the action of the hormone insulin and the mTOR (mammalian target of rapamycin) pathways, genes associated with cell survival and reproduction are activated. This results to synthesizing the proteins necessary for your cells to grow and divide themselves. This cellular state of growth and reproduction turns off genes that are contrary to this state. In particular, these genes are the ones responsible for fat metabolism, damage repair, and stress resistance.

When you start a fasting phase, you are setting up the conditions required to deactivate this growth state that your cells are going through. Your blood sugar starts to decrease as your cells continue to use them even without the continuous supply of calories from food. Eventually, your body will run out of glucose. This will start a state wherein the body will start to look for a fuel source other than glucose.

This state is ketosis. While in this state, the body would start metabolizing its fat stores. However, glucose is still an energy requirement for some cells in your body, like those found in your brain. This is where the liver comes in by providing ketone bodies as an alternative.

Even with this source of energy being available, the body stays in a fasted state as long as there's no food introduced to your digestive system. This causes the ketone bodies to increase in your bloodstream. This increase causes signaling molecules to prompt your cells to start a new state known as autophagy.

Autophagy Explained

To understand autophagy, you must first realize that your body's cells experience wear and tear just like any other part of your body. This could be in the form of worn out organelles, damaged proteins, and damaged membranes. Also, toxins and oxidized particles are created due to the processes inside your cells and the substances and conditions that your body encounters. Although your cells and your body can deal with these in the short term, it can be harmful over time, since it will eventually accumulate and cause disruptions in the cell. Moreover, having this would limit the capabilities of the cells to handle biological stresses. Because of the potential harm present, the cells undergo a process known as autophagy to eliminate the organelles, toxins, free radicals, and damaged proteins in it.

The word autophagy literally means the process of eating itself. This eating of "self" is how the cells solve their trash problem. They will break down the by-products, toxins, and damaged parts into molecules that the cell can use. These can be used as a source of energy to fuel the cell or as raw material to create new and fully functioning organelles to replace old and broken ones. As a result, the cell gets a cleaner and fully functioning system that helps return itself to full efficiency while preventing the harm caused by the accumulation of its trash.

The Different Ways Autophagy Can Start

There are two ways cells can start the process of autophagy. The first is when the cell detects it needs to clean up toxins, by-products, damaged organelles and proteins, and other sub-cellular debris in it. The second is when the cell detects a condition outside of it. These conditions can be divided into two categories: when the cell detects a declining level of blood sugar, and when stressors from the environment are detected. It is under the second way that we can consciously create the conditions required for autophagy. Here are the ways that you can trigger it in your body.

1. **Lower blood sugar**

As previously mentioned, the body's preferred source of energy is the glucose (or blood sugar) it gets from your diet. This is due to three characteristics of glucose. First, glucose is easily converted from the carbohydrates found in what you eat. Second, your body can easily store excess amounts into fat cells and convert it back if it needs it. Third, the body requires the least amount of input in converting blood sugar to energy compared to other energy sources.

When this convenient and preferred energy source becomes scarce, the body would start looking for more glucose from its stores. These, in the form of glycogen, are made whenever there's an abundance of it. Glycogen is stored in the muscles and the liver and is broken down back into glucose when the body needs it.

Eventually, this store of glucose would also decline (around 14 to 24 hours of fasting). When this occurs, the body would respond by lowering its levels of insulin hormone. This decrease in insulin causes the increase of a hormone known as glucagon, which would then induce autophagy.

In this kind of autophagy, the body is eating up the damaged organelles, by-products, toxins, and old and damaged cells. It does this since these are easily accessible, so it can quickly provide the fuel the different cells in your body need.

The body goes through this natural process whenever it runs out of blood sugar as an easy energy source. It was how pre-agricultural humans were able to go through their day to hunt or forage for food on an empty stomach. It just seems foreign nowadays since food is so accessible that we can easily have at least three full meals in a day to anticipate our body's needs.

You can replicate what our ancestors went through and lower your blood sugar by restricting certain food types, or by following a schedule of your meals and snacks. Choosing food intake can be done through a low carbohydrate diet, like the keto diet, to restrict your body's source of glucose. On the other hand, scheduling your food intake is done through fasting, which will help deplete your blood sugar.

2. Exercise

Your body requires a quick replenishment of its cells' energy stores during exercise. The body would adapt to it by switching from metabolizing glucose with oxygen to metabolizing glucose alone for energy. This helps cells get the energy that they need immediately.

The problem with producing energy without the help of oxygen is that it produces more by-products. The body and the cells involved anticipate this by starting autophagy. However, autophagy caused by exercise is only limited to the cells involved in metabolic regulation. These cells are those found in the muscle, liver, adipose, and pancreas tissues.

There are also some cells in the brain's cerebral cortex that experience autophagy. Although not directly involved with the metabolic regulation, it has a region known as the motor cortex involved with the planning, control, and execution of the voluntary muscles of your body. The activity occurring during exercise in this region is enough to produce similar increase of the by-products from cellular metabolism.

It is no surprise that research has observed intense exercise is the best way to trigger autophagy. This is because of such exercises requiring the body to forego oxygen to produce energy at a faster rate. Furthermore, this level of exercise has the greatest demand for muscle repair and rebuilding afterwards since it demands more strength and power from your muscles.

3. Exposure to Hot and Cold Temperatures

Exposure to hot and cold temperatures can cause stress to your body. This stress is enough to trigger autophagy in the affected cells. However, hot and cold temperatures are not equal when it comes to causing autophagy.

Exposure to heat has a more direct effect on autophagy. High temperatures can cause damage to the membrane, proteins, and organelles of cells where the heat was directed. But, the temperature does not necessarily have to reach levels wherein it could result to burns. Temperatures between 40 to 50 degrees Celsius are enough to trigger autophagy in cells. This temperature is enough to cause damage to cell proteins, which are then eliminated through autophagy.

On the other hand, cold exposure is not as direct as heat exposure. Cold exposure does not cause autophagy on the cells where it is applied. Instead, it occurs on the nerves due to how the cold sensation affects nerves to communicate the stimuli to the brain.

You can benefit from both types of exposure by switching back and forth between hot and cold exposure. This can be done by having a hot shower for thirty minutes before switching to a cold shower for thirty minutes. Another way to do this instead of a shower is through sauna and an ice bath.

4. Food and Antioxidants

There are substances found in food that can indirectly trigger autophagy in your body's cells. Most of these are antioxidants that help your cells get rid of the toxins and free radicals present in your system. In some cases, timing antioxidant intake during a fast can enhance autophagy.

These antioxidants are all naturally occurring substances in the food that we eat. But, in most cases, it is best to obtain it from a supplement since those found in food usually do not have enough to cause a significant effect in your body.

How to Know if Your Body Is in Autophagy

There is no way to directly measure the degree of autophagy in the body. The latest studies have only measured it through human and animal cell culture, and tissue biopsy on animal test subjects. This method would be completely impractical due to its invasive nature.

However, there is a way to gauge it indirectly. The amount of glucose, glucagon, insulin, and ketone bodies found in the blood can indicate the state of the body's metabolism.

Foods, Antioxidants, and Supplements That Promote Autophagy

1. Coconut oil

Coconut oil contains medium chain triglycerides (MCT). These fatty acid helps improve your insulin sensitivity. An improved insulin sensitivity can help your body shift faster into autophagy. This is due to the increased sensitivity, helping your body improve how it regulates its insulin levels. It can result to your body requiring lower insulin levels to regulate blood sugar levels. With less insulin circulating in your system, it requires less time to reach the point for autophagy to start.

You can take two tablespoons of coconut oil during your fast or before breaking it. If you do not like its taste, you can buy pure medium chain triglycerides that have been isolated from coconut oil.

2. Vitamin D

Vitamin D decreases the expression of mTOR proteins in your body which triggers the start of autophagy in cells. Also, the introduction of this vitamin to cells promote the death of cancer cells, and the clean-up of harmful bacteria found in cellular organelles.

You can get Vitamin D just by going out and getting some sun. This approach works best during spring or summer. You can also take Vitamin D supplements. You can improve your body's absorption of Vitamin D by taking Vitamin K2 as well.

3. Lithium

Lithium is an essential mineral that triggers autophagy in brain cells. This clean-up process is boosted even further when it comes to breaking down proteins that contribute to psychiatric and neurodegenerative diseases. In greater doses, it is taken as medication to manage the symptoms of bipolar personality disorder.

4. Berberine

Berberine is a plant alkaloid that has antidepressant, anti-inflammatory, and neuroprotective effects. It does this by inducing autophagy in the brain cells. This plant alkaloid triggers autophagy indirectly by activating the body's AMPK pathway. The activation of this pathway also improves insulin sensitivity and triggers fat metabolism.

Berberine works well with medications taken for diabetes. However, proper care should be done if you are taking anticoagulants and other blood pressure medications since it can also lower blood pressure by thinning your blood.

5. Nicotinamide

Nicotinamide, or niacinamide, is a form of Vitamin B3. It can trigger an autophagy that improves the quality of the mitochondria in human cells. This improved quality translates to more efficient energy production and a longer replicative lifespan. A cell that has a longer replicative lifespan means that it can have more generations of newer cells before it loses its ability to reproduce.

6. Acetyl-L-Carnitine

Acetyle-L-Carnitine is the amino acid carnitine's acetylated form. It induces autophagy in the brain cells that helps reverse functional decline and increases protection from oxidative damage. Supplementation with this particular form of the amino acid has been observed to lessen the effects brought about by chronic fatigue, effect improvements on the mood, increase alertness, and cause improvements in mental cognition.

7. Omega-3 fatty acid

This fatty acid has a significant anti-inflammatory effect on our nerves and brain cells. It can help you feel fuller by reducing your hunger and appetite. This effect has been observed in people who consumed fewer calories than their usual meals. Moreover, obese individuals experience a greater effect from the fatty acid's appetite suppression.

Also, it has been observed to cause autophagy and increase BDNF signaling in our brain. This results in observed effects such as improved cognition, memory, and mood. It also decreases the risk for degenerative diseases of the brain such as Alzheimer's disease, dementia, and mild cognitive impairment. Omega-3 fatty acid can also induce autophagy in the cells of the pancreas, prostate, and cell death in tumors.

Omega-3 fatty acids are fatty acids that your body cannot produce. It must acquire them from dietary sources like sardines, herring, black cod, and salmon. The most convenient way to get your Omega-3 fix is from a supplement like fish oil or krill oil. Just make sure that it is sourced responsibly, and distilled to remove heavy metals and other toxins.

8. Berries

Acai berries, blueberries, and strawberries contain polyphenolic compounds that can activate autophagy in human cells. The activation of autophagy is derived from the complete inhibition of proteins that prevent its activation. Direct supplementation of these polyphenols have resulted in reduced oxidative stress and inflammation markers. These also have improved the elimination of toxic proteins present in the cells prior to supplementation.

9. Epigallocatechin gallate

Epigallocatechin gallate or EGCG is a type of plant compound known as cathechin. This compound is found in high amounts in green, white, black, and oolong tea. It is also found in apples, peaches, avocados, pecans, hazelnuts, and pistachios. Out of all of these sources, the best source seems to be green tea due to the concentration of the compound found in it.

EGCG causes autophagy that has a specific anti-inflammatory action. It does this by activating the mechanism found in cells that fight inflammation. This same mechanism also protects the cell from the toxic effects of high lipid concentration, and promotes the cell's survivability against toxins and oxidative stress.

10. Ginkgo biloba

Ginkgo biloba induces autophagy by targeting the mTOR signaling pathways. The results brought about by its autophagic effect include decreased cell death caused by stress, a protective effect on cells making up the blood vessels, and reduced inflammation. Furthermore, gingko biloba is able to decrease the damage brought about by diabetic atherosclerosis on the blood vessels.

11. Curcumin

Curcumin is the plant compound that gives turmeric its characteristic yellow color. It triggers autophagy in the cells by inhibiting the activation of the mTOR pathway by causing moderate oxidative stress. The autophagy brought about by curcumin has been observed to halt the growth and replication, and to induce the death of pancreatic cancer cells. The same effect has been observed on other cancer cells while leaving healthy cells untouched.

12. Black Coffee

Coffee without any dairy, cream, sweetener, or sugar can help your cells induce autophagy while fasting. This effect is derived from the polyphenols present in coffee. This boost in autophagy has been observed in liver, muscle, and heart cells. The effect lasts one to four hours after drinking black coffee.

However, there are people who do not respond well to coffee. This response will often be stronger during a fast. If you feel anxious or irritated after drinking coffee, you are among the third that should not be drinking coffee while in a fast. This is often due to a sensitivity to caffeine that often precedes an increase in cravings and hunger. Having these sensations would not help and could make you prematurely break your fast.

You can try decaffeinated coffee and see if it does not come with these undesirable effects. Since the autophagy inducing effects of coffee is derived from its polyphenols, you can still benefit from it even with most of the caffeine removed during the roasting process. Just make sure that you are drinking freshly brewed coffee and not one that you made from instant coffee powder. A freshly made brew contains the most number of polyphenols since the manufacturing process to create the instant variant often destroys these beneficial compounds.

13. Caffeine

Caffeine causes autophagy by stimulating the AMP-activated protein kinase (AMPK) pathway of cells found in the body's skeletal muscles. This action of caffeine on the muscles is believed to be how it improves muscle activation time and muscular endurance.

14. Resveratrol

Resveratrol is an antioxidant compound found in dark chocolate, grapes, raspberries, and red wine. It induces autophagy in the brain. After inducing autophagy, it resulted in neuroprotective effects in healthy brain cells and accelerated recovery in injured ones.

Moreover, it helps the body improve its insulin sensitivity. This resistance has been observed even among those who consume a diet high in calories. It has even been observed to prevent the development of immature fat cells and growth of existing ones.

Although you can get this antioxidant from food, it is best to find a good supplement for it. The resveratrol content found in food is not enough for your body to reap its benefits.

15. Reishi mushroom

Also known as Ganoderma lucidum, it is a fungus that contains hundreds of bioactive compounds. It is a popular herb in traditional Chinese medicine used for supporting the immune system health, regulating inflammation, alleviating anxiety, and boosting brain function. According to research, its use in Chinese culture is justified due to how it can induce and regulate autophagy in the brain.

16. Ginger

Ginger contains an active compound known as 6-shagol. This compound inhibits the activity of mTOR pathways that regulate autophagy. 6-shagol triggers cell death in old and malfunctioning cells so that its components can be reused as energy for fueling the metabolism or as raw materials to build healthy cells.

However, this effect is unique to lung cancer cells. Despite this limited effect, it shows a promising potential as a supplement for limiting or stopping the progression of lung cancer during its initial stages.

17. Oleuropein

Oleuropein is a polyphenol found in olive oil that triggers autophagy. Because of this, it has potential in preventing or managing Alzheimer's disease and cognitive impairment. Aside from triggering autophagy, it improves the likelihood for cells to undergo autophagy by repairing the organelles in cells that play a role in its activation. The best source of this polyphenol is extra virgin olive oil, olive leaf extract, and argon oil.

18. Sulforaphane

Sulforaphane is a compound found in broccoli, Brussels sprouts, and other cruciferous vegetables. It causes autophagy by inhibiting proteins that lead to its regulation and suppression. The clean-up occurring within the cells goes beyond breaking down damaged proteins, old organelles, and toxins. It has also been credited to the cellular destruction of cells found in colon cancer and breast cancer tumors.

19. Galangal

The galangal is a ginger variant native to Thailand. It has a very similar look to ginger but has a sharp and crisp scent similar to citrus fruits. It contains a compound known as galangin that can induce autophagy. It has a high anti-tumor activity characterized by halting the cell cycle, promoting cell death and destruction, and reducing the proliferation of cancer cells.

The Progression of Autophagy

Usually, autophagy starts 18 hours into a fasting phase. This is when the ketone bodies reach amounts of around 0.6 to 1.0 mmol/l in the blood. The cells respond to this by releasing the signaling molecules that prompt itself to reduce inflammation and repair damaged DNA.

At the 24-hour mark, the cells start to break down its old and damage components, and unused proteins. When these are broken down, these are used as raw materials to create new components as replacements. In the case of proteins, the resulting amino acids can be used as raw materials or as fuel after being converted to glucose.

Intermittent fasters reach the maximum benefit from autophagy at this point. This is due to the maximum fasting phase having a duration of 24 hours in an intermittent fast.

WARNING: People new to intermittent fasting are highly advised not to do a fast that lasts for more than 24 hours. These fasting phases are beyond what one could consider as intermittent fasting. Those that go through with it undergo a screening and preparation process facilitated by their doctor to avoid any complications. Qualified medical professionals often monitor them throughout the duration of their fast, and provide emergency healthcare if necessary.

From the 48th to the 54th hour of the fasting phase, your body's growth hormone levels average up to five times the normal amount. It is also at this stage that your insulin levels decline to their lowest point. This causes a complete stop to the signaling pathways that involve mTOR and insulin. Also, with the absence of insulin in your system, the body gains a relative increase to its insulin sensitivity.

Upon reaching 72 hours of fasting, insulin-like growth factor 1 (IGF-1) starts to decrease. IGF-1 promotes the growth in every cell in the body. This decrease would eventually lead to a complete stop to cell growth. These cells would then start to breakdown and recycle old and damaged cells, and damaged and dysfunctional proteins in them. It is also at this point that stem cells increase their stress resistance and regenerative capacity.

It should be noted that autophagy can occur at a faster rate. It would depend on how well your body can shift into a fat-burning state. A faster shift would require your body a shorter amount of time during a fasting phase for the ketone bodies to build up and for your cells to shift into autophagy. Because of this, your body might be able to achieve the full effects of autophagy with only 24 hours of fasting through intermittent fasting in the long-term.

How the Body Shifts Back from Autophagy

Like anything that occurs in the body, there is such a thing as too much and too little autophagy. This is why autophagy starts and stops with minimal input from the body. For one induced by low blood sugar through fasting or a ketogenic diet, autophagy immediately ends when the body detects any increase of glucose in your blood. This could be as little as 50 calories from carbohydrates or from protein containing the amino acid leucine.

For intermittent fasting, these calories are introduced during the first meal of your eating phase. Where you get these first few calories is important if you want to maximize the clean-up that your body experiences during autophagy. It should come from a balanced and nutritious meal that contains a substantial amount of vegetables, plant fats, and plant fiber. Protein should come from lean cuts of meat while carbohydrates should come from whole sources and legumes.

Benefits of Intermittent Fasting

You have read what happens in your body when you do intermittent fasting. You have also read how it influences certain hormones, and how it affects certain organs and systems. In this chapter, you will have a closer look on how exactly intermittent fasting causes these changes. You will learn why these changes are important for your goal of losing weight and your overall health.

Weight Loss

To lose weight, you have to consume consistently fewer calories than how much your body needs. This lower calorie consumption results in a calorie deficit that forces your body to turn to an energy source other than glucose. At first, it will burn glycogen. When this runs out, it will start burning the body fat that we are aiming to lose.

The common approach to induce a caloric deficit is by following a calorie-restricted diet. However, this would require you the tedious work of counting the calories of your every meal, which is impractical, especially if you are eating out. And, with our caloric requirements varying for every single day, your calorie deficit would rarely be consistent.

This is where intermittent fasting can make weight loss easier for you. All you would have to do is follow a schedule for when you can and cannot eat. This would naturally make you lose some meals for the day, which puts your body at a calorie deficit.

Out of the two methods, intermittent fasting is easier to do. And, with one study stating that both methods can provide similar weight loss results, you are basically getting the same benefit for less work with intermittent fasting.

However, fasting provides even more weight loss benefits than simple fat loss. Intermittent fasting also increases the insulin sensitivity, human growth hormone production in your body. These help your body even further in losing unwanted weight from body fat. Here's how these help you in achieving weight loss:

Less body fat stored

Every fasting phase while intermittently fasting depletes the glucose present in your blood and the glycogen stored in your muscles. This helps the body get used to requiring less than its usual insulin levels to respond to increased blood sugar levels. This decreased requirement for insulin means that the body has regained its sensitivity for the hormone.

The increased insulin sensitivity makes the body more efficient in using glucose for energy. With less insulin going around, your blood sugar goes to where it is needed. It would not go to your body fat cells, which will make you regain the weight you lose while fasting or exercising.

Better muscle growth

Fasting increases your body's production of human growth hormone. By itself, an increased production of this hormone does not have any effect on weight loss. But, when it's combined with calorie restriction, a higher production of human growth hormone can accelerate weight loss by helping you burn fat. The increase in fat burning occurs due to human growth hormone increasing the breakdown and use of fat for fueling the body's metabolism.

Do not worry about looking bulky. Women naturally have lower testosterone levels. Because of this, your muscles do not grow in the same way or rate as men. Of course, there are women that choose to bulk up in such a way. However, these are often achieved with external intervention to boost testosterone production.

Maintain lean muscle mass

The problem with most weight loss and fat loss diets is that losing weight comes with losing muscle mass. Losing your muscle mass is the last thing you want when losing weight. It decreases how much calories your body needs on a daily basis. With reduced calorie needs, your body would eventually reach a caloric surplus even if you maintain your caloric intake. This risk of caloric surplus becomes even greater once you achieved your weight loss goal and stop restricting your diet. Either way, you would eventually gain the fat that you lost.

In intermittent fasting, this rebound is not likely to happen since it can preserve your lean muscle mass even when the body is deficient of calories. One study has observed that intermittent fasting can maintain lean muscle mass while promoting fat loss among obese individuals. This helps your body maintain its metabolism while getting rid of unwanted body fat. Because of this, you would not reach a caloric surplus even as long as you maintain your caloric intake.

Maintaining this lean muscle mass is crucial if you aim to have a defined figure when you finally shed the unwanted body fat from your physique. Doing intermittent fasting instead of focusing on restricting calories for weight loss will help you avoid getting the flat muscle look most women get that result from such diets. Of course, maintaining this definition when you achieve your intended fat loss requires that you already have created a foundation of muscle mass for it or working towards it. If you are working towards it while intermittently fasting, you would have to do resistance training.

Improves keto-adaptation

Our bodies normally use both glucose and fat as energy sources. However, due to a diet of high carbohydrates being the norm, we lost the ability to easily switch between using glucose and fat for fueling our metabolism.

Intermittent fasting helps you regain this ability by frequently depleting your body's glucose and stored glycogen. Once this is depleted, the body has no choice but to resort to a fat burning state. Eventually, the body will have an easier time to keto-adapt, which is its ability to switch from glucose to fat for energy.

Better keto-adaptation gives you more stable energy levels so you would have less cravings for food. Also, since your body switches to using fat more quickly, you are burning fat even when the body is only at standing or sitting down.

Decreased food cravings

Normally, when you think that you're hungry, you are actually just craving for food. These instances of food craving are brought about by the rapid or prolonged increase of your insulin levels. Intermittent fasting helps your body learn what it actually means to be hungry by helping it regain its insulin sensitivity. Once it reaches healthy levels of insulin sensitivity, the body stops producing more insulin than it actually needs. As a result, you are less likely to have sugar cravings despite having normal blood sugar levels.

Intermittent fasting also decreases food cravings and increases your tolerance against hunger. It also improves the response of the body when releasing the hormone inducing the sensation of fullness and satiety. As a result, one is less likely to overeat since they can immediately feel when they have eaten enough.

This greatly benefits women doing an intermittent fast. This is due to women being more likely to experience food cravings on a daily basis. To make it worse, food cravings experienced by women are for sweet foods like pastries, chocolate, and ice cream. The increased insulin sensitivity, improved hunger tolerance, and more responsive satiety can help manage these cravings, especially during the culmination of your monthly menstrual cycle when these cravings are at their strongest.

More manageable appetite

Intermittent fasting lowers your appetite. This results to you eating less and helping you maintain or lose weight. This decreased appetite arises from the effect of intermittent fasting on the hormones that regulate your hunger and satiety.

The body decreases its production of leptin and ghrelin after going through a schedule of intermittent fasting. This helps you have more manageable meals than a simple calorie restricted diet. You are essentially eating less since you do not feel like eating more and already feel satisfied with what you ate.

Promotes muscle gain and fat loss at the same time

An intermittent fasting regimen provides the best conditions to make it possible for you to gain muscle and lose fat at the same time. Training during the fasting phase helps your body to use more of its fat stores for energy. Then, when you break your fast after your workout, your body gets the nutrients it needs for recovery and building new muscle proteins. This was what has been observed in a study involving recreationally active individuals following an eight-week schedule of intermittent fasting and resistance training.

Furthermore, intermittent fasting increases your body's production of human growth hormone. Human growth hormone stimulates the various tissues in your body to release IGF-1. IGF-1 promotes amino acid uptake and its synthesis of muscle fibers. As a result, your body gets to recover and adapt to the stresses placed upon it by your workout.

It should be noted that the benefit of losing fat while gaining muscle requires more than following an intermittent fasting regimen. The same rules still apply when it comes to gaining muscle: you need to progressively train your strength and have a diet that supports its growth. You would also have to be smart about your choices for carbohydrates and caloric intake if you also want to lose fat.

Improved recovery from workout

Due to increased insulin sensitivity, your body is more efficient in allocating glucose to where it is needed. This means your muscles get the energy needed to recover from your workout. This energy can be used in helping the muscles recover and grow new muscle proteins.

However, it should be noted that muscle gain can suffer if the body is not getting what it needs from its diet. You have to consume enough calories to provide the energy needed to build muscles. You should also consume enough branch chain amino acids so your body has the necessary building blocks for muscle growth.

Also, with fasting inducing autophagy, your body becomes better at recovery and building muscle. This is due to autophagy improving the efficiency of the cells involved in repairing muscle cells and creating new muscle proteins. The more efficient cells can also help those who experienced muscle damage and trauma since autophagy also improves regeneration of muscle tissues.

An easier method to improve conditions of obesity

Other than problems with a person's genetic make-up, obesity is caused by a lifestyle of low physical activity and high carbohydrate and fat consumption. Those that find themselves in such a situation would usually resort to restricting their calories to lose weight. Unfortunately, most obese individuals often find this approach a drastic approach since the caloric restrictions are far below than what they are used to.

This is where some researchers turned to intermittent fasting as an alternative to help obese women ranging from 35 to 70 years of age. According to the study, intermittent fasting is effective in weight loss even without restricting food intake. The weight loss recorded is an average of 5 percent of their starting weight. Furthermore, if combined with a diet restricting food intake to 70 percent, participants lost twice the weight lost by intermittent fasters that have no dietary restrictions.

It should be noted that doing an intermittent fast without restricting the diet is only good for the short term. It can increase one's fasting insulin levels, which can be detrimental to long-term weight loss goals. This approach is useful as a starting point so obese individuals can gradually reduce their food intake.

Reduces visceral fat

Visceral fat is a body fat type found in your abdominal cavity. It can be found near, attached to, or surrounding your stomach, liver, arteries, and intestines. Unlike subcutaneous fat (the one you find under your skin), visceral fat increase your likelihood for serious health disorders like Alzheimer's disease, type 2 diabetes, liver insulin resistance, colorectal cancer, and breast cancer. Also, this fat increases the inflammation in your body, which could promote the accumulation of plaque in the arteries. Eventually, it could lead to a heart attack, ruptured or blocked arteries, and stroke.

Intermittent fasting can reduce the existing visceral fat in your body in two ways. First, it restricts caloric intake by having a limited time for eating. This helps your body burn body fat – both subcutaneous and visceral. Over time, the body metabolizes visceral fat tissue deposits until these are reduced to harmless amounts.

Second, intermittent fasting induces autophagy in the body. The body's self-eating mechanism protects the body from the formation of these harmful fat deposits. This helps manage and prevent new visceral fat deposits from forming as you are losing the existing ones. As for the existing fat deposits, autophagy increases the rate the body metabolizes visceral fat tissue into energy.

Lower risk for Type 2 Diabetes

Type 2 diabetes is a complication brought about by chronically elevated insulin levels. This causes the body to resist the effects of the hormone. With glucose unregulated, it can easily accumulate in your bloodstream. At its initial stages, the symptoms include increased hunger and thirst, frequent urination, sugar in the urine, blurred vision, and headache. In the long term, it could lead to complications in the cardiovascular system, nervous system, kidneys, eyes, bones, and joints.

Intermittent fasting helps to manage the blood sugar levels by restricting food intake at a set timeframe. The body does not get a new supply of blood sugar while it is restricted from eating. This forces the body to use up the glucose available in its bloodstream. This causes a decline in blood sugar levels. The body detects this decrease and lowers the insulin in its bloodstream.

Furthermore, there is an increase in insulin sensitivity every time a fast ends due to the release of glucagon-like peptide 1 (GLP1). This increased insulin sensitivity frequently occurs with intermittent fasting. In the long run, the body returns its insulin sensitivity to healthy levels.

Aside from this, intermittent fasting improves the overall function of the pancreas. Poor pancreas function is one of the factors believed to worsen conditions of type 2 diabetes. This reduced function is caused by pancreatic fat, malfunctioning pancreatic beta cells, or both. With intermittent fasting, these fat deposits in the pancreas are metabolized by the body for energy.

And, with a fast-induced autophagy, the dysfunctional and damaged organelles in the pancreas are broken down into reusable components. These are then used to build new organelles that let the pancreatic cells secrete insulin into the bloodstream.

Alternate day fasting is the method that works best to lower the risk of type 2 diabetes and improve pancreas function. This method was what research has observed to be effective. In this particular regimen, those that experienced improvement followed a 75 percent energy restriction during their fasting days.

Maintains and enhances brain health

Anti-aging benefits

As you age, the nerve cells of your brain go through natural changes. These are evidenced by slower reflexes, increasing difficulty in memory recall, reduced cognition, and slower decision-making as we grow old. Unfortunately, aging can be accelerated by the oxidative stress, toxic exposure, and amyloid beta-accumulation on our brain and its cells.

Intermittent fasting can help slow down these effects caused by aging. In some cases, these effects are even completely reversed. This anti-aging effect arises from the use of ketone bodies as an energy source while the body is under a fasting phase.

The use of ketone bodies causes neurons in your brain's hippocampus to produce more mitochondria for energy production that increases the efficiency of each cell in doing its job.

It increases the expression of the BDNF protein. This results in the inhibition of brain cell death, which helps preserve old brain cells so it can be repaired or reused by the body through autophagy. It also boosts the adaptability of the synapses of brain cells, which helps in its ability to change and adapt to the new information our brain receives or transmits.

Ketone bodies also prevent the production of free radicals in neurons. This is due to free radicals being a by-product of glucose metabolism. In addition to this, ketones stimulate the antioxidant activity present in neurons.

Aside from introducing ketone bodies to the brain, the repeated switching between fat and glucose metabolism boosts the resilience of your brain's cells and its neuronal circuits. The shifting strengthens the stress resistance of activated brain cells and increases the preparedness of these cells to transmit signals through the nervous system. This effect seems to be caused by the molecular recycling and pathway repair occurring in the cell due to the autophagy induced by fasting. This is combined with the creation of new neurons, synapses, and mitochondria when the body shifts into growth upon breaking the fast. Due to the nature of intermittent fasting, these two phases occur repeatedly in a cycle. This translates to a compounding effect of increasing efficiency for the existing cells and promoting cell, synapse, and mitochondria growth.

Lastly, when breaking a fast, the body releases the hormone glucagon-like peptide 1 (GLP1). The GLP1 hormone promotes insulin release from the pancreas and increases the insulin sensitivity of various cells. It does this by interacting with the neurons found in your spinal cord and those that connect it to your different organs. This interaction has an added effect of improving the signal cognition, stress resistance, and synaptic plasticity of these nerves. This results in the nerves being more efficient in transmitting signals between your brain and the various organs found in your cardiovascular system and digestive system. Moreover, since it can cross the blood-brain barrier, these benefits are also felt by your brain cells.

Reduces the occurrence of epileptic seizures

Epilepsy is a disorder of the central nervous system. It causes abnormal brain activity that triggers seizures, episodes of unusual behavior, weird sensations, and loss of awareness. The seizures that occur are the distinguishing symptom of epilepsy. This could be in the form of a blank stare that lasts for a few seconds or in the form of repeatedly twitching limbs.

Half of those with epilepsy cannot be determined as to what caused it to occur in the first place. For others, their condition has been attributed to their genes, to a traumatic injury on the head, to brain tumors and strokes, to infectious diseases, to developmental disorders, and to prenatal injury.

Treatment is limited to the management of its symptoms, particularly the seizures. However, the medication used to manage epileptic seizures only work for two out of every three patients.

An alternative treatment to anti-seizure medication is intermittent fasting. It turns out intermittent fasting helps reduce the occurrence of epileptic seizures through a neuroprotective effect. This has been observed among patients that followed a modified 5/2 method wherein they can only eat two meals on two days every week. But, there's a greater decrease in seizure frequency for those that fasted for 24 hours once a month.

As you might have noticed, the fasting method done by the patients are not as restrictive as what a normal 5/2 method or eat-stop-eat method would entail. This is due to these patients are all below the age of 10. They cannot fast as adults can or else they can experience complications that can affect their growth. If you plan to use intermittent fasting to manage epileptic seizures, you might be able to do a fasting schedule that stays true to the mentioned methods. Keep in mind that you should still consult your doctor before doing so in order to ensure your safety and long-term health.

Assist in the treatment and recovery from brain damage

Brain damage is any kind of injury that results in the destruction or weakening of your brain cells. It is not a degenerative disease or a congenital defect caused by birth trauma or genetics. Furthermore, the damage it causes is confined to a local area. This remains the same even in cases of closed head injuries wherein the damage is diffused to multiple areas of the brain.

Brain damage can be divided into two categories – acquired and traumatic. Both of these have similar symptoms that vary depending on the severity of the injury. Mild injuries are temporary and do not cause noticeable symptoms. Moderate ones lasts for a longer time and cause symptoms that are more noticeable. Serious brain damage can cause debilitating and permanent conditions.

Traumatic Brain Injury

Traumatic brain injury is damage resulting from an external force. This external force can be caused by falls, physical assault, sports injuries, and accidents. The primary damage caused by these events cause secondary brain damage attributed to increased inflammation, high oxidative stress, and brain cell death. Physical, speech, and occupational therapy rarely addresses these aspects of traumatic brain injury due to brain cells having a different mechanism for recovery. Fortunately, intermittent fasting has been found to have a positive effect on these conditions.

This effect from intermittent fasting is attributed to autophagy. It provides the brain protection from oxidative stress and inflammation. At the same time, it prevents cell death by replacing old and damaged parts, or by breaking down harmful substances that built up due to the injury. If this is not possible, the body recycles the components of damaged cells to create new ones.

Using intermittent fasting to help recovery from traumatic brain injury is only limited to moderate damage. Furthermore, the benefits have only been observed if the fast only lasts up to 24 hours.

Acquired Brain Injury

This type of brain injury is acquired through the lack of oxygen caused by drowning, strangulation, stroke, aneurysm, tumor growth, or a heart attack. These causes the brain cells to lose access to oxygen that arises from the body not being able to breathe air or having its blood flow cut off from a part of the brain.

Intermittent fasting through an alternate day fasting schedule can improve conditions of acquired brain injury through autophagy. This was what had been observed from test subjects that had experienced a stroke or a heart attack. The brain cells that lost access to healthy blood flow displayed reduced tissue damage and increased functionality. It shows that brain cells can be repaired and help patients to regain, at least, a part of their brain function after experiencing blood and oxygen deprivation.

As for brain tumors, a fast-induced autophagy can help manage during the early phases. Tumor growth is suppressed due to the cleanup of damaged organelles and recycling of molecules in the brain cells. However, it can make the condition worse in the later stages by promoting the survivability of cancer cells.

Decrease risk for degenerative disorders of the brain

As it ages, brain cells accumulate a formation of proteins inside. Although it is not clear what purpose this protein has, protein accumulation in brain cells disrupt its overall efficiency. This loss in efficiency is characterized by the poor transmission between neurons, decreased organelle function, and weaker synapse between multiple brain cells. Eventually, if the protein accumulation does not stop, it could eventually lead to a neurodegenerative disorder like dementia, Parkinson's, and Alzheimer's disease.

Intermittent fasting can help manage or stop the progression of such disorders by increasing the production of the BDNF protein in nerve cells. BDNF, or brain-derived neurotrophic factor, helps support the learning, processing, and memory function of your brain. It increases the stress resistance and survivability of the nerve cells. And, more importantly, it promotes the production of new nerve cells in the brain.

Aside from this, the autophagy induced by intermittent fasting improves the efficiency of the brain cells. It does this by breaking down the protein that have been building up into amino acids, which are used to grow new cells or organelles. Moreover, damaged and dysfunctional cellular components are broken down and reused for creating new ones. This results to brain cells working better than it previously did.

The ketone bodies produced by the liver while on a fasted state also improve markers indicating neurodegenerative disease. These particular markers are the accumulation of neuron plaque and neurofibrillary tangles, both of which contribute to Alzheimer's and Parkinson's disease. Furthermore, cognition improved among those that showed brain function deterioration while fasting or after consuming medium chain triglycerides.

Increased cellular repair

Intermittent fasting increases the production of human growth hormone in the body. This hormone activates the Foxm1b gene in various cells, which triggers responsible for healing and regeneration. The importance of this gene in our bodies is evident with how tissue repair becomes impaired as the levels of human growth hormone decline as we age. To confirm this, one study inserted Foxm1b gene into old animal test subjects. The study observed tissue regeneration similar to the rate observed in younger test subjects.

This same effect has been observed in humans. Human growth hormone was able to promote kidney growth in patients with chronic kidney failure. Although it is still being testing, it shows potential for addressing problems involving organ failure caused by a chronic condition.

Cellular repair is also enhanced thanks to autophagy. This is an expected benefit since autophagy is essentially the mechanism of our cells to repair itself and its organelles. It was already mentioned that it can repair and revive damage neurons in the brain. But, autophagy is more than just a measure in preventing neurodegeneration. It also repairs the cells found in your liver and heart, which are both incapable of self-regeneration without the assistance of autophagy.

It also repairs the cells found in your bones and joints. It is believed that increasing autophagy on older individuals can prevent the degeneration of your bones and joints, which eventually leads to osteoarthritis. Moreover, this repairing actions was also observed in tissues that are already degenerating. Because of this, some medical researchers suggest that that it has a therapeutic potential for treating osteoporosis and other bone diseases.

Overall anti-aging protection

Intermittent fasting increases the lifespan and oxidative protection of your cells. The increased resilience results from the manageable stress placed on the body by intermittent fasting. This process is known as hormesis. To illustrate, think of it as your cells lifting weight through intermittent fasting so it can lift the weight of actual oxidative stress.

The same increase in cellular longevity has been observed in cells after undergoing autophagy. It does this by replacing old and damage cellular parts by breaking them down and using the materials to build new ones or repair what can be repaired. This cleanup and repair inside the cell fixes age-related defects in the tissues and organs of the body and rejuvenate the cell as a whole.

Increased energy

Intermittent fasting can help your body acclimate to using body fat as a fuel. When you achieve this, your body has an easier time metabolizing nutrients for its energy needs. This is due to fat and ketone bodies only requiring three steps for the body to use it as fuel. This is in contrast to glucose needing 11 steps before it can provide energy to the body. This results in a greater endurance before feeling exhausted in doing high-intensity exercises and lasting longer in steady-state cardio exercises.

This increased energy also benefits your day-to-day life. With your body having adapted to easily switch between glucose and fat burning as needed, you would rarely, if not never, feel low on energy when your blood sugar drops. This is due to your body having a ready supply of fat that it can easily use as a fuel source.

Improved cardiovascular health

1. Manage high blood pressure

High blood pressure, otherwise known as hypertension, is a condition that develops gradually for most people. If left untreated, it can lead to complications such as loss or degradation of eyesight, stroke, heart failure, and kidney disease. There are a variety of health conditions that can lead to it. The most common include obesity, high cholesterol, and type 2 diabetes.

Intermittent fasting can lower blood pressure as confirmed by a study done on humans. It involved more than a thousand individuals that followed a fasting schedule for 21 days. The observation was that the improvement in blood pressure can be attributed to the increase in insulin sensitivity, increased activity of BDNF, and higher norepinephrine production. Unfortunately, blood pressure returned to its hypertensive levels once the study participants finished their 21-day intermittent fasting schedule. However, a similar study that went for five weeks observed a more permanent improvement. This shows that intermittent fasting requires a longer timeframe for results to remain once you stop fasting.

For women, it is important to have a proactive approach in managing blood pressure. This is due to the risk of developing it increases dramatically once you reach around 55 to 65 years of age. It is also best to avoid lifestyle choices that contribute to hypertension like smoking, a sedentary lifestyle, and a high sodium diet.

2. Lower blood cholesterol

High blood cholesterol is the condition wherein the blood contains unhealthy levels of bad (LDL) cholesterol. This can be caused by type 2 diabetes upsetting the balance between LDL and HDL cholesterol, high blood sugar levels, high carbohydrate diet, and oxidative stress. Having this condition increases your risk for a stroke, coronary heart disease, atherosclerosis, and peripheral vascular disease due to its tendency to cause plaque buildup along the arteries. Hypertension often comes together with this condition due to cholesterol buildup causing blockages or narrowing of blood vessels and hardened arteries.

Intermittent fasting helps improve high blood cholesterol by improving the balance between the good and bad cholesterol. It does this by increasing HDL levels while reducing total cholesterol levels in your blood. Furthermore, the body's state of ketosis shifts the body's metabolism into fat burning mode and looks for fat that can be used for energy. Visceral fat is among the fat stores targeted to fuel the body's energy requirements. This particular body fat increases LDL concentration in the blood by increasing VLDL particle concentration and insulin resistance. With it reduced to a certain level, this increased production of LDL cholesterol stops.

While the body is in a fat burning state, LDL cholesterol levels and total cholesterol balance is improved even further. One of the ketone bodies produced by the body can trigger the liver's niacin receptors. When this is triggered, the liver stops synthesizing LDL cholesterol while maintaining the one for HDL cholesterol.

It should be noted that intermittent fasting should only be done on the short term if you have high blood cholesterol. Doing it in the short term can improve LDL levels but long term intermittent fasting can increase bad cholesterol levels again. Also, it is also best to consume a healthy and well-balanced diet while doing an intermittent fast and to just stick to the 16/8 method. This helps in minimizing the risk of high blood cholesterol as observed in those following the alternate day fasting method.

3. Reduce arterial plaque

The formation of plaque on your arteries leads to a condition known as atherosclerosis. Other than cholesterol, these deposits contain fibrin, calcium, cell waste products, and fatty substances. The specific location of plaque would vary from one person to another. Because of this, atherosclerosis does not always cause the same complications. Conditions usually caused by plaque formation include coronary heart disease, carotid artery disease, angina, peripheral artery disease, and chronic kidney disease.

Aside from decreasing blood flow to heart muscles or the kidney, atherosclerotic plaque deposits can also cause complete blockages in an artery. This can be by a broken off plaque deposit that got stuck in a blood vessel, or a blood clot forming between a narrow channel between the plaque and the blood vessel's wall. If this blockage occurs in the brain or heart, the body can experience a heart or a stroke. In other cases, it could block of blood flow to your extremities that can result in tissue death.

Autophagy induced by intermittent fasting can help clear these deposits and reduce the risk of conditions that arise from atherosclerosis. Unlike the one that prompts cellular repair, the autophagy that occurs focuses on clearing excess cholesterol and preventing the expansion of these deposits. This is done through the action of fatty acids floating in your bloodstream.

This autophagy on plaque deposits works at a slower rate of breakdown. It provides cell protection on the healthy smooth muscle cells of the artery while breaking down and reconstructing damaged components in these cells. Combined, the plaque deposits remain firmly attached to the arteries and does not have a risk of breaking off.

Better Skin

Your skin quality deteriorates as you age. It incurs UV light damage from its exposure to the sun. It loses fibers known as elastin that help keep your skin's tightness. This results in the skin sagging and wrinkling, pores increasing in size, and skin looking thinner. For some, the skin gets more age spots, moles, freckles, and other skin pigmentations.

Autophagy can help bring back the youthful years to your skin. This was observed in one study wherein fasting increased skin stem cells, which could lead to younger looking skin thanks to better quality skin cells. Also, the skin regains its collagen for its youthful glow through the increased turnover of skin cells.

It is not only aging women that can enjoy this benefit brought by autophagy. Women who just gave birth or lost weight can also benefit from it. The stretching of the skin from weight gain or pregnancy would leave them with excess skin cells in the form of stretch marks and loose skin after losing weight or giving birth. Autophagy can fix this by clearing out cells that have no use, like the loose skin or stretch marks. Some people that lost their weight by using intermittent fasting from the very start say that it prevented stretch marks and loose skin.

Manages Type 2 Diabetes

Intermittent fasting forces your body to metabolize all its glucose and glycogen stores during the fasting phase. By using this up, the body returns to a state wherein it can relearn how it feels like to have no sugar in the bloodstream. This helps their cells regain insulin sensitivity little by little. Over time, the body regains a healthy response and stops excessive insulin release to regulate glucose levels.

Because of this effect, it is not surprising that people with type 2 diabetes can improve their condition through intermittent fasting. One study observed this improvement from their participants after 18 days of intermittent fasting through an alternate day fasting plan or a weekly three-day fasting plan. Their improvements reached the point wherein they can stop taking insulin and reduce their oral medication for managing type-2 diabetes. They experienced significant loss in terms of body weight, waist circumference, and glycated blood cells. All of these indicate that their blood sugar is properly regulated and that they have a healthy response to insulin.

Intermittent fasting also works for those with obesity-induced type-2 diabetes. Although it works the same as the average diabetes, this is caused by the stresses placed on parts of the cell membrane, which leads to the suppression of insulin receptor signals. Intermittent fasting was able to improve the transmission of insulin receptor signals in these cells. At the same time, it improved the how well the pancreas responds to changes in the blood sugar and tolerates elevated levels of glucose. It does this by improving the survivability, efficiency, oxidative stress tolerance, and regeneration of pancreatic cells.

Improved Immune Response

Although autophagy is naturally activates as part of your body's immune response, fasting can still enhance your immunity through a fast-induced autophagy. This improves your immune system's response by making your white blood cells more efficient. These cells adapt more quickly, have higher survivability, and have healthier and more efficient organelles. This results in an adaptive immune system that learns faster as it encounters toxins and infectious pathogens, and experiences the stresses placed on the body by itself and its environment. It also improves how well it retains what it learned from these so it can respond more easily when it occurs again in the future.

Furthermore, autophagy eliminates the toxic and infectious substances floating around in your body. These are broken into simpler forms and reused for its components for the body's raw material needs. This cleans up the body of harmful substances and infectious organisms that can cause harm to the body if left alone.

Helps prevent and fight cancer

Intermittent fasting can help prevent cancer by improving insulin sensitivity that prevents excessive amounts of the hormone from circulating in your body. Insulin resistance increases your risk for having cancer. In fact, women who are insulin resistant have three times the risk for breast cancer than those who are insulin sensitive. This increased risk is also true for cancers of the colon, endometrium (inner lining of the uterus), kidney, liver, ovaries, and pancreas. The culprit behind this is the high levels of insulin, which can promote cell growth in your body. Unfortunately, insulin does not discriminate which cells grow and, as a result, it can promote cancer cells to grow.

Moreover, since intermittent fasting induces autophagy, it can also have a more direct influence in preventing cancer. Cancer cells start as normal healthy cells that became defective at some point. Autophagy helps the body remove these cells in your system by breaking them down. In some cases, it can prevent this cellular malfunction from happening in the first place by targeting the defective parts in the cells. It does not even have to destroy these parts since autophagy can also repair a cell organelle if it can still be salvaged.

As for fighting cancer with intermittent fasting, it is a possible measure for those that do not suffer from malnutrition or severe weight loss. It is effective in preventing growth and reducing the mass of certain tumors. Furthermore, it widens the window available for cancer treatments and helps the body increase its tolerance for chemotherapy. This helps decrease the side effects of the treatment, which makes it possible to decrease antibiotic use and increase the dose or frequency of treatment.

However, proper care and consultation should first before using it as an aid for treating cancer. Intermittent fasting is not recommended as a measure to treat or aid in treating certain types of cancer. Fasting also limits a person's nutrient intake, which is the last thing a cancer patient would need since the body uses micronutrients to fight it and cope with the treatment. Furthermore, the research looking into the viability of short term or long term fasting is still in its infancy. There is still a lack of knowledge what it can do to the body given the different variables that could exist in a person's unique situation.

Decreased Risk for Metabolic Syndrome

Metabolic syndrome is a condition that results from the combination of various health problems. These include high belly fat, high body weight, high blood pressure, high LDL cholesterol, low HDL cholesterol, and high triglycerides. This eventually leads to insulin resistance. Once this happens, it increases the risk for type-2 diabetes together with the already high risk for a heart attack or stroke.

Intermittent fasting is effective in improving metabolic syndrome for the simple reason that it will help in making a person lose fat and in regaining healthy levels of its metabolism. This comes with regaining healthy levels of HDL and LDL cholesterol, blood pressure, and triglycerides. Together with this, the body would also regain its insulin sensitivity that provides great effect in preventing or reducing complications with type-2 diabetes.

Younger Biological Age

Your chronological age is the number of years that you have been alive. But, your chronological age does not indicate how young or old our bodies are. This is where biological age comes in. Unlike your chronological age that stays the same regardless of your choices, it takes into account the impact of various lifestyle choices like your diet, daily exercise and activity level, stress, and medications.

To determine this, tissue samples of a person and the genes found in it are catalogued. What was catalogued would then be compared to a list of 150 genes that give a person their "healthy gene score". Basically, if you get an equivalent gene score expected of your age, you have the health expected for your chronological age. If you get a better score, you are healthier than most of your generation and have a younger biological age. The opposite is the case if you get a lower score, which implies that you are more likely to have a degenerative or chronic disease sooner than those in your chronological age group.

Someone's biological age can also be hinted by one's appearance. Although it can be inaccurate, people who look and move younger than their age indicate they have a younger biological age than their chronological age. You would usually notice these in people who consistently exercise and have follow a good sleeping schedule. This is not a coincidence since these two activities can trigger autophagy.

Whether through fasting or exercise, putting the body into autophagy helps your cells return to its vitality. It removes any debris inside the cells that may disrupt it from functioning at its best. It basically gets rid of the old and dead, and reuses what it can get from to make things in tip-top shape.

Furthermore, autophagy and fasting improves the function of existing mitochondria and the quality of new ones built later on. This particular organelle is an important indicator for one's biological age since those with stronger mitochondria have been found to live longer.

Why Women Should Take Advantage of the Benefits of Intermittent Fasting

Women aged 25 to 34 have an increased risk of gaining weight. This risk is even greater for women who have a history of obesity in their family, who have issues with their hormones, who have post-traumatic stress disorder, and who are taking certain medications. Every woman should consider this risk and take measures to mitigate it. This is due to overweight women being more likely to increase their risk for various health conditions.

Overweight women are at risk for 13 different kinds of cancer. This includes cancer of the breast, endometrial, gallbladder, throat, kidney, thyroid, liver, colon, rectal, meningioma, ovaries, and pancreas. They are also twice as likely to develop type 2 diabetes and metabolic syndrome. They also have poorer cardiovascular health markers that indicate their higher chance for cardiovascular events like a heart attack or a stroke. They will also have more trouble getting pregnant and increase their chances of complications during pregnancy, such as preeclampsia, high blood pressure, and gestational diabetes.

This is where the benefits of intermittent fasting, particularly those on weight-loss, come in. Intermittent fasting can help women lose their weight by triggering the body's fat burning state. The weight lost is also easier to maintain by increasing insulin sensitivity. And, since intermittent fasting does not require the work most diets do, women will have a better chance of success since they are more likely to stick to it.

Intermittent fasting also brings about the body's natural self-cleaning and self-repairing mechanism. This plays a role in reducing the risk of so many degenerative diseases that women are at a much greater risk of acquiring. For example, diseases like Alzheimer's disease, osteoporosis, osteoarthritis, and stroke. In addition to these, there are also diseases unique to women that can lead to fatal consequences such as cancer of the breast, ovaries, and cervix. Through autophagy, the risk for these diseases are dramatically reduced due to its effect on keeping the cells that make up these tissues, organs, and systems in top shape.

As you can see, other than health conditions that could be aggravated, there is no reason why women should not do intermittent fasting. In fact, it should even be encouraged that women attempt should at least try a decent attempt for it for a month or two. Such a short time could already have positive effects on their health. And, by doing so, maybe they can see that it is not such a big deal to start eating your meals at a later time. It cannot even be placed under the same view as the calorie restriction diet, which is often viewed as a short-term punishment for long-term gain. It is a weight loss strategy that is very sustainable given the fact that it can be, and are being, done as a permanent fixture in their lifestyle.

What Women Need to Watch Out For

The physiological differences between men and women results in differences in experience when doing a diet or a workout plan. This is the same case for intermittent fasting. Also, if done in the exact same way as some male fitness experts would suggest, intermittent fasting can result in more harm than good for your body.

So, before getting started, you need to first realize what you might experience from intermittent fasting that is unique to women. There would be things that you should watch out for if you want avoid negative effects on your health. Also, there might be changes that you have to implement so you can avoid these. Such considerations are even more important if one is at risk for a disease, pregnant, breastfeeding, or menopausal. Here are the considerations you must take into account when doing an intermittent fast and some suggestions to avoid or manage these effects.

Negative Effects on Fertility

Men and women have the same glands that regulate the release of their hormones. These glands also release the same hormones – gonadotropin releasing hormone (GnRH), luteinizing hormone (LH), and follicular stimulating hormone (FSH). The difference between men and women is how their reproductive system works.

Men do not follow a schedule when producing testosterone and sperm. On the other hand, although their bodies continuously produce estrogen and progesterone hormones, women go through a cycle before they release mature egg cells and be fertile. This cycle requires precise release of the hormone GnRH. If the timing is interrupted, it will disrupt your reproductive cycle. Unfortunately, GnRH is highly sensitive to changes in the body and the environment. These changes include those that affect your sleep, stress levels, and food and nutritional intake.

Because of this, it is not surprising that some women experience irregular reproductive cycles when they do intermittent fasting. This irregularity often results from at least one of two things – poor protein consumption or elevated stress levels.

Poor protein intake

Low protein intake has this effect on your reproductive cycle due to it providing the amino acids necessary to activate your estrogen receptors. Activation of these receptors result to the liver producing IGF-1, which would trigger the thickening of your uterine wall and the progression of your reproductive cycle.

Elevated stress levels

Intermittent fasting increases your body's stress levels. This is nothing bad and just one of the body's reactions in maintaining your health. In fact, too little of is associated with inflammation, poor immune health, chronic pain, fatigue, and unstable blood pressure. The opposite is also the same as it is this abnormally high stress level that disrupt your body's reproductive cycle.

Now, the stress placed on the body by intermittent fasting does not reach the harmful levels. In fact, it contributes to the self-cleaning and self-repair effect caused by intermittent fasting through autophagy. But, each person's body is unique and would have a unique reaction to each situation. For intermittent fasting, it could be fasting beyond a certain timeframe would trigger unhealthy stress levels.

In addition to this, there are other factors that contribute to a person's stress levels such as lack of quality sleep, lack of or excess of exercise, and poor diet. Even if intermittent fasting alone does not cause you unhealthy amounts of stress, you can still reach such levels if other factors in your life are pushing making your life stressful.

Knowing these two causes already gives you a hint on how you can manage this unwanted effect by intermittent fasting. First, you must ensure that you are consuming enough protein in your diet. You can get what you need through red meat or through protein or amino acid supplements.

Second, you have to manage your stress levels. It could be as simple as getting enough sleep by going to bed early. In some cases, you might have to set up the conditions that can help you sleep better. You might also want to consider your lifestyle and eating habits. If any of these might contribute to elevated stress levels, you might have to change some of it to minimize stress. You can also alter your intermittent fasting schedule to shorter fasting phases. In this way, your body can adjust back from its stressful fasting phase sooner.

Hormones Go Beyond Your Fertility

Even if you do not plan on getting pregnant yet, your hormones should still concern you. The role of estrogen goes beyond your reproductive system. It also plays a role in your metabolism. And, if you want to create positive results with intermittent fasting, you better make sure that your metabolism is working as it should be.

Estrogen plays a role in modifying the amino acids that signal the release of hormones that make you feel full or hungry. It stimulates your neurons that starts or stops the regulation of your appetite. Moreover, if your estrogen levels drop, you are more likely feel hungrier than you actually are.

Intermittent Fasting for Pregnant Women

Many studies on fasting involve individuals following the Muslim tradition of Ramadan, which involves fasting from sun up to sun down. Some of the research participants are pregnant women who chose to fast even when they are exempted from doing so. What researchers found was that their insulin, glucose, and triglyceride levels improved. Furthermore, their babies have similar weights to the babies of mothers who did not fast.

However, it should be noted that there's a lower frequency in fetal movement for pregnant intermittent fasters. A low frequency of fetal movement is considered a warning sign regarding the baby's health. There is also not enough evidence suggesting that the infant did not experience adverse health effects that may appear later in life.

If you are considering intermittent fasting while pregnant, you must remember that it is during this time that your body needs to focus on helping your baby gain weight and develop its body, providing nutrients for brain development, and developing fat stores for breastfeeding.

It is important to first have a conversation with your doctor before attempting any kind of fast while pregnant. There are already doctor-approved methods that you can do to manage your weight. You can do moderate exercises such as walking, stationary cycling, and swimming. In fact, exercise can be good for you since it can shorten your labor, and reduce your risk for cesarean delivery and gestational diabetes.

For Women with Polycystic Ovarian Syndrome

Intermittent fasting can help those with polycystic ovarian syndrome (PCOS) lose weight. Those with PCOS find it difficult to lose weight due to their body's tendency to produce high insulin. Intermittent fasting helps improve this by improving their insulin sensitivity. This helps their body get better control on its insulin levels and indirectly assist in efforts to lose weight.

Furthermore, intermittent fasting can improve the chances of women with PCOS of getting pregnant. It can increase the levels of their luteinizing hormone, which one of the important hormones for your ovulation. And, with better chances for weight loss, PCOS women experience further benefits in their reproductive health by improving their menstrual cycle, fertility, and ovulation. The reduction in insulin resistance and cardiovascular disease risk also reduces the complications that women with PCOS are more likely to encounter during pregnancy and while giving birth.

Intermittent Fasting While Breastfeeding

Intermittent fasting can lower the milk supply of breastfeeding mothers. This is because of breastfeeding mothers not getting sufficient nutrients by doing an intermittent fast. To put this into perspective, those who are breastfeeding their child are advised to consume around 300 to 600 additional calories per day.

Furthermore, doing an intermittent fast will reduce the amount of food that you eat that contains the variety of macro and micronutrients. This can decrease the quality of the breastmilk. Although it may be not harmful, it can still cause potential risks in the future for the baby. According to a study, intermittent fasting can reduce the concentration of lactose and potassium, and the overall nutritional content of breastmilk.

Again, consult your doctor first if you are breastfeeding. You can still achieve weight loss or improve your insulin resistance through a healthy and well-balanced diet.

Intermittent Fasting During Post-menopause

Intermittent fasting can help women who are at their post-menopause stage. It can help post-menopausal women with their weight loss and management. The observed benefits include improved levels of total cholesterol, triglycerides, and fasting glucose.

Addressing Concerns About Intermittent Fasting

It is not surprising that the concept of intentionally missing meals, which can last for a full 24 hours in some days, would raise some concerns. And, no one can blame those who are wary about intermittent fasting. After all, it goes against everything we believe and what is commonly known about nutrition and maintaining our health.

In order to put these worries to ease, here are some of the most common concerns about intermittent fasting. The answers that have been provided might have appeared in an earlier chapter. But, sometimes, these concerns are best answered directly and the best way to do it is by reiterating some points that have been previously made.

Is intermittent fasting safe?

Fasting has been around for years. Although intermittent fasting is being done for the purposes of one's health, religions have been practicing it as part of their spiritual traditions for centuries. These traditions have not caused serious health complications. Furthermore, both intermittent fasting and religious fasting have the same exceptions on who can and cannot do it.

Furthermore, your body has measures in place when you have no access to food in the form of body fat. It was how humans in before the advent of agriculture survived. They did not have the convenience of easily accessible food. In order to eat, they had to hunt or gather, which can sometimes take days before they can even do so.

Of course, this does not mean that you can immediately jump into intermittent fasting or start with 24-fasting phases. You would have to do it gradually until you can do the fasting phase that work best for your lifestyle or needs.

How can autophagy be good when it literally means "self-eating"?

The common belief seems to be is that nourishing our bodies is always good. This is true but only for the case of infants, toddlers, children, and teenagers. These are people who actually still have to grow. But, for the case of fully-grown adults, constant growth becomes harmful. Once a body reaches adulthood, balance (or homeostasis) should take priority.

Now, what does this have to do with eating and fasting? Well, as long as your body is metabolizing food, your body is in a state of growth. When everything you ate has been broken down and used up, your body will start a state of breaking down damaged and malfunctioning parts to fuel itself.

These two contrasting states maintain a balance within your body. If growth is unregulated, your body will get sick. Just look at cancer, it is simply uncontrolled growth of malfunctioning cells. This is the same for autophagy. If the body is left in a state of autophagy, the body would eventually deteriorate and experience various complications.

Will it slow down the body's metabolism?

You probably heard before that meal skipping or fasting can slow down your metabolism. This concept came from the belief that our bodies need three full meals per day. This is actually not the case.

To correct this belief, you must first know what "metabolism" actually means. It is just a term to describe all of the chemical reactions occurring in your body to maintain the life of your cells and your body. Now, from this definition alone, you will realize that autophagy is one of these reactions that can be counted as part of your metabolism.

In fact, although it might be taking the belief "meal skipping is bad" out of context, constantly feeding your body with calories and macronutrients is harmful for your body. It is always in a state of feeding that it does not have a change to achieve stability. And, as you have read in earlier chapters, constant supply of nutrients can cause adverse effects in your body. It can be in the form of insulin resistance, liver and kidney disease, and weight and fat gain.

Will it cause nutritional deficiency?

Nutritional deficiency does not have anything to do with the amount of food you consume. It has more to do with the quality of what you eat and what you absorb into your body. If you are limiting what you eat to only a few food items, you are most likely deficient in nutrients not found in what you eat. It would not even matter if you eat more than what you need since it would still not give your body all the nutrients it needs.

Although it is possible that you can experience nutritional deficiency in intermittent fasting, the cause behind it has more to do with what you eat than how often or when you eat. You can avoid it through proper monitoring of your diet and smart choices on what you eat. This is where eating a diet rich in vegetables and healthy fats with lean protein and moderate carbohydrates will help you. Such a diet will give you an adequate supply of macro and micronutrients that your body would need. If you are still in doubt, you can take nutritional supplements to fill in the nutritional gaps that you might be missing from your diet.

Can it cause eating disorders?

Intermittent fasting can provide a lot of benefits for your health. But, if it will cause something that can harm your health, it is best to avoid. People who are at risk, currently going through, or previously had eating disorders are advised to avoid intermittent fasting.

If you are unsure if you are at risk, you can check your family background if a family member had a history of an eating disorder. Other signs of eating disorder risk include perfectionism, impulsivity, and mood instability.

Will it make me feel weak?

The feeling of being low in energy or tired is common among those just starting intermittent fasting. This feeling is associated with your declining blood sugar as you are in the middle to the latter parts of your fasting phase. This is normal since your body has not yet adapted to using fat for its metabolism.

Also, the psychological effect of your beliefs is quite powerful. We have been fed with the belief that we need frequent meals for our well-being. It can make you feel worse than you actually are.

To overcome these, you just have to push through your first few days in intermittent fasting (provided that you do not have any health conditions like anemia and hypothyroidism). Your body will eventually adapt in a little more than a week. Once it does, you will feel the mental clarity and the increased energy associated with the body's fat-burning state. As for the psychological barrier, your mind will eventually learn to differentiate actual hunger from cravings.

It is important that you start with a time restricted fast like the 16/8 method. It is unreasonable to expect your body to not feel weak in a 24-hour fast if it is your first time in intermittent fasting. In some cases, it is even advised to start with an 8- or 10-hour fast. This will give you a better chance of sticking through your intended schedule for intermittent fasting.

Will it cause muscle loss?

Intermittent fasting can cause muscle loss. But, if you eat well and do intermittent fasting right, you can maintain your muscle mass while losing fat. It is advised that you consume adequate amounts of protein so your body has ample supply of amino acids to maintain its mass. Getting enough protein from your diet becomes even more important if you are working out while doing an intermittent fast. It will supply your body the amino acids that it needs to repair and grow its muscles during the eating phases of intermittent fasting.

In some cases that there was muscle loss, it was minimal and most of it only consists of what you would call water weight.

Is it safe to do this in the long-term?

Generally, intermittent fasting is safe to do in the long term for both men and women. It was how our bodies are wired. But, you have to make sure that you are getting all the nutrients that you need. Although it might be inconvenient, you can keep track of your macronutrient intake. And, since long-term intermittent fasting has less to do with weight loss and more to do with weight maintenance, you will just have to make sure that you are consuming enough to maintain your weight.

Furthermore, you have to listen to your body. If you feel and look well doing it, you can continue intermittent fasting. If you feel a lack of energy or appear to be losing weight, you have to check your diet and adjust accordingly. If you do not feel good about it at all, it would probably be best to decrease the time for your fasting phase or completely stop it.

Regarding the best method for long-term intermittent fasting, it is best to stick to the 16/8 method. This method is more realistic and doable in the long-term. It will give you the benefits that you can get from intermittent fasting while still getting the nourishment you require on a daily basis.

All of the answers provided in this chapter are no substitute to your doctor's expert opinion. We are not bioidentical and it would not be reasonable to expect the same exact experience would happen to you in intermittent fasting. What might work for you might not work for you and vise-versa. It is important that you set things straight first in regards to your health. If you are sure that you can go through this, then you can start slowly. If at any time you do not feel well and continue to do so even after trying for a week or so, it would probably be best to reassess your health and see if you have an existing health condition.

Individuals That Should Not Do Intermittent Fasting

Intermittent fasting requires a level of commitment that might be impractical for some situations. You can easily do it if you have done some kind of diet before and integrated it to your life successfully. Factors like work, family, and personal life can affect how you do intermittent fasting. If doing it will negatively affect how well you do in these areas of your life, you will find it difficult and could even cause repercussions in the said areas.

This does not mean that doing it is impossible. It will just be more difficult. You can work around these challenges and find out how to make it work. However, if working around these challenges is impossible or too difficult, intermittent fasting might not be for you. Your work, family, and personal life is not worth sacrificing, especially that there are alternatives to intermittent fasting.

Other than these lifestyle factors, you should also consider where you are in terms of your health. If you are pregnant, breastfeeding, or planning to conceive, do not even think of doing intermittent fasting. The same also applies for the following:

- Those with a history or currently have eating disorder/s
- Underweight individuals
- Type-1 diabetes patient
- Below 18 years of age
- Individuals taking prescribed medication
- People with insomnia
- People who are chronically stressed
- Employees in performance-oriented or physical-intensive jobs
- Employees that work the night shift
- People who have no experience with exercise or dieting

    Some of these are not actually health conditions. But, if these individuals did intermittent fasting, they would likely experience fatigue or underperform on their jobs.

If you find yourself included in this list that should not do intermittent fasting, you still have other options to lose weight. A calorie-restricted diet has similar weight and fat loss potential as intermittent fasting. If you are interested with the effects of autophagy for your health, you can also achieve the same effect through exercise, antioxidant supplementation, and the ketogenic diet.

Why Intermittent Fasting Is Better Than Other Diets

Now, if you passed the "test" from the previous chapter, you are probably ready to read on how to get started. But, if you are still on the fence about it, this chapter will tell you why intermittent fasting is the best option that you have for weight loss and general health.

Convenience

There are many different ways that you can do intermittent fasting. This makes it easy for you to make it fit your lifestyle or preferences. For example, if you are doing a 16/8 method, you can schedule your fasting phases from seven in the evening until 12 noon the next day. In this way, you can coast through your fasting phase asleep. You also do not have long to wait until you can eat for the next day. This set-up makes it easy for those just starting with a full intermittent fasting schedule.

Also, if you happen to miss the start of your fasting schedule, you can easily adjust the start and end of your fasting phase. Using the previous example, let us say that you went out with your friends and missed the start of your fast because of it. Although not ideal, you can shift your schedule and just count from the time you ended your last meal. In this way, you can still fully benefit from its benefits and you do not have to completely break your schedule.

The same can also be said for 5/2 and eat-stop-eat method. You can reschedule your fasting phase when an occasion comes up. You can't say not eat in these events. Doing so would be terribly rude to the hosts or your friends. It would also be difficult since everyone else around you would be eating.

You can also easily set your meal plans for intermittent fasting since there are no restrictions on what you can and cannot eat. All you have to remember are the times when you can start eating and when you have to stop. You can be strict and precise with what you eat but, even if you choose not to, you can still experience the benefits of intermittent fasting.

Benefits

Intermittent fasting is proven in helping people lose weight. It can even help maintain your muscle mass while shedding body fat. It also goes beyond weight loss, which is what most diets focus on. It prompts your body to undergo a natural process to clean and repair its cells, and to prompt reactions that help delay aging in your body. Because of this, even if you do not intend to lose, you can still benefit from intermittent fasting.

Can Accommodate for a Nutritious Diet

You can do intermittent fasting in your own terms. You can set up your diet to be at a caloric deficit to help in your weight loss. On the other hand, if you want to maintain your lean bodyweight or support your workout goals, you can set your diet at a caloric equilibrium or surplus. What's great about this is you can still experience autophagy in both cases. You would still benefit from intermittent fasting in some way.

Moreover, you do not have to restrict yourself from eating certain types of food. You can eat whatever you like: carbohydrates, protein, fat, or vegetables. Because of this, you can easily avoid experiencing nutritional deficiencies from your diet. Although it is discourage, you can even eat junk food since all the benefits from this results from intentional depletion of glucose and glycogen in your body.

The Different Methods of Intermittent Fasting and How Each Can Benefit You

You have already read in the first chapter the different methods that fall under intermittent fasting. In this chapter, you will be taking a closer look on each of those methods. You will learn how to do each method and from there you can see which one would work best for your lifestyle.

16/8 method

The 16/8 method is the most popular way to do intermittent fasting. It got its name from the 16 hours of fasting and 8 hours of eating involved. It is often called interchangeably as the Lean Gains method. But, for the sake of discussion, this book will consider the 16/8 method and the Lean Gains method as different methods of intermittent fasting. Although Lean Gains method is the original 16/8 method, the generic 16/8 method known today took on a life of its own that, if you ask someone what it is, it is completely different from what bodybuilder Martin Berkhan designed.

How to do the 16/8 method

Doing the 16/8 method is simple. You just have to pick an eight-hour window that would be the only time that you can eat for the day. You are free to decide when you want this eating period will start or end. Some might say that a certain time is the best to end a fast or to start one due to some claim regarding weight loss, muscle gain, or appetite suppression. But, there is no evidence stating or supporting their claims. Just set it according to what works best for your lifestyle and personal preferences.

During the eating phase, you are free to eat. The objective during this time is to give your body the nutrient and calories it needs. It is recommended to eat your well-balanced meals with equal intervals between each other. This will help stabilize your blood sugar as you would not gorge yourself of food and cause it to increase rapidly.

Once this time ends, you are prohibited from consuming or drinking anything that contains calories. This will last until the eating phase for the next day starts.

14/10 variation for women

The 14/10 method is a variant of the 16/8 method. The two are almost exactly the same. The only difference is this method involves 10 hours for its eating phase and 14 hours for its fasting phase. It was created for women to prevent the negative effects of intermittent fasting done on their hormones. Also, the longer eating phase gives you more meals for the day. This can help in ensuring that you get enough nutrients, especially protein, to maintain a healthy hormone production in your body.

Lean Gains method

The Lean Gains method is the original form of the 16/8 method. Nutritional consultant, bodybuilder, writer, and personal trainer Martin Berkhan created it. It still operates with the same time restrictions of 16 hours of fasting and 8 hours of eating. However, unlike the 16/8 and 14/10 method, Berkhan instructs that the eating phase start at noon. This is to ensure that you are in a fed state during the afternoons and evenings. This schedule is meant to decrease the stress that you would get from work. Berkhan states that the eating phase can start later if you would be working late into the night.

Training is a big part of this method. It was formulated with the expectation that intermittent fasting would not stop a person's normal workout program. Because of this, this method can be done in four different ways. All were made with the consideration that each person would have different preferences on when and how they choose to schedule their workouts while doing intermittent fasting.

Furthermore, this method takes into account how diet and nutrient timing can help someone achieve their weight loss goals. However, unlike most diets, Lean Gains makes it easy since you only need to remember three things. First, you need to keep your caloric intake on the level that would help your reach your weight loss goal. Second, you need to eat fewer carbohydrates during non-workout days. Third, you need to follow the schedule and proportion of meals on your workout days.

For the workout days, the post-workout meal should consists of the majority of calories you would eat for the day. If the schedule allows for a pre-workout meal, it should provide the body with enough energy to do well in the workout. These should consist of 50 to 60 percent of carbohydrates and 40 to 50 percent of protein. The carbohydrate content would take care of your body's energy needs while the protein would maximize your muscle's protein synthesis and induce satiety. Fat is optional and can be used to add flavor to the pre-workout meal.

The key to the Lean Gains method is patience.

The Different Lean Gains Protocols

The protocols below only apply on workout days. If there is no workout, the protocols below do not apply and would follow a normal 16/8 method. There are a total of three meals for each eating phase and the last one is taken an hour before the eating phase ends.

The meal after the workout will always contain the most calories, carbohydrates, protein, and fat. The last meal always has the least amount of calories and carbohydrates with the exception of post-workout meals.

1. **Fasted training**

Training starts an hour before the eating phase starts. It is done on an empty stomach other than 10 grams of branch chain amino acids or of a similar mixture taken 5 to 15 minutes before the workout. The BCAA taken before the workout stimulates protein synthesis and metabolism. The small amount of amino acid is enough to halt the body's fasted state.

There is no pre-workout meal. The carbohydrate and calorie content of each meal decrease gradually as you go through the day.

2. **Early morning fasted training**

Training starts first thing in the morning after waking up. 10 grams of BCAA is taken 5 to 15 minutes before the workout. Another BCAA dose is taken an hour after training and another one at three hours after training.

3. **One pre-workout meal**

The first meal in the eating phase is the pre-workout meal. It consists around 20 to 25 percent of the day's total caloric intake. Workout is scheduled two to three hours after the pre-workout meal. Post-workout meal is schedule immediately after the workout.

This protocol is best for those who have the flexibility in their work or class schedule.

4. **Two pre-workout meals**

The first and second meal each has 20 to 25 percent of your total daily caloric intake. Training is done two to three hours after the second meal. Post-workout meal is taken an hour before the eating phase ends.

This is best for those who can only work out from five in the afternoon and until an hour before the eating phase ends.

You can adjust the Lean Gains method using the 14/10 fasting and eating schedule. You will still be fasting and benefit from the benefits of proper meal timing and nutrition of the Lean Gains method.

But, it could be best to try the Lean Gains method first by using the 16/8 eating and fasting schedule. You and your body would probably have easier time doing the fasting phases since you will be eating enough to satisfy your caloric needs so you would not be at a caloric deficit. Furthermore, the method places an emphasis on adequate protein intake. This ensures that you would get enough protein to supply what your body needs to produce hormones and to keep your reproductive cycle uninterrupted.

The Lean Gains method might look intimidating especially for an intermittent fasting method. The creator of this diet admits that it takes more work than your average fasting method. But, this is a much simpler approach compared to diets and strategies for those with goals of losing fat while building muscle. It also beats the other diets since Lean Gains method can be implemented using whatever type of diet you want. As long as you consume the right amount of calories, the right macronutrient proportions, and time your nutrient intake, it would not matter if you do a paleo, vegan, vegetarian, or Mediterranean diet.

Eat-Stop-Eat Method

Brad Pilon created this method while he was in his graduate studies. It was first introduced through his book "Eat Stop Eat."

The Eat Stop Eat method is done by fasting for 24 hours once or twice per week. The fasting phase can start any time as long it lasts for 24 hours before eating another meal. The 24 hours of fasting should be non-consecutive days if you choose to implement a two days per week fasting schedule.

This schedule would limit your calories to the amount you consume during the five or six days of the week that you can eat. This would put you automatically in a calorie deficit for the week. For example, if you consume around 2,000 calories per day, you would have a calorie deficit of 2,000 per week if you have one fasting phase per week, or 4,000 calories per week if you have two fasting phases per week.

During the eating phase, you will eat the amount of food that you would normally consume when you are not fasting. It is strongly advised to avoid making up for lost calories or bingeing on food after you end your fast. You should take the mindset that you will only consume what you normally eat in a day.

You are also free to choose what you eat. You can follow a diet to improve your health like the ketogenic diet, paleo diet, or a Mediterranean diet. But, you have to make sure that you are consuming enough to satisfy your caloric needs for the day. Also, these diets should not place additional stress on your self-control. Intermittent fasting is already hard as it is, especially for one that has a 24-hour fasting phase. Adding another factor like a diet will make it more difficult for you.

5:2 Method

The 5:2 method involves a fasting phase that restricts your food intake to 25 percent of your total caloric consumption. As its name suggests, this method involves five days of normal eating days and two days of fasting days. Although it recommends that women eat less than the calories indicated for fasting days, the chapter about differences between men and women indicate that their bodies should actually be eating more to avoid disruptions on their hormones. Because of this, it is best for women to consume around 28 to 30 percent of their total daily calories.

During fasting days, you can choose to eat what you would normally as long as you stay within the limits. But, if you want to avoid the feeling of hunger, you would have to be smart about what you eat. The best food choices during these two days are those that do not contain much calories but will make you feel fuller for quite a long time. These food items are green leafy vegetables, small cuts of roasted lean meats, soups, and salad.

You can set up three meals for your fasting days. But, based on other people's experience, a meal or two works best in managing their hunger or appetite. They also schedule these meals at lunch and dinner. They found it easier to skip breakfast than going without food lunch or sleeping without having eaten anything.

Unlike the Eat-Stop-Eat method, the creator Kate Harrison did not place any restriction on whether the fasting days can be done consecutively or not. However, she did state that fasting should not exceed 48 hours. She also does not recommend this method for pregnant women, nursing mothers, teenagers, children, and people with eating disorders. She also recommends anyone with diabetes or chronic medical conditions to first consult their doctor or specialist before doing the 5:2 method.

The method allows for exercising during fasting days. But, the calorie allowance for the day should be followed. Exercising would not allow to have additional calories so you can eat more food. If you do choose to exercise, you have to be careful and immediately stop once start feeling unwell.

You can vary the number of fasting days depending on what suits you best. Some people choose a 6:1 eating and fasting schedule if their lifestyle does not make it possible for 5:2 schedule or if they are just aiming to maintain their weight. You can also increase it to three fasting days as long as you do not exceed more than 48 consecutive hours of fasting.

You can choose to do this method for the long term. But, Harrison recommends to stick to a 5:2 or a 6:1 eating and fasting schedule.

Alternate Day Fasting (ADF)

The alternate day fasting is a method of intermittent fasting where in you would be completely restricted from food or calories every other day. If you would include the number of hours of your sleep to it, you will be fasting for 30 to 32 hours. From the number of hours involved fasting, this method is obviously not for beginners. It also involves going to bed after having a day without eating anything.

This is best for those looking to benefit from the effects brought by a fast-induced autophagy to the body. Most studies researching the effects of a fast-induced autophagy usually use the alternate day fasting to trigger autophagy in the body. If you are only interested in losing weight, this might not suit your goals due to its difficulty. Also, the other methods with shorter or fewer fasting phases already does fine in regards to weight loss.

If you still want to do this method, you have to keep in mind that this is an advanced method of intermittent fasting. People who have done alternate day fasting had to work their way to being able to do it for a length of time that will create results. Usually, the time frame is around four to six weeks. In order to last that long, they have to be already experienced with intermittent fasting. This experience is usually a year of doing 16/8, 5:2, or eat-stop-eat.

ADF is only done for the short term. It is not like the 16/8 or 5:2 method that you can do on the long-term. If you plan to continue on intermittent fasting, it is best to return to your previous method or pick another one that can be done long term.

Based on anecdotal evidence, experienced intermittent fasters who did alternate-day fasting did not feel weak or terribly hungry on fasting days. Although it was difficult at first, their hunger levels remained the same throughout the day. Hunger was no longer an issue around two to three weeks into alternate day fasting.

Those who regularly worked out were able to do so while doing ADF. Some took a strategic approach of eating the night before and working out first thing in the morning on their fasting day. However, most women felt terrible, especially if they had a workout, when they did not have enough protein or healthy fats during their previous eating day.

The Warrior Diet

The Warrior Diet is Ori Hofmekler's method for intermittent fasting. It attempts to mimic the way Paleolithic humans ate, which involves frequent eating of produce (fruits, nuts, and vegetables) during the day and feasting during the night with a hearty meal before going to sleep. Unfortunately, the original method is quite impractical with how complicated it went with the carbohydrate and calorie cycling involved, the restrictions placed on the diet to closely mimic a paleo diet, and the specified workout that should be done. For the case of this book, the Warrior Diet is stripped to its essentials to stay true to the regimented-approach of intermittent fasting. This modified version only involves 20 hours of fasting and 4 hours of eating every day.

You can schedule the eating phase whenever you want for the day. But, it is best to schedule it during the night – around 7 or 8 in the evening is the best time to start. This is for your body to wake up in a fasted state on the next day. Since your body is already in a fasted state, your insulin levels will be low and your body can enter a fat-burning state earlier in the day. As you go through your tasks for the day, you are burning fat. This will only stop during the eating phase when your body digests the carbohydrates from your only meal.

The Warrior Diet works best if you already follow a workout regimen. The workout is best done on a fasted state since it will maximize the amount of fat that your body metabolizes. As for the time of the workout, it is more manageable to do it in the morning. Your meal the previous night will still fuel your body through your exercises.

Like Alternate Day Fasting, this method is not for beginners due to the 20-hour period of fasting from anything that contains calories. It is also a method designed for maximum weight loss. Therefore, this should only be done if you want to lose weight or fat. It is not done on the long term and should only last for four to six weeks. You would eventually have to switch to more sustainable method like the 5:2, 16/8, or Lean Gains method.

One Meal a Day (OMAD)

One Meal a Day, or OMAD, is a method of intermittent fasting that involves a fasting phase lasting for 23 hours and an eating phase lasting for only an hour. Its name is derived from how an hour is only enough a single meal. Similar to the Warrior Diet, it uses the premise that ancient civilizations, particularly the Romans, only ate a single large meal each day and that the modern diet is giving the body more than what it needs.

OMAD is done best with a meal that fully satisfies the body's needs. This satiety is an indication that the body got what it requires and can stop eating for the day. There are those who have done OMAD in the long-term and state that they feel fine and function well throughout the day. They can exercise normally. They feel more energetic and lighter compared to how they felt with a "normal" eating regimen or a shorter fasting regimen. They also rarely got sick and, if they do, their body responds and gets better faster.

On the other hand, there are those who state that it is not possible long-term and that they cannot exercise at all. But, most people who state these are those who did not stick to it for more than a week or so. They also seem to have jumped straight into One Meal a Day instead of starting with an easier intermittent fasting method.

Due to the nature of this method, those with health conditions are highly discouraged from using this method. It is best that they use methods with shorter fasting periods. Of course, they should first consult their doctor before doing so.

As for beginners, this will be a huge adjustment from eating at least three meals a day. It is best to start with a 16/8 method and work towards the OMAD method.

The Four Keys to Success with Any Intermittent Fasting Method

Regardless of your preferred method, you need four things to succeed in intermittent fasting – quality food, proper nutrition, consistency, and patience.

Good food quality

You are free to eat whatever you like in intermittent fasting. But, you experience better results if you nourish your body with quality calories from whole foods and not junk or processed items. Your body will get the nutrients it needs from good quality food. It is a better option than getting empty calories that would not do much in feeding your body beyond its metabolism.

Proper nutrition

Intermittent fasting is a weight loss strategy that does not focus much on adequate calorie consumption or balanced nutrition. This idea comes from the belief that the limited time window would force you to have fewer meals. There is also an assumption that you would not binge on food whenever you can and that you would listen to your body when full.

However, if you do binge on food during your eating phases, you will eat more than your body needs. It will place you at a calorie surplus and make your body slower in reaching a fasted state. This is also the same if you have more meals than you actually need during your eating window. Both of these would not benefit your efforts in your pursuit of weight loss. It could even be enough to increase your weight in methods with shorter fasting periods.

The opposite is also true. You cannot eat too little or else your body would not have enough nutrients for its needs. Your body needs more than calories or glucose for its metabolism. It needs protein to form amino acids, fat and oils for fatty acids, and vitamins and minerals to support your body's functions. If you do not get enough of these, your body will get sick. You can experience digestion problems, unusual food cravings, muscle weakness, palpitations, menstrual issues, sleepiness, and decreased mental function.

Consistency

You have to stick to a method for a period of time. You cannot expect results to happen after only a week of intermittent fasting. It takes at least one to three months of consistent effort in following a method to get the best results.

Patience

You have to be patient. Your body need time to adjust. You will experience difficulty at first due to how it adapts. Also, it will take some time to achieve your goals for weight loss, fat loss, or better body composition. Depending on your present situation, you might have to do shorter fasting phases before you can do one of the methods mentioned. You might also have to adopt intermittent fasting for a longer period to achieve weight loss.

The Food and Drink Guide for Intermittent Fasting

What not to eat or drink during intermittent fasting

While in a fasting phase, you are obviously restricted from eating anything that contains calories. When you enter the eating phase, you are free to eat whatever you want. But, if you want to lose your weight faster, you better avoid the following food and beverages listed below:

Anything Containing Refined and Added Sugar

Removing refined and added sugar in what you eat or drink is the first tip you would always get in any strategy to improve your health. Intermittent fasting is not different.

Sugar does not nourish your body in any way. It is only in what you eat and drink to add flavor. It can rapidly increase your blood sugar levels and elevate your insulin levels, which will make it difficult for you to lose fat.

Here are the food and drink that contain refined or added sugars:

- Energy drinks
- Soft drinks (even diet soda)
- Sweetened juices and fruit drinks
- Chewing gum
- Candy bars
- Sweets
- Pastries
- Sweetened chocolate

Alcoholic beverages

In terms of calorie content, you can drink a bottle of beer in your eating phase. But, if you consider what alcohol can do to your body, it is best to avoid it for the whole duration of your intermittent fasting. This is because of alcohol's ability to hinder fat burning in an individual.

Also, it can decrease your insulin sensitivity. Even drinking it during your eating phase can cause drawbacks to your progress, especially in improving your body's insulin sensitivity.

Processed food and canned goods

Processing and canning food are done to preserve food. To preserve food, large amounts of salt are added. Although salt does not contain significant calories, it stimulates your appetite and makes it difficult for you to sense if you already had enough food.

Furthermore, most processed food items are low in nutrients. Eating such items would only add calories but would not give your body precious vitamins, minerals, and antioxidants.

Simple carbohydrates

Simple carbohydrates are grains that have been stripped of its fiber and nutrients to make it taste or look better. In some cases, it is also done to improve its shelf life. It is a poor source of calories due to its low nutritional content. Also, simple carbohydrates are quickly digested and absorbed into glucose by the body.

Deep fried foods

Deep fried food items contain high levels of unhealthy fat and salt. It also contains high calories but low nutritional value, especially in the case French fries, potato chips, and similar food items.

Frozen meals

These meals contain high amounts of salt as a preservative. It is also pre-cooked and have likely lost a significant amount of its nutritional value because of it.

What to eat or drink during intermittent fasting

If it is not found on the previous list, you can eat or drink it. This list will not provide all items that you can eat or drink in intermittent fasting. Generally, as long as it is not on the "do not eat or drink" list, you can eat or drink it during your eating phases. The items mentioned below will be a few that you should eat more of while doing intermittent fasting (and while under a normal eating schedule). These food and drinks will help you have a healthier body and experience better results in intermittent fasting.

Whole carbohydrates

The best source of carbohydrates is those that have only been minimally processed. These still have their fiber intact and it did not go through a process that stripped it of its nutrients.

Moreover, because of its intact fiber, your body does not digest it as fast as simple carbohydrates. The body digests and absorbs it at a slower rate so your blood sugar levels would only experience a gradual increase.

Vegetables

Vegetables contain vitamins and minerals that support the various functions in your body. These also contain antioxidants that can induce autophagy for fighting toxins and suppressing free radicals in your body. Vegetables can help your digestion and make you feel fuller.

Water

It has no calories so you can drink it in both your fasting and eating periods. Aside from keeping you hydrated, it can reduce your hunger, maintain the health of your digestive system, regulate your body's temperature, and help flush out toxins and waste in your body.

But, avoid water that has been sweetened or artificially flavored. These contain sugars that would break you out of a fasted state.

Black coffee

By itself, coffee does not contain any calories. You can drink it during your fasting and eating periods. It can help manage your hunger by making you feel satiated.

But, drink coffee moderately when doing intermittent fasting since it enters your bloodstream on an empty stomach. Some coffee beans can make your stomach feel acidic if taken on an empty stomach. Avoid drinking more than two cups of coffee a day as it can cause anxiety, a jittery feeling, and weakness.

Tea

Like coffee, tea does not contain calories if drinking it without sugar or milk. It contains antioxidants that help manage free radicals and oxidative damage in your body. It also contains beneficial contents for your gut health and detoxification.

Milk

Milk is a great source of calcium, fat, and protein. It should be consumed in moderation. This is due to it containing lactose, which is a form of sugar. Avoid buying or drinking milk with added sugar in it.

Apple Cider Vinegar

Apple cider vinegar can prevent rapid glucose increase in your blood. It also contains acetic acid, which promotes fat burning and slows down the rate that your body stores fat.

Nuts

Almonds, cashews, hazelnuts, and walnuts contain a significant amount of good cholesterol and antioxidants. It's a great snack for your eating window.

Protein

Chicken, eggs, seafood, and beef are great sources of protein. Protein can give you better satiety and is a great way to feel fuller, especially for the first meal after your fast. It also provides your body with the amino acids for building and maintain muscles, and for regulating hormones.

Beans and legumes

Beans and legumes are great non-meat sources of protein. These are also rich in vitamins and minerals.

Medium chain triglyceride oil

Drinking medium chain triglyceride oil (or coconut oil) is a great way to break your fast. It does not contain carbohydrates but it suppresses your appetite. It provides your body energy through its fat content, which would be easily and immediately converted into ketone bodies. This influx of new fuel for the body would make your appetite more manageable as your break your fast. If you want to avoid overeating on your first meal, take one to two tablespoons of MCT oil or coconut oil at the start of your eating phase. After 30 minutes, you can start to eat your first meal for your eating phase.

Common Mistakes and How to Fix Them

A simple mistake can prevent you from benefiting from intermittent fasting. But, if you are making two or more of these mistakes, you are likely making things worse for your body by losing muscle mass or gaining weight. Here are the mistakes you want to avoid to prevent this from happening and how to fix them so you can actually lose weight.

Ignoring previous eating issues or disorders

There is nothing more harmful than the possible consequences if one chose to do an intermittent fast despite a history with eating disorders. Consult your doctor first before doing intermittent fasting. Also, seek alternative weight loss strategies that you can do.

Getting into it too fast

If this is your first weight loss plan, it is best to slowly get into intermittent fasting. Any diet or eating regimen will cause stress to your mind. If you are used to eating every two to four hours, you would not have a good experience jumping into a 16-hour fast immediately.

It is best to start with a shorter fasting period. You can start by reducing your number of meals. You can set a maximum number of meals for the day and set a schedule for it that you would follow. Once you get used to it, you can start by delaying your breakfast for a two to four hours in the morning. You can then adjust it until you reach the desired number of hours for your fasting period.

Not taking nutritional supplements

Regardless of how much food and variety is in your meals, it is difficult to acquire the full spectrum of vitamins and minerals for your body. You would need to take nutritional supplements if you want to your body to get the best nourishment. You can get what you would generally need from a daily multivitamin, a fish oil supplement (or similar omega-3 supplements), calcium supplement, and vitamin D supplement.

Eating too much carbohydrates and/or protein

Eating too many carbohydrates or protein than you need will cause your body to store excess energy into body fat. If you are not losing fat with intermittent fasting, you are probably making this mistake.

Generally, your total calorie intake for a day should consist of 45 to 65 percent of carbohydrates while 25 to 35 percent of protein. If you are aiming for fat loss, your carbohydrate intake should be lower while your protein consumption should increase.

Too much fat in the diet

If you eat too much fat, your body will prioritize burning the fat from your diet for energy. Again, you will find it difficult to lose weight and body fat if this is the case. To avoid this, keep your dietary fat intake to 20 to 35 percent of your total daily calories.

Eating too much calories

The intermittent fasting will put you on a calorie deficit. This is how you will lose fat. If you eat too much calories, you will find it difficult to lose fat and even experience weight gain.

To avoid eating too much, do not eat foods that will increase your appetite like keto bombs and salty food. You can also add more fiber and lean protein in your diet since it will help you feel more full.

Also, if you find yourself looking forward to breaking your fast, you might not be ready for your fasting schedule. Start with a shorter fasting period and gradually build it up.

Not enough calories

You do not need to restrict your calories in intermittent fasting. Your body will do it for you by feeling satiated after a meal. Restricting calories in intermittent fasting will just result in having too little calories available for your needs. Your body will respond by slowing down its metabolism, which will lead to weight gain.

The solution to this is to eat a meal with an amount close to how much you normally eat from a single meal without intermittent fasting.

Not enough water and salt or minerals

If you feel hungry but already had your meal, you are probably just thirsty. This is the stomach accumulating acid because it is empty for a long time. Drinking water prevents this accumulation and any complications caused by it.

However, you must balance this out with adequate salt intake by drinking a glass of water with a pinch of Himalayan pink salt at least once a day. It holds in the water you drink and prevent you from just eliminating it immediately through your urine.

Feeling too hungry

If you feel abnormally hungry in the middle or at the end of your fast, your fasting method is not suitable for your body's current state. This is usually the case for individuals who are not yet keto-adapted. This often results to overeating or eating anything even if its low quality calories.

To avoid this, start with a 10 or 12-hour fasting period and increase the time once you can go through it without being bothered by hunger.

Lack of exercise

Exercise provides a lot of benefits for your health. Not doing it due to intermittent fasting is the contrary to your pursuit of a healthier life. You have to figure out on how you can do it with intermittent fasting and just do it.

Walking and resistance training are the best form of exercise with intermittent fasting. Walking would not increase your stress levels while resistance training will increase your growth hormone production.

Stressful lifestyle

High emotional and physical stress will increase cortisol levels. If you combine this with intermittent fasting, you will like lose lean muscle mass, and gain weight from fat. This elevated stress is often a combination of poor sleep, poor stress management, and a busy lifestyle. If you cannot fix these causes for your increased stress, it might be best to handle these issues first before doing intermittent fasting.

Drinking Bulletproof coffee

Some would suggest that drinking Bulletproof coffee would not break your fast. But, this belief is completely wrong. Bulletproof coffee contains butter and MCT oil. Both of these contain calories,

Drinking Bulletproof coffee will not break your fast since it does not change your blood sugar levels. But, it will stop you from losing weight. Since you introduced butter and MCT oil into your body as sources of fat, the body will stop using your body fat to make ketone bodies for energy.

Repetitive eating pattern

Your body will eventually get used to your intermittent fasting method. Once it gets used to it, you will eventually stop progressing in losing weight. This is easily solved by switching to the other intermittent fasting methods in this book. It is important that you keep your body guessing and prevent it from getting used to a routine.

Getting Started with Intermittent Fasting

You now know what you need to get started. This chapter will take you through the steps so you can do intermittent fasting successfully in the short-term and on the long-term.

1. Identifying your goals

Before you start intermittent fasting, you must identify what you want to achieve from it. Whether you want to lose weight or have a better body composition, you would have to be specific about it. How much weight do you want to lose? How much lean muscle mass do you want to gain? How much body fat percentage do you want to end up with?

By identifying the specifics, you can gauge how much work you need to do to get there. It can give you a realistic timeframe on when you can achieve it if you stay consistent and do the right things.

You can also see if you would have to do the methods with the longer fasting periods eventually. You can even set a plan ahead of time so you can work towards the more advanced methods from day one of your intermittent fasting journey.

2. Know your daily calories

Intermittent fasting will only work if you know how much calories your body needs on a daily basis. You can find caloric intake calculators on the internet. These would give you an estimate based on your age, height, weight, gender, and activity level. Some calculators will also provide a daily amount for each macronutrient.

You will then divide this amount by how many meals you have per day. This would give you how much calories each of your meals should contain. You will use this to estimate how much you should eat for each meal while intermittent fasting.

This value is just an estimate. Actual calorie requirements vary on how your day is going. You would have to observe and feel how your body is doing. For example, if you are feeling too weak, you might be not eating enough. Or, if you are gaining weight, you are probably eating too much. From these observations, you can learn how to adjust your meals.

3. Pick a method that works best for you

The most suitable intermittent fasting method for you is not the one that would give you the fastest results. But, it is the method that you can consistently do long enough to reach your goal. If you are just starting out, it is best to begin with the 16/8 method or its variants – 14/10 method or the Lean Gains method. If you already have experience in intermittent fasting or have become comfortable with the 16/8 method, you can start aiming for doing the methods with the longer fasting periods like the One Meal a Day, Warrior Diet, 5:2

method, and eat stop eat. Once you have become comfortable with 20 to 24-hour fasts, you can then move on to alternate day fasting.

To avoid placing too much stress on your body, it is best to revert back to the 16/8, 14/10, or Lean Gains method if you plan to change your method to another fasting method. Most intermittent fasting enthusiasts use the 3 methods with 16 hours or less of fasting phase as their long-term methods. They use is as a way to bridge between methods that involve longer fasting hours or long and frequent fasting phases.

4. Set yourself up for success

Before you get started, you first have to prepare yourself and your environment for succeeding in intermittent fasting. The first step you must take is removing all the food and drinks included in the "do not eat or drink" list in this book. Switch these out for items included in the "eat or drink" list. You might have to talk to your family, roommate, or partner about this if you are living with them. Doing so will help you avoid temptation while in an intermittent fast.

Next, start getting enough sleep. It will make your intermittent fast more easy and effective. You also have to stop snacking and focus on getting your caloric needs from your meals. It will also help to gradually remove refined and added sugar from your diet. Applying these two fixes to your diet would make the first two weeks of your intermittent fast easier.

As you are doing these fixes, you can start scheduling your meals. This will help you get used to only eating at a certain time. For example, you can set all meals to have at least four hours interval. You can also restrict meals at a certain length of time like you can't eat between 8pm until 8am the next day. In this way, you are training yourself to be above the influence of your appetite or hunger.

5. Get started

Now that you have prepared yourself, you can now get started with intermittent fasting. You can immediately go straight to a 16/8 method if you find it easy skipping breakfast. But, it is also fine to transition into it, or a 14/10 method, by slowly increasing the time between your dinner the previous night and your first meal for the day.

However you choose to get started, it will be difficult at first. This is new for your body. You might not feel it on your first day but you will feel hunger during your first week. Just be patient and consistently follow the method that you set for yourself.

During your fasting phase, keep yourself hydrated. When you enter your eating phase, break your fast with nutrient-rich vegetables, lean meat, and fiber-rich whole carbohydrates. Continue this with the rest of your meals and snacks by getting most of your calories from items listed in the previous chapter. You must also take nutritional supplements to ensure that you are getting enough of the essential nutrients that your body needs.

6. Observe, feel, and adapt

Even if you research on medical journals and other people's experiences, you will still have to learn firsthand on how your body reacts to intermittent fasting. This is why you have to start slow so you can see if your body is taking it well. A gradual approach will also make it easier for you to change your plans, adjust your diet, or shift your fasting periods.

You must also keep track of your progress. Take note of your weight, muscle mass, and fat loss. If you are doing resistance training, you can compare how you did before and after you started intermittent fasting. You can also keep track the difference on how you progressed in your training. And, if you find that you are plateauing in your progress, you can choose if you want to take it further, change your goal, or maintain your current state. From there, you can start all over again in choosing a new method for more progress or a method for long-term intermittent fasting.

Doing Intermittent Fasting with a Ketogenic Diet

The ketogenic diet helps your body maintain a fat-burning state. It consists of low carbohydrate, moderate protein, and high fat proportions. This dietary composition causes similar benefits to intermittent fasting since it uses the same mechanics of reducing insulin resistance, stimulating fat metabolism, and promoting autophagy in the body. Because of their similar effects, you might find yourself wondering if you can do both at the same time.

The short answer to this is YES. You can combine the keto diet and intermittent fasting. But, it will be difficult. So, it is best that you have consistently done one of these two for a few months before combining it with the other. Here are the rules that you have to follow for a ketogenic diet:

- Macronutrient proportions are at 75 percent fat, 20% protein, and 5% carbohydrates.
- Macronutrient proportions are based on a person's daily caloric needs to maintain weight.
- You are restricted from food and beverage containing sugar, simple carbohydrates, alcohol, citrus, and fructose.
- Other forms of sugar are not allowed, such as maple syrup, honey, coconut sugar, and agave syrup.
- Starchy vegetables, beans, legumes, grains, and grain products are not prohibited.
- Unhealthy fats, like margarine and vegetable oils, should be avoided.
- Processed and packaged foods are not allowed.
- Food and drinks with sweeteners, preservatives, and artificial coloring in the ingredients should be avoided.

When combining a ketogenic diet with intermittent fasting, you have to make sure that you are getting enough calories and nutrients. You have to be sure that you are eating enough calories. Since you will be restricted from eating carbohydrates, you have to place an emphasis on your diet for nutrient-dense keto-approved food items. These include food high in healthy fat like avocado, high quality animal and plant source of protein, coconut oil, and leafy green vegetables.

Furthermore, you have to closely track the levels of your ketone bodies. You need to stay in ketosis without reaching the levels that indicate diabetic ketoacidosis (240 mg/dl). Because of this risk, you need to use glucose meters with a ketone measurement feature. Warning signs of diabetic ketoacidosis include vomiting for more than two hours, queasy feeling, stomachache, fruity breath, difficulty breathing, tiredness, dizziness, and confusion.

Lastly, you have to take a similar approach to how you started intermittent fasting. You have to take it slow. In this case, you will gradually decrease carbohydrates in your diet. This will help your body get used to having no access to carbohydrates and to being in an almost constant state of ketosis.

The same precautions from intermittent fasting apply in this combination with the keto diet. You have to observe how your body is doing. You have to make sure that you do not feel like you are not getting enough calories. You also have to ensure that you feel well doing it. Lastly, you have to adjust the diet and the fasting length if you ever find it necessary to do so.

Intermittent Fasting Shopping List

Meat

Meat will provide your body with the protein it needs. The best meats that you can incorporate in your diet are lean red meats like beef, pork, mutton, and venison. These particular meats are rich in Vitamin B12. It is best to choose unprocessed meats since processed ones are high in salt and lower in micronutrient content.

Although it's not meat, eggs should be part of your list. This is an excellent source of protein and is quite versatile for different recipes.

Vegan Sources of Protein

If meat is not something you wish to eat, there are plant-based sources of protein. Soy-based products are one of the highest sources of plant-based protein. There's also lentils, chickpeas, and beans that are not only versatile food items but also contain fiber, potassium, and iron.

As for vegetables, you can find significant amounts of protein in kale, mushrooms, and broccoli. There are also seeds high in protein such as hemp seeds and chia seeds, and grain like quinoa and seitan.

- Tofu
- Edamame
- Tempeh
- Beans
- Green or red lentils
- Chickpeas
- Chia seeds
- Hemp seeds
- Quinoa
- Seitan

Vegetables

Vegetables contain vitamins and minerals that support your metabolism. This metabolism should be at its best shape if you want to lose weight. Buy vegetables that contain the most number and variety of micronutrients for your body.

- Asparagus

- Beet root
- Broccoli
- Carrot
- Cauliflower
- Celery
- Chili peppers
- Lettuce
- Pumpkin
- Spinach

Fish and seafood

Fish are rich in omega-3 fatty acids. It is essential for you're the health and function of your bones, brain, and heart. The best sources for this fat include sardines, mackerel, tuna, anchovies, and wild salmon.

Vegan sources of omega 3 fatty acids

Omega 3 fatty acids are a part of a healthy diet. Fortunately, there are vegan sources available that can provide a comparable amount to fish.

- Chia seeds
- Edamame
- Seaweed
- Kidney beans
- Hemp seeds
- Flaxseeds
- Walnuts

Nutritional Supplements

Your body does not stop needing the micronutrients it requires. Unfortunately, it is very difficult to get all of vitamins and minerals you need through only your diet. You have to take nutritional supplements if you want your metabolism and your body at its best.

- Daily multivitamin for vitamins and minerals
- Omega-3 supplement of your choice
- Vitamin D

- Calcium

If you are doing the Lean Gains method, you would also need a BCAA supplement and Whey protein for your pre-workout.

Dairy

Dairy is an excellent source of protein, calcium and fat. The best dairy products are those that went through very minimal processing.

- Organic dairy
- Cottage cheese
- Yogurt
- Greek yogurt

Fats

Fats are a great way to satisfy your appetite and make you feel fuller. Furthermore, using these oil in your diet will give your body nutrients. Some of these are also better cooking oils for cooking the recipes in the next chapter.

- Coconut Oil (and/or MCT oil)
- Heavy cream
- Olive oil
- Butter

Fruits

Fruits contain vitamins and fibers. It's a great snack in between meals. Since it does not contain much calories, you do not have to worry about overeating because of snacks in your eating phases.

- Apple
- Avocado
- Banana
- Berries
- Grapefruit
- Grapes
- Lemon (to flavor water or for salads)
- Melon
- Orange

Beverages

Non-caloric beverages are a great way to ease your mind during your fasting phase.
- Green tea
- Black tea
- Herbal tea
- Coffee (unsweetened and no cream or dairy)

Intermittent Fasting Recipes and Meal Plans

Essential Intermittent Fasting Recipes

Smoothies

Avocado Breakfast Smoothie

Serving size: 1

Total calories: 1,099

Carbohydrates: 42.6g

Fiber: 27.8g

Fats: 104.6g

Protein: 14.1g

Ingredients
- 1 avocado
- 1 cup coconut milk
- 1 cup spinach or kale
- 1 handful blueberries
- 1 tablespoon chia seeds

Instructions:

Blend all the ingredients.

Avocado Protein Shake

Serving size: 1

Total calories: 564

Carbohydrates: 21.3g

Fiber: 8.6g

Fats: 42.6g

Protein: 31.2g

Ingredients
- ½ avocado
- 1 handful spinach
- ½ cup water
- ½ cup milk
- 1 scoop protein powder
- 1 tablespoon fresh parsley
- 1 tablespoon coconut oil
- 1 tablespoon walnuts
- 1 teaspoon cacao powder
- 1 teaspoon cinnamon powder
- 1/3 teaspoon sea salt

Instructions

Put all the ingredients in a blender. Blend for 1 minute.

Cashew Milkshake

Serving size: 1

Total calories: 398

Carbohydrates: 53.3g

Fiber: 6.8g

Fats: 17.6g

Protein: 14.3g

Ingredients
- 1 medium banana
- 1 cup soy milk
- 3 tablespoons cashews
- 3 teaspoons cacao powder
- A pinch of Himalayan salt

Instructions

Put all the ingredient in a blender. Blend.

Meals

Banana and toasted oatmeal

Serving size: 1

Total calories: 700

Carbohydrates: 100.4g

Fiber: 11.3g

Fats: 24.7g

Protein: 24.2g

Ingredients

- 1 cup rolled oats
- 1 ½ cup milk
- ½ tablespoon butter
- 1 banana, sliced

Instructions

1. Heat a pot over medium heat.
2. Add and melt the butter. Toast the rolled oats.
3. Once toasted, add the milk and boil.
4. Reduce the heat to low once it boils. Simmer for three minutes while stirring occasionally.
5. Transfer to a bowl and add the sliced banana. Serve.

Beans and Brown Rice

Serving size: 4

Total calories: 271

Carbohydrates: 47.8g

Fiber: 8.8g

Fats: 5.3g

Protein: 10g

Ingredients

- 15 oz black beans, undrained
- 14.5 oz stewed tomatoes
- 1 ½ cups instant brown rice
- 1 onion, chopped
- 1 tablespoon olive oil
- ½ teaspoon garlic powder
- 1 teaspoon dried oregano

Instructions

1. Heat olive oil on a small pot over medium high heat.
2. Add onion and cook until translucent. Add the beans and tomatoes. Stir.
3. Add the oregano and garlic powder. Stir then bring to a boil.
4. Once it boils, add and stir in the brown rice. Cover and reduce heat. Simmer for five minutes.
5. Remove from the heat and let it rest for five minutes.
6. Serve with your choice of protein.

Liver Burgers

Serving size: 1

Total calories: 947

Carbohydrates: 13.2g

Fiber: 0.3g

Fats: 39g

Protein: 129.4g

Ingredients

- ½ pound ground beef
- ½ pound ground beef liver
- ½ teaspoon cumin powder
- ½ teaspoon garlic powder
- Salt and pepper to taste
- Olive oil

Instructions

1. Mix all of the ingredient in a bowl
2. Heat olive oil on a skillet over medium-high heat
3. Cook the burgers to desired doneness.
4. Serve with salad or with whole wheat burger buns and preferred salad dressing.

Scrambled Eggs with Smoked Salmon

Serving size: 2

Total calories: 471

Carbohydrates: 22.2g

Fiber: 6.1g

Fats: 31.6g

Protein: 27.5g

Ingredients

- 8 midi vine tomatoes, halved
- 3 large eggs
- 1¼oz smoked salmon, roughly chopped
- 1 tbsp chopped chives
- 1oz fresh watercress, to serve
- 1 tablespoon olive oil
- freshly ground black pepper to taste

Instructions

1. Season the halved tomatoes with pepper. Heat the olive oil on a pan over medium heat. Cook the tomatoes until soft while stirring but without breaking.
2. Scramble the eggs and season with pepper. Add the salmon and chives.
3. Pour the scrambled egg mixture into the pan and cook it gently while stirring gently. This would take around three to four minutes. Remove from the heat and continue the gentle stir.
4. Add the watercress and serve.

Salmon and Roasted Vegetables

Serving size: 1

Total calories: 983

Carbohydrates: 7.9g

Fiber: 0.4g

Fats: 67.4g

Protein: 90.4g

Ingredients

- 1 pound salmon or other fish of choice
- 2 tablespoons fresh lemon juice
- 2 tablespoons ghee
- 4 cloves garlic, finely diced
- ½ cup vegetable of choice
- 1 tablespoon coconut oil

Instructions

1. Preheat the oven at 400 F.
2. Mix the diced garlic, ghee, and lemon juice.
3. Place the salmon in foil and pour the mixture on top.
4. Wrap and seal the salmon in the foil.
5. Place it on a baking sheet with the vegetables.
6. Drizzle the vegetables with coconut oil.
7. Roast for 15 minutes or until the salmon is cooked through.

Easy and Healthy Chicken Recipe

Serving size: 4

Total calories: 255

Carbohydrates: 16.4g

Fiber: 0.7g

Fats: 8.3g

Protein: 28.3g

Ingredients
- 4 skinless and boneless chicken breast, halved
- 1 onion, chopped
- 3 tablespoons tomato paste
- 2 tablespoons soy sauce
- 2 tablespoons lemon juice
- 1 teaspoon ground black pepper
- 2 tablespoons olive oil

Instructions
1. Heat olive oil over medium high heat.
2. Sauté onion. Once it becomes translucent, add chicken and brown on all sides.
3. Combine and mix the tomato paste, soy sauce, lemon juice, and pepper.
4. Pour over the chicken and bring to a boil. Cover and simmer for 25 to 30 minutes.
5. Serve with beans and brown rice or salad/

Easy Beef Stir-fry

Serving size: 4

Total calories: 255

Carbohydrates: 16.4g

Fiber: 0.7g

Fats: 8.3g

Protein: 28.3g

Ingredients

- 1 pound beef sirloin, cut into 2 to 2.5 inch strips
- 1 ½ cups of fresh broccoli florets
- 1 red bell pepper, cut into thin sticks
- 2 medium carrots, thinly sliced
- 1 green onion, chopped
- 2 tablespoons soy sauce
- 2 tablespoons toasted sesame seeds
- 1 teaspoon minced garlic
- 1 tablespoon olive oil

Instructions

1. Heat olive oil on a large skillet over medium-high heat.
2. Cook the beef until brown. Move the beef to the side and add the broccoli florets, carrots, bell pepper, garlic, and green onion on the center.
3. Cook while stirring vegetables for two minutes
4. Mix the beef and the vegetables. Add soy sauce and sesame seeds. Mix well until vegetables become tender.
5. Serve with salad or beans and brown rice.

Tuna Salad Bowl

Serving size: 1

Total calories: 866

Carbohydrates: 16.7

Fiber: 10.3g

Fats: 71.3g

Protein: 44.2g

Ingredients

- 120g canned tuna, drained
- ½ avocado, sliced
- 1 large handful watercress, washed and dried
- 1 large egg, boiled, peeled, and halved
- ¼ red onion, finely sliced
- 10 walnuts, halved
- 10 putted black olives
- 1 tablespoon mayonnaise
- 1 tablespoon olive oil
- 1 teaspoon sesame seeds
- Pepper to taste

Instructions

1. Preheat the oven to 400 F.
2. Place the walnuts on a baking sheet and roast for 6 to 8 minutes or until golden. Take it out of the oven to cool.
3. Place the watercress in a bowl. Add the olives, egg, avocado, and walnuts.
4. Mix the olive oil and mayonnaise. Drizzle the mixture on the contents of the bowl.
5. Add the tuna and sprinkle the sesame seed on the salad. Season with pepper to taste.

Recipes for a Ketogenic Diet

Delicious Cauliflower Rice

Serving size: 1

Total calories: 1011

Carbohydrates: 104g

Fiber: 24.4g

Fats: 54g

Protein: 42.4g

Ingredients

- 24 oz cauliflower florets
- 6 oz broccoli florets, chopped
- 2 carrots, peeled and grated
- 2 large eggs, beaten
- ½ cup corn
- ½ cup peas
- 2 green onions, thinly sliced
- 2 cloves garlic, minced
- 1 medium onion, diced
- 2 tablespoons low sodium soy sauce
- 1 tablespoon sesame oil
- 1 tablespoon freshly grated ginger
- 2 tablespoons olive oil, divided
- ½ teaspoon sesame seeds
- ¼ teaspoon white pepper

Instructions

1. In a food processor, pulse the cauliflower until it is broken down to a similar appearance as rice. Set aside.
2. Whisk the soy sauce, sesame oil, ginger, and white pepper in a small bowl. Set aside.

3. Heat half of the olive oil in a medium skillet over low heat. Cook the scrambled eggs until completely cooked through. Flip once to cook the other side. Transfer to a plate and let it cool. Dice the cooked scrambled egg once cool. Set aside.

4. Heat the rest of the olive oil in the skillet at medium high heat. Saute the garlic and onion. Once the onions become translucent, add the the broccoli, corn, carrots, and peas. Stir constantly the contents until the vegetables become tender.

5. Add the cauliflower rice, and the mixture of green onions, eggs, and soy sauce. Continuously stir until the cauliflower rice becomes tender. This means that all of the contents have been heated through.

6. Garnish with sesame seeds. Serve while hot.

Greek Garlic Chicken

Serving size: 4

Total calories: 338

Carbohydrates: 6.2g

Fiber: 2.4g

Fats: 19.2g

Protein: 35g

Ingredients

- 1 pound chicken thighs
- ½ pound asparagus, ends removed
- 3 cloves of garlic, minced
- 3 tablespoon olive oil, divided
- 1 zucchini, sliced in half moon shapes
- 1 teaspoon oregano
- 1 lemon, juiced
- 1 lemon sliced
- Salt and pepper to taste

Instructions

1. Combine 2 tables spoons of lemon juice, olive oil, oregano, and minced garlic in a large-sized bowl. Whisk until combined.
2. Toss the chicken thighs into the bowl and coat it with the mixture. Cover the bowl with plastic wrap and marinate the chicken in the refrigerator. Take it out after 2 hours.
3. Season both sides of the chicken thighs with salt and pepper.
4. Preheat the oven to 425 F. Heat the rest of the olive oil in an ovenproof skillet over medium high heat. Place the chicken thighs on the skillet with the skin-side down. Pour the marinade onto the skillet.
5. Let the skin-side of the chicken thighs become golden (10 minutes). Flip the chicken thighs then add the asparagus, lemon slices, and the zucchini.
6. Transfer the skillet to the oven. Cook for 15 minutes, or until the chicken gets thoroughly cooked and the vegetables become tender.

Keto Omelet

Serving size: 4

Total calories: 288

Carbohydrates: 6.8g

Fiber: 1.3g

Fats: 23.9g

Protein: 12.9g

Ingredients

- 2 medium eggs
- ¼ cup diced tomatoes
- ¼ cup diced onion
- ¼ cup shredded lettuce
- 2 tablespoons cream, full fat
- 1 tablespoon butter

Instructions

1. Whisk the eggs, cream, tomatoes, onion, and lettuce in a bowl.
2. Heat the frying pan over low medium heat.
3. Melt the butter in it and pour the egg mixture. Swirl the frying pan to evenly spread the egg in the skillet.
4. Cover the skillet with a lid and let it cook for two minutes.
5. Remove the lid, and use a spatula to transfer from the pan on to the plate.

Keto Beef Stroganoff

Serving size: 10

Total calories: 353

Carbohydrates: 3.4g

Fiber: 1g

Fats: 23.5g

Protein: 30.1g

Ingredients

- 3 pounds fat-trimmed beef brisket, cut against the grain into half-inch pieces
- 1 white onion, finely chopped
- 16 oz fresh mushrooms sliced
- 1 /12 cups beef broth
- ¾ cup sour cream
- ¼ cup mayonnaise
- ¼ cup avocado oil
- 2 teaspoons minced garlic
- 2 teaspoons ground thyme
- 2 tablespoon apple cider vinegar
- 1 ½ teaspoon xanthan gum
- ¾ teaspoon salt
- ½ teaspoon black pepper

Instructions

1. Heat a large saucepan over medium heat. Add the avocado oil, finely chopped onions, and minced garlic into it. Sauté contents for 3 minutes or until fragrant.
2. Add the cut beef brisket pieces, pepper, salt, and thyme. Sauté contents for 8 minutes or until beef is cooked. Make sure to stir frequently so the beef is browned evenly.
3. Turn down the heat to medium low. Add the beef broth and apple cider vinegar into the large saucepan. Simmer the contents for 30 minutes. Do not cover.
4. Add the mushrooms. Cover the pan and simmer for an hour and 30 minutes.

5. Remove the saucepan from the heat. Stir in the sour cream and mayonnaise in increments of a ¼ teaspoon. Incorporate it completely into the contents of the saucepan.
6. Add the xanthan gum until the liquid contents thicken.
7. Cover the saucepan with a lid and let it sit for 10 minutes.
8. Once the ten minutes is done, serve in bowls.

Meal Plan

You can use the smoothies in the provided recipes to break your fast. These are low carbohydrate meals that can be quickly digested and absorbed. Moreover, since these are high in fat, you will feel fuller compared to a regular meal.

If you prefer an actual meal to break your fast, you can do the oatmeal recipe. It consists of whole carbohydrates so it will not be absorbed easily by your body.

As for the rest of your eating phase, you can eat the other meals. These contain enough calories to bring up your total to 2,000 calories. You can adjust it according to your personal daily calorie intake.

Even if you are using a method that only allows for a single meal or a short eating phase, you can use these recipes and still get your required calories. You can choose a meal with meat or fish and combine it with a salad or the beans and rice. If you are still hungry, you can make a smaller portion of one of the smoothies.

If you are following the lean gains method, you can use one of the smoothie recipes as a pre-workout meal. However, you have to reduce the amount to coincide with the methods' limits. You can aside the rest for your post-workout meal.

Conclusion

Intermittent fasting provides women a simpler and more convenient method of losing weight. If done right, it also serves as a better weight management plan in the long term. It does not diminish the body's metabolism rate unlike in calorie restrictive diets that result in the body adapting a slower rate of metabolism. Because of this, women using this are less likely to experience the yoyo effect from most weight-loss diets.

What is great about intermittent fasting is that it goes beyond helping people lose weight. It triggers the body's natural self-cleanup and repair process known as autophagy. It places the body into a balance with the state of growth it constantly experience with the modern diet and lifestyle. Because of this balance, the body is at a lower risk for diseases associated with today's diet and lifestyle.

People who did intermittent fasting have experienced great benefits for their health. Several studies have observed improvements on people with high blood pressure, type 2 diabetes, high insulin resistance, metabolic syndrome, neurodegenerative disorders, and cardiovascular disease. Aside from managing these conditions, researchers have also observed intermittent fasting of helping those at risk for these degenerative diseases reduce their chances of preventing them. Even those who are not at risk experience benefits from their health, normal healthy individuals help their body fight aging, improve its immunity from infectious diseases, and increase its energy levels through intermittent fasting.

Despite these benefits for women, this book does not gloss over fact that it has risks. It recognizes the conditions unique to women that intermittent fasting could aggravate. The most important one discussed in this book is how the eating regimen affects hormone production. Although it eventually continues to its normal rhythm, small interruptions are enough to cause issues for the fertility, menstruation cycle, and overall reproductive health of women. It might seem small for those who are not planning to get pregnant soon. But, these hormones also affect other aspects of the body's health.

Fortunately, this risk is easily managed. It just requires an adequate protein intake that maintains one's hormonal balance. If this is not enough, adjustments to the time and frequency of fasting phases can also be done. Overall, contrary to what critics say, it is not a deal breaker for intermittent fasting but just something to be aware of.

Compared to other weight loss strategies, intermittent fasting is the least restrictive. In fact, one can say that no other diet or eating regimen compares to the amount of flexibility it allows. Beginners do not have to do something that they find to be too difficult. They can do a method that suits their current state of health, keto-adaptation, or lifestyle, and they would still benefit from intermittent fasting. Likewise, more advanced intermittent fasters have options to prevent a plateau in their efforts for weight loss. They can adjust their current method to lengthen or increase their fasting periods. Or, they can choose another method that would force their body to adapt to a new pattern.

Moreover, intermittent fasting can be tweaked to accommodate a person's lifestyle. If they cannot fast due to their work, they can adjust the fasting phases to accommodate their responsibilities. If they have health goals that require more caloric intake, they can increase their calories but they would still benefit from the effects of fasting. Even those who cannot do the full intermittent fasting experience can use its concept by scheduling their meals at only certain times. Basically, it is just your schedule for eating. It just turns out that it provides these amazing benefits for your body.

Of course, this book did not leave you merely knowing things about intermittent fasting. It provided you some of the priceless information that other intermittent fasters have experienced. The book revealed the common mistakes of those who failed in this regimen and provided the possible solutions of those who succeeded to overcome or prevent the said mistakes. It also provided what women should watch out for due to their dietary needs and solutions that they can apply for a successful and healthy intermittent fast.

You also know the steps to take so that you can get started with intermittent fasting. You know the importance of setting your goal. You were provided some strategies on how to help your body adjust to fasting phases even before you get started.

The steps on how you can start intermittent fasting

Important health considerations were also brought up and the risk when intermittent fasting is concerned. Moreover, common mistakes when doing intermittent fasting is discussed and some suggestions for solutions were given.

With the knowledge provided and the actionable information provided in this book, you can now take on the task of getting yourself ready and getting started with intermittent fasting. You know what to and what not to eat and drink so you will keep your eating and phases on point for your goal and your overall health. You also have the knowledge of what to watch out for, and how to adjust your regimen to avoid mishaps and succeed in achieving your goal. The only that is missing is you getting started.

Everything that you have learned from this book is worthless if you do not use it. You can start by attempting your first 12 hour fast and see how it feel. Or, you can start timing your meals so you only eat during the time you specify for yourself. However you choose to get started, the important thing is that you start.

Book #4

Autophagy Secrets

Promote Longevity and Anti-Aging, Burn Fat, and Achieve Peak Performance with Intermittent Fasting and Autophagy

Introduction

Autophagy literally means "self-eating" from the Greek.

It may sound cannibalistic at first but if you consider the fact that it happens in the cellular level then it doesn't sound so morbid. In this book we highlight medical research that has been done that highlights the benefits of this naturally occurring bodily process that promotes self-healing and cellular recycling.

The medical world still doesn't understand how it fully works but we at this point know enough to be able to take advantage of this metabolic process. There are strategies that you can employ today to help you maximize the health benefits from autophagy.

Imagine being able to induce healing at the cellular level. You will enable your body to heal from insulin resistance, burn body fat, repair skin cells, heal brain cells, and a host of other benefits just because you gave your body a chance to let its inherent natural ability to regenerate and heal itself.

This is an exciting field of ongoing study and this book shows you how to make use of present-day techniques to enhance your body's autophagic processes. We will cover the pros and cons as well as a bit of the science behind it. The terms and jargon have been simplified as much as possible so that you the lay person can understand the bodily processes being described.

Thanks for purchasing this book, I hope you enjoy it!

Chapter 1: What is Autophagy?

The word autophagy is derived from the Greek words auto, which can be translated to "self", and phagein, which is translated to "to eat." You put those two together and what you have is that autophagy means "to eat the self"—that sort of sounds macabre to a certain degree.

This "eating of the self" that occurs in the human body is actually more of recycling than actually consuming or digesting one's body parts. Big hint: all of this occurs on the cellular level. It's not like your body's digestive system will go gung ho and start acting on your other organs.

Autophagy and Apoptosis

Autophagy is actually a wonderful thing—it is the body's way of recycling its own broken-down parts. Yes, again that is usually done on the cellular level. The old and worn out machinery of our cells like the cell membranes, proteins, organelles, and such will be broken down and then reused since there is no longer enough energy to sustain it as a part of the functioning whole.

Note that this is not a wild viral thing that happens in the body. It is actually quite an orderly process and it shows how well our bodies have been designed. An old cell that undergoes autophagy is degraded, broken up, and then recycled down to its cellular components.

Another similar bodily process is called apoptosis. Apoptosis means a preprogrammed cellular death—yes, equally morbid sounding as autophagy. What this really is in simple terms is that when the body's cells have undergone several times of cell division it is programmed to die.

It would sound like the body is some huge ingrate getting rid of things after it has gained all the benefits from them. However, that is not the case. Both autophagy and apoptosis are actually beneficial to your very own health.

How is that?

Well let's use a certain analogy—think of a brand-new car. Every cell in your body is like that car. When it was brand spanking new it was efficient and it was very helpful. Of course as the years went by your car gets an oil change, you get it tuned up, and maybe you added some decals and perhaps you even upgraded or customized certain parts.

However, as the years roll by your car gets older and it will get beat up from all the use and abuse you give it. After driving it for more than a decade or two, the maintenance costs for what used to be a wonderful piece of machinery will keep going up.

It was a great car—no doubt about it. It has given you a lot of great memories but it's just that it is no longer beneficial to keep it. It breaks down more than you are driving it since its serviceable life has already passed.

What's the best option for you at that point? It is to sell the car, break it down, and maybe reuse the parts for other projects that the buyer may have in mind. What do you end up with? You get to buy a new car.

The same thing happens to the cells of your body—believe it or not.

But the body's cells are more efficient than we think we know when it comes to these matters. The usable life of each cell has already been predetermined or pre-calculated. After so and so number of cell divisions it has been predetermined that the original cell is already old and clunky.

These old cells are no longer functioning at optimum levels. It costs more to maintain them than to get new ones so the body opts for the better option—apoptosis. That way you don't need to worry about the proverbial car breaking down at the worst possible moment—when you need it the most.

Looking at It at the Sub Cellular Level

Think of autophagy as the process that happens before apoptosis. Autophagy is the maintenance period where the cell can still go on and it just needs replacement for certain parts. If after some time that no longer works then apoptosis kicks in so that an entire new cell will take the place of the old one.

Going back to the car analogy, sometimes all a car needs is a new battery, maybe a replacement spark plug, or some other part and then it will be good to go. This very thing happens to the cells at a sub cellular level. For instance only certain organelles are destroyed so that the cell can make new ones.

The old organelles can then be removed along with the rest of the cellular debris. Do you know what that roughly translates to? It means your body is naturally getting a detox at the cellular level. Now that is what a real detox is – the old and bad parts that no longer function is discarded and thus the working and functional environment of a cell is optimized.

Discovery and Short History

The bodily process of autophagy was first discovered in January of 1962 at the Rockefeller Institute by Professor Keith R. Porter and Thomas Ashford, his student. In their studies they noted that after adding glucagon, they noticed an increased number of lysosomes. Lysosomes are that part of the cell that is responsible for breaking down parts that are no longer needed. It was Christian de Duve, a Nobel Prize winner, who eventually coined the term "autophagy."

More studies on autophagy were conducted in the 90s. One of the discoveries was that there were genes that were related to the process. Michael Thumm and notably Yoshinori Ohsumi discovered starvation-induced non-selective autophagy. Ohsumi eventually was awarded the Nobel Prize in Physiology or Medicine in 2016.

It was in this turn of the 21st century when the field of autophagy research has gained a lot of traction. We don't know everything about it but we are learning a lot. There is plenty of scientific research that have been and are being conducted especially those that are related to cancer, aging, and other neurodegenerative conditions.

Chapter 2: Understanding Its Pros and Cons

Now, even though the name of this bodily process kind of sounds like it is a bad state of affairs, it is a proverbial fountain of youth. From the discussion in the previous chapter we have learned that it is one of the ways the body renews itself from the core of our beings.

There is ongoing medical research on how to use of autophagy as a kind of therapy. That is one of the many uses that experts are looking into. However it should be pointed out that autophagy as a therapy is not for everyone.

It also has downsides. In this chapter we will go over both the pros and the cons of using autophagy as a therapeutic approach.

It May Preserve and Lengthen Your Life

Autophagy as a therapeutic approach may save your life—okay that sounded like something from an infomercial. However, take note that it is accurate, scientifically speaking. It is after all a core mechanism of the body that occurs naturally.

Our bodies enter different states of autophagy at different times and at different degrees. It is a process that your body performs to basically save your life. It basically kicks in when you are sick, when you are in a state of starvation (especially when in a prolonged starvation mode) , when you are suffering from an infection, and of course when you are under a lot of stress.

It is used by the body to maximize the repairs that can be done and to ensure minimal damage in case a virus or any invading bacteria or otherwise has come to threaten your bodily systems. Is it possible to induce autophagy without illness or anything life threatening? The answer is yes.

That is best achieved with the help of intermittent fasting. That is the best known way to put the human body in that state of "self-eating." But studies have also shown that adding some fat in intermittent fats as well as other nutrients and other kinds of food can also help boost the autophagy process.

When you do intermittent fasting your body enters starvation mode every now and then. Doing so will also starve an infectious intruder of the glucose it usually feeds on. Since the body's glucose levels go down it also produces another effect—inflammation is also reduced.

Since inflammation is reduced the immune system is given a bigger legroom to do its job since it can concentrate on fighting off the infection instead. In short, autophagy gives your body's immune system an easier time taking action.

We see this in nature a lot of times and we just didn't know it back then. Animals have basically evolved based on their body's autophagy process. When they are sick they conserve energy and refuse to eat. They go into low energy and starvation mode so that their bodies can beat the infection. Well, they don't have medicine after all.

Wild animals also enter this state when food sources are scarce. You can say that it is their way to extend their lives. How does that translate to us humans? Autophagy is a critical part of our bodily systems (particularly the immune systems) as well. When it kicks in you are better able to handle illnesses and researchers have found that it can also help reduce one's risk of developing cancer.

Improves Quality of Life

Autophagy actually has anti-aging effects, which is one of the ways it can help improve your quality of life. It helps to make your skin healthier since the skin cells get renewed, which means newer and younger skin replaces the old skin. However, the benefits of this natural bodily process is not only skin deep.

Recent studies have shown that autophagy improves your overall cellular health. That means every cell in your body can potentially benefit from this process. Remember that it was explained in the previous chapter that autophagy is more like a recycling process.

The damaged parts are taken down and recycled and newer parts of the body's cells are grown in their stead. This same process of recycling and renewal also gets rid of toxic materials that get lodged in the body and it is all done naturally. You can say that this is the body's automatic and natural method for detoxification.

By reducing the toxic damage the body has received you are actually improving your biological age. You may be older chronologically (i.e. according to the day you were born) but you are internally younger physically. The better your body is at repairing itself will dictate how young you really are in terms of biology.

Fine Tuning for Your Metabolism

One of the parts of the cell that gets removed, recycled, and replaced during autophagy is the mitochondria. You can think of the mitochondria as the engine of your cells. They make each cell work as efficiently as they can. Of course just like a car's engine, the cellular engine will also come to a point when it will break down.

Just like an engine, mitochondria burn the body's fuel (mainly fat) and then it produces the needed energy called ATP or adenosine triphosphate. ATP is an organic chemical that gives the cells and the entire body in general the energy that it needs to function.

ATP is used by your muscles so they can contract. They are used by the body for chemical synthesis (i.e. chemical processing). They are also used by your nervous system propagate nerve impulses so that your brain can better control your body. ATP is used everywhere in short.

Now, it isn't that hard to imagine that if the mitochondria has been damaged or plagued by toxins then it gets damaged and/or comes to a point when it can no longer function properly. Thus it will also need to be repaired or recycled and then replaced with a new one. And that is what autophagy is for. It basically gives your cell's engine a tuneup—well it's more of an overhaul actually.

Reduce Risk of Neurodegenerative Diseases

Neurodegenerative diseases are the kind of medical conditions that occur in the brain. They usually don't happen in a day, month, or even a year. They are the diseases of the aging brain and they usually take many years to develop. By the time you know it they have already entered into their full blown state.

They develop that way because it takes many years for proteins that are found around as well as in your brain cells to accumulate, develop, and get mis-folded. In time they eventually don't work the way they should anymore.

Again, researchers believe that it is possible for autophagy to be a big help in this department. In this case the process of autophagy aids in the clean-up of the proteins in the brain that are no longer performing, which helps reduce their build up. This process reduces the build-up of amyloid in Alzheimer's patients. In the case of Parkinson's patients it helps to reduce α-synuclein build up in the brain.

There are researchers who believe that dementia somewhat goes hand in hand with another medical condition—diabetes. When someone consistently has high blood pressure, this state or condition actually prevents the body from activating the autophagy process. That means the cells of people with diabetes and related diseases have cells that are already clogged up.

Inflammation Regulation

The process of self-eating can both increase inflammation and also reduce inflammation. It is important that we put that out in the open. When germs, bacteria, or viruses invade the body, the process of autophagy helps to boost the immune response.

The immune system already has less clutter to deal with so it performs better. This means whenever it is needed, your body's immune system can more effectively increase the level of inflammation in an area of the body as needed.

However, that isn't actually always the case. Most of the time autophagy actually reduces inflammations in the body. The cleanup process clears away any excess antigens (i.e. the proteins that trigger the immune response) thus inflammations are reduced.

Cellular Toxin and Microbial Removal

Remember that the cleanup process that occurs during autophagy is in the cellular level. There are microbes, viruses, as well as toxins that get into the cells. Examples of which are HIV and Mycobacterium tuberculosis. These get dumped out of the cells during autophagy along with the toxins that can produce food borne illnesses.

Muscular Performance

Every time you exercise you create micro tears in your muscles. That means pumping iron or running doesn't really make your muscles more defined and larger. It is the repair that happens after you work out that creates those abs and other well defined and toned muscular features.

It requires energy to exercise so that your muscles can perform how they're supposed to and it also requires energy to repair them when you rest. When your body undergoes a cleanup the cells in your muscular tissues will require energy both when they are in use and when they are being repaired. This balance in the use of energy helps to provide more energy for the repair process of your muscles and also reduces the risk of any future damage that will be made when you exercise.

Preventing the Onset of Cancer

Since autophagy aids in the control of chronic inflammation then it is a big help to prevent the onset of cancer. Research also suggests that it may also suppress other bodily processes like DNA damage response and genome instability that also lead to the formation of cancer cells.

However, this is a double edged sword as one research points out [1]. Researchers suggest that yes autophagy may help prevent the onset of cancer but for those who already have cancer autophagy may not be as beneficial as people may have thought.

As cancer progresses, the cancer cells can also activate autophagy but not to clean up cells. It uses the process of degradation and recycling of cells to obtain their much needed fuel. It is also their way to hide from the body's immune system.

Note that when it comes to this field of study there is still a lot of research that needs to be done. We know that chemotherapy induces damage to cells that are non-cancerous and this will also trigger autophagy.

One interesting subject that researchers are looking into is the comparison of chemotherapy and autophagy as a treatment. The goal is to see if autophagy can trigger an immune response that will attack cancer cells and comparing its effectiveness to treatments like chemotherapy.

Adding Glow to Your Skin

The biggest organ in the body is obviously the skin. It is the organ that is used to represent yourself to the world as it were. And since it is the organ that is one of the organs that are directly exposed to the environment it does take a lot of beating.

The skin takes punishment from environmental conditions, chemicals we apply on it, changes in humidity, and the changing temperatures from heat to cold and back. Oh, our skin also gets physically damaged from bruises, cuts, and other physical injuries.

Now, we know that our skin cells tend to change often due to all of this stress that it goes through. However, toxins still tend to accumulate on our skin and when that happens the skin tends to age. Left on its own it just can't cope with all that punishment. Using autophagy as a treatment may be able to boost the rejuvenation that the skin needs.

Weight Management

The science that purportedly supports the use of autophagy for weight loss isn't completely there yet. There are studies that suggest that it might help people maintain a healthy weight but more studies are required to confirm everything.

Here are some of the factors that lend credence to the use of autophagy for weight management:

- The body's fat burning processes must be activated first before autophagy can be induced. When that happens fat is burned but proteins are spared in the recycling process. However, do take note that if the duration of your fasting tends to get longer, then your body will also begin to lose protein mass. Keeping fasting periods shorter is the way to go to lose unwanted fat and help the body make use of protein.
- Autophagy helps prevent chronic inflammation. It has been observed that chronic inflammation will raise insulin levels in the body. Increased insulin levels then causes an increase in weight. That is why reducing inflammation may help people lose weight.
- Autophagy is all about making your metabolism more efficient again. When the body's cells get that much needed repair the metabolism also gets some fine tuning, which may help the body burn more fat.

Improving Digestive Health

The cells in our intestines tend to do a lot of work albeit constantly. They usually need a lot of repair as well as restoration and autophagy can help boost that process. It will help improve your gut health thus allowing your gastrointestinal tract some time to heal itself.

Not for Everyone

According to the same study cited earlier autophagy can help suppress tumors. However, when the cells are under stress autophagy tends to turn on you. Tumor cells can take advantage of the ongoing autophagy process for them to survive. In this way autophagy is both good and bad for the body. In another study it is suggested that autophagy promotes the survival of the fittest cells of the human body[2].

Again, do take note that the science behind the use of autophagy in cancer treatment isn't completely there yet. There are studies that show that the lack of autophagy in the body can lead to the reduced production of genes that suppress tumors [3]. However, it should be noted that these studies lack actual human trials.

The bottom line here is that promoting autophagy or inducing autophagy is not for everyone. If you have a preexisting medical condition prior to practicing any form of induced autophagy then you should first consult with your doctor before you attempt anything.

Chapter 3: Ten Ways to Induce Autophagy

In this chapter we will go over different ways to induce autophagy. There is no doubt that the best way to bring your body into autophagy mode is to go on a fast. Well basically because that the exactly what the body needs to be in—starvation mode (well sort of).

But fasting and starvation are two different things. We'll go over the itty gritty details about that in the next chapter. In this chapter we will have an overview of the things that you can do to activate autophagy besides fasting.

There are several and natural ways that you can influence it. By doing this you are reaping a host of benefits such as reducing your risk for neurodegenerative disease, inflammation, depression, and other related symptoms.

In this chapter we will go over lifestyle habits, food that you can eat, and other things that can help get your body started on autophagy. However, it should be stressed here that the real best way to induce it is nothing more than by fasting.

You can use the information here and combine it with a fasting regimen in order to better prepare your body to enter into autophagy mode. There is no magic bullet that will work for everyone and that is why researchers, dieticians, and other experts have looked for ways to induce autophagy.

Option 1 – Fasting/Intermittent Fasting

Let's get this one out of the way and we won't go over this in detail because we have an entire chapter on intermittent fasting in this book. Fasting is no less than a biological stressor that solicits a reaction from the body—just like exercise (see details below).

Fasting deprives the body of nutrients and the body will react to that. Studies have shown that fasting can greatly induce autophagy in the human brain as well as in the other organs as well [4, 5, 6].

The challenging part is that you will have to stay fasted for 24 to 48 hours in order to get the highest levels of autophagy and also the best benefits from this metabolic process [7].

The big problem with this is the length of the fast. It is usually not practical and it is not a realistic option for many people. The good news is that there are a variety of fasting regimens that you can try.

You may be able to find a suitable one for you and you can combine that with the other autophagy inducing techniques/methods discussed in this chapter. Remember that studies suggest that even shorter fasts can promote better neuronal autophagy [8].

Option 2 – Exercise

Aside from fasting, another way that you can lower your body's blood insulin levels is through exercise. In fact, this is one of the best methods to induce more autophagy to happen in your brain—where it matters the most.

There are of course different types of exercises and not all of them are better suited to promote autophagy. So, which type of exercise should you focus on? Researchers have found out that aerobic exercises are your best option at inducing autophagy [9].

Resistance training should also be part of any exercise regimen and it will help keep the body healthier. But if you are looking to increase your chances of activating autophagy mode you will focus on aerobic exercises.

Aerobic exercises are the ones that will usually make you pant a lot or pause and catch your breath. People usually call them cardio exercises. Aerobic exercises improve cognitive function and experts believe that this is due to autophagy [10].

Exercise produces stress in the body and autophagy is one of the ways the body copes with stress. Studies suggest that it only takes 30 minutes of aerobic exercise to induce this stress and to trigger a level of autophagy [11].

As a result this metabolic state becomes a huge benefit for overall brain health. It reduces neurodegeneration and at the same time it increases neurogenesis. That is way researchers highly suggest exercise—aerobic exercise especially—for obtaining optimal health for the brain.

You don't have to stick to jogging or treadmills. The idea is to find an aerobic exercise—say swimming?—that you enjoy doing and keep doing it. That way you tend to commit to it thus increasing your chances of success.

Option 3 – Go Through a Protein Fast

According to one study, going through a protein fast has the same effects as undergoing a calorie restriction[37]. How is a protein fast done? You might have to measure your protein intake per week when you do it.

You should first account for all the protein sources that you eat for each week that you plan to go on a protein fast. Yes, you may have to go semi-vegan too. Plant proteins should also be avoided if you have already reached your limit.

So pick a week or two in each month when you plan to go on a protein fast. On your protein fast week(s) pick two days in that week when you will go on your protein fast.

On your protein fast day you have 2 options:

   a. Don't take any protein for that day—both from plant and animal sources (no proteins!)
   b. Limit your protein intake to 15 to 25 grams per day.

Why do you want to do this? Well, it gives your body a protein break. You are giving your body a full day to recycle the proteins that you already have. Are there direct benefits aside from inducing autophagy?

Yes, there are other benefits. First off your cells go on a deep cleanse without getting any form of muscle loss. Another benefit is that it helps promote the reduction of inflammation.

If you are already used to protein restrictions then you can also schedule 1 protein fast day each week.

Option 4 – Try a Ketogenic Diet

Dr. Colin Champ once said that "Ketogenesis is like an autophagy hack. You get a lot of the same metabolic changes and benefits of fasting without actually fasting." A keto diet is one that is characteristically high in fat and low in carbs.

Of course medical experts are referring to healthy fat sources when they say that you should eat more fat. Ketosis is also seen as a way to reduce neurodegeneration [12]. Even though ketosis and autophagy are not directly related (i.e. you can experience one without the other) they usually occur at almost the same time.

In fact ketosis supports autophagy and vice versa. Autophagy also reduces the amount of amyloid beta in the brain, which will be very helpful for people with Alzheimer's disease [13]. Studies suggest that ketosis can help to reduce brain injury[14]. We have an entire chapter on the relationship of ketosis and autophagy so we will deal with subject there in much greater detail.

Option 5 – Exposure to Hot and Cold Temperatures

Studies have shown that exposure to hot and cold temperatures can also trigger autophagy. One study suggests that heat stress contributes to the stimulation necessary to induce autophagy [15]. It is not yet clear how the heat shock phase and autophagy are exactly connected but studies confirm that one thing does lead to the other and it helps in the body's repair process [16].

In some cultures taking a sauna is part of the daily routine especially during the cold months. There are also other treatment modalities such as cold plunges and some even try cryotherapy. Of course before you try any of these treatments you should first consult with your doctor especially if you are at risk for certain medical conditions. We will go over cryotherapy along with how to use hot and cold exposures later in this book.

Option 6 – Deep Sleep

Sleep is the phase or mode where the body heals. That is why getting enough quality sleep is one of the keys of obtaining a state of autophagy. It shouldn't come as a surprise that poor sleep is one of the contributors to poor cognitive function.

Not getting enough sleep, studies say, negatively affects autophagy especially when you wake up intermittently through the night [17, 18]. There is of course the question of which is more important the length of time sleeping or the quality of sleep.

The answer is both length and quality are important. Experts recommend at least 7 hours of quality sleep each night—that means uninterrupted sleep of course. So how do you improve the quality of your sleep? It is done by taking care of your circadian rhythm and also by promoting the production of melatonin.

Researchers have found that there is a connection between the human sleep-wake cycle (i.e. your circadian rhythm) and autophagy. This interconnection plays a role either in the improvement or decline of cognitive function [19].

When we sleep well at night the brain is better able to produce more melatonin. Melatonin is a hormone secreted in a small gland in the brain called the pineal gland. Studies suggest that melatonin can induce autophagy and also helps to reduce one's risk for neuropsychiatric disorders [20, 21]. We will cover how to increase the quality of your sleep in order to activate autophagy later in this book.

Option 7 – Acupuncture

Acupuncture is an alternative healing method that has been around for centuries. An acupuncturist inserts needles in specific parts of the body to produce a reflex reaction. According to one review, studies suggest that acupuncture can improve learning and memory and also induce autophagy [22].

Another study showed that through this process brain cells are protected via the up-regulation of the pathways for autophagy. It is also suggested that acupuncture can help clear the proteins from the brain that are contributory to Parkinson's disease [23].

There is also testimonial evidence that suggests that acupuncture can also help wean people off their psychiatric medication. Note that some antidepressants can be habit forming and this type of alternative medicine can help with withdrawal symptoms.

You should get this alternative treatment from a licensed acupuncturist. Some even suggest that ear acupuncture is a lot better for inducing autophagy in the brain than other types.

Option 8 – Hyperbaric Oxygen Therapy

Hyperbaric oxygen therapy or HBOT is a treatment modality that is used for brain injury. It is particularly useful for the recovery of the central nervous system after it has experienced an injury.

In this form of therapy, patients will be placed in an HBOT chamber where they are made to inhale 100% oxygen. In this chamber the oxygen is no longer transported through the blood's red blood cells. It is dissolved into all the body fluids which allow the oxygen to penetrate deeper where it is needed.

Since the dissolved oxygen is carried deeper, it is better able to reach areas which were previously blocked off due to injury. Oxygen also is now able to reach areas where blood circulation has diminished.

Studies have shown that HBOT elevates autophagy especially in the nervous system [24]. The big downside here is that HBOT is rather expensive and you have to find a specialized clinic that has the facilities to perform this type of therapy.

Option 9 – Foods That Help Induce Autophagy

It may sound counterintuitive to eat certain foods so that you can induce autophagy. Note that there are different levels or types of autophagy depending on the cells that undergo this metabolic process.

The following is a list of different food that may help boost autophagy.

- **Coffee/Caffeine**

Which coffee is better decaf or regular coffee? Studies suggest that both are equally helpful at inducing autophagy [25]. You should be careful about how much and how frequent you take coffee since caffeine in the coffee can disrupt sleep.

- **Green Tea**

Green tea has been found to restore the brain's autophagic flux [26]. The active ingredient in green tea that contributes to autophagy is EGCG (Epigallocatechin-3-Gallate).

- **MCTs (Medium Chain Triglycerides) in Coconut Oil**

MCTs are the compounds in coconut oil that helps to increase ketone levels in the brain and other parts of the body [27]. If you don't like adding coconut oil to your meals you can just take MCT supplements instead.

- **Reishi Mushrooms**

Reishi mushrooms are rich in bioactive compounds. Studies suggest that some of these compounds may contribute to the activation of autophagy [28].

- **Ginger**

Ginger is another nutrient rich Asian herb that also contains lots of bioactive compounds. Some of these compounds have been found to support autophagy [29].

- **Turmeric**

The curcumin in turmeric has been found to be protective of the brain's cells, which also aids in autophagy [30].

- **Thai Ginger**

This type of ginger may be a bit hard to find and it is not actually ginger to be exact. It is a totally different kind of spice. You usually find in Thai, Malaysian, and Indonesian cuisine. Studies suggest that galangal (i.e. Thai ginger) can help boost autophagy [31].

- **Broccoli Sprouts**

Broccoli sprouts contain lots of sulforaphane a phytochemical that may help increase autophagy in brain cells [32, 33].

- **Acai Berries**

Acai berries of course have been made popular by Oprah (or at least that is where I first heard of it through mainstream TV). These berries are rich in antioxidants, some of which stimulate autophagy in the brain[34]. If you can't find acai berries then you can just get some strawberries or blueberries instead—they too have been found to have the same beneficial effects. Blueberries contain Pterostilbene has been shown to help induce autophagy [35].

- **Extra Virgin Olive Oil**

Extra virgin olive oil is rich in Oleuropein a phytochemical that is contributory to the induction of autophagy. It has also been found to help reduce cognitive impairment.

- **Omega-3 Fatty Acids**

Omega 3 acids are of course essential and beneficial nutrients that aren't produced naturally in the human body. They have been found to be helpful in the treatment of many neurodegenerative diseases. They also increase BDNF signaling which enhances autophagy [36].

Option 10 – Take Supplements

There are certain nutrients that can help induce autophagy. The following is a short list of these nutrients:

- **Probiotics**

Researchers have found that the SLAB51 probiotic formulation can help reduce cognitive decline as well as brain damage [38]. There are other probiotics that may also help as well.

- **Ginkgo Biloba**

Ginkgo Biloba is one of the herbs/supplements that is used to treat mood disorders, improve blood flow to the brain, boost attention spans, and increase mental energy. It is even a prescribed herbal medicine in Germany. Its compounds have been found to be helpful for the treatment of dementia and Alzheimer's and also for the induction of autophagy [39].

- **American Ginseng**

American ginseng is another type of ginseng from the Asian variant. Researchers suggest that it may help induce autophagy and reduce mitochondrial dysfunction[40].

- **Vitamin D**

Research suggests that you can induce autophagy by activating the Vitamin D receptor[41]. Other studies also link Vitamin D deficiency with defective autophagy[42].

- **Acetyl-L-Carnitine**

Acetyl-L-Carnitine has been found to have cognitive-enhancing as well as neuro-protective effects. Research suggests that it can help reverse cognitive decline as well as support the functions of the mitochondria in cells[43]. It does that by inducing autophagy in the brain.

- **Vitamin K2**

If you are taking Vitamin D you should also take Vitamin K2 since this vitamin also helps to induce autophagy. In fact these two vitamins go well together[44].

- **CBD**

CBD or Cannabidiol is one of the active cannabinoids that can be extracted from marijuana. Don't worry this one won't make you high. It is actually beneficial and researchers have found that it both activates as well as enhances autophagy[45].

- **Lithium**

Lithium orotate has been found to significantly increase the production of myelin, which improves overall brain health. It does that by enhancing the autophagy in the brain [46].

- **Berberine**

Berberine is usually extracted from a variety of plants. This alkaloid has been found to promote neurogenesis[47]. It also helps to prevent and reduce inflammation. Through these actions berberine is able to help protect the cells of the brain and induce autophagy[48].

- **Rhodiola**

Rhodiola is also known as the arctic root. It is also known as the golden root in Asia. It is actually a pretty popular herb used to increase both mental and physical stamina. It does this by reducing neurodegeneration via increasing autophagy in the brain[49].

- **Schisandra**

Schisandra is a berry and it is frequently used in traditional Chinese medicine. It is traditionally used to improve someone's mood, reduce stress, and it is particularly helpful for women going through menopause.

Studies also suggest that it can also enhance autophagy[50].

- **Resveratrol**

Resveratrol is known to prevent the development of a lot of Alzheimer's and other neurodegenerative diseases. Studies show that it helps brain cells recover and heal after an injury[51].

- **Spermidine**

Spermidine is a compound that can be found in potatoes, pears, mushrooms, chicken, fermented soy, and aged cheese. If eating these foods will ruin your fasting or diet then you can just take it as a supplement. It has been found to be effective in reducing the aging of the synapses of the brain and this compound also helps induce autophagy [52].

Chapter 4: Activating Autophagy through Fasting

Experts say that fasting is the fastest and most effective way to help the body to get into a state of autophagy[53]. How does that happen? Fasting deprives the body of nutrients which signals the body to activate autophagy. When we stop eating the body's insulin levels go down. And to compensate for that drop in insulin drop, the body produces more glucagon. When you have more glucagon it triggers autophagy[54].

Researchers like the award winning Yoshinori Ohsumi and plenty of others recommend fasting (particularly intermittent fasting) as a means to activating autophagy. There are other methods of course, such as the Ketogenic diet for instance, but we will go over those in a separate chapter. In this chapter we will focus on fasting and how you can use it to induce autophagy.

What is Fasting?

Isn't fasting the equivalent of starvation? Well, not exactly—but yes you will starve at one point. The big difference between general starvation and the practice of fasting is control. Starvation is involuntary—you are forced to it due to the lack of food. On the other hand fasting is not—you chose not to eat.

Starvation can lead to severe health problems and even death. Fasting on the other hand is controlled and deliberate and you can stop any time you want. Yes, you will suffer from the lack of food in both cases but you as you can see you have control when you fast.

Fasting for Religious and Spiritual Purposes

People have been fasting for a lot of different reasons for thousands of years now. Some do it for health reasons while others do it for spiritual reasons. Yes, spiritual reasons.

For instance, Muslims go fasting during the month of Ramadan—they fast for an entire month. Catholics on the other hand do fasting every Good Friday and on Ash Wednesday. On Yom Kippur, Jews undergo a six day fast.

Hindus on the other hand have several new moon fasts like the Shivarati, Saraswati, and Puja. Mormons go fasting on the first Sunday of every month. Other religious traditions that include fasting are those from Jainists, Taoists, and Buddhists.

Fasting for Health and Fitness

Fasting as a practice has been around for thousands of years. So, it's not really new. But you don't have to be religious to go on a fast. Fasting is also a practice for people who are not underweight. Some people try fasting to lose weight. Note however, that if you have health issues you should consult with your doctor first before trying any form of fasting.

Bodybuilders in particular have been looking to cut down on body fat through fasting. You see, when the food supply is cut, the body will start to use its stored energy to survive—the stored body fat to be exact.

During fasting you choose not to eat for health reasons—maybe to cut weight, stimulate autophagy for healing, and other reasons. Food is readily available. You will also have a designated fasting period. After the fasting period you will have to eat and thus end your fast.

Some undergo fasting for a day up to several days with medical supervision. Sometimes you will be required by your doctor to fast before undergoing a medical procedure. But that is a different subject altogether.

You may not know it but you actually undergo fasting every night. You've been doing it your entire life. Do you know where the word "breakfast" comes from and what it means?

Break-Fast

This term actually comes from "break fast"—it is the meal that people eat to break their fasting period. You eat breakfast in the morning; that means you were actually fasting as you slept at night. That implicitly means we all fast at night and it is something that we do daily.

However this nightly fast is actually a short term fast usually lasting anywhere from 6 to 10 hours. Some people sleep longer for various reasons. Body builders and people who are sick need to sleep in order to recuperate.

Benefits of Fasting

- ***Weight Loss*** – as stated earlier there are people who undergo fasting to lose weight. Any extra that gets digested and doesn't get used by the body will end up getting stored for later use. That stored unused body fuel is called fat. Since fasting means not eating the body will switch to using fat for sustenance.
- ***Promotes Longevity*** – as you grow older your metabolism slows down. This condition will later lead to a gradual loss of muscle tissue, which is known as sarcopenia. The good news is that fasting helps to speed up your metabolism, which prevents sarcopenia and the degradation of muscular tissue. On top of that fasting triggers autophagy.
- ***Detoxifies the Body*** – nutrient deprivation is interpreted by the brain as a form of stress or threat and it reacts protectively or defensively. The brain starts up its adaptive stress response and that includes looking for alternative sources of energy. The liver is then triggered to produce glycogen as an alternative source. After that the body turns to fat stores—when that happens the toxins in the fat get released in the conversion process when fat is used as an energy source.

- **Metabolic Boost** – as it was explained earlier, the body gets a metabolic boost when you go fasting. According to one study[55], fasting can boost the body's metabolism by up to 14%. According to another medical study, people who undergo fasting experience an increase in neropinephrine in their blood. This is a neurotransmitter that increases the body's metabolism.
- **Improves Brain Function** – studies suggest that undergoing fasting may help to improve overall brain function. It promotes the production of BNDF or brain-derived neurotrophic factor. BNDF helps protect the brain from degenerative conditions such as Alzheimer's and Parkinson's disease. According to one study, it is suggested that fasting helps to improve memory[56]—this is according to the Society for Neuroscience. Another study suggests that fasting also promotes the growth of new nerve cells[57].

In the next chapter we will go over what intermittent fasting is and its various forms.

Chapter 5: Intermittent Fasting

We have gone over the benefits and also some of the downsides of fasting in the previous chapter. The next question is what is intermittent fasting, how do you use it to induce autophagy, how to go about it, and how to get started with this type of fasting.

What is Intermittent Fasting?

Intermittent fasting is a method of fasting where you cycle between fasting periods and then eating periods. Currently this is one of the more popular diets and weight loss regimens. It has also become quite popular as a method to improve one's health.

Some believe that intermittent fasting is an ancient secret to better health. Believe it or not it has been practiced by human beings all throughout human history. It is secret well because everyone has forgotten about it in modern times. It is actually more of a habit in certain cultures and only noticed in the west. Thus it is virtually forgotten by many people.

People are actually rediscovering this practice. The interest in this mode of dietary intervention spiked sometime in 2010 when Google searches for the search term "intermittent fasting" went up by 10,000 percent. It became an instant fad and it went on for almost a decade.

Note that intermittent fasting can only be beneficial to you if you do it properly. Yes, at times people do it the wrong way. Some people have reported that they have reversed type 2 diabetes with the help of intermittent fasting. Some also credit it for their weight loss. Obviously when you go on fasts regularly you save money and also time since you no longer have to spend money or time buying or preparing meals.

Warning: Intermittent Fasting is NOT for Everyone

Intermittent fasting does carry it with it some dangers. Well, it is fasting and as it was pointed out in the previous chapter, fasting is not for everyone. Intermittent fasting is still a controversial topic despite its proven benefits.

For one thing it entails certain potential dangers for people who are taking medication. If you are a diabetic and you are already taking prescribed medication then fasting intermittent or otherwise may not be an option for you.

But that doesn't mean diabetics can't go on a fasting routine. In some cases the dosages of some of your medication may need to be adjusted so you can go fasting. But in some cases it is just not possible to go on fasting. The best way to find out for a diabetic is to consult with their doctor.

Apart from diabetics, there are also other people who should not undergo intermittent fasting. They include the following:

- Those who are already underweight.
- People who are suffering from eating disorders such as anorexia
- Women who are breastfeeding and those that are pregnant
- Anyone who is under the age of 18 should not undergo intermittent fasting

A Tool for Weight Loss

At the very core of this dietary practice it is actually just a way to give your body a break from processing all the food that you have eaten. Some people eat way more than they really need and fasting can help the body take the necessary time to either clean up the gunk that has accumulated in its systems and also process the rest of the food that is still in the digestive tract.

It also allows the body to use the stored energy that may have been sitting there accumulating. And for some people they have accumulated way more reserved energy than necessary. In a way you are giving your body a chance to burn off those excess fats.

It should be emphasized here also that human beings have evolved through the centuries to include fasting as a part of the daily routine. In some cultures, like in some Native American tribes and other tribal peoples in the world, fasting is a daily experience. Some can even go on only 1 meal a day and they are living healthy lives.

As it was explained earlier in this book we all go through short term fasts each night. That means people can go on shorter fasts that can last for several hours—and there are those who can go on fasts that can last for days without incurring any consequences with regard to their health.

Remember that body fat is nothing more to the body than a type of food energy. It is something that has been stored away for future use. In order for the body to actually make use of that stored food energy is to stop eating.

When you have stored so much food energy it is a signal that you have lost balance, which is what life is all about. Eating and fasting is part of a balancing scale that we need to go through in order to regain our health. Eating is the flip side of fasting that is why when you aren't eating you are fasting and vice versa.

The Role of Insulin in Fat Storage and Use

Insulin is the key hormone involved in the storage of food energy in the body. Usually when we eat we take in more food energy (i.e. calories) than what is readily needed by the body. That is why the body naturally stores that energy away since it isn't necessary at the moment.

Every time we eat insulin levels in our body rises. This helps the body to start storing excess food energy in two different ways or two separate processes. The first one is when carbohydrates are broken down into glucose (a form of simple sugar). These broken down pieces of glucose will be organized into long linked chains which later forms into glycogen.

Glycogen is then stored in the muscles (for immediate use when muscular action is required) as well as in the liver.

Note that both the muscles and the liver don't really have a lot of storage space. They can only store so much—remember that glycogen in the muscles is for immediate use. When all the storage spaces both in the muscles and in the liver are already full then this triggers the liver to convert the glucose chains into fat. This process of transforming glucose chains into fat is called de-novo lipogenesis, which literally translates to "making new fat."

Now, the liver also has some storage space for fat but not that much. Most of the fat that gets converted by the liver is stored elsewhere in the body. When the body reaches that phase then the storage space available is much larger than what the muscles and the liver can provide.

In a way, the amount of fat that can be stored at this point is virtually limitless. This stored food energy will be used only when there is no more available glucose or glycogen.

From this we gather that the body has 2 ways to store excess food energy:
1. Readily available food energy stored as glycogen but stored in very limited spaces.
2. Reserve food energy (i.e. fat) that has virtually unlimited storage but this food energy is much more difficult to access.

Insulin is the bodily hormone that is the key to both the creation of new fat and also the body's consumption of that hard to reach stored energy.

Fat Creation Process

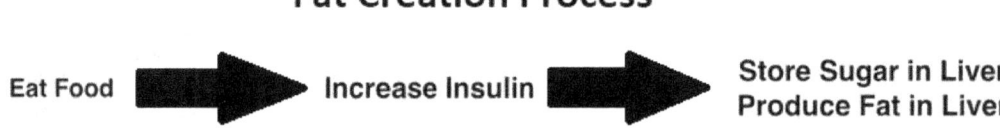

The graphic above shows process 1 where the sugar called glucose is stored in the liver and how body fat is also produced in the liver. Note that this process goes into reverse mode when insulin levels decrease.

Please note the graphic below:

Fat Burning Process

As you can see the process reverses when you go into fasting. This occurs in short amounts or periods every night—except of course if you wake up in the middle of the night feeling hungry and grab a midnight snack.

Remember that the digestive process continues even if you are asleep. Technically you are fasting when you sleep at night whether you had dinner or not. You break that nightly fast if you wake up at 1 am and grab a cookie and then go back to bed.

When you fast and there are no food to digest then the body looks for glycogen—remember the long chains of simple sugars called glucose? Those are the first things that get used up. Glycogen chains get broken up and turned into the simpler glucose which the body can readily use.

If all the glucose gets used up and there is still no food being digested then the body turns to the stored fat. The body will break down fat to convert it into readily usable energy.

From this we can gather the following:

1. The body has two fundamental states.
2. The first state is the high insulin state where you have eaten something
3. The other state is the low insulin state where there is no food in the digestive tract (i.e. you didn't eat anything).
4. Your body switches from one state to the other.

So, if you begin eating the moment you roll out of bed then you trigger the body to enter the high insulin state. And if you stay fed the entire day all the way to the night then you are always in the high insulin state. That is the state when your body is producing fat.

If you continue in that state day in and day out, you are likely going to store more fat unless your metabolism can keep up with the fat production going on. Well, most likely we can't keep up due to the type of diet we have in the modern age.

Intermittent Fasting: Restoring That Balance

Intermittent fasting actually restores that needed balance. It allows your body to switch from the high insulin state to the low insulin state. What you need to do therefore is to increase the amount of time your body spends burning fat rather than making it.

Should you always be in fasting mode? Of course not—that is why you make an intermittent schedule of eating and fasting. There is totally nothing wrong with fasting. It is how our bodies are naturally designed. That's how bears, cats, dogs, and other mammals do it. And that is how we human beings are supposed to do it just as Mother Nature has designed.

Chapter 6: The Different Stages of Fasting

We have just gone over the general steps in the fasting process that goes on when you do intermittent fasting. In this chapter we will dig into the details of fasting in general. Going deeper into these details will help you understand how autophagy fits into the picture.

Yes, we have gone over how the body naturally breaks down glycogen and fat but where and when does it enter into the cellular level? We'll go over that in this chapter.

The Cell Growth Mode

As a kind of recap, when you are in the high insulin state that means that means you are well fed. Whenever you are well fed the cells of your body enter a growth mode. The insulin and something called the mTOR pathway are telling your cells to process proteins and also to cell divide i.e. to grow. Note that when these pathways start to go overactive they tend to help the growth of cancer cells.

mTOR stands for mammalian target of rapamycin. This pathway loves having lots of proteins and carbs. When the mTOR pathway is active in the body it tells the cells not to bother doing any kind of autophagy. That means there is no clean up being done on the cellular level and there is no recycling going on.

The cells are then made too busy cell dividing and growing. They basically have no time to recycle and cleaning up. Thus they end up losing efficiency.

In this growth mode there are different genes in the cells that get activated such as the ones for cell proliferation. When that particular genes get turned on it tends to switch off other genes like the ones used for damage repair and fat burning. That means even at the cellular level your body gets programmed not to burn fat and turn off autophagy when you are in a high insulin state or when you are well fed.

How the Preservation Mode Kicks In

On the cellular level we have a well preserved starvation program. This can kick in when food isn't readily available. Well, not all kinds of food but glucose, yes that simple sugar, isn't available.

We mentioned the mTOR pathway and high levels of insulin earlier and how they trigger the growth mode of the cells. As you might have guessed there is always something that balances something else off. If there is high insulin levels and mTOR, there is also low insulin levels and AMPK.

Think of AMPK as the signaling pathway that steps on the brakes for mTOR. Not only does it make mTOR stop it also signals the cells to enter a self-protecting mode. It also tells the cells to enter into autophagy and thereby start breaking down stored body fat.

Fasting also triggers another internal chain reaction that is related to drinking red wine. Wine has a molecule in it called resveratrol. Now, how is that related to all of this? When you go fasting the number of molecules called NAD+ increases in the body.

Normally NAD+ gets converted due to the presence of proteins and sugars that you eat. Since there aren't any new proteins and sugars coming in the number of NAD+ molecules increase. They accumulate and they become the precursor to Vitamin B3.

Vitamin B3 as part of this chain reaction activates SIRT1 and SIRT3. These are sirtuins, which are proteins that stops cell proliferation (they signal the cell to stop cell division). When the cells stop cell dividing they will turn to other things like the creation of new mitochondria and start the self-cleaning process.

Ketosis Kicks In

When you start fasting ketones eventually are produced in the body. Yes this is another process that goes on when the body isn't busy digesting and processing food energy. It's pretty busy actually come to think of it. The body actually has a lot of other things to do when there isn't a lot of food lining up in its digestive tract. Ketones turn on the body's genes that are related to damage repair as well as antioxidant processing.

Again the trigger here is the level of insulin in the body. That's how the body knows that it has finished digesting food. Now that you have at least some sort of idea what happens in the background when you stop eating and go on a fast, we can now move on to the stages of fasting. We'll be covering fasting in general, which will include long term fasting and intermittent fasting.

Stage 1 – The First 12 Hours

In the first 12 hours of fasting you will enter a metabolic state called ketosis[58]. This is the point when your body starts to accumulate ketones as it was described earlier.

The stored body fat by this time is being broken up bit by bit and then burned or used as an energy source for the body. Some of this fat is used by the liver which continuously produces ketones or ketone bodies. Ketones also serve as an alternative energy source for your brain.

During your resting state the brain uses up to 60% of the glucose that your digestive system is processing. The liver then produces ketones to provide energy to the brain which requires a lot of energy. Ketones are only part of the overall reserve nourishment of your brain cells. Think of ketones as nutritional substitutes for glucose.

There are those who point to ketone usage by brain cells as one of the reasons why you get mental clarity when you undergo fasting. As your brain consumes more ketones the more positive your mood becomes. That is why fasting is so hard during the first few hours because the brain starts to run low on glucose and your grumpiness starts to kick in.

When ketone bodies are metabolized (i.e. used as alternative fuel) they don't produce a lot of inflammatory effects unlike when glucose is metabolized. Another benefit to inducing ketosis is that it kick starts the production of BDNF, the brain's growth factor. The body's repair mode has kicked in well within this phase.

Stage 2 – The 18 Hour Mark

After 18 hours of fasting your body has already switched to fat burning state. Your body is now producing ketones at a significant rate, which is enough to compensate for the lack of glucose. At this point your body fat is now the primary source of energy for your body.

By this time your doctor can perform tests to measure how much ketone bodies are produced by your body. Your doctor can compare it with your baseline values, which should be around 0.6 to 1.0.

When the volume of ketone bodies in your blood increases they can then act as a kind of signaling molecules just like what your body's hormones usually do. Some of the things that ketone bodies signal to your cells include stress stopping pathways, initiate the repair of damaged DNA, and the reduction of inflammations in the body.

Stage 3 – The 24 Hour Mark

At 24 hours into your fasting the cells in your body are now recycling their parts at an increased rate. A lot of repairs are now getting done such as breaking down of any misfolded proteins, which are linked to diseases like Alzheimer's[59]. This phase of brain repair is a huge part of the process called autophagy.

If the human body isn't able to go into a state of autophagy a lot of bad things tend to develop. One of those things is the development of neurodegenerative disease. Since there is no mechanism for tissue rejuvenation at the cellular level misfolded proteins in the brain start to occur more frequently.

Stage 4 – The 48 Hour Mark

When your body operates with very few calories or totally without calories for 48 hours the hormone levels tend to jump up to as much as 5 times when you started fasting[60]. You can achieve this state also consuming very little amounts of proteins and carbs.

Remember that ketones induce the increased production of growth hormones in the brain as well as in other parts of the body. Growth hormones help to preserve the body's lean muscle mass so that your bodily systems do not start feeding off muscle tissue.

Another hormone is secreted called Ghrelin and that too helps to stimulate the production of growth hormones[61]. The production of growth hormones is especially important in people as they age.

Growth hormones are particularly helpful when it comes to maintaining cardiovascular health as well as in healing wounds. Thus experts are conducting further studies on growth hormones suggesting that these hormones may have a role to play in terms of human longevity.

Stage 5 – Insulin Levels Drop to the Lowest Level

This stage occurs around 54 hours into your fast. It should be noted that the body at this point is at its most insulin sensitive level[62]. Note that lowering your insulin levels actually carries with it certain important long term as well as short term benefits.

Apart from helping to trigger autophagy in the body, lowered insulin levels help to make you more sensitive to insulin. In other words you become less insulin resistant, which is something really important to people who are at risk of developing diabetes. Lowered levels also help to prevent chronic diseases related to aging as well as cancer.

Stage 6 – Old Immune Cells get Replaced by New Ones

The next stage in fasting occurs 72 hours into a fast. This can only be achieved through much persistence and practice. No one expects you to reach this level until you have learned how to fast for a few hours first. We will go over how you can properly fast and the different methods that can help you achieve autophagy in a later section of this book.

At this point several signaling pathways that reduce insulin-like growth factor IGF-1 and PKA can now be found in almost every cell of the human body. These signaling pathways help to promote the survival of the body's cells and stimulate growth.

When PKA and IGF-1 are suppressed old proteins as well as old cells get recycled. Prolonged fasting also promotes the regeneration of blood stem cells[63]. Patients undergoing chemotherapy may also benefit from long term fasting as studies suggest. It helps preserve healthy white blood cells.

Stage 7 – Feeding Stage

The last stage of intermittent fasting or any kind of fasting for that matter is the feeding stage. You can't really end a fast without eating again. Every fast must be broken or stopped since the body isn't designed to maintain autophagy for really prolonged periods of time.

The eating phase is just as important as any fasting phase. However it should be noted that breaking a fasting period should be done with a healthy and nutritious meal. That means you shouldn't end your fasting with a ton of carbs. According to the National Institute of Aging, eating a healthy meal after a fast improves the body's insulin sensitivity, promotes synaptic plasticity, and increases the overall resistance of human cells to stress[64].

In the next chapter you will get an overview of the different ways to do intermittent fasting. We will then go over each of them in detail later on in this book.

Chapter 7: Different Ways to do Intermittent Fasting

Intermittent fasting is a blanket term for a lot of fasting methods today. That having said, you should expect that there will be different ways to do intermittent fasting nowadays.

It is no secret that it has become quite a trend nowadays. Some people swear by it saying that intermittent fasting has helped them lose weight. Some credit their extended lifespan to this mode of fasting and others give testimonies as to how intermittent fasting has helped them become healthier.

It shouldn't come as a surprise that different ways to do intermittent fasting have sprung up. Note that there are no hard and fast rules as to how one should do it. However, you should choose the best one that would suit your needs. Not every mode of intermittent fasting will be effective for you. The goal is to make it as effortless as possible.

In this chapter we will go over the common methods to do intermittent fasting. We will discuss each in detail in a later chapter.

The 16/8 Method

The 16/8 method or 16:8 method means that you will fast for 16 hours each day and eat only within an 8 hour window. There are no exact figures but generally you will be expected to fast anywhere from 14 to 16 hours and restrict your eating time to 8 to 10 hours only.

This method of intermittent fasting is known as the Leangains protocol and it was made popular by Martin Berkhan. This is perhaps one of the simplest ways to do intermittent fasting. You can actually get this type of fasting done by just not eating anything after dinner and then follow that up by skipping breakfast.

Let's say you have dinners at 8 you should make sure that you don't have any post dinner evening meals or midnight snacks after that. When you wake up in the morning you should skip breakfast. Let's say you had your dinner at 7 pm and finished it at 8 pm at 8 pm you should refrain from eating anything at all.

The next thing you will eat is lunch the following day. You will skip breakfast, yes. And technically you have already fasted for a total of 16 hours if you do it that way. That is the program for the men. It is recommended that women have a slightly shorter fast, which should be about 14 to 15 hours.

Now this fasting isn't called a dry fast. A dry fast is where you avoid both food and water. That means you don't eat and you also don't drink. Experts say that 24 hours of dry fasting is the equivalent of 3 days of water fasting. Of course dry fasting is going to be a very difficult practice especially if you haven't done any form of fasting.

You can drink water when you go on an intermittent fast. You can also drink some coffee or tea while you fast. This can help reduce the hunger pangs that you feel. However, do take note that you can't take in any alcoholic beverages during your fast.

On top of that during your eating window you are supposed to eat a balanced diet. If you're still eating fast food during the hours when you're supposed to eat then don't expect to see any good results.

Some people do low carb diets in conjunction with the 16:8 intermittent fasting schedule. Whenever you feel hungry during your fasting window then drink water or tea.

The 5:2 Method

The 5:2 Method is also known as the 5:2 Diet and also the Fast Diet. This method of intermittent fasting was popularized by Michael Mosley, a doctor and British journalist. This is another simple strategy where you eat regular meals 5 days a week and then in 2 selected days you will restrict your calorie intake to 500 to 600 calories.

Men are recommended to take in only up to 600 calories during the 2 fasting days. Women on the other hand are supposed to take only 500 calories during those days.

So let's say you want to go fasting on Tuesdays and Fridays. On those two days you will count your calories eating only 250 calories per meal for the ladies and 300 calories for the men.

Critics of this dietary method say that there are no studies that support its effectiveness but we have plenty of people who swear by it. Some don't even consider it as a form of intermittent fasting.

Eat Stop Eat Method

The eat stop eat method will require a full 24 hours to complete. You will also be required to fast two days in a week. This mode of fasting was popularized by Brad Pilon, a fitness expert.

So, how do you do the eat stop eat fasting method? Here's how—let's say you finished dinner on Tuesday and you want to start fasting. You will begin your fast after dinner on Tuesday night. The following day you will not eat breakfast and you will skip lunch. Your next meal will be on Wednesday evening—dinner time.

So, essentially this is a dinner to dinner fast. Note that this is not a kind of dry fasting. You can have water, coffee, tea, and other non-alcoholic drinks during your fasting days. The only restriction is that you should not eat any solid foods.

People use this type of fasting to lose weight. It is also important that you should eat a healthy and balanced diet during non-fasting days. You are not supposed to eat like it's your last meal during the dinner before your fast begins.

That will just defeat the purpose of your fast. You are also not supposed to eat more food during your non-fasting days. It would be as if you are stock piling food for the upcoming fast.

Of course this type of fasting isn't the easiest one to try and it is not recommended for beginners. Note that the drop-out rate for this type of fasting is pretty high and many people will find it very difficult at first. The last few hours before you can eat again will be the most challenging because people usually become ravenously hungry since they are expecting a meal in a few hours.

You don't have to go dinner to dinner if that is not the best option for you. You can do the eat stop eat fasting going breakfast to breakfast or lunch to lunch. You can follow whatever fasting schedule that works for you. Note that this is a challenging fasting method and some people tend to just eat their next meal after the fast rather early.

Alternate Day Method

Now, if you think that the eat stop eat method is tough the alternate day fasting method is even tougher. Again, this is also another mode of fasting that is not recommended for beginners.

Using this method you will be fasting every other day. Note that you will be doing a full 24 hour fast on fasting days. However, there are also other versions of this fast where you will be allowed to take in around 500 calories during your fasting days. Again that will be 250 calories for women and 300 calories for men for 2 meals.

Note that there are studies on intermittent fasting that have test subjects use this fasting method (or some version of it). The results of course vary for each version. Now this fasting method is not suitable for the long term. No one can keep up with this fasting schedule without feeling miserable. It's a great option if you are looking for healing and rejuvenation but it isn't sustainable. You can have a fasting week once each month but you are already asking too much if you want to do it every single week.

Spontaneous Meal Skipping

This type of intermittent fasting calls for you to skip meals whenever it is convenient. Unlike the other methods for intermittent fasting, this type of fasting doesn't have any structure to it.

In other words you are just skipping meals from time to time. You can just go on fasting when you don't feel hungry come dinner, lunch, or breakfast. You can also just opt to go fasting if you're too busy to cook or you still have a lot of things to do and you don't really feel hungry. Again, in short, you go fasting when it is convenient for you.

You will be surprised that the human body is more than well equipped to skip one random meal any day. You may be traveling and you can't find any food that you like then you can go on a fast until you can find a suitable meal.

You can skip 1 meal or 2 it's up to you and that can still be considered as a spontaneous meal skip fast. That of course falls into the category of intermittent fasting. The only restriction here with this strategy is that you should eat a regular amount for each meal and that you should eat healthy food with each meal.

The Warrior Diet

The Warrior Diet is another popular diet and it was made famous by Ori Hofmekler, a fitness expert. This is a 24 hour fast—well almost since you will have a 4 hour eating window.

In the Warrior Diet you will be eating small meals consisting of raw veggies and fruits. Come night time you will have a feast. You can eat all you can within that 4 hour window at night.

This was one of the popularized diets to incorporate a form of intermittent fasting. Note that this diet also encourages a diet that is similar to the Paleo Diet. That means you can only eat unprocessed foods. The only food allowed is from natural sources.

Note that there are a few common denominators to all of these intermittent fasting methods. One of them is eating regular healthy meals. Another one is that you should shift from an eating phase and a non-eating phase which is why intermittent fasting is a great way to induce autophagy.

Chapter 8: Long Term Fasts vs. Short Term Fasts

There is no question that fasting is the best way to induce autophagy. However, since we have already covered some of the most popular ways to do intermittent fasting, the next question is which is more effective, short term fasts or long term fasts?

These are loose terms actually and there is no governing health authority that has categorized fasts strictly into short or long term. So, just for the sake of comparison we shall include all fasting methods that last 24 hours or less as a type of short term fast and those that require more than that amount of time as a long term fast.

Characteristics of Short Term Fasts

Again, any fasting regimen that requires a fasting period of up to 24 hours will be categorized as a short term fast. Now, when it comes to intermittent fasting there will be a lot of those that will fall into this category.

Note however that we are not saying that there is a best method of fasting. All of these fasting regimens will work for different people and will have varying degrees of success. There is no right or wrong answers when it comes to these things. It sometimes boils down to what works for each individual since each person will have a different health constitution.

Some of the short term fasting regimens will allow low caloric or non-caloric drinks. And there are fasting regimens that fall under the same category that don't allow any liquid intake. That means some fasting methods are dry fasts while others aren't. Both types are still acceptable in this category.

Dry fasts or absolute fasts are the most difficult type of fasting. That is why many fasting regimens today do not incorporate that type of fasting. A dry fast will always be accompanied by some degree of dehydration which may be detrimental to the health of others.

Varying Durations

There are no standard durations for different fasts whether you are talking about long term or short term fasts. Fasts can range anywhere from 12 hours up to a full 3 months. Some fasts require even more time.

You can actually fast once a month, once each week, or once each year. It all depends on the conditions of your health. As it was explained in an earlier section of this book not everyone can fast. There are of course other ways to induce autophagy besides fasting. However, don't expect to get the same results as fasting.

Short term fasts are more suited for people with metabolic diseases such as fatty liver and diabetes 2. You should also work with your doctor when treating more significant diseases via a fasting regimen. Some have found that long term fasting (i.e. those lasting more than 24 hours) can give faster results.

Note also that there is a break in period that occurs for people who haven't fasted in a while. This initial break in period will help people determine which fasting regimen they would prefer. A greater number of people usually prefer short term fasts to long term fasting. However, you can engage in a long term fast every once in a while.

12 Hour Fasting Method—The Original Daily Fast

The 12 hour fast was the way everyone fasted for hundreds of years. There are also versions of the old 12 hour fast today. Just like many short term fasting regimens, the 12 hour fast is expected to be done routinely every day. This one as it was described earlier happens every day when we go to sleep at night.

Everyone had their dinners around 7 pm and then they went to bed. Everybody then woke up 12 hours later and had breakfast. That used to work for everyone for centuries. There was no such thing as obesity back then—well at least it wasn't common. However, something changed.

The change happened in the 1950s when the meal standards changed—actually, it was the standard meal that changed. There came an influx of high carb foods into the standard diet. On top of that the meals were also formulated so that there will be less fat in the everyday diet for most people.

The other thing that changed was the frequency of the meals. Yes, we human beings didn't use to eat 3 square meals a day. No we didn't. As soon as we changed the frequency of meals eaten in a given day it reduced the frequency of our fasting periods.

The 12 hour fast would have still been quite alright even today but there are a lot of things that you should change. You need to remove all processed foods in your diet. You should also avoid excessive amounts of sugar in your diet. On top of that you shouldn't have any significant insulin resistance to begin with. However, given what we have in our meals today the 12 hour fast would not be enough to reverse a lifetime of insulin resistance.

16 Hour Fasts

Another short term fast strategy is the 16 hour fast. You will have 16 hours of fasting each day and that would mean that you will skip breakfast. We have covered the details about this fast in the previous chapter. Yes, this is the one known as the 16:8 fasting.

Martin Berkhan, a pro bodybuilder, wrote about it extensively in his blog which made the fasting regimen quite popular while he was out promoting it. He blogged about it from 2007 to 2010. However, it kind of lost steam and you don't hear much about it from Berkhan through his blog since then.

However, his website is still around which means Berkhan may be off to other forms of business other than just promoting his book and his fasting regimen. You can check him out at his blog at www.leangains.com to see updates. Last time I checked he was taking clients with whom he works with one on one.

I guess nowadays Berkhan is just content letting his books do the talking and he gets to demonstrate his unique concepts about intermittent fasting directly to clients. It would appear that the lean gains diet or 16 hour fasting method works quite well even for bodybuilders. For more information on how his diet works you can check out his book or sign up for one of his coaching sessions.

20 Hour Fasting

The 20 hour fast is otherwise known as the Warrior Diet, which we also mentioned and covered somewhat in the previous chapter. As it was explained earlier, this is a one meal a day fast. Well, not exactly one single meal. It's a one big meal and several tiny meals.

With this diet or fasting system your insulin levels are bound to spike only at night when you have that one huge meal. For the most part during the day your insulin levels will drop down and trigger fat burning and also autophagy i.e. the body's repair mode.

This diet and fasting regimen became popular in 2002. It stresses that the timing of the meals is just as important as the amount of the meal, which is really important when you do intermittent fasting. In other words when you eat is just as important as what you eat. Both elements are equally important.

Hofmekler, the guy who popularized this diet, drew upon the diets of ancient warrior societies like the Spartans and the Romans. During the day even though you are allowed some snacks you will still have to eat unprocessed foods. On top of that you will have to do some intensive physical training to make the most of the calorie burn and fat burn that will be going on for most of the day. The snacks are only there to help you get over the hunger pangs and nothing more. It wouldn't be hard to imagine that this short term fasting method would work for busy people and those who tend to travel a lot.

Are Short Term Fasts for You?

Note that whatever type of short term fast you choose they all have one singular point to everything. They all allow insulin levels to go down during the day (or for a specified amount of time) more than the usual time it goes down when you go to bed at night.

Doing these short term fasts tends to break the insulin resistance that we all feel due to the type of diet that we have in our modern society. The goal of course is to allow the body to reach a state of homeostasis.

Short term fasts seem to be more favorable for more people. Well, the human body is a thing that prefers narrow range events and activities. Any stimulus or activity that is prolonged is usually something that becomes uncomfortable and the body would most likely try to resist it eventually.

Prolonged periods of high level insulin in the blood will result in insulin resistance. The same is true, staying fasted for too long will also be detrimental to your health. What do you think will happen if the body runs out of stored fat?

That is why for most people short term fasts is the way to go. However, if you are looking to treat insulin resistance on a much better scale then a long term fast will be better for you (yes, something that can last more than 24 hours).

Characteristics of Long Term Fasts

Long term fasts are those that last longer than 24 hours. Note that the 24 hour limit is only arbitrary. There is no actual standard that divides which type of fasting is long term and what type of fasting is short-term. Some might feel and believe that 24 to 48 hour fasts should be included in the short-term fasting category.

Fasting for 72 hours is already pushing yourself to a higher limit and your body will be resisting the effort a lot by that time. On the other hand, with some practice, a 24 hour or even a 48 hour fast will seem doable for those who have been fasting for quite a while.

Note that long term fasting should be done less frequently. The actual duration of a fast will usually be up to you. If you can only do 12 to 18 hour fasts for now then stick with that fasting regimen. There is no need to force yourself to fast for longer hours especially if you have a preexisting medical condition.

After fasting for quite a while you will notice that your hunger pangs will increase significantly on day 2 of any fast. Any amount of fasting on day 1 can be bearable. You will find a way to tolerate it as well as you can. But as soon as you reach day 2 the temptation to reach out for food will become quite strong.

It's anywhere from day 2 to sometime in fasting day 3 when hunger and desire for food will be at its peak. After that your hunger pangs will gradually decrease. This is important to know since it will make or break the effort. At least you know what to expect when you undergo a long term fasting.

24 Hour Fasts = Long Term Fasts? Really?

There are people who consider 24 hour fasts as long term fasts. Well, if you haven't done any fasting then not eating for 24 hours will seem long term. That is why I recommend that you start with at least an 8 to 12 hour fast.

Again, take note that you aren't going around with no food in your belly in a 24 hour fast. Let's say you ate breakfast today and you want to start fasting afterwards. What happens is that this breakfast will be the last and only meal you will be having today. You will then skip lunch and also dinner. The next time you will be eating will be during breakfast the following day.

The same thing holds true if you do your fast lunch to lunch or dinner to dinner. Now, some may have already noticed that this type of fasting is kind of similar to the Warrior Diet that we talked about earlier. If you try the 24 hour fast you should count exactly how many hours you haven't been eating. Sometimes you may have to move your breakfast (or whatever meal you had last time) an hour after.

But why stick to the 24 hour or longer starvation period? Well sometimes it's just 20 hours and that will still be fine in some instances.

Now that is a good question. The goal here is to ensure that your insulin levels go down significantly to make your body switch from burning glucose to burning fat. For people who have more insulin resistance. That means the longer the fast the more effective it is. Yes, you may get some benefits from short term fasts but the impact won't be the same as the ones you get from long term fasts.

Note that when you do 24 hour fasts you will still be eating. This is advantageous for people who need to take medication. They can take their meds during their eating window. So for instance, you can take your aspirin, iron supplements, or maybe metformin with the one meal you are having for that day.

Another advantage of 24 hour fasts is that they are easier for people who go to work. They can be incorporated into your daily life. Some people prefer to have dinners as their one meal for the entire day. That way they can still share a meal with their family at the end of the day.

Note that you will not go hungry during long term fasts because you can still have beverages all throughout the day. You can have a cup of tea or coffee in the morning to get you started. You can skip lunch or just have another beverage for lunch. You can spend your lunch time continuing your work with a cup of your favorite drink as you work.

Now, you don't have to do 24 hour fasts every day. Remember that long term fasts should be done with less frequency. Only short term fasts should be done on a daily basis. The maximum for any long term fasting should be 2 to 3 days a week.

Will you lose muscle mass when you do long term fasting? There are studies on this very subject and none of them have reported any loss of lean muscle mass in people who fasted in the long term. In fact, in one study test subjects fasted every other day (i.e. alternate day fasting) for 22 days. Their body weight steadily increased but their lean muscle mass stayed the same.

Slow Rise in Popularity

You would think that with all the hype about fasting in the late 2000s that it would have become quite popular since then but the fact is that it didn't. Sure pioneers like Brad Pilon and Martin Berkhan saw some success but their marketing efforts didn't prove to be quite viral.

It was not until Michael Mosley's 5:2 fasting approach when fasting started to hit the mainstream media. The big difference is that Mosley was a TV producer apart from being a physician. His programs on BBC put fasting on the health and fitness roadmap globally.

Mosley appeared in TV program called Eat, Fast, and Live Longer. Apart from the documentary show on BBC he also published a book called The Fast Diet. Fasting as part of a dietary regimen became a hit sensation gaining intense interest from the public especially in the UK.

Mosley's book became a best seller in the UK of course and then he came up with follow up books as well.

Scientifically Backed Fasting Diets

Mosley's 5:2 fasting diet of course wasn't backed by science although there is already medical research on fasting in general. Greater interest in the form of clinical studies will later follow after the link between autophagy and fasting will be made in later years.

So, which fasting regimen has the most research behind it?

That would have to be Alternate Daily Fasting. The bulk of the research on this dietary regimen was conducted at the University of Illinois in Chicago with Dr. Krista Varady leading the team.

She wrote about it and published a book entitled The Every Other Day Diet but the book wasn't a big hit, which is a shame. Well, because the diet itself is backed by actual scientific studies. That means the recommendations that Varady made in her book/dietary fasting method is proven to work. Perhaps she needed a better marketing strategy which would have made her book a much better success.

Risks and Complications

Long term fasts are actually better at inducing autophagy than short term fasting. However, long term fasting also comes with its own risks and complications. The benefits do accrue the longer you fast but be aware that there are certain dangers associated with fasting longer, which is why long term fasts should be supervised by a medical professional.

Doctors may recommend long term fasting regimens for people who have obesity that are harder to treat or type 2 diabetics. Nevertheless, you should also be aware that these doctors will also closely monitor these patients, doing the blood work, checking their blood pressures, and checking for other factors.

Note that if at any time you feel sick during your fast then that is a clear signal that you should stop fasting. Fasting should still make you feel healthy and well.

Doctors should also closely monitor your medication intake. This can be a major issue for diabetics who undergo fasting regimens. Those who take the same dose of diabetes medication while fasting run the risk of hypoglycemia. That can be quite a dangerous condition if it all comes to that, which is why your doctor will keep a close eye on diabetics as they fast.

Your blood sugar going down is not really a complication. That is actually what you want to achieve when you go fasting – make your blood sugar drop. However, when your blood sugar is already low and you still take your usual dosage of meds then that may cause some problems. It also translates to the fact that you are already overmedicated at that point, which is why your doctor should adjust your prescriptions for your fasting days.

The dosage of diabetic meds should be reduced and the schedule of intake of certain drugs should also be adjusted. Note that there are medications that can cause an upset stomach when taken without a meal. Examples of such drugs are metformin, iron supplements, ASA, and NSAIDS.

36- and 42-Hour Fasting

If you really want to try going without food or drink (or mainly just solid food) then you can try a 36 hour fast. In many clinical practices patients with type 2 diabetes may be recommended to undergo a 36 hour (or longer) fast for 2 to 3 times a week.

This type of fasting usually produces better compliance among patients and it brings results faster. 36 and 42 hour fasts are better for diabetics due to their higher insulin resistance. This type of fasting regimen has been observed to be much better than shorter but more frequent fasting periods. But that doesn't mean shorter fasting protocols don't work—they do but they don't bring in results as fast as long term fasting.

Is it possible to fast for 42 hours or longer?

A 42 hour fasting routine can be easily incorporated into your daily grind. It's a lot easier than you think. However, remember that this type of fasting should be carefully supervised.

If you are used to having a quick breakfast maybe just some coffee or some other drink to get your day started then this kind of fasting strategy might just suit you. If your mornings are a rush and you usually don't have time for breakfast in the morning then this might just be the fasting habit that will work for you.

That is exactly what you will be doing in a 42 hour fast. You will make it a daily routine to skip your regular meal in the morning (aka no more solid breakfast). The entire morning still counts as part of your total fasting hours.

You will then break your fast at noon time. It is important not to binge eat during lunch as it will ruin the purpose of your fast. If you notice this is the setup for the 16:8 fasting regimen. Yes, it is a short term fast.

What you need to do now is to add a bit of long term fast in between those regular daily fasts. What you can do is to combine that with a 36 hour fast. So let's say you're already used to skipping breakfast having only your regular coffee and water in the morning—you're already doing that 7 days a week Mondays to Sundays.

Let's say you want to do a 36 hour fast on Tuesday. So, you will skip breakfast as usual on Monday and then have your regular lunch and dinner. Come Tuesday morning you will skip everything from breakfast to dinner—essentially living on a liquid diet the whole day Tuesday. The next meal you will be having is on Wednesday at lunch time. Count the number of hours you fasted during that time and you will have done a 42 hour fast.

It is important though that you should not implement any calorie restriction during actual meal times. A lot of times those who have made fasting a daily habit would lose appetite. The ideal thing to do rather is to eat until you are satisfied during your eating period. Eat to satiation not until you can't eat any more.

Why Do Appetites Decrease During Long Term Fasts?

There is a good reason why people start to lose appetite during long term fasting. As your body starts to break its insulin resistance cycle, the usual high insulin levels in your blood decreases steadily.

Insulin is the hormone that regulates BSW or body set weight. If the insulin levels are usually high then the regular BSW is also high. That means your body will want to gain weight i.e. you will get hungry plenty of times.

But when your body breaks its insulin resistance cycle the insulin levels go down. Since there isn't a lot of this hormone in your blood then there will be fewer hunger pangs triggered. In essence, your body wants to go down in terms of BSW. At the same time as your appetite goes down, the body's total energy expenditure also goes down and is better maintained.

Chapter 9: The Effect of Ketogenic Diets

Is it possible to trigger autophagy through a ketogenic diet? If you remember in a previous discussion in this book we talked about ketosis as one of the phases that will be reached on the way to autophagy. How long a fast does it take to induce ketosis and autophagy? Those are the two questions that we will cover and more in this chapter.

Ketosis and Autophagy

Keto diets and fasting diets are some of the health trends today. These are not fad diets since both of them are backed by actual scientific studies. On top of that there is a lot of testimonial evidence for them as well.

Many people have tried them some under the supervision of a physician or some other health worker—like a fitness coach for instance. People do it for different reasons. Some do it for weight loss, some do it for their overall wellbeing, and many people are on these diets looking to resolve or address their individual health problems.

Experts are beginning to understand the role of fasting and ketosis to deep internal healing in the body through both of these diet regimens. *But, what is the difference between ketosis and autophagy?*

We have already established that autophagy is the body's process of recycling cellular parts and it occurs when the blood insulin levels go down. That basically happens when you enter into starvation mode.

Ketosis on the other hand is a metabolic state (which is what autophagy is too) where the body produces more ketone bodies and makes use of them a lot more than usual. As it was explained earlier the liver produces more ketone bodies when the body's glycogen stores are depleted.

Ketone bodies are used as a substitute for glucose. There are two ways to induce ketosis. The first way to do it is to go on fasting. The other way to do it is to go on a ketogenic diet—a diet which is essentially low carb.

Note that autophagy and ketosis are metabolic states that support one another. However, it should also be pointed out here is that these two states or bodily processes are not inclusive of each other. That means you can go into a state of ketosis but never reaching the point of autophagy. The reverse is also true that you can also be in a state of autophagy without essentially be in a ketogenic state.

However, a lot of times ketosis and autophagy accompany one another or occur at the same time because they both follow the self-same principle.

Will Autophagy Require a State of Ketosis?

The next question is whether or not a state of autophagy will require a state of ketosis? We know that ketosis will occur first before autophagy sets in. The key here is to understand what regulates both of these metabolic states.

What Regulates Ketosis

Your body achieves a state of ketosis via glucose restriction. The primary mechanism or driving condition that causes a state of ketosis (i.e. the creation of ketone bodies in the liver) is the depletion of glycogen in the liver.

A deficiency in carbohydrates can also cause the increased production of ketone bodies. Is there anything that can cause carb deficiency in the body? Well, we know that protein can help increase the synthesis of carbs. It happens through a process called gluconeogenesis.

Note however that gluconeogenesis is a secondary factor in the production of ketone bodies. That means this process doesn't affect ketogenic production that much. This also means you can achieve ketosis without having to lower your blood insulin levels—but lowered insulin levels do tend to happen.

That means you can eat food that is rich in protein and achieve ketosis. However, since the calorie content of that food will still maintain the insulin and mTOR levels in your body then you don't achieve autophagy.

What you have achieved is something called nutritional ketosis. In this state your mTOR signaling factor will still be high. That factor will inhibit the state of autophagy. Note that the reverse is also true—you don't need to enter a state of ketosis in order to achieve autophagy. You can be in a state of autophagy for several days and still not achieve ketosis.

How is that possible? It all depends on how keto adapted a person is. But it should be emphasized here that being in a ketogenic state already meets a lot of the requirements to induce autophagy.

In other words even if you are unable to achieve autophagy yet, getting into a state of ketogenesis is already one huge step forward. Some of these requirements include lowered mTOR levels, low levels of blood glucose, and reduced blood insulin. You just need to make a few adjustments in your dietary regimen (e.g. make adjustments in your fasting or include fasting in your regimen).

Measuring Ketone Levels to Estimate Autophagy

There is actually no exact way to measure autophagy in human beings. The studies that have been conducted where a state of autophagy has been determined were largely done on rats and other animals as test subjects.

What we really have are close enough estimates. What your doctor will do is to check your insulin to glucagon ratio and also look at your glucose ketone index. That's as close as we can get at the moment but that doesn't mean we may not be able to find a viable way to measure autophagy. There is still a lot of research going on and this is one of the interests in the ongoing studies.

Experts estimate that it takes anywhere from 48 to 72 hours of fasting to activate autophagy. However, there is no actual timeline and we currently do not know for sure when autophagy has already been achieved.

The length of time needed for fast to induce autophagy depends on the actual nutrient status of the person who is fasting. That is why it will be different from one person to the next. We don't have the means to exactly point out whether the current mTOR and insulin levels have become low enough to achieve that metabolic state.

Key Factors to Consider

There are several indicators that will be considered when estimating the instance of autophagy in human beings. They include the following:

1. When the insulin to glucagon ratio is lower this it indicates that there is nutrient deprivation, fat oxidation, gluconeogenesis, ketogenesis, and more catabolism.
2. A lower score on the glucose ketone index will indicate more AMPK and higher ketosis. This index indicates the insulin to glucose ratio in the body.
3. Higher insulin to glucagon ratio on the other hand will indicate nutrient storage, elevated blood sugar, higher insulin levels, and a lot more anabolism.

The actual length of the fasting period before autophagy finally is induced will be determined by the body's nutrient status. The presence of certain nutrients like ketones, glucose, and amino acids will be telling.

That means if you do not take in too much protein or carbs on a daily basis then you are better poised to enter into autophagy compared to someone who does. That is because you no longer have to burn through a lot of calories to get to that point.

Here's how the glucose ketone index formula is computed by your physician:

1. Your blood glucose is measured
2. The blood ketones are also measured
3. The amount of blood glucose is then divided by 18
4. Divide the result with the number of ketones that was measured in step 2

NOTE: if you are measuring the glucose ketone index (GKI) in mmol/L then you should do step 3. However if you want your figures in mg/dl then your doctor will skip step 3.

Entering Autophagy While in a State of Ketosis

As a recap, remember that the most effective and also the most natural way to enter into a state of ketosis and autophagy is of course through fasting. However, it should be stressed here that you should fast for several days in order to induce your body to enter into these metabolic states. The goal behind it all is to cause energy depletion in the body, which will ramp up the production of ketone bodies in the liver.

Studies have shown that in order for ketones in the body to be synthesized, you will have to enter into a state of autophagy[65]. This is one of the interesting connections between autophagy and ketosis. Gluconeogenesis is not affected by the reduced production of ketones in the liver.

What does that indicate? It means that autophagy is essential if you want to achieve ketosis. It is also an essential state that the body should enter into in order to become more keto adapted. If there is not enough autophagy going on, then the body will stay in a sugar burning state.

According to another study, ketosis actually promotes a different type or level of autophagy called brain macro autophagy. This is accomplished by activating Sirt1[66]. That strengthens the connection between these processes that goes on in the human body.

Ketone bodies also play another role when it comes to autophagy. They help to stimulate CMA or chaperone mediated autophagy. This particular metabolic state will usually make use of specific types of substrates as well as certain amino acids[67].

This gives us a huge impetus for elevating the levels of ketone bodies in our systems since they are very beneficial to our overall well-being. There are two ways to elevate the ketones as well as the Beta-hydroxybutyrate in the human body. The first way as you might have guessed is to go fasting forcing your body into starvation mode. The second way to do it is through eating a ketogenic diet.

We all go through ketosis naturally, just a bit of FYI. It isn't something special that you have to induce. It is not a reserved state of the body that only gets activated in the rarest occasions. People go into ketosis at certain times during the cold winter months.

We also enter this metabolic phase when we eat more protein than carbs. Well, people tend to eat more meat during winter season. The combination of limited carbs, calorie restriction, and larger protein intake makes the body more flexible since it is not restricted in its diet. This combination also allows the body to better activate autophagy and therefore it is much better suited to entering into ketosis.

CMA: Ketosis Providing Support for Autophagy

Eating a ketogenic diet will definitely bring your body to a state of ketosis. When your body is in that metabolic state it can provide a lot of support for autophagy state or phase. That means your body's cells are better able to recycle and repair the needed parts including specific types of protein. This is called chaperone mediated autophagy or CMA.

Do you need to go on fasting to enter CMA mode? Well, not necessarily. The important thing is to keep the protein and carb intake really low for a sustained amount of time. This is one way to allow your body to enter into ketosis while in a ketogenic diet. That way your body can remain in ketosis as it recycles specific types of protein.

If you aren't to eat a lot of protein and you're not going to consume carbs that will fuel the production of glucose in the body, what should you eat?

The answer is that you should eat healthy fats. This is one of the modalities seen as a way to decrease neural injury in patients that have been experiencing seizures. In a way it mimics a lot of the aspects of a body's physiology when there is lowered mTOR and insulin.

Certain fats like coconut oil as well as MCT oil can help increase the body's production of ketone bodies. The only downside is that including too much healthy fat in your diet can ruin your fast since fats are calorie rich and they contain a lot of macronutrients. In other words they can still raise your insulin and mTOR levels if you have too much.

In that case what does a ketogenic diet look like?

The ratio of therapeutic macros in that kind of diet will have to be 5% carbs, 15% to 20% proteins, and 70% to 80% fats. This will help you maintain a keto diet and help achieve autophagy. As you can see you can eat a little more proteins or fats and still stay within a ketogenic ratios.

Now, here's an important detail about all this. You can eat more protein and also more carbs and still stay within ketogenic limits. With that sort of percentage in macros your body will still produce more ketone bodies. The downside is that exceeding those limits will already break your fast.

Which is Better Ketosis or Autophagy?

A ketogenic diet may be low in carbs but it does look like it is a doable diet, right? You won't get hungry due to the amounts of healthy fat that you will be consuming. If you check out keto recipes and keto meals they still look like the regular food that you eat, which means it won't feel as restricting as other diets.

That is why some ask if ketogenic diets can be a better alternative to fasting when it comes to producing the desired effects. Effects would be repair and recycling of the body, rejuvenation, anti-aging effects, etc.

Again, there should be no question about it that autophagy is way better than ketosis when you're looking at health and metabolic benefits. That is if you compare fasting induced autophagy versus keto diet induced autophagy. The level of metabolic benefits from fasting far exceeds the benefits from a keto diet thus fasting wins almost every time.

However, there are instances where a ketogenic diet is better suited for people who struggle with weight loss issues, insulin resistance, seizures, and diabetes. Now, here's a big tip – you can magnify the health benefits of a ketogenic diet by adding some intermittent fasting in between. If you want to maximize the benefits of a ketogenic diet then you should incorporate an extended fast every now and then into your dietary schedule.

Instead of thinking which one is better, the better thing to ask is how you can combine both of these regimens in order to reap the most benefits. A low carb keto diet that doesn't overdo the amounts of protein is a great basal template that you can follow.

It will help you maintain better metabolic health. It also primes your body to go into autophagy a lot faster—that means you don't have to fast too long to enter into autophagy.

So, What Foods Can You Eat On A Keto Diet?

Here is a sample list of foods that you can eat while on a keto diet:
- Cauliflower, zucchini, spinach, and other low carb veggies
- Eggs – note that they are absolutely low carb
- Shellfish and fish – both are also low carb and they are good protein sources
- Meat from grass fed sources – the goal here is to get high quality protein sources
- Yogurt and cheese – high calcium and high protein options
- Butter and cream – these foods barely have carbohydrates in them
- MCT oil, Coconut oil, and olive oil
- Avocadoes
- Seeds and nuts

If you are interested in finding out all the food that you can eat while on a keto diet, we have a list of those foods at the end of this chapter.

2 Important Benefits from a Keto Lifestyle

Researchers attribute certain health benefits from a keto lifestyle. The two most important benefits they cite are the following:

- **Weight Loss** – a lot of people go into a keto diet in order to lose weight. People lose weight for different health reasons. Some need to lose weight because that will help them cope with diabetes. Others lose weight for cardiovascular health. A keto lifestyle is appealing because it helps make the body more efficient at burning fat. You remain full in the process even though you only consume fewer calories. People who suffer from epilepsy have shown great improvements after undergoing a keto diet. It induces the body to produce ketones as well as decanoic acid which are beneficial for preventing seizures.
- **Improved Insulin Sensitivity** – again a keto lifestyle is a huge benefit for people with diabetes. Other than helping these people lose weight they also become more insulin sensitive. A keto diet can lower blood sugar levels.

Safety Issues

The next question that people ask if the keto diet is a safe diet. It is important to point out that this kind of diet does pose some risks. Putting your body in a state of ketosis also has downsides too, which you should know before you jump into it.

Here are some of the side effects of a ketogenic diet:

- Lowered blood sugar levels (this condition may be a problem for some but a benefit for others)
- Indigestion
- Constipation
- Bad breath

The first few days of trying a keto diet can be a quite challenging due to an overall feeling of being sick even though you are eating perfectly healthy meals. Some people experience some form of insomnia while on a keto diet while others report feel nauseous. There is also a risk for potential dehydration and since you will be eating more meat, there is also that chance of developing kidney stones.

Should You Go On a Keto Diet?

Note that no one really knows today what the long term effects of a keto diet are. And that is one of the things that everyone should consider before they try it. It is still best to ask your dietitian or your family doctor before you embark on any dietary change keto or otherwise.

Remember that the keto diet can make extreme changes in your lifestyle. If your body is used to taking in lots of carbs, then the reduction or total removal of carbs on your diet will have a significant impact on your well-being. If you are Asian and rice is a staple in your diet then you may find the keto diet to be quite challenging. The same is true for anyone who has a carb staple in their meals.

If you are experiencing seizures then your doctor might recommend that you go on a keto diet. In that case it has been deemed a good option for you. Your doctor will incorporate this mode of treatment in case seizure medications aren't working for you. Note however that your doctor or dietitian will closely monitor your progress and can call off the diet as he deems necessary.

If you have kidney issues or problems with your liver then you definitely should consult your diet first before trying the keto diet. Note that this type of diet will put more strain on these vital organs. It can even lead to fatigue and loss of muscle tissues despite the fact that you are taking in proteins.

Chapter 10: Keto Meal Plan to Boost Autophagy

In this chapter we will provide you with a sample meal plan in the ketogenic diet. This is not intended to be a comprehensive guide. There are other works that cover this topic a lot more extensively.

The goal here is to give you an idea about the meals that you can prepare, that way you can gauge whether this type of diet is for you or not. Your doctor may also prescribe this diet to you if you have any preexisting medical conditions such as the following:

- Acne
- Brain injuries
- Polycystic ovary syndrome
- Parkinson's disease
- Epilepsy (the keto diet was primarily designed for people who have epilepsy).
- Alzheimer's disease
- Cancer
- Heart disease

After going over the meal plan and the recipes, you can look for other keto recipes. You can find a lot on the web, which means you will hardly run out of options. We will also go over some tips that can be useful to you especially when you have to outside.

Foods to Avoid/Consumed Less Frequently

Note that in the keto diet any food that has high carb content shouldn't be eaten or should be consumed in minimal amounts. The following foods should either be avoided or reduced.

- *Sugar free diet foods* – yes they may say "diet" on the label but diet food and drinks are usually highly processed. On top of that, they usually contain a lot of sugar alcohol which have a huge impact on the body's ketone levels.
- *Alcohol* – alcohol usually has high carb content, which is why they aren't allowed in any keto based diet. They can literally knock you out of ketosis.
- *Unhealthy fats* – mayonnaise, processed vegetable oils, and other unhealthy fats should be limited.
- *Sauces and condiments* – be careful about sauces and condiments. Make sure that they do not contain any unhealthy fat or any form of sugar.
- *Diet products or low fat products* – diet sodas are out in this diet. Be cautious of any kind of diet- or low fat products. A lot of them are made from highly processed products and are high in carbs.

- *Tubers and root veggies* – this includes parsnips, carrots, sweet potatoes, and potatoes.
- *Legumes and beans* – this includes chickpeas, lentils, kidney beans, and peas.
- *Fruit* – all kinds of fruit intake should be reduced. Remember that a lot of fruits naturally contain sugar. However, you can take very small portions or reduced portions of berries.
- *Starches and grains* – you should avoid eating cereal, pasta, rice, and any kind of wheat product.
- *Sugary foods* – this includes candy, ice cream, cake, smoothies, fruit juice, and of course soda.

Sample Meal Plan – Week 1

The following is the meal plan for week 1.

Monday

- Breakfast – Fried eggs with bacon
- Lunch – burger (no bread) with salsa and cheese
- Dinner – steak and eggs with a side of salad

Tuesday

- Breakfast – spinach, egg, and white fish cooked in coconut oil
- Lunch – cheese and ham slices with a side of nuts
- Dinner – cheese omelet with veggies and ham

Wednesday

- Breakfast – burger with bacon (minus the bun), cheese, and egg
- Lunch – beef stir fry with a side of veggies (use coconut oil to fry)
- Dinner – yogurt (sugar free) with stevia, cocoa powder, and peanut butter

Thursday

- Breakfast – stuffed chicken with veggies on the side. Stuffing can be cream cheese and pesto.
- Lunch – guacamole, salsa, celery sticks, and a handful of nuts
- Dinner – avocado and omelet.

Friday

- Breakfast – pork chops with salad, broccoli, and parmesan on the side
- Lunch – shrimp salad on olive oil
- Dinner – keto milkshake

Saturday

- Breakfast – meatballs with veggies and cheddar cheese
- Lunch – peanut butter, almond milk, with milkshake with stevia and cocoa powder
- Dinner – goat cheese omelet with basils and tomatoes

Sunday

- Breakfast – salmon and asparagus
- Lunch – chicken salad with feta cheese
- Dinner – eggs, bacon, and tomatoes

Sample Meal Plan – Week 2

The following is the meal plan for week 2.

Monday
- Breakfast – scrambled eggs
- Lunch – Asian beef salad
- Dinner – keto pesto chicken casserole

Tuesday
- Breakfast – keto cheese roll ups
- Lunch – keto caprese omelet
- Dinner – keto meat pie

Wednesday
- Breakfast – keto frittata with spinach on the side
- Lunch – keto chicken soup
- Dinner – keto carbonara

Thursday
- Breakfast – dairy free keto latte
- Lunch – keto salad with avocado, bacon, and goat cheese
- Dinner – keto pizza

Friday
- Breakfast – mushroom omelet
- Lunch – smoked salmon
- Dinner – keto tortilla with ground beef

Saturday
- Breakfast – baked bacon omelet
- Lunch – keto quesadillas
- Dinner – Asian cabbage stir fry

Sunday
- Breakfast – keto pancakes with whipped cream
- Lunch – Italian keto plate
- Dinner – pork chops with green beans

Keto Snacks

There are days when you will have to fast during the week. In the meal plans that you will make you should indicate which meals you will have to skip on your fasting days. You get to choose which type of intermittent fasting you will do.

In case your fasting strategy requires you to have lower calories during meals then you can use these snack ideas. They will also become useful in case you do get hungry in between meals and you really need something to eat.

You may have to break your fast at some point but at least you are still maintaining your ketosis. That way you can give your diet a bit of a push later on and still induce autophagy rather easily than not putting yourself into a keto state.

The following are keto snack ideas. However, do take note that some of these snacks may have more calories than you can imagine. It would be a good idea to do some calorie counting during your fasting days to be sure.

- Smaller portions of leftovers
- Celery with guacamole and salsa
- Strawberries with cream
- Full fat yogurt
- Low carb milkshake
- Nut butter and cocoa powder
- 90% dark chocolate
- 2 hard-boiled eggs
- Cheese and olives
- A handful of your choice of nuts or seeds
- Cheese
- Fatty fish
- Fatty meat

Eating Out/Fast Food While on a Keto Diet

This is probably one of the concerns that people who go on a diet usually have in their minds. You are on a strict and obviously different diet than most people. That means your food options are not the typical ones that you will find in your everyday menu—unless of course you're eating in a keto friendly restaurant.

Keto Friendly Restaurant Options

However, the good news is that it isn't really that hard to make regular restaurant food keto friendly. Remember that a lot of restaurants usually offer menu options that are either fish based or meat based. You can order that option and just ask to have the carb ingredients replaced with veggies.

Other than meat or fish based foods, egg meals are also another option. Omelet and bacon is a staple in low carb diet plans like keto. If you order burgers, you can ask to hold the buns and replace the fries with veggies. If you dine in a Mexican restaurant then you're in luck. You can enjoy their meat type dishes and ask for extra cheese, sour cream, salsa, and guacamole.

Keto Friendly Fast Food Options

Choosing the right fast food can be the most challenging thing to do when you're on the keto diet. Note that the keto diet is definitely a restrictive diet, which makes it kind of hard to find compatible menu options.

The hard part is in the fact that a lot of fast food options are usually high in carbs. However there are fast food chains that also serve keto friendly items on their menu. Here are several ideas on how you can make fast food keto friendly.

1. **Bunless Burgers**

The high carb levels in burger options in McDonald's, White Castle, or any other burger chain is from the buns. If you want to make these burgers keto friendly all you need to do is to get rid of the buns.

You should also ask to have some of the high carb toppings removed. Examples of these toppings are breaded onions, teriyaki sauce, ketchup, and honey mustard sauce among others.

Of course you can still have toppings on your bun-less burger. Just make sure to use keto friendly options such as tomatoes, regular onions, ranch dressing, lettuce, mustard, avocado, fried egg, salsa, and mayo.

Note that a lot of fast food stores will be happy to serve you bunless burgers if you just ask. So, how many calories will you get on the average bunless order? Here are a couple of figures that might interest you:

- Wendy's Double Stack Cheeseburger minus the bun will have 260 calories with only 20 grams protein and 1 gram of carbs
- A McDonald's Double Cheeseburger minus the bun will have 270 calories, 20 grams of protein, and 4 grams of carbs

2. **Egg Breakfasts**

There are many egg based breakfast options served in different fast food chains. To make them more keto friendly you can remove the hash browns, bread, and other carb sources that come with the egg. You can substitute veggies and other keto friendly options instead.

- The Burger King Ultimate Breakfast Platter minus the biscuit, hash browns, and/or pancakes gives you 340 calories total, 16 grams of protein, and only 1 gram of carbs.
- The McDonald's Bacon, Egg and Cheese Biscuit but holding the usual biscuit that is served with it gives you 190 calories, 14 grams of protein, and 4 grams of carbs.

3. **Low Carb Salads**

When we think of salads we think that they are usually nutrient rich foods that are low in carbs and just loaded with all the good stuff, right? Well, that is just not the case with fast food salads. A lot of them are actually loaded with carbs.

Here's an example: the Apple Pecan Chicken Salad from Wendy's sounds really safe for dieting right? But it actually has a total of 52 grams of carbs and not to mention its sugar content, which is about 40 grams per serving.

So where do all the carbs in these salads come from? They're actually found in the additives. That means you need to skip some of the usual ingredients to make them more keto friendly.

For instance you may have to remove the dried fruit, marinades, certain dressings, and toppings. Pay attention to the ingredients that are high in sugar. That means you need to avoid those sweet dressings. That means you need to stick to keto friendly dressings like ranch, vinegar, and oil.

For instance, take away all the usual carb sources from Moe's Taco Salad, you will get 325 calories, 22 grams of protein, and just 10 grams of carbs. You can keep the guacamole, cheddar cheese, jalapenos, and chicken adobo as additives. You will still be within keto bounds but you should pay attention to serving sizes.

Remember that you need to stay within the allowed number of calories to stay within a fasting zone. As it was described earlier, some fasting regimens allow around 500 to 600 calories or so per day even on a fasting day. You should avoid croutons, breaded chicken, tortilla shells, and candied nuts in order to stay within the limit of your fast.

4. **Burgers in Lettuce Wraps**

The good news is that fast food companies are catching on to the keto craze and they want to cash in on the rising number of customers who are opting for keto based options. That is why they are adding more keto friendly options on their menus.

An example of this is the lettuce wrapped burger. They still get to serve burgers but cutting away the majority of the carbs. Wrapping burgers in lettuce makes for a fascinating low carb option.

Here are a couple of examples:

- The Protein Style Cheeseburger from In-n-Out Burger packs around 330 calories, 18 grams of protein, and only 11 grams of carbs
- The Lettuce-Wrapped Thickburger from Carl's Jr. packs 420 calories, 25 grams of protein, and only 8 grams of carbs.

5. **Low Carb Burrito Bowls**

Do you know that a burrito wrap packs 50 grams of carbs which translates to 300 calories? That's just the wrapping alone—you're still not getting the entire burrito. And then comes the burrito bowl.

It's a burrito minus the wrap, basically. They have that low carb base made of leafy greens, healthy fat choices, and protein. You should avoid corn, sweet dressings, beans, and tortilla chips which are carb heavy options.

Again, you should pay attention to the calorie content and plan your meals ahead of time. Some of the burrito bowls served by popular fast food chains still have plenty of calories in them.

Here are a few examples:

- Moe's Southwestern Grill Burrito Bowl (394 calories)
- Taco Bell Cantina Power Steak Bowl (310 calories)
- Chipotle Chicken Burrito Bowl (525 calories)
- Chipotle Steak Burrito Bowl (400 calories)

If it is a fast day or you just have to cut back on your caloric intake, you can always eat half of the burrito and have the rest to go so you can keep it in the fridge for later.

6. Keto Beverage Options

It is no secret that a lot of beverages served in fast food restaurants have lots of sugar in them. Sure they call the iced tea, diet soda, sugar-free this but they are still sweet and they may have enough sugar (or sugar based substitutes) to break your ketosis.

For instance, if you order the Dunkin' Donuts Vanilla Bean Coolatta, you are still getting 88 grams of sugar. That is the equivalent of 22 teaspoons of sugar.

That is why when you order your beverages make sure that you are getting the keto friendly ones, which include the following:

- Water
- Soda water
- Hot tea (minus the sugar of course)
- Black iced coffee
- Coffee with cream
- Unsweetened iced tea

Well, what if you want to sweeten your beverage? Now what? Well, you may have to bring some zero calorie sweeteners like Stevia. Yes, it can be a bit of an inconvenience but that is a little adjustment that you will have to make if you want to maintain a ketone balance enough to induce autophagy.

Chapter 11: The Exercise-Autophagy Connection

Everyone knows that there are a lot of benefits if we engage in physical activity. The effects are of course well-known and well-researched. Well at least on the macro level. However, the cellular processes behind all those benefits have only become clearer fairly recently.

Treatment of Disorders in Skeletal Muscles

One of these relatively newer findings is the link between the prevention of the dysfunction of our muscles with exercise. One of the dysfunctions in particular that researchers are beginning to shed light on is the loss of stimuli. This frequently occurs in the skeletal muscles. Note that this is the type of muscle that makes up the most of the body's mass.

This loss of stimuli isn't because of the skeletal muscles themselves. It has more to do with the nervous system instead. The dysfunction occurs as an aftermath when the sciatic nerve gets injured.

This neural injury usually occurs on people who are bed ridden and also on people who sit for long hours such as bus drivers. Medical intervention is required in order to treat these patients and eventually improve their quality of life.

According to one study[68] from the University of São Paulo, Brazil, this type of dysfunction is due to the increased production of processed proteins in the skeletal muscles. This resulted in muscle wasting and eventual weakening of the muscular tissues.

Why was there a build-up of proteins which eventually resulted in both muscular and nerve damage? According to researchers this build up is due to the impairment of autophagy.

The loss or lack of stimulus in skeletal muscle tissues is a degenerative disease. Researchers were able to demonstrate that with exercise the skeletal muscles can be primed for autophagy. The test subjects in this study were subjected to aerobic exercises. Aerobic exercise resulted in the delay of the observed muscular atrophy.

According to Julio Cesar Batista Ferreira, daily exercise can sensitize the autophagic system. That means it doesn't only happen in the brain—it can also greatly affect the muscular tissues of the body (and perhaps other parts of the body as well).

Exercise on a daily basis facilitates the removal of dysfunctional organelles in the cells of the body—we've already touched on that several times in this book. However it should also be emphasized at this point that autophagy is also the process that eliminates unnecessary proteins that build up in the muscular tissues.

The removal of these dysfunctional components is definitely important. They are unnecessary so the body (well, the muscles in particular) don't really need them. They have no use and they have no function. But when they accumulate overtime they will become toxic. Researchers suggest that they can even contribute to muscular impairment and eventually death.

Dr. Ferreira often uses a fridge analogy to describe this kind of muscular dysfunction. He says that the muscles are like a fridge, which of course needs electricity to function. The "electricity" of course is supplied to the muscles by the sciatic nerve. Once the connection between the electricity and fridge is lost the fridge stops to function.

In the case of the muscles, the neurons stop innervating them. The food in the fridge will start to decompose or spoil. The speed of the spoilage of the food items will depend on the composition of the food. The same is true with the proteins of the muscles—they "spoil" at different rates.

How Autophagy Can Help

But Ferreira clarifies that there is a difference between a fridge and the human muscles. The muscle tissues and cells are fortunate to have an early warning system. This early warning system will activate the autophagic system at the onset of the degradation.

It isolates and "incinerates" as it were any defective material (i.e. the proteins and other toxins) that is found in the muscular tissues. This process will prevent the spread of the damage. This is basically how the autophagic system works in the muscles.

All of that is well and good. But what if autophagy is impaired? It does happen since skeletal muscles do lose stimuli. Dr. Ferreira explains that if the muscles stop receiving the right electric signals and if it continues for an extended period of time then this early warning mechanism of the muscular tissues stop to work. The result is the collapse of the cells of the skeletal muscles.

The proteins in the muscles that no longer function properly form the toxins that build up eventually. These toxins will then start killing the other cells in the muscular tissues. If autophagy is activated the process would isolate these toxic proteins and they will later be destroyed and recycled.

As you can observe from the process described above, the severed connection results in cascading effects. The end result of that series of events is the death of useful cells.

Exercise and training has been observed to increase the autophagic flux. This clean up or recycling process in the cells reduced the number of dysfunctional protein cells. At the same time exercise also improves the muscles ability to contract.

So how does that happen? Dr. Ferreira explains that exercise is a type of transient stress. This type of stress tends to create muscle memory. When human beings or any other organism is exposed or pre-exposed to certain kinds of stress it is better able to combat and respond to degenerative dysfunctions.

Dr. Ferreira's team however stresses that their research was not designed to find a solution or treatment to sciatica (i.e. the loss of stimuli to the sciatic nerve) or any other dysfunction in the muscles. They were just laying the groundwork for other research in the future.

The goal is to understand what happens to the muscles when they are subjected to exercise on the cellular level. They hope to develop a drug or a treatment regimen that may be used for patients with degenerative muscle diseases. Maybe further research can be made that may also help people with impaired limbs.

Recovery and Protection of Cardiac Muscles

Regular exercise is part of the overall treatment for heart conditions, particularly heart failure. Heart failure is a condition wherein the heart is unable to pump enough blood to supply for the entire body.

Exercise is of course beneficial to people with other related medical conditions. It is beneficial for the treatment of a variety of conditions from arterial blood pressure to cachexia (severe loss of muscle mass and weight).

We know that exercise promotes improved cardiac function. Exercise has also been found to postpone degenerative processes in heart tissues. It can help to prevent the progressive death of heart cells. Degenerative cardiac diseases are considered very serious conditions since 70% of all patients who have them tend to die from it within just 5 years.

According to one study[69] that was conducted in the University of São Paulo, Brazil, aerobic exercise has been seen to improve autophagy in the heart and protect this vital muscle. So, how does autophagy benefit heart health?

Researchers say that aerobic training increases the removal and replacement of mitochondria in the heart that are no longer functioning properly. As it was explained earlier, the mitochondria are the power house of the cells. In other words they are responsible for providing the needed energy to the cells.

When failing mitochondria is removed and eventually replaced, this improves the delivery of ATP to the cells of the heart muscle. ATP again is short for adenosine triphosphate, the molecule that stands as the energy source of the cells.

But that is not the only benefit of autophagy in the heart. When dysfunctional mitochondria are recycled the same process also reduces the production of toxic molecules in the heart. Examples of which are reactive aldehydes and oxygen free radicals, which tend to build up in the cardiac area. Excessive build-up of these toxic molecules damages the structure of the heart cells.

Putting It All Together: Exercise and Cellular Maintenance

These studies cited above confirm and reaffirm the need for exercise in the lives of people in today's modern age. Our current couch potato and sitting all day in the office culture needs to change. From the two cases—both for skeletal and cardiac muscles—we see the value of daily aerobic exercise and ability to induce autophagy.

Experts say that exercising daily will help to sensitize the body's autophagic system[70]. Exercise facilitates the removal of dysfunctional cellular components. This is important because the accumulation of these dysfunctional components whether they be mitochondria, proteins, or others will cause a toxic build up and eventual degeneration and impairment of nearby muscular tissues. The final effect of this toxic build up is cellular death.

Aerobic vs. Anaerobic Exercise

In the studies that we highlighted, the researchers used aerobic exercise as the primary exercise regimen to induce autophagy. Now the question here is that do just do aerobic exercises or can we do anaerobic exercises as well?

Well, before any of that we should first identify the difference between aerobic and anaerobic exercises. To put it all simply, aerobic exercises constitutes any light activity. If it is an exercise that you can do and sustain for a long period of time then that is considered as an aerobic exercise.

Examples of these exercises include jogging, walking, swimming, and cycling. These are exercises that you can keep doing for hours on end without getting absolutely fatigued. That is not the case with anaerobic exercises.

Anaerobic exercises are the types of activities that will leave you running out of breath within a few minutes. They are more of bust exercises that can only be done for a very short span of time. Examples of these exercises include sprinting and weight lifting.

During aerobic exercises you are able to supply oxygen to the body since you have enough power left to inhale and exhale while performing the said exercise. That is not the case with anaerobic exercise. In that mode the activity that you are doing is so difficult and your actions so vigorous that you hardly have enough time or energy to breath. You will be forced to stop exercising just to be able to breathe.

So, which one is better?

The truth is that both types of exercise burns fat. Both of them will give your metabolism a boost. And that caloric burn will go on for a few hours even after you have worked out. That means in order to give the biggest boost to your autophagic system you should incorporate both exercises when you work out.

Aerobic exercises increase muscular endurance. It also improves your cardiac health. Anaerobic exercises help you burn more body fat and also helps you gain lean muscle mass, which is important to prevent muscular atrophy (aka muscle loss).

Aerobic and Anaerobic Exercise Samples

You don't necessarily have to go to the gym to exercise. You can do it all in th comforts of your own home. The following are examples of aerobic exercises that you can try:

- Ride a stationary bike
- Go bicycling around the block
- Play tennis
- Play badminton
- Ice skating
- Roller skating
- Swimming
- Dancing
- Follow an aerobic workout on TV or YouTube
- Jogging
- Run or jog on a treadmill
- Jog every morning or afternoon
- Jumping jacks
- Brisk walk around the neighborhood

The following are examples of anaerobic exercises that you can do at home. Note that you can purchase weights if you want or just find heavy objects that you can safely lift. Another option is to do bodyweight exercises (i.e. calisthenics).

- Sprints (you can do 2 minutes of running as fast as you can, rest for 1 minute, and run at a moderate pace for another minute, then rest for another minute and then repeat from the start).
- Weight lifting (again you can use weights but you can also just use objects that are sufficiently heavy like bottled water, a backpack full of books, etc.)
- Calisthenics like inclined pushups, pushups, sit ups, chin-ups, bench dips, and knee raises
- Plyometric exercises like jump rope, lunges, skipping, clap push-ups, and jump squats (note that some of these exercises can be intense for someone who hasn't done any exercise for a long time). I suggest that you reserve these exercises for later.
- Isometric exercises like forearm planks, low squats, triceps extension against the wall, prayer pose, high planks, bent over presses against the wall.

Tips for People Who Haven't Exercised in a Long Time

If you haven't done any cardio exercises in a while then you shouldn't go gung ho about it. Start slowly. You don't want to put undue strain on your limbs, which will take the brunt of the punishment.

Do things gradually and start out with just a short 5 to 10 minute workout (maybe brisk walking first?) each day for a week. Allow your feet, legs, and lungs to slowly regain their strength. Basically what you're doing is acclimating your body to workouts and exercises.

If 5 to 10 minutes of cardio every day seems too much then start with cardio 2 to 3 times a week. Do your cardio for 2 weeks or until your body has become used to walking or jogging.

The following week you can take things up a notch. You can either try a more intensive workout or just increase the time you exercise. Let's say you just used to walk on two separate days each week for 10 minutes, you can try walking 15 minutes every day next week.

Another option is to go jogging for 10 minutes on two separate days in the next week. The following week you can try jogging 5 minutes every day. And then the following week you can go jogging for 15 minutes every day in the morning or afternoon.

After that you can try running instead. But you should reduce your workout time so as not to strain your joints especially your knees. You can also switch to swimming or dancing which is more intense. You should do things progressively.

If you miss a day of workouts or if you are sore then you can of course take the day off and rest for a day or two. Give your body time to recover. Don't push yourself too much. What you want to happen is to incorporate exercise into your daily routine along with the other practices that we have covered in this book such as fasting and a keto diet. The end goal of course is to induce autophagy.

Should I Do HIIT?

HIIT or high intensity interval training transforms your usual cardio exercise into a very powerful aerobic exercise. Should you do HIIT? It depends on your fitness level and your diet.

Yes you will get the most of your workout time by doing HIIT but note that this type of training is really intense. It is one of the most demanding forms of training out there. If you are on the keto diet or any low carb diet then doing HIIT is a recipe for disaster.

If you plan on doing HIIT then you should be done with your low carb diet. That means you're back to the regular carb levels. If you haven't had a sandwich (not the keto approved breadless sandwich kind) then HIIT is not for you.

You should do this type of training after you have established that you can get back to fasting and low carb diet. If you're looking for workouts just to stimulate autophagy then HIIT is not for you. It may possibly end up in muscle loss or you may not be able to finish the training anyway.

What About High Altitude Training?

High altitude training is another controversial kind of workout. Yes, high altitude training is able to improve the function of skeletal muscles. However, there isn't sufficient evidence that this type of training regimen can positively impact or contribute to autophagy. In fact, you can also get the same autophagic stimulation if you do cardio for 2 to 7 days straight.

Until further evidence can be cited in favor of high altitude training, we can't recommend it as a method to induce autophagy—in short we're on a wait and see mode for now.

Chapter 12: Deep Sleep and Autophagy

One of the simplest things that you can do to help induce autophagy is to get some quality sleep. There is a link between autophagy and the body's circadian rhythm. The circadian rhythm is the sleep-wake cycle that we all go through.

It's a Matter of Cycles

As a matter of fact, a lot of things in this life and not just sleep and wakefulness have cyclic patterns. That also includes living and dying both on the macro and micro levels of life. Cycles are present not only in the body but also in our environment.

Circadian rhythms are more than just sleeping at night and waking up in the morning. There are a lot of physiological processes that go on behind the scenes while you are awake and while you sleep. These same processes govern the circadian rhythm as well as the body's autophagic systems.

And guess what—autophagy is a re-"cycling" process. Old cellular parts are cycled over to be reused. In that process there is also a clean-up that happens and waste is dumped out of the body's systems. It is again a cycle – in this case on the cellular level.

Autophagy itself is part of another cycle—one of feeding and not feeding. Coincidentally we feed usually when we are awake, unless you can go sleep eating of course but that's a different matter altogether. A lot of the info we have about the molecular systems involved that control the circadian rhythm come from the works of Nobel Prize winning physiologists Michael W. Young, Michael Rosbash, and Jeffrey C. Hall.

Sleep and Autophagy

Getting quality sleep is a crucial factor if you want to get the best benefits from autophagy. Melatonin is called the sleep hormone and it has been found to modulate the body's autophagic processes[71]. It is also a very powerful antioxidant.

It also controls a lot of the other repairs that go on in the body as you sleep. On top of that it also controls the release of the body's growth hormone. That is how vital this hormone is to the human body.

The growth hormone is also just as important as melatonin. Studies have shown that 70% of growth hormone pulses that we experience each day only happen during deep sleep[72]. It facilitates fat burning, regeneration, and other physical repairs. It also acts on the liver to stimulate or induce the autophagic process.

Again, remember that the growth hormone is stimulated by melatonin. That is why your body should be able to produce sufficient amounts of that hormone. How does your body produce it? Melatonin is produced only in the absence of green and blue light—it only occurs in darkness.

If you want to increase the autophagic processes in the body then you should optimize your sleep in order to increase melatonin production. You need to get enough sleep at night. That means you should get enough sleep time and you should also sleep at the right time.

It should also be noted that both AMPK and mTOR (the two pathways for autophagy and growth respectively) are also regulated by melatonin[73]. Remember that as it was described in previous chapters that AMPK promotes autophagy, cell breakdown, catabolism, and also ketosis. mTOR on the other hand promotes nerve proliferation, bone enhancement, protein synthesis, as well as cellular growth.

AMPK can be activated using calorie restriction, low carb diets, fasting, and exercise. mTOR on the other hand is activated by excess calories, increased insulin levels in the blood, eating lots of carbs, consuming protein, and resistance training.

Circadian Rhythms and Autophagy

It should also be pointed out that even the autophagic process has a diurnal rhythm as well. It can be observed occurring in the muscles, heart, and also the liver[74]. We know that fasting creates conditions that are optimal for the kick starting of autophagy.

However, an equally important thing to consider is the timing. When does autophagy usually take place? Studies show that autophagy gets activated usually during times of low metabolic activity—i.e. when your body isn't busy doing other stuff.

That usually happens during fasting—since you are not eating and there is no food that your digestive system is working on. It also occurs during times of caloric restriction (i.e. when you eat less food). It also happens when you experience energy stress (i.e. when you are exercising). And now we know that autophagy is also activated when we sleep.

Remember that when you are awake and the body is busy doing all the other processes dictated by your metabolism, then there is no time for it to perform any repairs. The body is said to be in its growth state at such times. But when it shuts down the growth phase (or an active phase) and moves on to other things, the body focuses on repair as well as in self-healing.

Quality sleep is an essential if you want to achieve autophagy. Even though you put in some time to fast short term or long term and you do regular exercises, it might not be enough to stimulate autophagy if you do not allow your body to enter into repair mode—that is why you need to put in some time to sleep (which should be around 7 to 10 hours at night).

That means everything that you do to prep your body to enter into autophagy gets stacked up as it were. They get installed and wait for something to happen before their benefits can be reaped. You finally get to reap those benefits when melatonin is produced in your brain—and then the work of autophagic processes rolls forward. In this essence getting quality sleep is essential to an overall plan if you want to induce natural self-healing.

How to Support Melatonin Production

Since melatonin production is critical to autophagy you should know how to help your brain produce more of this hormone. Here are a few tips that may help you get better sleep, improve melatonin production, and help you get a better circadian rhythm.

- When you wake up in the morning make sure that you expose your eyes to sunlight. This sets up your circadian rhythm.
- Turn off cellphones and even your home's WIFI. You should also shut down any other electrical devices in your room. What you want to achieve is the reduced exposure to EMF, which negatively impacts melatonin secretion.
- Avoid drinking any kind of alcoholic drink before going to bed
- Reduce stress (this can be a bit challenging for some people).
- Sleep in a dark environment. That means close the curtains and/or wear a sleep mask
- Avoid caffeine in the afternoon or in the evening
- Don't watch any scary, action packed, or otherwise stimulating movie or video before going to bed.
- Don't eat anything 3 hours before going to bed.
- Turn off sources of blue light at night—switch to non-blue light emitting bulbs at night.
- Maintain a regular sleeping schedule

Chapter 13: Time Restricted Feeding

What is Time Restricted Feeding?

According research all living organisms have a consolidated time for actively being awake and also sleeping. During this cycle they also go through a time for sleeping and repair/healing. This is the phase for inactivity and as it was explained earlier the healing is booted when you go fasting. We have a feeding plus awake phase of the cycle and a sleep plus fasting cycle.

And here is where the concept of Time Restricted Feeding (TRF) comes in. What is TRF? Simply put it means that you will eat food within a given time frame. This time frame should coincide with the body's circadian rhythm. Researchers say that the act of eating the calories that we consume has a huge impact on the brain's SCN or suprachiasmatic nucleus[75]. The SCN is the master clock inside of us.

Studies indicate that human beings usually have a 15 hour feeding period. Roughly 13 hours of that is done when we are awake during the day time and the last 2 hours are done during the night at dinner time, usually. Experts recommend that people should only eat within an 8 to 10 hour feeding period if you don't want your caloric intake to interfere with your circadian rhythm.

Whenever we fast—whether it is at night when we sleep or any time when we are awake—both the immune system and the digestive system are given time to make needed repairs and let the processes of autophagy do their thing[76].

TRF vs. Intermittent Fasting

Some people believe that there is a difference between TRF and intermittent fasting. The truth of the matter is that sometimes both of these terms are used interchangeably. So when you read text about them you should consider the context. But there are a few subtle differences.

We can also say that intermittent fasting is the blanket term that people use to describe any practice that involves the suppression of eating on a recurring basis. And TRF is a type of intermittent fasting—it can be considered as part of that blanket term or category.

But there are differences—so let's go over those a little bit. Intermittent fasting is more concerned about going through a cycle of eating followed by a period of not eating. An example of this is the alternate day fast where you fast in one day but then you have regular meals the following day. Extended fasting can also be seen as cyclic in a way since you will not eat for several days and then eat again in the next following days.

TRF on the other hand can also be considered as a form of fasting because you do not eat after a given time. On top of that you also follow a cyclic period. The big emphasis in time restricted feeding however is that you can only eat within a specified time frame. For instance, if you follow an 6/18 window then that would mean that you are only allowed to eat within 6 hours a day and you should not eat anything the rest of the day.

2 Types of TRF

There are actually two types of time restricted feeding (or time restricted eating). The first one is called Early TRF and the other one is Late TRF. Early TRF means that you will eat usually in the morning and stop sometime after lunch.

An example of early TRF would be having breakfast at 8 am and maybe having a snack before lunch. And then you can have your lunch at noon. And then after that perhaps one last snack at 2 pm could be placed in your schedule. After 2 pm no more eating will be allowed.

Late TRF on the other hand would mean that you are only allowed to eat during the later parts of the day. You are going to skip breakfast and you will schedule your lunch at a later time—not at noon. Let's say that your eating window starts at 2 pm, that is the only time when you will have lunch. You can schedule other meals until 10 pm. No more meals can be had after 10 pm.

Given the description of TRF, anyone who does the Warrior Diet, the 16/8 diet, or even the OMAD (one meal a day) are technically doing a type of intermittent fasting called TRF.

Benefits of Time Restricted Feeding

TRF does not necessarily reduce one's calorie intake. Yet studies have shown that it can prevent metabolic syndrome as well as obesity. Studies also suggest that it can also prevent the development of heart disease. Those who undergo TRF also experience improvement in glucose control[77].

The same research pointed out that eating the same amount of food within a window of 6 hours in TRF can improve one's blood pressure, insulin sensitivity, and glycemic control. This showed better results than people who ate food when they were given a 12 hour window for eating (i.e. they were allowed to eat for 12 hours instead of just 6 hours).

In that same review the effect of TRF was compared to men who were weight training. Both groups basically were doing resistance training. One group was given only a 12 hour eating period where they should eat their meals. After that no more meals were served. The other group followed the 16/8 fasting regimen as it was described in a previous chapter of this book.

The results showed that both groups had the same improvements when it came to muscle growth and strength (yes, you can still workout in the gym even if you are on a fasting regimen). But the group that went through the 16/8 method had better results when it came to fat burning. That meant that their autophagic systems were running well given their schedule.

These studies exemplify the great benefits of TRF. These benefits actually come from the fact that time restricted feeding is better at suppressing insulin. It also allows you to stay in a fasted state much longer. It also better allows the body to enter into a state of autophagy.

Early TRF or Late TRF: Which One is Better?

The next question that people ask is if Early TRF is better than Late TRF. There was one study that tried that[78] and here are their findings. The study involved 15 men who were already diagnosed as obese. They were required to go through TRF with a 9 hour eating window and they started with Early TRF.

They did that for a week having breakfast at 8 am and their last meal for the day at 5 pm. They ate normally, which meant that they did not binge eat or anything—just the same balanced diet. That also meant that they never went hungry at any time during the day.

After a week their stats were taken and then the test subjects changed their eating schedule. This time they went on Late TRF the following week. After that they ate normally to negate any adaptations that their bodies have undergone.

What they found out was that it doesn't matter whether you did Late TRF or Early TRF. You still get the same benefits from time restricted feeding. The men who went through both regimens practically reaped the same benefits—that is if you take only the glycemic control, insulin levels, energy expenditure, and other related results into consideration.

Adding Melatonin Production into the Equation

The big difference between Early TRF and Late TRF happens when you add melatonin production into the factors that you should consider. Remember that the pancreas tends to produce more insulin during the day than at night. That means blood sugar happens much better during the day time than at night[79].

The melatonin production levels in the body usually begin a few hours before the usual time you go to bed. The only thing that will stop this production is when you are exposed to a lot of blue or green light as it was explained in chapter 12 previously.

When melatonin levels increase they can bind better to their receptors that can be found in the pancreas. Now, we don't need to get too technical on that but that simply means the melatonin is signaling or telling the pancreas to stop the production of insulin. In other words this hormone is signaling your pancreas that bed time is almost near and your body doesn't need to process any more energy[80].

That is how it should work normally but there are things that can disrupt this pattern. One of those things is eating a big meal before going to bed—especially one that is high in carbs. If that is the case and the pancreas stops producing insulin, then there will not be enough insulin left in your blood stream to process the remaining glucose.

That will result in a strained system and you may not be able to sleep that well for the night. The quality of your sleep will be affected and thus autophagy may be impaired for that night.

But there is a huge BUT that we can throw into that mix.

You see, eating a huge meal at night and lowered insulin production may only affect you if you go on short term fasts. If you are already on a long term extended fast your insulin sensitivity may already be very high.

That means even if you ate a huge meal in the evening and you are still highly insulin sensitive then your body can still process the remaining glucose even if the pancreas has already reduced its insulin production.

Nevertheless, the big issue here is that if eating at night (or fasting at night) will disrupt your melatonin production then you should opt for Early TRF or some other fasting routine that won't make you eat at night.

Chapter 14: Heat Exposure

One of the methods to induce autophagy that was mentioned earlier in chapter 3 of this book is hot and cold exposure. This type of changing exposures creates cellular stress and this is the factor initiates or at least contributes to autophagy. In this chapter we will go over the possible use of saunas and heat shock response. In the next chapter we will cover cryotherapy and other hot and cold methods and how they may help to stimulate cellular repair in the body.

Saunas and Heat Shock Response

There are several medical studies that have tackled the subject of heat shock response and heat stress and how they can stimulate autophagy. According to one study autophagy and apoptosis can be induced due to heat stress. Several studies suggest that heat shock proteins are formed when the body is exposed to heat and these proteins are involved in the maintenance of healthy cells and of course autophagy[81].

Knowing that kind of gives you a hint that there is something about saunas that can be beneficial to one's health. In fact saunas or some other form of heat therapy are part of many cultures in the world. Heat therapy has long been recognized as therapeutic even before the modern medical world has noticed its benefits. Many people have been dipping in hot pools, taking hot baths, and enjoying saunas for thousands of years.

Today we have a lot of scientific studies that support the health benefits of heat therapy and its effects on human longevity. A sauna is basically just a heated room—some people call them sweat lodges.

Here are some of the benefits of heat exposure via saunas, sweat lodges, hot baths etc.
- According to one study, it is suggested that taking sauna baths around 4 to 7 times a week can reduce one's mortality rate by 40% [82].
- Heat exposure that produces heat shock response has been found to increase brain neurotrophic factors and also raise the brain's endorphin levels.
- Taking sauna baths have been linked to a lowered risk for Alzheimer's and dementia[83].
- Maintains a youthful appearance by clearing the skin
- Flushes the lymphatic system of pathogens and other toxins
- Increases the number of white blood cells and strengthens the immune system
- Improves the strove volume of the heart to increase one's physical endurance (*Thermoregulatory Responses to Acute Exercise-Heat Stress and Heat Acclimation. Kent B. Pandolf, Michael N. Sawka, C. B. W. Handbook of Physiology, Environmental Physiology, 2011.*)

- Improves blood flow to skeletal muscles and increases overall blood circulation
- Lowers the heart rate and improves overall cardiovascular health (*Hannuksela, M. L. & Ellahham, S. Benefits and risks of sauna bathing. The American journal of medicine 110, 118-126, 2001*)

In many cultures saunas and hot baths have other uses other than just for bathing, self-washing, and getting clean. In some cultures mothers give birth in saunas. In others, they wash their dead in saunas as part of the ritual in burial preparation. In many instances, the sauna or hot room is usually the cleanest part of the house.

The Production of Heat Shot Proteins

We mentioned heat shock proteins (or HSPs) as part of the benefits that are produced when you go through heat therapy (e.g. taking a sauna bath). But what are heat shock proteins?

HSPs refer to an entire family of proteins that are produced by the body when it experiences heat stress. It is one of the ways the body responds to experiencing heat—in other words the body produces HSPs to adapt to increased temperature. The body releases HSPs due to environmental conditions that give rise to water deprivation, hypoxia, starvation, heat stress, and inflammation[84].

HSPs actually have a number of health benefits, which include the following:

- Studies suggest that HSPs may be able to increase one's lifespan by at least 15% (*Khazaeli, A. A., Tatar, M., Pletcher, S. D. & Curtsinger, J. W. Heat-induced longevity extension in Drosophila. I. Heat treatment, mortality, and thermotolerance. The journals of gerontology. Series A, Biological sciences and medical sciences 52, B48-52, 1997*)
- HSPs have been found to be involved in cellular turnover and also macroautophagy
- They help promote the body's antioxidant capacity
- They prevent cell damage and the accumulation of free radicals
- They also promote the repair of misfolded proteins which is the same action that occurs during autophagy (*Naito, H. et al. Heat stress attenuates skeletal muscle atrophy in hindlimb-unweighted rats. J Appl Physiol 88, 359-363, 2000*).

The research suggests that there are plenty of benefits that can be gained from heat shock proteins as they are mediated by autophagy. However, some may ask if heat exposure can actually damage cells and eventually lead to cell death.

That is indeed a valid concern and it is also a natural phenomenon. If there is indeed too much heat then the cells will eventually die. But the body has a natural protective mechanism against heat stress on the cellular level—mitochondrial autophagy. This protective metabolic state turns on when the body experiences heat shock that can induce the death of cells (i.e. apoptosis).

This is one of the body's adaptations to environmental stress[85]. However, if the body's autophagic system is blocked or impaired then exposure to heat stress via saunas or other similar treatments may not be as beneficial as it should be.

Heat Stress Encourages Growth Hormone Release

In reality exposure to any kind of stressor from the environment has the potential to make the body stronger. This might remind you of the adage that what doesn't kill you only makes you stronger—it is very real in this case. Examples of environmental stressors can include exercise, fasting, calorie restriction, cold temperatures, and of course heat exposure. These things can make you healthier and also stronger through experience and adaptation.

Heat stress also aids in the release of the body's growth hormone. This growth hormone as it was described in previous chapters helps to inhibit protein breakdown. The growth hormone doesn't help you build muscle or anything instead it helps to prevent muscular catabolism.

When something is in a catabolic state or is in catabolism it breaks down its complex components into smaller ones. It is the opposite of anabolism, which refers to the build-up of something—in this case muscular anabolism refers to the building of muscles whereas muscular catabolism is its opposite. The growth hormone helps protect your muscles from breakdown during stressful conditions.

Combine that with fasting and you will see a growth hormone production boost of up to 2000%[86]. The catch of course is that you should stay fasted for at least 24 hours if you want to achieve that level of catabolism in the body.

That means it will be a pretty good idea to take sauna baths or at least a hot bath when you are fasting. Not only will this practice help you promote additional fat burning effects but it will also induce anti-catabolic effects. In other words, it helps boost the autophagic systems of the body.

Sauna Baths to Induce Autophagy

How do you take a sauna so that you can induce autophagy? There are a few factors to consider when answering this question. How long do you have to spend in a sauna? What is the optimal temperature that you have to set? How many times do you have to go into the sauna to get the desired effects? Can you do it every day?

Research shows that people should go into saunas and stay there for 15 to 30 minutes to get the most benefits from it. The temperature for each sauna session should be anywhere from 156°F to 212°F or 70°C to 100°C.

Experts recommend that people do saunas around 2 up to 4 times a week. Do take note that doing more saunas will not translate to reaping more health benefits. You see it's going to be like that crab in hot water phenomenon. You put a crab in a pot and slowly raise the temperature ever so slowly.

The crab won't notice the subtle increase in temperature. It slowly acclimates to the warm environment. And before long it is cooking in its own bath as it were. The same is true for human beings, unfortunately.

If you have too many frequent saunas your body will get used to the heat, which means you will have to increase the temperature to induce hormesis (i.e. the point where your body reacts to the heat and trigger that adaptive healing response). That simply means it isn't a good idea to do saunas every day.

Supporting Medical Studies

There are medical studies that suggest that heat exposure via saunas promote longevity in the human body similar to the effects of intermittent fasting. There was a study in conducted in Finland where one group of test subjects had saunas 2 to 3 times each week and another group had saunas only once a week.

The results suggest that those who had more frequent saunas had reduced their chances of dying via cardiac related conditions down to 22%, which is much lower compared to the group that only had one sauna session per week. It was also suggested that the more frequent you go to the sauna increases your survivability from cardiovascular disease by 50% to 63%.

Infrared Sauna Autophagy

The sauna sessions that we have been describing thus far have been those of traditional saunas where steam and other usual heating methods are used. These are the saunas that can reach temperatures of 70-100°C.

There are other types of saunas. Well they are more modern versions of the traditional sauna known as infrared saunas. These modern saunas heat the body directly unlike the traditional ones that heat the air surrounding the body. They generally have a higher heat range anywhere from 120 °F to 140°F or 50 °C to 60 °C.

Now, even though they have a different mode of action when it comes to heating they also provide you with the same health benefits. They can also help reduce inflammation, improve blood circulation, promote better sleep, and induce relaxation.

Regular saunas on the other hand can stimulate lymph flow and open the skin's pores—something that infrared saunas can't mimic. However, infrared saunas have their unique set of benefits such as deeply penetrating into the body's organs, muscles, and joints.

The big downside to using infrared saunas is the fact that they emit electromagnetic radiation (EMF). That is why if you are in the market for an infrared sauna unit or before you step into one, you should check whether or not it is low EMF type.

Safety Rules for Using Saunas

Over exposure to heat can be dangerous no matter how much autophagy it can stimulate. If you have preexisting medical conditions then a sauna may not be a good idea. Make sure to check with your doctor before proceeding with it.

Here are a few safety precautions and rules to help you stay safe when you take a sauna.

1. Don't stay in a sauna for too long. If it is your first time and you aren't accustomed to the heat then shorten your stay to a few minutes. On average your max time per session should be around 15 to 20 minutes. The most that you can stay is 30 minutes but never longer. Note that the length of time the body can tolerate the heat in a sauna will vary from one person to the next.
2. Remember to rehydrate after a sauna session. You may also want to eat something a bit salty since salt enhances water retention in the body.
3. Rest for at least 10 minutes after your session. Give your body time to recuperate. This is the period when your body is stimulated to heal itself.
4. Never go alone as much as possible. Some people may pass out due to the heat and you don't want to be alone in such circumstances. You can't always count on the staff of a spa to come rescue you. There is a good reason why saunas are shared with other folks.
5. Take the time to cool down—you may even want to take a cold bath after, which follows a tradition in Finland. Well, they jump into the snow after a sauna but you can take less extreme means to cool down like maybe a cold bath. Doing so may help to prevent the reabsorption of the impurities that your body has just eliminated via the heat exposure.
6. Never drink alcohol while having a sauna. The National Stroke Association has correlated taking alcohol during a sauna to cause stroke and possible death.
7. Don't have a large meal after a sauna session
8. Leave the sauna immediately if you feel dizzy, nauseous, or you feel a headache coming on.
9. Don't bring your cellphone with you in the sauna
10. Don't have a sauna if you are pregnant
11. Don't go into the sauna naked—some people do but you shouldn't do it. It's unsanitary.
12. Don't wear any jewelry. Don't even wear your watch—remember that metal heats up quickly. There is usually a timer in there.

Chapter 15: Hot and Cold Therapy

One of the safety tips mentioned in the previous chapter mentioned a Finnish tradition where people jump into icy cold water or the snow right after a sauna. This hot and cold exposure is believed by researchers to promote neural autophagy[87]. These studies of course are in their initial stages but there is reason to believe that there is a strong correlation between hot and cold exposure to inducing autophagy, though indirectly.

This has something to do with the production of cold shock proteins (CSPs) in the human body. Just like HSPs, cold shock proteins are produced by the body as an adaptive and protective response but this time as an adaptation to cold temperatures.

CSPs and Their Benefits

Cold shock proteins are one of the most reserved proteins in the body. They are reserved for special circumstances—when you are exposed to extreme cold. Note that CSPs are also present in other organisms especially the ones that hibernate during the winter.

Note however that the term CSD is a blanket term that is used to refer to an entire family of proteins that are produced in response to cold temperature. Some CSDs are particularly targeted for cancer therapy like the Y-box protein-1 [88].

As you may have already guessed there are benefits that can be gained from the induction of CSPs in the body—and they can also help to induce autophagy. Here are some of their benefits:

- Winter swimming has been observed to reduce uric acid levels in the body[89].
- Cold exposure activates the body's brown adipose tissue which can improve the function of the mitochondria in cells[90].
- Increasing CSPs in the body coincides with the increased production of adiponectin, which can help regulate insulin in the blood[91].
- Cold exposure also increases the production of norepinephrine, which can reduce inflammation and provide other health benefits[92].

Do CSPs and Cold Exposure Induce Autophagy?

The short and sweet answer to the question above is no—cold exposure does not *directly* influence autophagy in the cells. However, heat shock does[93] induce autophagy. What happens is that cold exposure indirectly influences this metabolic state. It follows a different pathway to help induce it.

Combining cold showers or ice baths after a sauna can boost the health benefits that you can gain from HSPs. You can also do it the other way around. You can take a mildly cold shower and then go rewarm yourself through either a hot bath or a sauna. This cold to heat process encourages the production of the LC3 protein, which is known to promote autophagy[94].

How to Safely Do Hot and Cold Therapy

You should take care when you do hot and cold therapy just as you would take precautions before do a sauna. For starters, you can sit in a sauna for 5 to 10 minutes. Make sure to follow the safety rules mentioned in the previous chapter.

You should have an ice bath prepared beforehand. This can be made of a tub with water and ice. The ice bath doesn't need to be freezing cold. It should at least be cold enough so that you can tolerate the cooler temperature. After your sauna you can take a dip in the ice bath for 2 minutes and then dry off.

Another way to do it is to sauna for 5 minutes followed by a cold shower for 2 minutes and then back into the sauna again for another 10 minutes. After that you cool off and hydrate.

Conclusion

I'd like to thank you and congratulate you for transiting my lines from start to finish.

I hope this book was able to help you to understand what autophagy is and how you can enhance it. Remember that there is still a lot of ongoing research about this subject. We may not have yet been able to produce a pill or a treatment protocol that can induce or enhance autophagy. But the strategies mentioned here in this book can help prime your body so that it can enter into a state of autophagy for increased healing and wellness.

Thanks for reading, and I wish you the best of luck.

Book #5

Vagus Nerve Unlocked

Guide to Unleashing Your Self-healing Ability and Achieving Freedom from Anxiety, Depression, PTSD, Trauma, Inflammation, and Autoimmunity

Introduction

Researchers will know that feeling, the small euphoria of that "eureka" moment when a person finds that everything he has studied so far fits together like some splendid jigsaw puzzle. That was what I felt when I first discovered the existence of the vagus nerve.

Let me back track a bit. I had always had some interest in the study of diseases, and how they form. I know that the human body is a massive interconnected network of organs and feedback systems, even as it is also connected to the outside world. I was thinking, "what if it is possible to boil down the causes of a lot of diseases into a smaller set of factors?" Sure, we already have things like diet, lifestyle, genetics, and the like. What if it could be further narrowed down? I was going for something like an amateur's version of the Grand Unified Field Theory, only this time related to the formation of diseases.

So I read, researched, even took a few courses to understand what I was reading. In the course of my study, I found a word that has been mentioned in passing in various literature:

"Vagus nerve"

Here it mentions that the disease affects the vagus nerve. There it mentions that the effects can be seen in the vagus nerve. Another research paper claims that managing the vagus nerve could help calm the symptoms of the disease I was looking up at the time.

Now, I wouldn't have paid much attention, had it not been for the fact that I saw the word in absolutely different types of research papers. I saw it pretty prominently in research on epilepsy, then in passing on a paper about the good effects of lactobacilli in the gut. I saw it again on a study on cardiovascular illnesses, and then once more in pulmonary injuries. I was intrigued. It was like seeing an Easter egg appear here and there, a vaguely familiar factor that keeps persisting. So I did what any sane man would do: I Googled.

And that's when the floodgates opened.

Somehow, everything I studied in the past came together in the image of a bundle of nerve fibers.

A New Focal Point

Science, like the media, likes to have its darlings. In the field of technology and gadgets, for example, engineers are struggling to fit more and more computing power in as small a space as possible. In the field of rocket science, physicists are perpetually trying to break records of payload and fuel efficiency.

In the field of medicine... well, the darlings can be quite numerous. That's partly because the discipline is broken down into a huge number of smaller ones, each one trying to pursue a different thread that when woven together hopefully brings us better health.

But there are times when these disciplines bump into each other in discovery, as they find common ground. These are the focal points of health, and they are of great interest when they appear because they represent a single factor that has the ability to influence a massive host of other factors. The DNA was such a focal point when it was discovered and eventually mapped. Before the DNA, the discovery of the cell was a huge focal point.

Now, as I found, the discovery of the vagus nerve and its various implications appear to be the next big focal point in the field of health.

What is it to you?

You're probably wondering now why you should spend your time going over this "vagus nerve". I'll answer this one up front — this might be the biggest health-related idea you have come across with in forever, and you would want to know just how the proper stimulation of this nerve could improve your daily life. I won't be exaggerating when I say that this could change your future, with regards to your health. With this knowledge, you can avoid a landmine of possible health issues, and even turn back the hands of time to resolve illnesses that have already taken hold. I won't even be exaggerating when I say that knowledge of the vagus nerve can *literally* affect the welfare of the future generation! You'll see that in shocking detail at the last part of this book.

These pages are the culmination of my lengthy study on the concept of the vagus nerve, and the various health factors that it influences. I tried my best to make complicated medical information as accessible as possible, even as I explore various theories. I also did my best to make the book as practical as possible, so that you can have takeaways that you can also share to others. Within these pages, you will find not just theories and results of various studies, but also a generous helping of self-care tips you can then use at *any* moment. I know you're investing precious time reading this book, so I strived to make the knowledge presented as easy to apply as possible, while not compromising on the impact it could bring to your life.

So strap in, and prepare for a wealth of cutting-edge knowledge about your health and how you can improve it! Believe me when I say that all it takes is a few deep breaths and soothing touches — but what you will learn before you get to that conclusion will blow your mind!

PART 1:

The Basics

Chapter 1: The Vagus Nerve: A Tale of Many Cities

"New roads; new ruts." -- Gilbert K. Chesterton

The human body may be one of the most precious things Nature has ever created. It is a complex array of organs and cells, each one with specialization, and yet each one dependent on each other to survive. While some might argue the case of animals and other creatures with much more complex structures, the human body is unique simply because it is the only one endowed with as much brain power.

And, while it's still debatable, this brain power stands at the very core of what humanity is all about. Our ability to grow and evolve, to learn and to plan, to invent and to theorize, to do high-order cognitive tasks, all reside in our brains. Our brains allowed us to progress from caves and trees to the creation of virtual realities.

But while the brain is amazing, it would be completely useless without its supporting cast. Every organ, every system, has at least some role that relates to the protection of the brain. The rest of the nervous system, for example, consists of pathways for signals to travel from the brain to other parts of the body.

And this is where it gets interesting. The brain would be an isolated city of ultimate complexity if it were not connected by the "roads" that are the neural network. Can you imagine a world where each city, prosperous as they are, would be isolated from each other because of the lack of connections? That wouldn't be much of a world. In history, the creation of roads and other transport routes have been one of the greatest catalysts of progress. The human body, too, has many great cities -- but what truly defines them is how they are connected to each other.

In the body, there are set "roads" that travel to other "cities" in the body, sending instructions on how they can make the body better as a whole. But two sets of roads stand out from all others.

One of them is the spinal cord, essentially an extension of the brain, a superhighway through which the brain sends signals to other parts of the body. Break this superhighway, and the brain ceases to have control over motion and other voluntary functions. The function of the spinal cord is very well-known, and has been subjected to much study.

But there is another superhighway in the body that isn't as popular, but could be just as important. This one does not lead to the voluntary muscles that power the body's movement. Rather, this one is connected to some extremely important and sensitive organs -- the heart, the lungs, and the stomach to name a few.

This nerve actually connects the core of life. Take out one of these organs, and the whole body dies. In contrast, some people have been known to live through spinal cord damage (albeit with debilitating effects). Indeed, it would be possible to lose function in some parts of the spinal cord and still live, while significant loss of function in this other superhighway of nerves would mean an agonizing death. The implications of this nerve's connections has pretty recently seized the attention of researchers as a possible answer to many health issues. Many have considered this to be the holy grail of modern medicine — a panacea that could end a host of modern diseases with minimal effort.

Enter the Vagus Nerve

What if I tell you that there is a single bundle of nerves in your body that controls your whole well-being? You would probably be laughing now, but it actually exists.

onsider this. A single, overpowered nerve bundle has the power to control such diverse aspects of your personality as:

- Heart rate
- Memory
- Breathing
- Healing
- Relaxation
- Hunger and satiation
- Emotion

This may be a very short list, but what a diverse list it is! You can immediately see how this nerve, called the vagus nerve, can have an incredible impact on your life.

The Hard Science

The vagus nerve goes by many names. In the olden days, it was called the "pneumogastric nerve" due to the way it connects the brain and the lungs, and the stomach. Another designation is "CN X", or Cranial Nerve X. Despite being a paired bundle, it is commonly described as a singular nerve. As such, it is the longest nerve of our autonomic nervous system. This is that part of the nervous system that controls the "autonomic" processes of the smooth muscles and the various glands, thus having a vital role in our body's function and development.

The name "vagus" came about when physicians realized that the nerve takes a "wandering" course throughout the body. It is literally a wandering nerve, coming from the skull and making its way down towards the abdominal cavity. The word "vagus" is also the root of the word "vagabond".

In the past, the vagus nerve was simply thought of as that nerve that connects various important parts of the body, helping them function. Today, however, more of its unique and fascinating functions have been uncovered.

Vagus Nerve Structure

The vagus nerve is what is called a "mixed nerve", a nerve that is composed of both "efferent" (signal-sending) and "afferent" (signal-receiving or sensory) fibers. The vagus is about 20% efferent and 80% afferent, which is important because this combination allows it to effectively communicate with a huge group of organs. Most of the other nerves in the autonomic nervous system is efferent, since they are mostly used to control other parts of the body. But the afferent qualities of the vagus nerve allows not just for control but also for a feedback mechanism. This way, the brain (on the other end of the nerve) doesn't just tell the body to start or stop a certain process. The body can also tell the brain more about the status of the process, whether it has been started or completed, and what potential issues may have arose from the performance of the process.

The vagus nerve stems from the base of the brain (the brainstem), going down through the neck, the chest, and down to the abdominal section. As the nerve traverses this line, it also has several branches that touch various organs such as the pharynx, larynx, lungs, heart, and the gastrointestinal tract. In the brain, the ends of the nerve are connected to other important regions including the amygdala, hypothalamus, and thalamus.

Stimulating the Vagus Nerve

Because it is so expansive, the vagus nerve can be accessed ("stimulated") in a wide variety of ways. Its first recorded roots (at least, if we go by medical records) reaches back to the 1880s, when it was found that manually massaging and compressing the carotid artery in the neck's cervical region could help suppress seizures. This was the first time medical professionals attributed the stimulation (albeit a crude one) of the vagus nerve to the suppression of seizures. In the 1930s and the 1940s, the electrical stimulation of the vagus nerve was experimented on, to understand the influence of this segment of the autonomic nervous system and in the electrical activity of the brain. Animal experimentation determined that the nerve had a role to play in other types of brain activity. Later, it was confirmed that the vagus nerve plays an important role in the treatment of convulsion (though the relationship was first reached when experimenting with dogs, and not with human samples).

After this, the connection of the vagus nerve to the diaphragm was established. This was when deep breathing and paced breathing were both considered effective means to influence the mind through the vagus nerve. The nerve's connection to both the heart and lungs had been postulated to be among the reasons why there is a positive cognitive and emotional stimulation when we do cardio-respiratory exercises. In fact, ancient exercise like yoga and breathing techniques had been thought to be effective partly because of this same connection.

A time passed, dedicated experiments had been approved by the US FDA in order to determine other possible benefits of vagal stimulation. The first implanted device meant to stimulate the nerve was put into service in 1997. This was meant to treat refractory epilepsy. This device was itself later FDA approved, ushering in the era of further research on the benefits of vagus nerve stimulation. It is interesting to know, though, that the device didn't get the FDA certification as an epilepsy cure -- it was meant to help treat chronic treatment-resistant depression! This was also around the time doctors started understanding more about the role of the vagus nerve in the nurturing of mental wellbeing.

From depression, research quickly moved to other psychological conditions such as bipolar disorder and anxiety disorders. Other brain-related issues, from chronic headaches to Alzheimer's, also got the vagus nerve stimulation treatment. From there, researchers have started moving into lifestyle issues, such as obesity. While the body of literature on these subjects show some promise, none of them are as of yet definitive and hence none are yet FDA-approved. But just looking at this history shows that this bundle of nerve fibers shows much potential for improving not just a specific group of conditions, but also our entire wellbeing.

Measuring Vagus Health: Heart Rate Variability

Science lives on measurement, and something does not exist unless it can be concretely measured. Throughout this book, you will encounter nearly-unbelievable accounts of how much the vagus nerve can affect several areas of your life -- literally, the wellbeing of your mind, body, and spirit rests in this long bundle of nerves. But before that, we need to know just how you can measure whether your vagus nerve is doing well or not.

As we are talking about something that is deeply embedded in the body, the surest way to measure vagus nerve health is by sticking instruments into your neck and back and measuring the minuscule impulses that travel through your vagus nerve as your body responds to different stimuli. But that's like saying you can only measure your heart rate by getting a monitor to observe the beating of your heart. For a body part this vital and well-connected, there must be an easier way.

Since the vagus nerve's health cannot be measured in size and mass like muscles, or in visible functioning like organs, scientists have created a benchmark to measure how well the vagus nerve performs. This wellbeing is termed "vagal tone", and the benchmark is called "heart rate variability".

Heart Rate Variability (HRV) is, simply put, the time difference between heartbeats. It is the interval between one beat and another, and can be read on the electrocardiogram as the RR variability, which refers to the R waves that correspond to the depolarization of the ventricles. These measures have been found to correlate to the healthy balance between the sympathetic and parasympathetic nervous systems, and has been confirmed in empirical studies.

Further research has found that HRV has been correlated to the mortality rate of different diseases. For example, studies as early as 50 years ago have revealed that HRV marked the possible onset of fetal distress even before there had been actual, measurable changes in the heart rate. Today, HRV has been found to be a good indicator for various syndrome and diseases.

How does this relate to the vagus nerve? Since the vagus nerve is attached to the heart, and therefore plays a role in its contractions, it has been found that a weakening in the vagus nerve can actually be the root cause in the heightening of disease mortality rates. These correlations become even more manifest when a medical procedure has been done which may have touched or damaged the vagus nerve's heart connection, such as cardiac surgery. HRV can also be a determinative factor in predicting the severity of conditions such as rheumatoid arthritis, some autoimmune diseases, and even bowel diseases.

These findings also come in contrast to the previous idea that it was these diseases that cause a decrease in the vagus nerve activity. For some time it was taught that diseases caused a concomitant neural damage, weakening the vagus. It has since then been found to be the other way around. This is especially pronounced in diseases that cause inflammation. Since the vagus nerve is also an important part of the anti-inflammatory circuit of the nervous system, what would have been normal inflammatory responses become aggravated because of the weakened vagus nerve.

Further studies have established the vagus nerve as the "grand central station" of nerve pathways where the most important functions of the body meet. Without specialized (and highly intrusive) equipment, it would be impossible to tell just how well the vagus nerve is functioning. Our best, and scientifically proven bet is Heart Rate Variability, which is the most readily available indicator to measure how well one of the most important bundle of nerves in the body is doing its job.

Takeaways:

- The vagus nerve is responsible for a huge array of bodily processes.
- The vagus nerve's health is important, and it can be measured through heart rate variability.

Chapter 2: Fighting the Undefined: The Secret Powers of the Vagus Nerve

"Now comes the mystery." -- Henry Ward Beecher

Hopefuls in the scientific and medical community have long been looking for that silver bullet of health that can destroy the many health issues that have plagued man. It's not a new endeavor, either -- the alchemists of old have spent their lives (and massive resources) looking for the Elixir of Life. In the modern day, science keeps on discovering new and interesting ideas that inch us closer to that panacea. Among these is the vagus nerve.

There are many reasons why the vagus nerve has become a fairly hot topic recently. Recent research has proven that the vagus nerve not only touches several organs in the body, but also several aspects of life that we thought are simply too abstract or too difficult to be directly addressed.

Think, for example, the concepts of rampant weight gain (or difficulty of weight loss), depression, and inflammation. The common denominator among these is the fact that all of them are multifaceted issues that are usually addressed by medication and therapy. But these medication and therapy approaches usually attempt to cure only the overt symptoms of the issue, while only rarely being able to go down deep enough to cure their roots.

Yes, these issues can be caused by a very wide variety of factors. Weight gain, for example, can be as much a lifestyle issue as it can be a problem of genetics or a physiological illness. Depression can be caused by a chemical imbalance, and it can also be a direct product of a toxic and repressive environment. Inflammation can be due to any damage, ranging from an injury to an infection. And yet, all of these issues have something to do with the way the brain interfaces with the body, where the brain causes reactions in the body sent through -- you guessed it -- the vagus nerve and similar nerve systems.

Recent research has found out that these three issues, otherwise undefined (or very roughly so) can be eased by activating the vagus nerve. This is among the many secret powers of the vagus nerve that most people are yet to discover.

Let's take a look at how the vagus nerve specifically relates to these issues.

Vagus Nerve and Weight Problems

Obesity is something that is almost a given in today's world. It is a rampant concern, made worse by today's sedentary, tech-oriented lifestyle and fast-food-first diet. We already know that obesity is a major factor in several lifestyle diseases, such as hypertension and diabetes. An obese person is also much more likely to die from stroke or heart attack.

Despite the many factors that surround obesity, science has found it undeniable that the whole idea of weight gain and weight loss is mediated in great part by the activity of the vagus nerve. The idea of using this connection to treat weight loss was first floated when a study found that depressed people who used vagus nerve stimulation devices also reported weight loss, completely independent from the improvement (or lack thereof) of their depressive states. These improvements prove that the vagus nerve acts a mediator of weight gain or loss independent of its effects on the psyche.

The vagus nerve is the one that mediates the signals of hunger and satiety. When you eat, the expansion in your stomach triggers the sending of signals to your brain saying you are already full. When your gut changes that there has been a change in the nourishment of your body, it can also start sending either hunger or satiety signals to the brain.

While the causes of obesity are different, researchers have found that most people who are obese also suffer from a lower sensitivity of the vagus nerve. This means that it cannot immediately relay the satiety signals from the stomach to the brain. When this happens, the person continues eating as if he was still hungry, stopping only when the signals are finally sent to the brain.

This insensitivity isn't caused by obesity per se. In fact, the food we eat is more likely to blame. A 2016 study has found that many food items that induce obesity are also responsible for reducing vagus nerve sensitivity at the same time. The same study has also found that the vagus nerve can be used as a treatment target for obesity. Current techniques used have resulted in a mixed bag of results for human studies, but research is still ongoing.

Aside from mediating the feeling of satiation, it has also been proven that a healthy vagus nerve can help reduce cravings. Vagus nerve stimulation is also more sustainable as a means of treatment, since the results have found that the loss of weight is proportional to the excess weight.

Later in this book, we will be looking at the different ways on how vagus nerve stimulation can be done, but right now, there are two opposing approaches to using the vagus nerve as a treatment staging point for obesity. First, there is the natural method of just stimulating the vagus nerve, in an attempt to make it more sensitive in transmitting the signals from your stomach to your brain. Then, there is also the method of blocking (or regulating) the activity of the vagus nerve, by bypassing the natural signal sending of the stomach and instead sending artificial signals to the brain.

The latter technique is done through an implanted device that interfaces with the vagus nerve. We will read more about these implants in a later chapter on electronic stimulation, but for now suffice it to say that such an implant (FDA-approved) can be placed through a minimally-invasive procedure. The device senses the stomach's activity, and sense satiety signals through the vagus nerve as soon as it detects that the stomach has received food. In effect, it dupes the brain into thinking that you are already full after just a few bites.

This is currently being looked at as an alternative to the more common obesity treatment that is gastric bypass, which aims to force the stomach into reducing its capacity, therefore sending satiety signals early. The advantage of the vagus nerve stimulator is that it is reversible, and therefore there is no danger of causing malnutrition or runaway weight loss.

Vagus Nerve and Depression

It has been predicted that by 2030, depression would be the second most dangerous disease humanity will face, only right after HIV. Unless science finds out exactly how depression develops so it could create a cure, the current social conditions seem to still point to this bleak future.

The vagus nerve has also been studied as the ideal treatment location for depression, specifically treatment-resistant depression. This is the type of depression that can no longer be treated by medication and therapy. This is actually a significant number, as it is noted that two out of three patients who suffer from major depressive problems do not benefit from the first prescriptions given by doctors. One third of all patients, on the other hand, do not respond to any prescription at all. In response, the FDA has approved vagus nerve stimulation devices for the treatment of depression back in 2005.

Depression treatment via the vagus nerve takes the form of "hacking" the brain -- this means attaching a device for electronic vagus stimulation, which delivers impulses directly affecting the part of the brain that affects the mood. Some experts also hypothesize that stimulating the vagus nerve in this way helps increase one's sense of focus, which is markedly one of the things lost during depressive episodes. After the surgery to implant the device, a person can feel alert and relaxed enough to resume normal physical, social, and emotional functioning. This may sound like pretty invasive procedure, but it is actually pretty safe and trials have produced a mainly positive result, especially when combined with traditional methods. Some studies have found that around half of test subjects responded favorably to vagus nerve stimulation, though around 40% of them relapsed soon after when the stimulation was stopped or removed.

Another way in which such devices help the depressed individual is by what is known as the "anti-convulsive effect", where the stimulation acts as an anticonvulsant system (similar to how it prevents the onset of epileptic seizures) to help relieve depressive symptoms. This is analogous to the use of some antidepressant drugs such as lamotrigine and carbamazepine, which are all also anticonvulsive.

Perhaps even more powerfully, the vagus nerve activation can cause changes in the local anatomy of the brain. The nerve has ends that are connected to the part that regulates mood, and some neurologists have hypothesized that stimulation can change how these areas of the brain work over prolonged periods of time.

Another way that the vagus nerve helps to reduce depressive episodes is in its regulation of the neurotransmitters noradrenaline and 5-hydroxytryptamine. These two substances are reduced during cases of depression, and some medications work to ensure that the brain has enough supply of these two neurotransmitters. It is believed that the vagus nerve, when activated, does the same.

One thing to remember, though, is that electronic VNS stimulation for depression treatment is not a quick treatment. In fact, it can take months (up to 9 months has been reported) before the effects can be felt. This is why one needs to practice conventional methods in tandem with electronic stimulation, in order to maintain one's welfare in between the start of treatment and the effect.

The side effects reported for this type of VNS is similar to the usual side effects reported for all types of electronic stimulation. This will be explored in detail later. The biggest issue with this type of treatment is the continuous operation of the pulse-emitting device. The battery will have to be replaced every now and then, and the operation needed for this would expose the patient to risk of infection. Still, this is an acceptable trade-off as the device can greatly enhance one's wellbeing.

Vagus Nerve and Anxiety

As alluded to in the previous section, one can gain reprieve from (often random) bouts of anxiety thanks to vagus nerve stimulation. Among the many signals carried by this superhighway of nerves are signals that relate to calm and nervousness, anger, and relaxation. This is tied to the vagus nerve's connection to the heart and lungs -- two organs that get really overworked when exposed to increased levels of anxiety.

An insensitive vagus nerve could fail to quickly perform its task of stopping the sympathetic nervous system from continuously sending signals. A person who is anxious engages this part of the nervous system, stimulating a fight-or-flight response. The vagus nerve, along with the rest of the parasympathetic nervous system, is charged with ceasing this response when the danger has passed (or, as the case may be, when there really is no dangers at all). When this happens, the sympathetic nervous system takes over the body, being able to send stress signals at will even when not necessary. This imbalance is at the root of most panic attacks. It also creates a vicious circle -- when the body is stressed, it creates more glutamate, which is a chemical that can provoke even more anxiety. This results in a host of physical issues, ranging from irritability and irrationality when making decisions to migraine, insomnia, and other health issues. It also hampers the formation of new memories, thanks to a reduced volume in the hippocampus (the part of the brain that facilitates the formation of memories).

Because the vagus is insensitive, anxiety has also been widely known to trigger discomfort in many of the organs facilitated by the nerve. This includes issues with the gastrointestinal tract (anywhere from hyperacidity to contractions) as well as difficulty in breathing and irregular heartbeats.

The good news is that you don't need an implant in order to control vagus nerve issues arising from (and causing more) anxiety. The usual natural methods, from deep breathing to the practice of enjoyable physical activities, can greatly help remedy the issue. This vagus nerve connection is the primary reason why such relaxation techniques, from deep breathing to the more advanced forms, have become so successful even since the olden times of yoga and such.

Perhaps even more interestingly, the vagus nerve has also been pointed to as essential in the enhancement of what psychologists call "extinction learning". Extinction learning is the term used when a person is exposed to a fear or anxiety-generating stimuli over and over again, until such time that he (and his mind) realizes that the stimuli does not carry any inherent danger. This effectively makes the fear extinct. Vagus nerve stimulation applied at the same time has been said to greatly increase the extinction process. Research done on this avenue has also tangentially produced results that point to the role of the vagus nerve in the formation of memory, and scientists are also exploring the fact that the vagus nerve may also be hacked to help a person remember things more easily! Such undefined factors as anxiety, fear, and memory are all vastly affected by the vagus nerve.

Vagus Nerve and Trauma

Trauma is often a touchy topic, arguably as much as (if not even more so than) depression. Deep psychological trauma such as that caused by extreme periods of stress or emotional states can greatly contribute to the downward spiral of a person. This is not the type of mental issue that can be treated just so by medications -- it needs a more personal, therapeutic approach. Aside from counseling, those who have undergone extreme bouts of trauma have been taught to practice meditation and other mindfulness techniques (incidentally, all practices that help stimulate the vagus nerve). But even then, these may not be enough.

Stimulating the vagus nerve, though, through concrete methods (short of electronic stimulation) can help improve one's trauma management and is essential in reinforcing the results of various therapeutic techniques. As we will see later, stimulating the vagus nerve is essential in increasing its connectivity, therefore improving the body's rest-and-digest system in order to let it recuperate. A good vagus nerve connection helps improve the natural stress management system of the body, and also helps reduce the brain's overreaction to stimuli.

A group of Swiss scientists have found out that the afferent bundle of the vagus nerve is directly related to how the body handles response to fear and anxiety. The Swiss research found that a healthy vagus nerve (measured through vagal tone) can help overcome one's conditioned fears -- a fact that is of great importance to people whose primary source of trauma is a fearful encounter, such as war veterans and people with PTSD. In the study, it was found that a healthy vagus nerve slows down the fear-related response from the body (specifically, the gut) to the brain, therefore preventing spikes from the sympathetic nervous system. The researchers have also tried blocking these signals altogether, and they found that this induced a longer retention of "learned" fears.

This is especially important for PTSD patients, as a healthy and stimulated vagus nerve can help re-associate stimuli from a person's surroundings. Stimuli that had once been associated with threatening situations can be reinterpreted to mean safer surroundings. The efficacy of direct vagus nerve stimulation to induce this state is still being studied, but current findings are very illuminating. As the researchers put it, it is remarkable how altering a simple signal path from the gut to the brain can result in complex changes in one's behavior.

Vagus Nerve and Epilepsy

One of the first therapeutic applications of vagus nerve stimulation has been done in the field of epileptic seizures. It is also one of the places where vagus nerve stimulation has become highly successful. Today, VNS devices and stimulation techniques have been the answer to epileptic cases that do not respond to medications (drug-resistant epilepsy).

The weird thing is that research has not defined exactly how stimulation stops the onset of epileptic seizures. We do know that epilepsy is caused by runaway electric signals in the brain, "shocking" the body into seizures. Regular, mild pulses sent through the vagus nerve does not really help disrupt these signals, but other mechanisms have been put forward. One is the fact that stimulation helps increase the blood flow to key areas in the brain, making them more resistant or less prone to seizure attacks. The process also raises some levels of neurotransmitters that control seizures, therefore increasing the body's natural ability to prevent these seizures on its own. It is also suggested that the regular pulses which the stimulation device emits helps change the overall EEG patterns during a seizure, preventing these effects.

The latest models of the stimulation devices have harnessed an additional dimension of the vagus nerve's connection to the brain. Research has found that around 80% of all people who experience seizures also experience heightened heart rate before the seizure begins. Newer devices can pick these heart rate changes, allowing the machine to provide an extra burst of pulses to prevent the seizure from even forming.

It is important to understand that vagus nerve stimulation is merely an add-on to existing epilepsy treatment methods, and not a standalone treatment -- unless in the express condition that the epilepsy is not treatable by any other type of medication.

Before being lined up for vagus nerve stimulator implantation, the person is first screened. First, physicians have to make sure that the cause of the seizure is epileptic, and not some other issue. Stimulation will only help if the seizures are caused by runaway electric activity in the brain. Some research have found that generalized epileptic seizures can also be improved by vagus nerve stimulation, but most of the curative results have been focused on focal seizures.

It is also important to test out and exhaust all other avenues for treatment. For example, the lack of effect by medications does not necessarily mean that the epilepsy is drug-resistant -- it can be a lifestyle issues, where the patient has difficulty taking the medications on time and regularly. There may also be other behavior affecting the intensity of the seizures, such as poor nutritional choices. A physician will first make sure that the appropriate medicines (different ones for different seizure types) are taken at the appropriate times and durations.

All these checks are done to ensure that vagus nerve stimulation will work as intended, as it can be dangerous for a person be installed with a stimulation device when the seizure is caused by different reasons. Because of possible side effects, a person undergoing non-epileptic seizures can, for example, have difficulty breathing at the same time, or may have his heart slow down or speed up at the same time. Combined, these factors could be very harmful. Follow ups are also made after the device installation, to adjust the intensity as needed.

The very first vagus nerve stimulation implant done on a human being was performed in 1988. This was way before the FDA approved the use of such devices for cure in cases of epilepsy. Further studies show that the later generations of such implants were so successful that they reduced the seizures by around 50% for the first year. This has increased to more than 64% in later studies.

Vagus Nerve and Brain Growth

It has been thought, long ago, that the brain does not grow new neurons during adulthood. However, new research has shown that there are parts of the brain that continued to grow even during later life, through a process called neurogenesis. This is especially pronounced in certain areas, and it has also been found that vagus nerve stimulation helps greatly in this growth. This knowledge is especially useful when one considers the case of people who have undergone brain operations. Long-term vagus nerve stimulation can cause a continued increase in the number of new brain cells persisting even if the stimulation is discontinued for some time.

This effect is directly brought about by the same mechanism that reduces depression through the vagus nerve. It has been found that increased levels of noradrenalin can increase the production of new cells in the hippocampal region. It has also been found that the stimulation of the production of serotonin helps in the same neurogenetic activity. This is connected to the fact that, in the past, studies have shown that anti-depressant drugs have actually helped trigger neurogenesis even in adults. It all boils down to the increased activity in the sites that produce the relevant neurotransmitters.

Vagus Nerve and Sleep Disorders

Because of the vagus nerve's important role in the rest-and-digest system, it also plays an important role in maintaining one's health during sleep. While it does not actually put the body to sleep, it plays a vital role in maintaining the other bodily functions that allow the body to function well when all conscious control is gone.

When the vagus nerve fails in this function, sleep disorders may occur. One of them is obstructive sleep apnea, which is a breathing disorder that causes the inability to breathe while asleep. As breathing is regulated by the vagus nerve, physicians have found that vagus nerve stimulation is also instrumental in resolving sleep apnea issues. To further highlight just how vital the vagus nerve is, it is also to be noted that sleep apnea is a concern that usually appears along with epilepsy.

Sleep apnea, obviously, causes difficulty sleeping. Even worse, it starts a downward spiral as the vagus nerve (and the whole parasympathetic nervous system it is a part of) can be greatly harmed by lack of sleep. The parasympathetic system is a part of a two-way system, and it activates best when its complement (the sympathetic axis formed by the hypothalamus, pituitary gland, and adrenal glands) is at rest. Sleeplessness causes this part of the nervous system to remain alert for extended periods of time, thus undermining the activity of the vagus nerve. This then contributes to other health problems, such as hypertension and weight gain. You may want to dial back on your caffeine intake to allow your body to rest some more. Sleep issues arising from other conditions, like insomnia, also has to be taken care of separately in order to ensure good vagus nerve health. While there are several possible causes for sleep disorders, from the physical to the psychological, there are corresponding treatments for all of them that you can look into to prevent further damage to your health.

Vagus Nerve, Inflammation, and Pain

In today's world, pain seems to be a constant companion, so much that painkillers and analgesics seem to be a part of everyday life. Technology has coerced us into working for extended hours without moving, a sedentary lifestyle that leads to chronic pain issues. Even those who workout daily and live a healthy lifestyle aren't exempt from the pain -- a single wrong lift, a few wrong movements, and you can bust a part of your body leading again to chronic pain.

The vagus nerve is, again, linked to how the body processes pain and inflammation. In fact, research on this subject has been one of the first clues that scientifically linked the vagus nerve to many of the processes now attributed to its functions. In the late 1990s, a New York-based neurosurgeon discovered that when an anti-inflammatory drug was injected into a rat's brain, the drug had the unusual effect of blocking inflammation elsewhere in the rat's body. This was despite the fact that the dosage injected was far too small to be carried into the bloodstream, to affect the other cells. During further research, he realized that the vagus nerve was responsible for carrying the anti-inflammatory signals from the brain to other parts of the body. This became the basis for future research on how the vagus nerve can help turn off pain and inflammation in other parts of the body. It was also the first actual proof that the brain and the nervous system is inextricably linked to the various organs of our body and their cells, not only regulating their functions but also their wellbeing.

The vagus nerve carries immune signals to the rest of the body. This is why it has also been studied as a treatment point for inflammatory diseases such as arthritis. It has been pointed out earlier that arthritis is also one of the diseases whose worsening can be predicted by HRV or Heart Rate Variability. In more recent studies, it has been found that aside from the brain using the vagus nerve to spread out immune signals, the brain also uses the vagus nerve to detect the overall state of the body's immune system, thus allowing the core of the nervous system to regulate its response. These studies have also begun looking into just which cytokines (proteins that mediate the interactions between the body's cells) produce which effect in the vagus nerve, possibly ushering in a new era of pain treatment and management.

Inflammation is not all about pain, too. In fact, inflammation is an immune response that could take different forms. For example, it can cause an upset stomach, or even histamine-induced itching. This is an important finding, because there are some medications for these same conditions that actually counteract how the vagus nerve naturally works to cure these illnesses. For example, there are certain medications that block the production and use of acetylcholine, which is how the vagus nerve communicates to the rest of the body. When taking medications for issues that can be connected to the vagus nerve, it is best to ask your doctor for more natural (or at least vagus-friendly) alternatives.

The idea that stimulating the vagus nerve (either naturally or through electronic alternatives) is a key element in preventing pain and inflammation has also been a major thrust of the new field called "bioelectronic integrative medicine". This field looks into how issues that used to be treated with medication (such as pain and inflammation, with analgesics) could be better aided by the use of neuromodulation devices. The use of implants and other vagus nerve stimulation techniques have been found to be effective in keeping the symptoms of pain and inflammation at bay, but for now science is still not able to permanently remove these symptoms. Stop the stimulation, and the symptoms resume. In the future, advances in the field could make pain and inflammation a thing of the past.

Vagus Nerve and Hypertension

Even if you are already hypertensive, you might not know that there are actually different types of hypertension depending on where the elevated blood pressure is. A specific type, for example, is Pulmonary Hypertension, where there is increased blood pressure in the pulmonary vasculature. Like other types of hypertension, it can cause a wide variety of accompanying diseases. A subclass of Pulmonary Hypertension, Pulmonary Artery Hypertension, is especially lethal with half of all diagnosed patients dying within seven years from their initial diagnosis.

Pulmonary Hypertension is complex, and it is very difficult to trace the interplay between the various cells and systems of the body leading to the illness and its effects. One thing for certain, however, is that the vagus nerve has a huge role to play in this illness. This knowledge, only recently studied in detail, comes in stark contrast with the way that Pulmonary Hypertension has been usually treated. In the past, it has been alleviated by efforts to inhibit the activity of the sympathetic nervous system, usually through medications. A more potent alternative, instead, is the restoration of balance through the activation of the vagus nerve, and along with it the rest of the parasympathetic nervous system.

In experiments with animal subjects, it has been found that stimulation of the right cervical part of the vagus nerve has led to a drastically improved survival of subjects with induced Pulmonary Hypertension. This is further aided by treatment using pyridostigmine, a type of acetylcholine-based substance that helps increase the activity of the parasympathetic nervous system. This has been previously used to help improve left ventricular function, and is now being used to blunt the tone of the sympathetic nervous system, thus allowing the parasympathetic half to catch up and balance. The study is just touching the tip of the iceberg, since it still has not been translated to success in human samples.

Vagus Nerve and Alzheimer's Disease

Dementia is one of the most dreadful effects of aging, and nowhere is it more dreaded than in Alzheimer's disease. This illness continues to fascinate researchers, its roots being a cocktail of genetic and lifestyle-related concerns. It is also the source of some of the major medical breakthroughs of recent years. There was a time when Alzheimer's was a dead end, with no cure. Today, there are several options (albeit mostly experimental) that could pave the way for a definite cure. And of course, the vagus nerve has a huge role to play in exploring these possible cures -- though maybe not in the way you thought of at first.

As already mentioned, the vagus nerve is the highway that links the brain to the digestive system, what many researchers call the "gut-brain axis". The gut is home to a huge host of microorganisms, many of which are very important in regulating the response of the immune system. What isn't known to many is that this biome of organisms also has a huge role to play in one's mental health, so much that the term "second brain" has arisen in some circles. While some may consider this an exaggeration, it is true that the gut and the brain work with each other through the vagus nerve. That is, the brain does not just control how the gut works, the gut also sends signals that affect the brain.

This becomes even more relevant to the topic at hand when we consider that an imbalance in the gut's host of microorganisms has been found to be among the roots of Alzheimer's. While age is still the primary risk factor in the onset of Alzheimer's, many other conditions have been found to be nearly as influential, among them obesity, issues with one's cardiovascular health (such as hypertension) and even depression. You would notice that these are also all conditions where the vagus nerve comes into play!

Recent research has focused on the treatment of Alzheimer's not from the brain, but from the gut and from the bundle of nerves that connect it to the brain. This research is given further impetus by the recent findings that Alzheimer's may partially be caused by infection from various types of viruses, in combination with a host of other factors. We already know that the vagus nerve has an important role to play in the regulation of the immune system, so this lends more credence to this emerging field of study.

Vagus Nerve and Memory Loss

But memory loss is not only exclusive for people suffering Alzheimer's. In fact, memory loss is very common, not only among the aging. For those who lack mental exercise, especially those with unhealthy diets and lifestyle, memory loss is a pretty common occurrence.

Again, the vagus nerve comes into play. The vagus nerve connects to the brain primarily through a relay network called the Nucleus Tractus Solitarius (NTS). This part of the brain connects the vagus nerve to the other parts that are related to memory and learning. Thus, stimulation of the vagus nerve can also lead to stimulation in these parts.

Memory improvement related to vagus nerve stimulation has not yet been thoroughly studied and conclusively proven in humans, but all signs thus point to this fact. For example, some studies in animal samples reported that those who underwent stimulation of the vagus nerve had better overall information retention and performance than those who did not. There had also been similar studies on human subjects with the same result, but a bigger sample set is needed for these studies to receive the stamp of scientific approval. It is to be noted that the changes noted were not immediate. Instead, they changed over time. This fact also calls for a longer study period to see just how far the memory-improving potential of the vagus nerve can go.

In all the examples so far, we have found how the vagus nerve, almost literally, has its fingers in all of the body's pies. It is one of those very important and yet very undermined parts of the body. Ignoring its importance can literally be a life or death situation.

Perhaps the most amazing is the fact that this bundle of nerves is so instrumental in fighting a host of so many illnesses that might appear too tough or too unusual to be dealt with by even the latest medications. It's all about understanding how the body works, and shifting the paradigm of treating these otherwise intangible illnesses to improving the restorative balance in the body.

Now that you have this information, how would you know if your vagus nerve is healthy? The next chapter deals with the specifics of vagus nerve health.

TAKEAWAYS:

- The vagus nerve's functions and connections allow it to influence a wide variety of diseases. These include:
    - Weight-related issues
    - Depression
    - Anxiety

- Trauma
- Epilepsy
- Brain damage
- Sleep issues
- Inflammation
- Pain
- Hypertension
- Alzheimer's Disease
- Memory Loss

- A healthy vagus nerve can prevent these issues from occurring, and can also help a person bounce back if they are already afflicted with such ailments.

Chapter 3: Is your Vagus Nerve healthy?

"The first wealth is health." -- Ralph Waldo Emerson

If you've never paid attention to your vagus nerve before, that's quite normal. In fact, unlike more famous vital organs in the body, the vagus nerve is very rarely heard of in normal conversations despite its importance. Those who might be hearing it for the first time would be forgiven to think of it as some pseudoscientific mumbo-jumbo -- in our world where nearly everything has one job and one job only, it seems inconceivable that something in our body aside from the brain (and perhaps the spinal cord) could be in charge of so many things at once.

However, this lack of knowledge about the vagus nerve can be quite debilitating. Put simply, there are lots of ill conditions that can occur due to a damaged or unstimulated vagus nerve. These issues are made apparent in the organs that the vagus nerve touches -- organs that are important not just in keeping our overall well-being, but also our vital processes.

Let's count the various injuries you may get from a damaged vagus nerve:

Starting with the nerve's attachment to the vocal cords, a damaged or inefficient vagus nerve can cause hoarseness and a strained feeling when talking. A voice that is unnaturally deep or hoarse, especially one that sets on without any actual damage to the pharynx or larynx can be a symptom of vagus nerve damage. You may also experience difficulty in swallowing, and the toning down of the gag reflex. The latter is important because it protects the body by automatically rejecting things that could choke us. A reduced gag reflex makes a person more susceptible to choking.

The vagus nerve is also connected to the ear, and plays a role in the brain's interpretation of sounds by carrying signals. Damage to this segment of the vagus nerve can result in partial or full hearing issues, ranging from the inability to distinguish sounds to deafness.

The organs inside the thoracic cavity are also innervated by the vagus nerve, so damage can also bring an increase in heart rate which can be harmful. This brings with it an increase in blood pressure, since the vagus nerve is responsible for the parasympathetic support to the cardiovascular system.

As for the esophagus, which is also connected to the brain through the vagus nerve, it can experience difficulty taking in food and drinks. The gut can also experience discomfort, or outright malfunction. Hyperacidity is a common symptom, which can damage the stomach's lining. The disruption of the established control mechanisms relating to gastric acid secretion can also lead to peptic ulcer due to the excessive secretion of peptic acid. This can also lead to other gastrointestinal issues such as dyspepsia.

When the part connected to the intestines are affected, this could cause problems in the process of peristalsis, the one responsible for moving food along for digestion and eventually absorption. Impaired peristalsis can cause constipation and other problems in the bowel movement. The urinary bladder is also touched by the vagus nerve, and damage can cause incontinence.

There are also several illnesses that can be caused or aggravated by a faulty vagus nerve, which sadly most people are not aware of. If you have one of the following, especially, read through this book as you will likely benefit from a healthier vagus nerve:

- Obesity or excess weight
- Depression
- Chronic fatigue
- Irritable Bowel symptom
- Irregular heartbeat, such as bradycardia (slowness of the heartbeat) and tachycardia (increased speed of the heartbeat)
- Rapid weight loss
- Peptic ulcer
- Chronic inflammation
- Gastroparesis
- Epilepsy

These is quite the varied list, and most of these diseases are caused by a list of factors. Because of the number of possible causes, most people don't even consider the importance of the vagus nerve in all this. But, together with the many ways one can rein in these diseases, taking care of the vagus nerve is also important.

Other, more generic symptoms of vagus nerve damage include the following:

Pain. This is the most common symptom, but also the one that tends to mask vagus nerve disorders the most -- simply due to the fact that pain can occur for a huge variety of reasons.

Pain due to vagus nerve is caused by the latter being pinched, often at the small exit through which it leaves the skull. While most other pains are sharp and stabbing, pain due to vagus nerve issues are mostly dull, and flat. It is also chronic, and while you can ease the pain through various means it is hard to completely get rid of it.

Cramps. Like pain, cramps are dreadfully common. Aside from the important organs we have mentioned, the vagus nerve is also connected to a few other muscles. While these muscles are not controlled by the vagus nerve per se, a malfunction in the nerve can also cause damage to the ability of the muscles to move. This includes cramps, which are different from those caused by a lack of electrolytes such as potassium and magnesium.

Fainting. As mentioned before, the vagus nerve also triggers fainting when overstimulated. When the nerve malfunctions, the same effect is achieved. Fainting per se is not life-threatening, but it does carry the risk of accidental injuries such as hitting your head or breaking a bone upon falling.

What causes vagus nerve issues?

Like most of the diseases enumerated earlier would suggest, certain lifestyle choices can greatly affect the vagus nerve' health. Here are a couple of the common activities that can degrade your vagus nerve's health. Note just how incredibly common these factors are in today's lifestyle, however. If you think that bingeing and boozing are destroying only very specific organs in your body, think again. That extra gummy bear might be leading to breathing difficulties in the future, thanks to the link between sugar, the vagus nerve, and the lungs!

Drinking. While occasional drinking isn't bad, chronic abuse of alcohol can greatly affect the nervous system as a whole, not just the vagus nerve. The more alcohol you take in, the more the nerves are damaged in a process called "alcoholic neuropathy". This causes severe problems throughout the whole body.

Sugar intake. Sugar is the main energy source of the body, and a healthy sugar intake (through complex carbohydrates) is also important. However, too much can cause diabetes, which can drastically change the chemistry of the nerve. This leads to such conditions as gastroparesis with symptoms including abdominal bloating, vomiting, and constipation. This happens when the stomach and the intestines are no longer able to properly push food through the digestive system.

Other causes of vagus nerve injury or malfunction are not related to the person's lifestyle, but rather are incidental to other issues:

Infections. Infections of the respiratory tract may redound to the vagus nerve. This can be pretty hard to pin down since symptoms can be indistinguishable between illnesses with infection at the root, and illnesses with the vagus nerve at the root. For example, both include runny nose, cough, and nasal congestion.

If these symptoms remain for long periods, however, it is likely that the vagus nerve is at fault, and it is also possible that a previous infection has caused it damage.

There are also infections whose symptoms include the inability to speak continuously, unusual tiredness of the throat, coughing, and the compulsion to clear the throat all the time.

Surgery complications. This isn't as common, but there are some times when operations done to the gut go wrong. A common surgery is the laparoscopic hemifundoplication, which is used as a treatment for one's gastric reflux. The damage happens when the surgery damages the vagus nerve connected to the stomach or the small intestine.

Repairing a damaged Vagus Nerve

Nerves are very fragile, which is why the most important bundles of nerves in our body are sheathed by tough layers of bone and cartilage. But the vagus nerve, alas, is pretty exposed -- exposed enough that when you press on your carotid arteries in the neck, you are essentially pressing on a part of your vagus nerve. Thus, the vagus nerve is far less protected from injury than other nerves.

For the most part, repair of the vagus nerve is symptomatic, meaning the symptoms are treated as they appear. Rarely, however, do such treatments actually go back to treating the vagus nerve itself. Fainting due to the overexcitability of the vagus nerve, for example, is treated by medication. Excessive or abnormal activity of the gastrointestinal tract is also treated by medicines, though some treatments have such side effects that most of them are reserved for more severe cases.

There is also the surgical alternative, though most only treat the symptoms. Patients with gastroparesis, for example, can go under the knife for stomach bypass or stomach staples.

Other symptoms of vagus nerve malfunction can be so subtle, however, that there are those who fail to detect them immediately and consequently don't take any steps to treat them.

Since it is currently impossible to isolate the specific part of the vagus nerve that is causing illnesses, there is no way to operate on it directly. The best option is a holistic approach that relies on stimulating the whole length of the nerve through the different points it is attached to. There are several ways of doing this, and it is even possible to address some issues directly through vagus nerve stimulation. We will be learning more about these techniques in the next chapter.

What to feed your Vagus Nerve

As we have mentioned, the best approach towards repairing and improving the vagus nerve is a holistic one. And there is nothing more holistic in approach than nourishing the body through the food we eat. Consider this section a rough guide on what food you should stock up on, in order to bring your vagus nerve back to tip-top shape. Of course, these are just general recommendations. If you think you have an injured vagus nerve, immediately go to a doctor who will give you specific advice on what to eat and what not to based on your individual circumstances.

The vagus nerve uses a type of chemical called acetylcholine as neurotransmitters. This acetylcholine transfers the information from the different organs the vagus nerve attaches to, towards the brain. The brain will then respond, sending acetylcholine down the vagus nerve towards the intended organ, mixed with other chemicals that would cause specific responses (such as anti-inflammatory ones).

Because of the importance of acetylcholine in the information transfer process between the brain and the organs, it is important to eat food that is known to help increase acetylcholine levels in the body. Here are the most common examples.

Egg yolks. Soft-boiled and raw eggs are great sources of choline. Cooking actually destroys the choline content, so if you are looking to use eggs as part of your vagus nerve diet, then it's best to keep it off the fire as much as possible.

Offal. Animal organs, such as kidneys and livers, are also great options for the improvement of one's acetylcholine levels. Pasture-fed sources are preferred, since these are less likely to contain harmful chemicals that can be absorbed by the body.

Lecithin granules. For the vegans, lecithin granules are perfect for building up the stock of acetylcholine in the body. These granules are usually made from soya, and sometimes from sunflower seeds. They can be added to different types of food and even drinks like smoothies.

Certain nutrients also help in the formation of acetylcholine, such as L-acetyl carnitine which can be found in meat. Various food sources such as squash and broccoli provide excellent sources of Vitamin B5, which helps in the creation of acetylcholine as well. If you like fish, you'd be happy to know that the methionine and lysine they provide can also be beneficial.

TAKEAWAYS:
- Like any other body part, the vagus nerve can be damaged. Damage can lead to a host of possibly debilitating symptoms, such as lifestyle diseases and chronic pain.
- This damage can be caused by lifestyle choices such as vices and improper diet, and also by injury caused by surgery and the like.
- However, the vagus nerve can be restored to health by proper stimulation and following a vagus-friendly diet.

Chapter 4: Jacking up the Vagus Nerve

"You have always to stimulate the senses." -- Henrik Fisker

Way back in 1934, a physicist found out that when the carotid sinus is pressed down, it produced a direct response in the circuit of the brain. This response cascaded into a difference in the person's heart rate and blood pressure. Such was science's entry into the field of vagus nerve stimulation that had been practiced without clear definition or direction for ages.

Only four years later, Bailey and Bremer noted that such stimulation caused changes in the reading of ECG results. In 1951, a different study showed that stimulation of the vagus nerve -- then isolated and severed -- had evoked changes in the thalamic regions of the brain. And finally, in 1985, there was the concrete observation that electrical stimulation from the vagal region inhibits some neural processes. This can change the electrical activity in the brain, and end seizures of an epileptic nature. This ushered in the era of using vagus nerve stimulation as a means of addressing illnesses.

Why stimulate the Vagus Nerve?

If the vagus nerve is so important, surely there is a way to make it better? If we can train the brain to be sharper, and our spinal cords to conduct instinctive movements faster, then maybe there's something we can also do for the vagus nerve. We know about muscles being exercised in order to strengthen them and improve their functioning. But how can constant stimulation improve the health of a nerve?

As an oversimplification, nerves are networks of neurons, "relays" that transfer signals (chemical impulses) from one part of the body to another. While neurons don't grow in size like muscles, it is possible to make the transfer of impulses faster and more efficient by "exercising" them through constant stimulation. This stimulation, when performed consistently over time, creates a physical change by improving the structure of the neurons, allowing them to be better at carrying signals. This is the principle behind such concepts as "muscle memory", which is in fact a certain set of neurons involved in the performance of an activity being conditioned to fire off faster and more efficiently.

The vagus nerve also benefits from the same concept. When the nerve is stimulated consistently, it becomes better at sending signals to and from the many organs attached to it. Thus, it improves several important functions of the body, from heart rate and respiratory rate to the digestive process.

Methods of Stimulation

Vagus nerve stimulation (which we'll call VNS, moving forward) can be classified into two. On one hand, we have the natural VNS methods, which are done without the aid of any electronic tools. We also have more modern methods that utilize implants and other devices that send electronic impulses directly stimulating the vagus nerve. In this chapter, we'll explore how both these methods work, and the benefits that each one has.

Natural Methods

Natural methods of stimulating the vagus nerve have been known to man since ancient times, but only recently have they been substantiated by scientific findings. Only recently had these same methods actually been connected to real-world physiological effects -- in the ancient times these practices were all about managing the flow of energy and creating a body that is one with the mind and spirit.

While natural methods have not been found to be as immediately effective or as well-targeted as their electronic counterparts, research has shown that there are concrete benefits to be had when stimulating the vagus nerve through these means.

Just like in electronic methods, natural methods can be done on demand and adjusted in "intensity" according to one's preference. However, since they don't target a specific part of the nerve, natural VNS methods give way to a "Goldilocks" principle wherein the person needs to find the perfect balance between stimulating and not stimulating the vagus nerve. For example, VNS may need to be done when one feels down or anxious, but too much stimulation can swing one's mood to the opposite direction and make him irritable and panicky. This cycle of ups and downs can alternate frequently, causing more issues than before. It is up to the user of natural VNS methods to find the middle ground.

Here are some of the most common ways to stimulate the vagus nerve naturally.

Humming. Since the vagus nerve passes through by the neck, attaching some of their ends to the vocal cords, it is possible to stimulate the nerve by simple humming a tune. In fact, humming has been found to be one of the easiest ways to influence the state of the nervous system.

When humming, do it with gusto -- you will know you are doing it right when you can feel the vibrations in your throat, and in your chest. When you have achieved a certain level of practice, you will also feel the vibrations reverberating in your head.

Immersion in cold. While most people shun the cold, it is actually essential in the stimulation of the vagus nerve and is as such instrumental in ensuring the nerve's health. In fact, multiple record-holder, Wim Hof attributes much of his incredible cold-related feats to an overall wellbeing that is primarily fueled by his cold-based training. He is not superhumanly resistant to cold, just like any human -- but his being accustomed to the cold has given him unusual levels of autoimmune development that allowed him to complete his feats.

A study suggests that as the body tries to adjust to the cold, the sympathetic nervous system slows down, and the parasympathetic system takes over. The sympathetic nervous system would be more familiar as the fight-or-flight mechanism, which is more active and is mediated by other nerves. The parasympathetic system (also nicknamed the rest-and-digest system) is triggered by ambient temperatures that are around 10 degrees Celsius.

Animal experiments also found out that sudden exposure to cold temperatures such as 4 degrees Celsius can greatly increase vagus nerve activation. This may be rooted to the fact that historically, creatures bathe in cold water in order to relax. Warm water was not easily available (in fact quite rare) even in the hotter regions. These conditions, before the advent of heating, seem to be the primary reason for the evolution of this response for the cold. Today, cold tubs are still popular in countries such as Japan, while many European countries neighboring the Arctic Circle also partake of cold ocean dips in special occasions.

If you want to try this out, but can't find the right conditions, taking a cold shower is a good place to start. You may pre-condition your body (and also your vagus nerve response) by dipping your face in cold water first. This will trigger the diver's reflex, which will be discussed in detail later.

Deep Breathing. Various deep breathing techniques can be used to influence the nervous system. The common denominator among these techniques is that the means of breathing employs the diaphragm, where the vagus nerve is attached. For most people, breathing is a matter of expanding the chest space through lifting the shoulders. This is an incorrect form of breathing, as it places undue stress on the upper chest, without actually working the muscle meant for breathing (the diaphragm). In correct deep breathing (and even regular breathing), the diaphragm moves and makes space for the lungs to draw in air. Physically, it looks like the stomach is bulging out, and the chest and shoulders stay in place.

The most effective deep breathing techniques for the stimulation of the vagus nerve involve slowing down the breath. The normal respiratory rate is at 10 to 14 breaths per minute, and deliberately slowing this down to about 5-7 breaths per minute can greatly increase stimulation in the vagus nerve.

One of the most common techniques not just for controlling the breath but also for managing stress is the "Box Breathing" method, so-called because of its technique of counting to 4. Basically, you breathe in for 4 seconds, hold the breath for 4 seconds, breathe out for 4 seconds, and hold it again for 4 seconds. Repeating the process has been known to calm the mind, especially in times of stress. It has also been known to reduce headaches and similar pain, which has been attributed to its ability to stimulate the vagus nerve.

Another technique one can use is prolonging the exhalation. A common counting system is breathing in for 5 seconds, and breathing out for 10 seconds. Aside from stimulating the vagus nerve, prolonging the exhalation helps ensure one uses up all the available oxygen upon inhalation.

A technique specific to the stimulation of the vagus nerve is the constriction of the back of the throat upon exhalation. This motion is similar to when one wishes to fog up a mirror or a piece of glass. The difference is that the air still passes through the nose instead of the mouth. This is a known yoga breathing technique, called *ujjayi pranayam*. There is a host of other yoga-related breathing techniques that you can try. Some of these techniques are downright unusual, but the common denominator is that they place a great strain on the diaphragm, therefore stimulating the vagus nerve attached to it.

If you feel like it, the breathing techniques involved with singing (particularly those songs with high notes and long verses) can also stimulate the vagus nerve. This is one of the driving forces behind the healing power accorded to meditative chanting. Singing hymns or repetitive chants can help activate the part of the vagus nerve that is at the back of the throat. A scientific study has found that for a group of 18 year-olds, singing can actually increase the Heart Rate Variability through VNS. Heart Rate Variability has been associated with better adaptation and resilience, along with relaxation. It also helps increase the efficiency of the body's rest-and-digest mechanism, an activity that is primarily overseen by the vagus nerve.

Later, in the second part of this book, you will be introduced further to the art and science behind breathing, and its place in the near-esoteric field of contemplative traditions. We will be breaking down the general ideas behind the concepts of meditation, mapping the science behind them, and from there building a new practice that you can use in your daily life.

Valsalva Maneuver. This may sound complicated, but it's actually just the act of exhaling (or, more correctly, attempting to exhale) when the airways are closed. This is a familiar technique for those who want to make their ears "pop" when boarding a plane, or when moving to a ground of different elevation. The maneuver is commonly used to equalize the air pressure in the ear, using the small ducts that connect the ears to the nose. However, the Valsalva Maneuver also helps increase the pressure inside the chest cavity, stimulating the vagus nerve from there.

The maneuver is done by simply keeping the mouth closed and pinching the nostrils shut, then trying to breathe out. Don't do this too rashly, as this may cause injury to the ear when forced. Test it out slowly at first until you can find the most comfortable intensity of exhaling.

Diving Reflex Stimulation. The "diving reflex" is essentially the body's ability to prepare for an underwater excursion. Such reflex changes the body's normal way of distributing oxygen, channeling the bulk of it to the brain and the heart, and reducing supply to the other organs and areas of the body. This is done in order to make the most of the oxygen stores and therefore prolong the ability to stay underwater without needing more oxygen. The vagus nerve is also involved in this process, and it is possible to do natural VNS by stimulating the diving reflex.

While diving reflex can be (weakly) stimulated by holding the breath, it can be better stimulated by contact with cold water. Splash cold water on your face, especially on the space between the lips and the hairline. You can also simulate this by using ice cubes in a

Ziplock bag. Couple the process with a moment of holding your breath, to trigger the redistribution of oxygen. If you don't feel like wetting your face, it is also possible to stimulate the diving reflex by dipping your tongue in lukewarm liquid. Hold the liquid in your mouth, and roll it around with your tongue, in order to evoke the reflex.

Making social connections. Weirdly enough, there have been studies that showed that the vagus nerve can be stimulated by positive emotions. In fact, it is possible to stimulate the vagus nerve by doing something that makes you feel happy and connected. This is different from simply feeling calm and at ease, since the latter (in the form of meditation) has been proven to be ineffective at natural VNS.

Another way to effectively stimulate the vagus nerve through making social connections is having a good laugh with a friend or family member. This is the reasoning behind the famous quote, "laughter is the best medicine". In fact, laughing has been proven in some clinical tests to be effective in natural VNS. One basic proof is the propensity of some people to faint while in a fit of laughter. This has been pointed out to be due to an overstimulation of the vagus nerve as well as other parts of the parasympathetic nervous system. Other means of overstimulating the vagus nerve can also lead to fainting. Another proof of the connection between laughter and the vagus nerve is the laughter elicited by electronic VNS in children with epilepsy.

Other studies seem to suggest that the *idea* of connection alone can increase the body's natural ability to stimulate the vagus nerve. A study involving a small group of people found that praying -- an act that elicits a feeling of connection to a higher deity or purpose -- helps increase vagus nerve activation. The group unanimously experienced an improved level of cardiovascular rhythms, and also had a drop in diastolic blood pressure. Other researchers pegged the VNS effect to the actual act of saying the prayer. Praying the rosary, for example, takes around 10 seconds for the reading of each cycle. When said orally, this effectively slows down the breathing pace of a person and regulates inhales to once every 10 seconds, thus producing the same VNS effect as measured breathing.

Probiotic intake. This is still an emerging field of study, but some research has suggested that the flora in the gut can have effects in the nervous system. Remember that the gut connects to the brain through the vagus nerve, so some researchers believe that good bacteria in the gut also translates to nourishment for the vagus.

There have been some animal studies that seem to prove this point, although in terms of scientific robustness they are still lacking. In one such study, mice which had been supplemented with a type of probiotic had experienced an improvement in the GABA receptors, among the many parts of the parasympathetic nervous system that is being regulated by the vagus nerve.

Physical Activity. There is more research to prove that a good dose of physical activity can greatly help improve the performance of the vagus nerve, stimulating it for better efficiency. Those into yoga, for example, will be happy to know that the mood improvements caused by the activity is greatly affected by the thalamic GABA levels increased when the vagus nerve is active.

Other forms of exercise help stimulate the flow of the gut part of the digestive tract, and this is caused by the concurrent stimulation of the vagus nerve connected to it. Like the probiotic angle, though, much research is still needed to support this claim, especially on human subjects.

Even if you don't like to move your body, you may still get good natural VNS by having a massage. Make sure to get a massage that reaches the neck area, as you need to target specific areas such as the carotid sinus. Research suggests that epileptics, or those who regularly get seizures, can get relief from this kind of VNS -- though it is not advisable to do it at home since overstimulation can result in fainting. The effectivity of such massage is so well-known in other regions that a neck massage is given to infants to stimulate their appetite (mediated by the vagus nerve). Finally, there are reflexology methods that purport to excite the vagus nerve as well, though these have been tested only in small experimental groups.

Diet Patterns. Since the vagus nerve is connected to the gut, there are ways to stimulate it directly from the changes we do to our diet patterns. For one, eating a diet high in seafood can give us EPA and DHA, omega-3 fatty acids that lowers the heart rate and heightens the heart rate variability. Heart rate variability is linked to the stimulation of the vagus nerve, and some scientists believe that this is a big reason why omega-3 fatty acids are so good for the body.

Zinc is also considered to be important to natural VNS through diet. In laboratory studies, zinc has been found to increase vagus nerve stimulation especially after a diet that is particularly deficient in it.

For those who are on a hard diet regimen, even fasting can help improve the health of the vagus nerve. Intermittent fasting has been shown to increase the heart rate variability in certain animals, and this is found to be a marker of vagus nerve stimulation.

As with many of the resources cited here, fasting still needs to be observed in bigger samples in order to establish its complete efficiency. One theory states that fasting mediates a reduction in a person's metabolism, in the same way that it mediates a change in a person's metabolic priorities in the diver reflex. This time around, the vagus nerve will detect a decline in the blood glucose levels, and a decrease in the mechanical and chemical stimuli coming from the digestive tract. This reduction has been found to increase the level of vagus nerve impulses from the liver to the brain, triggering the slowing of the body's metabolic rate. As always, check with your doctor when attempting to engage in any fasting regimen. As it stands, fasting can have more harmful effects than good one when done improperly, even if it does stimulate the vagus nerve.

Fiber, which is known as a very important component of a healthy gut, also has great effects on the vagus nerve as part of a diet. Studies suggest that fiber helps increase the occurrence of GLP-1, a satiating hormone that also has the effect of stimulating the vagus impulses to the brain.

On the other hand, it is also important to note that there are types of food that can serve to *inhibit* the vagus nerve instead of stimulating it. Carbohydrates, for example, increases the levels of insulin in the body. This insulin can compromise the function of the vagus nerve, which connects to the function of the liver. Capsaicin and ginger are also among the most potent ways of inhibiting the vagus nerve -- in fact, ginger's ability to stop vomiting and nausea is attributable to its ability to hinder the function of the vagus nerve.

Electronic Methods

Before we delve into the different methods of electronic vagus nerve stimulation, it's important to understand that these methods are not free from side effects. In fact, it is possible to feel these side-effects intermittently even while stimulation is not being applied.

These adverse effects, when present, can be felt in the organs that are connected to the vagus nerve. It is not that common, however, since as mentioned around 80% of the nerves in the vagus carry signals from the body to the brain, so only 20% are left with the ability to actually affect the body parts.

Different parts of the vagus nerve, when stimulated, can lead to different side effects. For example, left cervical VNS can cause changes in one's voice, as well as coughing. It can also affect the neck, causing pain. Dyspnea or shortness of breath is also a common occurrence. Right cervical VNS, on the other hand, has been known to produce bradycardia or the slowing of the beating of the heart. In extreme cases, especially when stimulation (or the device applying it) is misapplied, it is also known to cause asystole or the lack of contraction in the ventricle of the heart. This is a form of cardiac arrest, and is deadly.

Despite these possible adverse effects, direct electronic VNS is a very potent cure for various conditions as we will shortly see. The most important thing to remember is, like any other medical treatment, to have it done by a licensed medical practitioner well-skilled in the process. This way, electronic VNS can immensely improve one's quality of life.

Is it safe for me?

The adverse effects mentioned here can all be controlled by changing the parameters of the device used for stimulation. Generally, tolerance to side effects build up as exposure to the stimulation is prolonged. There are no known recurring adverse reactions which would endanger a VNS patient, and even children and pregnant women have been treated successfully by the technique. Its combination with medication has also been well-studied, and unless indicated by your doctor should have no contraindications.

The only limitation is that a person carrying a VNS implant could not undergo such radiation-based procedures as MRI, and shortwave, microwave, or ultrasound diathermy.

Diagnostic ultrasound is still permissible. The implant is also not affected by common radiation-emitting appliances such as metal detectors, microwaves, and cellphones.

Left Cervical VNS

In the left cervical VNS, stimulation is done by the implantation of a "pulse generator device". This is commercially available, and its "installation" is a quick outpatient procedure done under general anesthesia.

The generator is placed just under the skin, in the left upper chest. It has an electrode that is attached directly to the vagus nerve via another incision made in the left neck section. The electrode and the generator is connected via a lead wire. Since it is a relatively simple procedure, there aren't many things that could go wrong. The installation of the pulse generator is generally safe.

The generator itself is programmed by a handheld computer, interfaced with the device through a programming wand. The wand is passed over the skin where the device is implanted. There are various parameters that can be controlled, which the doctor can program. These parameters (intensity, charge, pulse width and frequency, etc.) are all optimized to deal with the specific illness the stimulation is treating.

These generators typically run continuously, and the only way to turn them off is to run a magnet over them. This is only temporary, though -- only the programming wand can turn it on or off completely. The battery life can change depending on the parameters set, and when spent can be easily replaced.

Right Cervical VNS

This is the technique used in order to help reduce seizures in animal models. It has also been looked into for the treatment of depression, but human tests on the matter is still inconclusive.

Like in left cervical stimulation, a device is also implanted in the body. However, an additional system has been developed for VNS stimulation leading to the treatment of heart failure. This device is implanted in the patient's right chest wall, and is connected via a cuff to the right cervical vagus nerve. This cuff is meant to activate specific efferent fibers of the vagus nerve, in order to fix the cardiac rhythm. The device has a stimulator which responds directly to the heart rate, shutting off when the heart goes past the threshold for bradycardia.

Studies have found that stimulation of the right cervical vagus nerve is not only safe, but also effective for the treatment of heart problems. In Israel, a similar system has been designed specifically to counter any possible VNS-related side effects. This device, in contrast, only activates the afferent fibers. This right cervical VNS device has been used in conjunction with the left cervical VNS-based treatment to improve the status of patients without causing any untoward side effects.

Transcutaneous Vagus Nerve Stimulation

There are also devices that can stimulate the vagus nerve at different locations through a person's skin.

For example, the outer ear carries the vagus nerve's auricular branch, and this nerve exclusively services some areas of the ear. One such area is the cymba conchae, which can be stimulated by applying an electrical stimulus. The stimulus can be felt by the person, but is still below the pain threshold. Such a stimulation can produce activity in the brain that is similar to direct stimulation in the left cervical vagus nerve. Hence, this can also be used to help treat epilepsy and some other types of pain.

Aside from being much less invasive than direct stimulation, another advantage of transcutaneous VNS is that it can be applied by the patient himself. What may be an issue, though, is the fact that there are no universally accepted clinical processes on the application of transcutaneous VNS. The manufacturer of the stimulation device (currently the only one approved for clinical use) says that stimulation sessions should last at least an hour, up to 4 times a day. The literature behind this recommendation is still unclear, but the device's effects are substantiated. Pilot studies have also been done on the product's efficiency for depression epilepsy, pain, and some other complications. While the results are yet to be verified by bigger studies, there is already a universal consensus on the product's safety.

A different device has been approved for use for the treatment of migraine, cluster headache, and headache due to the overuse of certain medicines. The device, called "gammaCore", is a handheld device with two flat surfaces that can be placed over the neck where the pulse is. The device then sends an electrical signal which lasts for about 90 seconds. The intensity is controlled by the patient, and the device may be used on demand when headaches come, or throughout the day to prevent headaches. While there is some literature supporting the effectivity of these devices, it still needs larger trials for further proof. Unfortunately, there are no trials yet to prove that the same device is useful for epilepsy and depression, two other areas where VNS should be helpful.

TAKEAWAYS

- A huge number of techniques can be used to stimulate activity in the vagus nerve. Stimulation is important to make the vagus healthier, hence improving its function and improving the overall health of the body.
- Vagus stimulation may be natural or electronic:
    - Natural methods can be done through variations of engaging the lungs (humming, deep breathing, singing, etc.) or engaging the reflexes of the nervous system (cold immersion, Valsalva method, etc.). It is also possible to stimulate the vagus nerve through psychological means such as fostering a healthy social life.

- Electronic stimulation is done by implants, targeting different parts of the vagus nerve. There are also implants that are done at skin level, which are less complicated and have a broader (less specialized) range of stimulation.

PART 2:

The Vagus Nerve in your Daily Life

Thus far we have discussed the scientific points of the vagus nerve along with the many options one has for stimulating it.

But what we have so far is a disparate set of information, things that are illuminating but not immediately practicable in daily life. It's like trying to learn how to train in martial arts by knowing only the descriptions and mechanics of various punches and kicks, and the materials one needs to have to train, but not really applying them in one's everyday living.

In this unit of the book, we will try to combine everything we have learned so far in order to distill a functioning "vagus nerve training manual", one that you can do even in the midst of your hectic schedule. After all, one of the main reasons why the vagus nerve weakens in the span of the modern lifestyle is because so few of us actually have time to train it. Here, we will try to remedy this by creating a set of vagus-stimulating activities that can fit in no matter what backdrop of activities you may have in your daily life.

Chapter 5: Vagus Nerve and Meditation: An Ancient Combination for Modern Life

"Meditation is not following any system; it is not constant repetition and imitation. Meditation is not concentration." -- Jiddu Krishnamurti

Thanks to popular media, the image is all-too-familiar to the modern generation. A lone man, well-advanced in his years, sits alone on a mountaintop, still and silent, deep in meditation. When he stands up to do his chores, he does it slowly and rhythmically, without any hurry. Approach this old man and you would be amazed at his wealth of wisdom, and his flawless recall. You would be even more amazed when you find out that this man must be nearly twice as old as he looks! If ever you make the regrettable decision of being mean to this man, you would also feel that his strength and coordination has hardly declined since his youthful days.

This image seems all too magical, a mere invention by people who glorify the ways of the old, who romanticize the quiet life of the mountain sage. Myth and legend are rife with such figures of impossible feats, but the fact that they no longer exist in the modern day makes their possibility patently questionable. And yet, in every story is an iota of truth. What if there *were* such people, with such traits? Sure, stories of their feats had been exaggerated, but where did people get the idea that a life spent alone and in meditation could unlock near-supernatural powers within an individual?

With the discovery of the vagus nerve and all its potential, we may have found the answer.

The Art of Contemplative Traditions

Earlier in this book, we have discussed that there are ancient methods that have been known to increase the vagus nerve stimulation. We have also discussed the many separate ways through which vagus nerve stimulation can be attained, either naturally or electronically.

Short of actually having a vagus nerve implant (which can only be had if one actually has an illness treatable by such a device), then what we need for daily life is a holistic approach that can serve to uplift our general wellbeing as much as it uplifts the vagus nerve. This is why for this chapter, we will look into one of the most time-honored "rituals" that can be embedded in one's life, as a thorough approach to VNS. We are looking at contemplation -- a very broad array of practices with the common goal of improving one's overall health. In study after study, science has also proven that these are among the best ways to improve vagus nerve health.

The Treasure Trove of Contemplation

Contemplation takes different forms. Some may be introduced to it in the modern takes on meditation. Others may be more focused on the schools of knowledge passed down in yoga or tai chi. All of these acts have ancient roots, and all of these have been found to have immensely beneficial effects on the physical, mental, and cognitive well-being of a person.

However, there haven't been many studies actually elaborating on how these practices achieve their efficiency. A 2018 research, however, posits that all of these practices have one thing in common, and it is this one thing that makes them so efficient -- in all of them, breathing is carefully controlled and guided. Yoga, tai chi, and simple meditation are not just a series of postures, they teach a form of regulated breathing that helps stimulate the vagus nerve. We have already gone into slight detail about how to help stimulate and tone the vagus nerve through simple exercises earlier, but this time we will look at these methods as something that can be applied to all corners of daily life.

For the purpose of this chapter, we will be referring to the collection of similar contemplative actions as "Contemplative Traditions" or CT. These CTs are usually done in order to help one achieve a more "balanced" life (though balance may be a word whose meaning slightly differs depending on the specific practice). They are also aimed (and proven effective) at changing one's state of mind. They appear in several forms, from praying to meditating. Let's dive into the understate treasure trove of these traditions with a brief history.

Meditation is a set of traditions that come from the Asian region, usually rooted in the Hindu or Buddhist belief system. There are different types of meditation from each country of origin. For example, China birthed the origin of Zen meditation, while India was the cradle of transcendental meditation and vipassana. There is also the loving-kindness meditation of Tibet. These have all seen popular resurgence, with various studies supporting their efficiency.

According to the 2018 study, these meditative acts can be generally classified into two: Focused Attention (FA) and Open Monitoring (OM). The former trains the person to focus on a single point, object, or action, and to shift the focus back to the object being meditated on should a rogue thought arise. Open Monitoring, on the other hand trains the person to spread his attention thinly across multiple stimuli, those things happening around and within him, so that no single item has his rapt attention. Some traditions blend from one meditative practice into another, with OM being seen as more advanced models of meditation than FA.

A broader classification of meditative processes, found in a 2015 study, is based on the emphasis in techniques. This resulted in a three-way classification: attentional, constructive, and deconstructive. Both FA and OM are then found under the banner of attentional meditation. Constructive meditation is aimed at internal improvement and the spread of such improvement to others. An example is loving-kindness meditation. Then, there is the type of meditation that removes the barriers of everything from habits to perceptions, from thoughts to behavior. This is exemplified by most forms of mindfulness meditation. Note that we are solely referring here to mindfulness as a meditative practice, and not as a state that is achieved after indulging in such practice. As a state, mindfulness can be the target of any other meditative techniques, particularly those of FA and OM.

Then again, there is a whole different subgroup of the meditative practice dedicated to the synergy of the movements of the mind and body. These include all forms of meditation that include stances and complex movements, along with those that include muscle relaxation techniques.

These classifications are important because the effects of vagus nerve stimulation are more pronounced in some categories than in others, simply due to the fact that there is a different set of instructions given for these meditative practices. But research has found that all of these practices have at least some type of effect in the various domains of wellbeing. Here are a few:

Improved cardiopulmonary functioning. Various CTs have been shown to decrease risk factors concerning a person's cardiorespiratory health. As much can be found from various meta-analysis studies that compared independent research on various CTs. Some practices, though, like qi gong, have not yet been efficiently studied due to a lack of long-term trials.

Anti-Inflammatory effects. Many CTs have records of improving immunological improvements, centering on anti-inflammatory effects. These effects have been quantified in the reduction of pro-inflammatory markers in the body, along with a reduction in the cytokines that ignite inflammation.

General physical improvements. This is where it gets pretty interesting, as many CTs have been found to improve bodily factors as diverse as bone density, physical balance, and overall strength. These changes also help alleviate pain, and this includes not just muscular pain but also illnesses such as migraine and osteoarthritis. Stress reduction has also been found to be a direct effect of these physical improvements. These effects are, in fact so strong that they are comparable to the medication used for chronic pain.

Decrease in stress-related issues. We have mentioned that stress-reduction is a common result of these CTs, and naturally the reduction of symptoms of illnesses related to stress would follow. These include symptoms of psychopathological illnesses such as PTSD, anxiety, and depression.

Improved cognitive control. Some studies have also shown that CTs can enhance the way the brain handles memory and other executive functions. These are the functions that rely on high-level mental processes, such as arithmetic and logic. These improvements can act as a remedy for many memory and logic issues related to age-related brain decline. These improvements are especially pronounced in mindfulness-type meditation. Just like in physical improvements, these mental improvements can be so pronounced that it is possible to induce them simply by short bursts of CT interventions. These effects could snowball after prolonged exposure to such practices.

Improved attention span. Most practitioners of CTs would attribute their improved ability to concentrate on everyday tasks to their constant practice at keeping their attention during the meditative stage. While the idea that "willpower is a muscle" still remains debatable, research lends credence to it thanks to studies showing a specialization on attention and focus for those who practice CTs.

When we say "attention span" here, we're not just talking about the ability to stay focused on one task. Different CTs offer different advantages according to their nature. For example, Focused Attention (FA) CTs increase one's ability to sustain attention on a narrow field for extended periods, while those who practice Open Monitoring (OM) CTs have the ability to jump from one mental task to another without muddling the ideas that come to mind. Both of these types show just about the same level of enhanced mental performance overall.

Improved creativity. Creativity is not something that is easily measured, so studies on the matter are limited to easily observable traits such as verbal creativity. Various CT researches have proven that practitioners have increased levels of creativity over time, coupled with an increase in the overall cognition ability. This latter metric consists of various thinking exercises such as convergent and divergent thinking. Practitioners are also better able to distinguish the many things happening around them in daily life, pointing towards a better level of awareness, which in turn helps fuel their creativity.

When we look at all these benefits from CTs, it is easy to draw the line between the observed improvements and the vagus nerve. All these improvements touch areas of the body, both physically and mentally, that are directly connected to the vagus nerve's many functions. Thus comes the proof that these meditative practices, discovered and practiced since ancient times, holistically improve the body by engaging the vagus nerve.

What makes these CTs so effective?

These CTs have their own unique traits, which we need to look into so that we can discern just what makes them so effective. After all, not everyone has the time to study yoga or tai chi, and not everyone has a place they can go to for Zen meditation. We need to determine what principles and techniques are at play, which make these practices so effective.

In 2011, a study on mindfulness meditation has revealed a formula-like set of activities that are common to most CTs. These include attention and affect training, the adjustment of "metacognitive recognition" (simply put, being aware of what one is aware of), awareness of the body (including its states and processes), physical activity, and the use of various breathing techniques. Let's take a look at these factors, and how each would affect the vagus nerve.

Attention and Affect Training. In CTs, the focus on attention isn't very clear cut. Several traditions train one to focus on an external object, while others teach one to focus on internal processes such as breathing. Still, some would push for a focus on abstract concepts such as thought, and the very idea of thought. Then, there are some CTs (such as the first incarnations of Zen meditation) where one isn't taught to focus on anything at all.

As stated earlier, the type of attention training would greatly affect the cognitive improvements one may reap. Some are able to focus on a task even better, while some are able to multitask without much distraction. Thus, it would be better to understand attention training as something that is more focused on control rather than on a specific result.

Affect training, on the other hand, is focused on training a person to handle one's emotions and moods. This means being aware of what one perceives to be negative feelings and ideas, and turning them into something that is useful or at least manageable. This is a more abstract equivalent of exposure therapy, wherein one is exposed to negative stimuli in the hopes of giving him time and means to process it so it makes less of an impact.

Most CT practitioners are instructed to "alter" their mental state by diffusing the intensity of the negative thought or emotion. Most practices would teach their students to consider that these are all just fleeting sensations, therefore allowing the student to detach himself from the idea that is observed. The detachment that then results protects the practitioner from forming any more of such ideas.

In effect, attention and affect training covers two important parts of the mind: the cognitive and the psycho-emotional parts. As discussed previously, these parts are both also affected by the vagus nerve. This is why VNS has become important areas of research in the battle against Alzheimer's (cognitive) and depression (psycho-emotional). Furthermore, it has been studied that a better grip on both one's conscious and subconscious thought processes is an effective way to prevent the onset of extreme stress. Reduced stress then allows the vagus nerve to start its own healing regimen, leading to better immune function and heart health.

Adjusting one's metacognitive recognition. CTs are well-known for their overarching concepts of oneness, unity in everything. This is also evident (perhaps not surprisingly) in how the common denominators of these CTs present a unified front. Case in point is metacognitive recognition, which is a direct effect of the techniques used in attention and affect training.

Metacognition is better put as "thinking about thinking". Therefore, adjusting metacognition is changing the way one thinks about thinking. At first blush, this is an idea that is meant to twist the vagus nerve and the brain into confusion, but in practice, it can be fairly straightforward -- just focus on changing the way your mind processes information.

The brain is very good at recognizing patterns, perhaps so much that most of the stimuli we encounter everyday have a "default" response as they go through a certain route in the brain.

These instincts and impulses then shape our reality. While these may be put to good use, such as in committing certain actions to "muscle memory" (really a practiced pathway from the brain to the muscles) for faster retrieval, sometimes these also lead us to spirals of negativity. This is why many CTs advocate "thought monitoring" in order to teach us how to deconstruct thoughts and how we process them, moving away from default responses and preconceptions to carve new processing routes and possibly new outcomes.

At face value, this seems to be the root of how creativity is improved for those who practice CTs. When practiced, it helps a person gain better control over how he processes information, getting rid of irrelevant ones and providing a fresh perspective on the relevant ones (potentially allowing for new and novel uses).

Such a process helps improve the overall health of the vagus nerve in a way that is different from most of what we have discussed so far. We have touched upon the idea of "muscle memory", which is in fact just an improvement on the pathways that send signals from the brain to specific areas of the body, in order to trigger a specific set of responses. The benefits of metacognitive adjustment to the vagus nerve runs in the same vein. Looking at old stimuli in a new light will transfer the information to new areas of the brain, passing through those areas of memory and emotion that are also served by the vagus nerve. When these stimuli elicit new responses, a different part of the vagus nerve may be activated in order to serve the flow of new information.

Nerves are "exercised" through the process of myelinization. Myelin is that substance that sheaths the nerve fibers around the axons, allowing for efficient transfer of signals from one nerve to another. The healthier the myelin sheath is, the faster the travel of information from one end of a neural network towards the other end is.

Myelinization is triggered by using the same network over and over again -- this is why we are able to pull off instinctive reactions to stimuli more quickly than newly-acquired responses. But if we are able to pull back from such preset networks to explore other possibilities, then other parts of the vagus nerve can also undergo the process of myelinization, therefore strengthening the whole network. In contrast, disuse of specific parts of the network, whether it is in the vagus nerve or in other parts of the body, would make the myelin sheath weak an inefficient at transmitting information.

Awareness of the body. Certain CTs instruct practitioners to be aware of the body and its different states, often focusing on the tension in the muscles or sensations in the skin. Still others would instruct practitioners to focus on what their "gut" tells them (though very few actually recognize the existence of the gut as a "second brain" as discussed earlier).

In keeping with the theme of oneness, this bodily awareness is also central to the whole affective process discussed before. Body awareness teaches the CT practitioner to treat the body as a separate entity, a vessel that contains the self, but that is not completely the self. This encourages a culture of interoception (this time connected to the idea of metacognitive recognition), and teaches one to be keener in understanding what it is the body feels. Studies have expressed the fruits of this practice as an increase in tactile acuity, and a resulting increase in the parts of the brain that process the signals being sent by the body. These, in turn, can produce vivid effects on the emotional and cognitive levels.

This benefits the vagus nerve in the same way that metacognitive recognition does, allowing the brain to intensively engage new sections and possibly new pathways through the vagus nerve.

Physical activity. Many would point to the physical activity practiced in different CTs to be the primary factor in their effectiveness as harbingers of wellbeing. However, this is just one side of the coin, as we have demonstrated with the effects mentioned above. Still, the physical benefits reaped from CTs that recommend activity stand out on their own, even while directly interplaying with the other benefits discussed above.

It is also to be considered that some CTs do not advocate any specific type of physical activity at all, such as the sitting meditation of later Zen meditation schools and the prayer meditation practiced in some religions. Still, these have not been found to be inferior to the more physical CTs. This points to the fact that overall benefits can be gained simply from the internal processes of CTs, especially the concomitant vagus nerve stimulation.

Like in benefits to mental acuity, the various improvements in physical ability would depend on the specific contemplative tradition that is being practiced. For example, some schools of yoga place special emphasis on flexibility and on aerobic endurance. Tai chi, on the other hand, focuses on balance and posture. There are some studies positing that aside from the physical benefits these actions provide, they also help increase a person's cognitive health since physical control is directly mediated by the brain. There have also been some studies that say these actions can improve working memory, though the results are still debatable.

One curious point here is the fact that there is no direct evidence to point to the physical activity involved in CTs as a direct source of the mood-enhancing effects that are attributed to such practices. A review in 2009 mentioned that even increasing the physical components of CTs don't correlate to actually increasing their mood-enhancing factors. This points to the fact that there are more important factors at play for those who wish to gain mental clarity from meditative practices. Also, it is noticeable that of all the CTs studied by various experts, only a select few actually have exercises significant enough to produce significant boosts in the physical makeup of a person.

Cardiovascular health, which is among the primary benefits of physical activity, is directly connected to the health of the vagus nerve. In the previous unity, we have already mentioned how cardiovascular health is inextricably linked to the vagus nerve, going so far as to determine a cardiovascular metric as a manifestation of the vagus nerve's health. While drowned out as a primary candidate for vagus nerve stimulation at least in the field of meditative practice, it is also interesting to note that activities that trigger increased cardiovascular excitement have their fair share in boosting the vagus nerve's health.

Before moving on to the next common denominator in CTs, let's pause for a moment to synthesize the different factors we have learned so far. Theorists have put forward separate ideas that serve as models determining the effectivity of CTs. Some of them have focused on the primacy of the CTs' focus on executive functions of the brain, pointing to these as the most useful aspect of developing the person. Others point to the synergy of mind and body, pointing to the superiority of mind-body movements coupled with exercises that focus on attention. There are researchers who encapsulate CTs as a form of "meditative movement". However, such researches may be faulted for relegating movement to simply motor coordination, almost completely omitting the aerobic benefits (however mild) that some CTs have.

TAKEAWAYS

- Contemplative Traditions hit the sweet spot on many different bodily issues. Incidentally, these same issues are also those touched upon by the vagus nerve, serving as the first hint towards their interconnectedness.
- There are various types of CTs, but they all have similar basic sets of rules. These rules then serve as the primary drivers of their effectiveness.
- When done properly, these rules complement each other to produce a snowball of health effects.

Chapter 6: Breathing, the Foundation of Life

"Breathing in, I am aware of my heart. Breathing out, I smile to my heart and know that my heart still functions normally. I feel grateful for my heart." -- Thich Nhat Hanh

We have saved the breathing discipline aspect of CTs for a separate chapter to highlight just how vital it is to the overall idea of meditative practice -- and also to highlight how it is the foundation of all that is vagus-stimulating in the practices we have highlighted so far.

You've already read how diaphragmatic breathing is a key to stimulating the vagus nerve, and you've also seen different techniques to induce such stimulation in a jiffy. But since we're going for a holistic system rather than a one-off technique, let's discuss breathing a little in-depth, and in the context of these contemplative traditions.

On top of the theories discussed in the preceding chapter, two researches (Gard, in 2014; Wayne and Kaptchuk, in 2008) have also put forward a breath-centric model to explain the ability of these CTs to induce wellbeing. The researches went on to describe the breathing patterns used in traditions studied to be "slow, deep, and diaphragmatic" -- just the exact combination needed for vagus nerve stimulation.

The breathing techniques are undoubtedly meant to slow down the respiratory cycle. For many traditions, the exhalations are much longer than the inhalations. The "focus" of breathing becomes the abdomen -- that is, the person should be conscious not of the air entering his nose and going down his chest cavity, but of the same air filling the lungs and the lungs pushing out the stomach. This is the "natural" breath, the type one can see in children and infants before they are conditioned by stress to take quick, shallow breaths. The only exceptions in CTs are some techniques that specifically use faster respiratory cycles, such as in a few yoga techniques. But these are in the minority. Some meditative traditions aim to make a synergy between these slower breaths and the movement of the body. In essence, the pace of the breathing is the foundation -- the rest of the body will follow.

Breathing, such a basic act, has been described in many a scientific literature -- but rarely in such a way that describes its role in the contemplative traditions. This is despite hard evidence showing that breathing is the single most effective factor in attaining the purported benefits of these meditative practices.

So let's take a look at what sparse evidence there is to see breathing in action. According to a 2008 study by Danucalov, there is an increased metabolism and oxygen absorption in the body during breathing exercises prescribed by yoga traditions (pranayamas). This is a surprising finding, since meditation usually invokes the idea of resting and relaxing.

Such breathing exercises studied included breathing in and holding the breath, then extending the exhalation as far as one can go. A 2009 study of the same set of pranayamas found that despite increased internal activity, there has been a registered drop in blood pressure for the subjects studied. There was also an accompanying reduction in heart rate. A more focused study on Sudarshan Kriya Yoga, also done in 2009, found a general activation of the parasympathetic nervous system to induce a rest-and-digest state, wresting control from the sympathetic nervous system.

Breathing by any other name

Some studies have also taken the breathing exercises out of the context of CTs and attempted to manipulate the regular breathing states of test subjects to see if they can influence the dials of the autonomic nervous system. A study, for example, quantifying the difference between normal (unconscious) breathing and diaphragmatic breathing found that the subjects had a reduced heart rate and a higher insulin content in the blood when they consciously breathed. Another study in 2001 found that a hypoxiated individual can oxygenate the blood faster by breathing in and out slowly rather than by regular breathing. These studies were duplicated in 2015, with the same results.

While there are a few researches with conflicting data, the bulk of the scientific facts currently available contend that conscious, diaphragmatic breathing -- the type espoused in a vast majority of CTs -- can on their own increase a person's wellbeing. The other techniques found in CTs are meant to build upon this vital bedrock, exploiting and multiplying its benefits.

Breathing Science: Linking it to the Vagus Nerve

Now, how exactly does the vagus nerve play a role in all these, especially in breathing? We know that the vagus nerve is stimulated by breathing, but where does it go from there?

To answer this, we need to look into a model called the Neurovisceral Integration Model. In this model, it is hypothesized that there is a bi-directional relationship between the autonomic functions of the nervous system and the cortices of the brain. The model posits a system called the "Central Autonomic Network", whose purpose it is to modulate the rest of the body's autonomic functions. The parts of the nervous system involved in this network then interface with the endocrine system (that collection of organs which are involved in secreting hormones to affect the other functions of the body). This interface is done through -- guess what -- the vagus nerve.

But the Neurovisceral Integration Model also suggests that the communication works both ways, and that the rest of the body, through the endocrine glands, can also communicate with the autonomic network through the vagus nerve. In effect, this creates a loop. The brain sends signals to the body, the body responds and sends feedback to the brain, which it then uses when sending another set of signals out. Other sequences are also possible, such as when the brain focuses on its executive functions and signals the body to relax.

Thus, a healthy and stimulated vagus nerve is both an indicator and a means of creating a sturdy link between a well-responding nervous system and a well-relaxed body.

To simplify things, breathing and CTs help stimulate and improve the overall wellbeing of the vagus nerve. This wellbeing, in turn, serves as the platform on which the body builds a working network of feedback and balance mechanisms. When done long enough, it is possible for these breathing practices and CTs to produce structural improvements in the autonomic network.

The Neurovisceral Integration Model also plays to the strengths of meditative practices. The stress-busting effects of mindfulness, for example, can be explained in terms of adjustments in the influences of external stimuli on the network. For example, an exaggerated response to a trigger may be reconsidered (and therefore be treated less as a stressor) by either reappraisal (top-down approach, stemming from the executive functions and moving down to the visceral level) or continued exposure (bottom-up approach, where visceral-level stimuli affect the executive function).

Boiling it all down

As we've mentioned, the reason we're going through all this trouble is so we could identify the most important factors that make contemplative traditions so much of a success, in an attempt to bring these lofty practices down to a level that can be called on at any time in our hectic lifestyle. Most contemplative traditions are steeped in philosophy, which can be a good avenue for a different type of learning and practice. But for those who just need to maintain vagus nerve health for daily wellbeing, something much more basic would suffice. Think of it as Cliff's Notes for contemplative practices. They can work on their own, but now that you know the science behind them, you can expound and make modifications whenever you wish.

Let's first take a look at the things we have distilled from our discourse into CTs, so far:
- Breathing is the central component of meditative practice, and the main stimulant for the vagus nerve. Slow breathing and slow exhalation is the most prevalent form in contemplative traditions.
- Awareness of the body, the mind, and the surroundings plays an important role in stimulating the vagus nerve by letting signals flow to various areas of the brain and body, in a way that makes new neural pathways or improves old ones.
- Physical activity is not a must, but it can also help build new neural pathways through the vagus nerve.

From these, we can now construct a new and more potent vagus nerve stimulation regimen.

TAKEAWAYS:

- Breathing is not just one of the most essential of bodily processes. Done right, breathing can also serve as the primary stimulant of the vagus nerve.
- Scientific studies have found that breathing not only helps relax the body, it also helps manage the various stimuli that enter our senses.

Chapter 7: Breath-Centric Stimulation

"To build may have to be the slow and laborious task of years. To destroy can be the thoughtless act of a single day." -- Winston Churchill

Contemplative traditions are very multi-modal, and they're not to blame. After all, if one seeks to attain purity in life, he would do well to occupy his time with useful stuff. Most meditative practices are made to occupy a man's time just enough so that he cannot be idle.

But this cannot apply to our daily lives. Today, we live in a world of perpetual avalanche. Everything just falls down endlessly, and to take time to breathe means to fall several steps behind. There have been very famous meditative techniques that invite a person to pause for at least a minute to "breathe in the present". But soon, that present becomes the past, and (with due respect to meditative schools that espouse the idea of the "eternal present") the time taken to meditate could just lead to further stress as one regrets the time he could have spent doing something.

This is not to disparage the contemplative arts. They are still highly recommended, and they can be truly life-changing experiences. But it would be difficult for the everyday salaryman -- the man most stressed, the man whose vagus nerve is most likely frayed beyond recognition -- to step away from the hamster wheel even for a moment. Thus the drive to create something that can be integrated seamlessly wherever one is, whenever one needs it.

And this has resulted in something *so* simple indeed that it would be harder not to use it in daily life.

"Bullet Time" Breathing

Here is a meditative technique where you do not need to stop whatever you're doing. You do have to slow down, to keep your breath in check, but at least you can balance your productivity with your vagal health.

It goes like this:
- Several times throughout the day -- as often as you need it, depending on your stress levels -- take one, big breath. This should be a breath that originates from the diaphragm, not from the chest cavity. Feel your diaphragm push your stomach out, and draw in as big a breath as possible. Then, exhale with force. This will serve as a mental cue of what happens next.
- For as long as you can afterwards, breathe in and out slowly. It is not necessary to count the seconds as you breathe in and out. Just be aware of the same sensation of air filling your lungs and of your diaphragm being pushed out. You don't need to

take your mind off your task at hand, either. Just relish the air going in and out, as slow as is comfortable. Note that your "slow" might still be fast at first, but constant practice will allow you to lengthen your breaths and lower your respiratory rate even further.

- As you do this, slow down in whatever task you are doing. The idea is to match the pace of your task to the pace of your breathing. If you are typing on your keyboard, for example, slow down just enough so that your fingers don't feel out of rhythm with your breath. If you are walking, slow down enough just so you could feel each breath. Here, you are making your breath the foundation of the moment -- and everything else afterwards is just an accessory to it. The slowing of your task is meant to provide as little distraction as possible to your breathing rhythm, since you are trying to maintain this for as long as possible.

- If you notice that you are breathing your normal pace again, that's okay -- you don't have to spend too much conscious effort trying to maintain your slow breathing. At first you won't last very long, but this will change with constant practice. It's even possible that constant practice will allow you to turn slow, diaphragmatic breathing into a normal habit! It is hence advisable that each time you notice that you're breathing fast again, to begin the process anew.

- If remembering to take that one big breath before you start slowing down is difficult, try setting an alarm or using different cues in your surroundings to remind you to take it slow. If your schedule permits it, you can also set something to guide your breathing as you enter this phase. A metronome, for example, could greatly help (make sure to set it on a slow beat). Other natural sounds such as the hum of the AC or the ticking of the wall clock may also be used as rough guides for breathing (just make sure not to follow the clock by the second -- the longer the interval the better).

Just like the iconic "bullet time" sequences in movies, this technique of slowing down carries with it just enough weight to let you see what may otherwise be imperceptible things (attention and affect), give you time to notice new things about old stuff (metacognitive recognition), allow you to observe your own motions by slowing down (bodily awareness, mixed with physical activity), all while exciting your vagus nerve through slow, diaphragmatic breathing.

Too Simple? Not Quite

There are those who would decry this type of technique as too simplistic, and not completely taking advantage of the many good things that true-blue meditation has to offer. And yet, it still ticks all the scientific checkboxes.

One may find it unusual that no special emphasis is given to maintaining the breath for a set period of time. In fact, the instructions are kind of vague when they talk about how long you should maintain the breathing pattern, and how slow it should be. But according to research of existing contemplative traditions, simply using the breath as an attentional focus will immediately yield changes in the respiratory rate. That is, a person who focuses on his breath will unconsciously slow it down. Deeper breaths automatically follow. The idea with the first conscious, deep breath is to set a template for the body to follow in its automated slowing down, while also conditioning the mind to be aware of the mechanics of deep breathing.

Another interesting fact about respiration-based vagus nerve stimulation is the fact that it is a bilateral process. This is as opposed to other vagus nerve stimulation systems, especially the electronic ones. Of all the vital functions in the body, breathing is the only one we have conscious control of, so any change in breathing pace would have a more profound effect on the whole body than any other conscious action. These effects can be classified into either direct or indirect functions:

Direct Function. Among the direct functions of "bullet time" breathing, mediated by the stimulated vagus nerve is the lowering of one's heart rate and blood pressure. This is due to the cardiorespiratory coupling through the vagus nerve previously discussed. This process is the one that famously reins in the sympathetic nervous system, and activates the anti-inflammatory pathways (with which, again, the vagus nerve is involved). This then helps reduce stress levels, and over time can increase cognitive control through the Central Autonomic Network.

Indirect function. After "bullet time" breathing has affected the nervous system, this relaxed nervous system would then send respiratory signals back to the lungs, this time signifying a low-threat scenario. Thus, the way one breathes is now being affected. The expansion of one's abdominal cavity to accommodate the lungs is more pronounced. This cycles back quickly to affect cardiopulmonary patterns. As the loop goes on, the anti-inflammatory effects of the parasympathetic nervous system are engaged, along with an increased cognitive control.

It is also to be remembered that this better breathing pattern causes an increase in the oxygen levels of the blood, thus providing more fuel for the brain and other organs. This also helps further sharpen the cognitive improvements charted from vagus nerve stimulation.

While the indirect route takes time to take hold, it is not any less important. In fact, the indirect functions are being investigated as the initiator of long-term improvements in vagal tone.

In contrast, other forms of stimulation would only result in one-dimensional improvements, and most of these are hardly sustainable. With "bullet time" breathing, however, it is possible to achieve all the long-term effects attributed to a healthy vagus nerve without needing to take precious time off your daily tasks. Such a routine can be carried out with minimal effort and can be squeezed into whatever you're doing. Whether you're indoors working on a project or outdoors making your way past the commute, you can take your sweet "bullet time" to get your life and your vagus nerve back in order.

TAKEAWAYS:

- Slowing down your breathing, and doing so in a mindful manner, is enough to get your daily vagus nerve exercise without taking time off work. The exercise filters all the best practices of contemplative traditions into a holistic yet unobtrusive process.
- "Bullet time" breathing exercises can be done as follows:
    - Take a deep diaphragmatic breath, and exhale with force.
    - Take all succeeding breaths as slowly as comfortably possible.
    - Try to maintain this breathing pattern. Slow down your movements by being synchronous with your breath.

Chapter 8: For that Quick Pick-Me-Up

"I don't fear death because I don't fear anything I don't understand. When I start to think about it, I order a massage and it goes away." -- Hedy Lamarr

There are times, though, when you might want a more sensory experience to wake up your vagus nerve. These may come at times when you quickly need energy, or when you need to perk up for an upcoming activity. As mentioned in the first part of the book, massage and reflexology can help stimulate the vagus nerve. But if you're all by yourself, you can also stimulate your vagus nerve through a massage.

In this chapter, we'll put together all we know about vagus nerve structure in order to create a routine massage you can use for a quick pick-me-up.

Step 1. Start from your collarbone. Put your fingertips in that fleshy part where your collarbone meets your neck, and massage upwards. You may increase the sensation by going for one side first, then the other.

Step 2. Place your fingers behind your earlobes, in that soft part right under the skull. Massage in a circular motion.

Step 3. From there, move your fingers downward. The target this time is the back of the neck, on either side. Massage the area slowly downwards.

Couple this massage routine with slow, diaphragmatic breathing, and you will feel relaxed. And yet, you will be energized enough to gain additional focus on the task at hand.

To cap it all off, you also need to mind your posture when performing your tasks. Man evolved an upright form not just in order to stand out from its fellow animals, but also to alleviate pressure in its internal organs — this includes nerves, such as the vagus.

A poor posture restricts the flow of information in the vagus nerve. This is especially prevalent when adopting a posture where the head juts forward or backward, thus putting pressure on the vagus nerve that goes out from the base of the skull. This can disrupt the nerve's functions, the most common effect of which is poor digestion and difficulty in breathing.

Today's gadget-dominated lifestyle has increased the risk of incorrect posture more than ever, that for some people their default posture is already broken. If you are among these, it might be good to visit a physical therapist for corrective therapy.

TAKEAWAYS:
- A "vagus nerve massage" is a good way to get your vagus nerve perked up immediately for those times when you need to perform harder.

- Proper posture is also important in maintaining vagus nerve health.

PART 3:

The Future of Vagus Nerve Stimulation

Thus far, we have gone through the current state of knowledge and technology with regards to vagus nerve stimulation, though we have ventured into some theoretical discussions along the way. This time around, let's focus on the theory and emerging fields of research in the topic of vagus nerve stimulation. What exactly does the future hold?

Chapter 9: The Vagus Nerve Versus the World

"I never think of the future - it comes soon enough." -- Albert Einstein

Aside from the vagus nerve, there is perhaps one other discovery on the nervous system that has shocked the scientific community, allowing research to strike off in new dimensions that could have unprecedented fruits. This is the fact that the brain is not a permanent blob of neurons -- that is, it can be molded and reprogrammed almost at will.

Now, we have the magical vagus nerve, and scientists are quick to make the link between the nerve and the brain's plasticity. Now, new avenues of research are looking into the vagus nerve as a means of engaging this ability of the brain to reshape itself.

This idea is the foremost being brought to bear on the topic of neurological diseases. Preliminary research has found that the brain's plasticity can be triggered by the norepinephrine and acetylcholine bursts that the vagus nerve excites. Thus, VNS is being looked at as a safer and more effective means of healing the brain.

It's a Plastic World

The concept of plasticity is straightforward enough. When the environment changes, the brain has the ability to change its "form", pretty much like a plastic can take on different shapes depending on the mold. Such plasticity can be called on for all kinds of tasks, from something as mundane as learning something new to something as staggering as recovering after a comatose or a debilitating injury. There had been reports of people waking up after years of coma, after their brains rewired themselves to go around the damaged portions. This is, so far, the upper limit of brain plasticity that we have registered.

Currently, the concept of plasticity is also being applied to treat all kinds of disorders. For one, there's the case of amputees who experience phantom limbs and phantom pain. Certain therapeutic methods are used to help rewire the brain's maladaptive behavior, helping it "realize" that the part of the body a small section of it is serving has been severed. This reorganization of the brain is usually induced through a variety of means, but in the future it is hoped that vagus nerve stimulation will play a part in making the process faster.

The same idea has been thought of as a possible research point in the treatment of tinnitus, which like phantom limbs perceives that something is there (this time, sound) when in reality there is none. As of the time of this writing, research is still lacking the correct neural map that the vagus nerve needs to stimulate in order for the renormalization process to proceed.

The Vagus Nerve as a Helping Hand

According to some studies, the existence of transmission in the brain can either promote or inhibit its ability to create new neural pathways. By "transmission", we mean the presence of chemicals that are associated with mental activity, such as norepinephrine and acetylcholine -- the two neuromodulatory transmission agents induced by the vagus nerve.

The lack of such transmission agents has been found to reduce the brain's ability to reorganize itself as needed by its surroundings. This comes up as a problem not only during moments of neurological damage, but also during times when the brain needs to adapt to external stimuli (such as when we are learning something new). Studies have observed the loss of plasticity in such wide-ranging mental functions as seeing and movement.

On the other hand, the presence of transmission agents in the brain have been found to enhance its plasticity. Some experiments have tried directly injecting acetylcholine to the brain during certain activities, and the brain responded accordingly by making minuscule adjustments in the spot. Over time, this resulted in better performance in test tasks. Like in inhibition, such effects have been observed in wide ranging functions, which have also included seeing and movement. It has also been found that when the brain already has previous experience performing the tasks being boosted thanks to the presence of neurological transmission agents, such experience can be brought to bear in helping the brain strengthen its newfound connections.

The same principles have also been studied in brain activities that do not demand immediate action, such as in learning new concepts and theories. Research has found that the same level of plasticity can be leveraged during the acquisition phase, or that part where the brain collects all the necessary information to learn something new.

Oddly enough, the effect seems to fade during the consolidation phase, or when the brain actually tries to store all the gathered bits of information. From this, we can infer that the presence of neurological transmitters could increase one's ability to gather new information and store it as temporary memories (the amygdala, where short-term knowledge is stored, has been shown to be especially active in this stage) but whether or not the same information can be recalled after some time depends on other factors entirely.

This is very exciting news, as we are now seeing the birth of vagus nerve stimulation as applied in learning and training. While the above-mentioned example has included the technique of directly injecting neurotransmitters into the brain as a sort of supplement, such an approach is impractical in everyday life. The only other alternative is to use the nervous system itself to stimulate the production of the same chemicals. And -- you guessed it right -- this can be done through stimulation of the vagus nerve.

Your Brain, the SSD

In the world of technology, we have created storage devices that have increasingly faster read/write speeds. Solid State Drives (SSDs) for example have unprecedented access speeds, allowing us to store and retrieve data faster than ever before. Wouldn't it be nice if our brains could also attain greater access speeds, so we can store stuff better and faster?

But this has been found to be almost possible now, thanks to an outcrop of the research above. Simply put, there has also been evidence that plasticity can be used as a driving force to "control" memory.

The vagus nerve is also responsible for relaying information from the peripheral nervous system to the central nervous system. It relays two types of data -- one is "good" data, which soothes the brain (the feeling of satiety, or the feeling of relaxation, for example) and the other one is "bad" data (the feeling of stress, or the feeling of inflammation). These bits of information are then used by the central nervous system to help build memories on.

Because of this, an arm of research has also been thrust towards the idea of controlling memory through nerve relays and the transmission of this peripheral data. The extent is not yet completely known, but the vagus nerve has been showing participation in a lot of neuromodulatory tasks involved in the induction of plasticity in the brain. Electrical stimulation has already been shown to increase the activity of plasticity-driving chemicals in the vagus nerve. In the same experiments, a different link was also established -- without the presence of enough neuromodulators in the brain, even electronic stimulation would not have much of an effect in changing the behavior of the central nervous system through the vagus nerve. This points to the primacy of more natural methods of stimulation that rely on a healthy vagus nerve, not just one that electronically beats it into submission. The "bullet time" breathing technique described above makes for a good candidate for natural interventions to create the environment for such a healthy vagus nerve.

The Vagus Nerve as a Neurosurgeon

We have already touched upon the possible use of vagus nerve stimulation as a means of curing such conditions as tinnitus and phantom limbs, but if we are to push the boundaries of its ability to control plasticity then we might as well apply them to much more serious diseases. Among them is the dreaded stroke.

Stroke can be so debilitating that around 85% of stroke patients suffer from some sort of impairment in the upper limbs. Strokes cause a blockage in the blood flow to the brain, thus leading to cell death in the motor cortex. This death interferes with other motor-related circuitries, therefore leading to impairments in coordination and motor function.

As of this moment, there are no clear ways to reverse the effects of stroke. The only hope is to do therapy in order to regain some of the lost movement, and to hope that the brain heals itself. Now that the ability of the vagus nerve to induce plasticity has been uncovered, researchers are now looking at VNS coupled with motor therapy in order to help rewire the brain and regain complete motor function. Earlier research (from as far back as 2001) had revealed that the brain can reorganize its motor cortex much faster when VNS is used together with therapy. Tare are no known studies yet done on stroke patients, but this just remains part of the unexplored potentials of vagus nerve.

What other debilitating neurological issues can you think of? Some diseases likely to come to mind would be Parkinson's and spinal cord injury. And yes, both of these can also be helped by the vagus nerve's ability to stimulate neuroplasticity. The idea comes directly from the nerve's ability to help in the therapeutic treatment of stroke, and though the pathology of the three conditions are far apart from each other, the future ability to perform targeted plastic therapy can greatly promote healing by engaging undamaged circuitry in the brain. Brain damage due to trauma may also be helped by the same technique.

Aside from curing physical ailments, plasticity may also be invoked to help those with a cognitive disorder. These include those suffering from anxiety, stress, PTSD, and the other issues we have discussed earlier. This can also be extended to cover such issues as drug addiction, bipolar disorder, schizophrenia, and ADHD. While these are all issues with widely differing pathological origins, they all have a common denominator — they all include some form of cognitive issue, coupled with maladaptive plasticity. The entry of VNS in the field of possible treatments for these issues mark another landmark, and that is the attempt to address the underlying pathological issues of these illnesses. For a long time, treatment for these have also been symptomatic and their complex origins are undermanaged. Now, we have a way to try and fix how the brain works by fixing it through its own terms. As a plus, VNS might just be that flexible treatment platform which could address the special need for less regimented strategies for these health issues.

Note that this is not something of a magical cure to otherwise debilitating diseases. The idea of inducing neuroplasticity does not mean the brain can immediately repair itself. It is a mere boost to the usual process of therapy and recovery. Yes, it has the potential to drastically cut the time needed for recuperation, but there is still a huge gap between existing research and actual results.

One of the more pressing research questions is, just how much vagus nerve stimulation is needed to induce plasticity. The word is not yet final, but what we have is pretty encouraging.

Just add a pinch of VNS

According to recent findings, the frequency that's needed in vagus nerve stimulation for the process to be helpful in inducing plasticity is lower than the currently approved frequencies used in vagus nerve stimulating machines. As we have discussed in earlier, some of these machines deliver frequencies that can be felt by the user. For the most part, the sensation is tolerable, and one can easily grow into it. However, it would still be better if the frequency is left under the radar.

Studies have found that the current needed to induce plasticity via VNS is about 100 times less than that which is advocated in current protocols. This is foreseen to have fewer side effects. This same level of current has also been tested for the improvement of motor control through plasticity, and it is also the current used to help stroke victims during experiments of VNS use for recovery.

This, however, does not discount the possibility that the current recommended level of intensity for other applications of VNS (such as epilepsy and depression, where one needs a 30 Hertz pulse every 5 minutes, each one lasting for 30 seconds) would remain. There are other benefits from increased stimulation, such as the increase of neurotransmitters which could help drive other benefits not achievable with lower stimulation levels. Then, there is also the difference in the natures of plasticity-targeting VNS and existing commercial electronic VNS. For the latter, stimulation becomes more effective after a prolonged exposure. Meaning the issue being treated becomes more responsive to the pulses. For plasticity, however, the effect lasts only for as long as the stimulation is applied. This means VNS will have to be done at the moment it is needed, as the effect wears off immediately after.

As of the time of writing, researchers are yet to be able to map the exact frequencies needed to induce specific effects. When such a mapping is done, it would be much easier to customize frequencies as needed for electronic stimulation.

On Demand Sensory Relief

We've already discussed how the vagus nerve helps mediate pain and inflammation, and how stimulation can help eliminate these issues. Moving on from this knowledge, we can also look into the possibility of the vagus nerve as a means of controlling sensory perception and curing sensory dysfunction.

ain may be an important indicator of danger to limb, but it is at the core a type of sensory dysfunction. Vagus nerve stimulation may be just the perfect tool to remove the use of potentially addictive oral medication from the pain treatment equation, and it is also an ideal tool to help "normalize" sensations received elsewhere in the body. Sensory dysfunctions can be anywhere from irritating to debilitating (from phantom pain and itches to phantom limbs) and the vagus nerve can help reduce the intensity of dysfunctions so they don't drown out normal sensory input.

The Vagus Nerve as a Health Barometer

By now, you should be able to link a huge variety of health issues to the vagus nerve. You might mean it as a tongue-in-cheek idea, but you're not really far from the truth — at least according to a concept paper completed and published in 2018. It turns out that the vagus nerve is indeed THAT tied to overall health that its activity can be used as a barometer of wellbeing, sans the presence of communicable diseases.

This runs through the whole gamut of the Global Burden of Diseases (GBD, and yes that is an actual term), from cardiovascular diseases, to pulmonary issues, to cancer. Despite a disparity in their origins, it is possible to distill their roots to reveal a set of lifestyle factors (think stress, diet, and vice). The paper leverages known neuro-immunology data to use the vagus nerve as a predictor of the onset of such diseases.

According to the paper, the vagus nerve's connection to the front of the brain makes it related to an individual's conscious decision to make unhealthy lifestyle choices (which ultimately leads to diseases in the GBD). High activity of the vagus nerve, read through a high HRV, has been found to predict a reduced risk of GBD illnesses. The same level of activity has also been seen to increase one's hopes of bouncing back when beset with such a disease.

The paper also shows high hopes that this understanding of the vagus nerve can help alleviate not just the symptoms but also the roots of these GBDs, and advocates additional study on populations that have these illnesses.

The Vagus Nerve as an Antiseptic

Sepsis, stemming from bacterial infection of the body, is a huge medical problem. The issue arises for a multitude of reasons, and while medicine has made incredible headway in addressing septic issues, it still remains a multi-billion dollar thorn on the side of modern medical practice. But, maybe, advances in vagus nerve research can help stop the scourge once and for all.

We already know that the vagus nerve has mechanisms that allow for the control of inflammation, allowing the body's parasympathetic nervous system to soothe symptoms. But this is just the top of the iceberg. Research has showed that the same mechanism has pushed back the progress of sepsis in a number of patients, by regulating the release of the body's natural defenses against such infections. The increase in acetylcholine triggered by the activity of the vagus nerve has allowed the body to launch a chemical counteroffensive against the invading bacteria, stopping the spread of infection even without the use of pharmaceuticals.

These findings are especially important in the case of neonatal sepsis, or the type of infection that causes a significant mortality rate among newborns. These infants have underdeveloped immune system, making the very susceptible targets for infection. At the same time, they do not have built-in tolerance for a wide variety of pharmaceuticals, so a drug-free way to control infection is much sought after. The only blocker right now is the development of a device or technique that will allow newborns to have enough VNS to push back infection without using implants.

The research that made these findings had another, curious result. They found that the same vagus nerve stimulation needed to reduce infection has also been the same stimulation needed to arrest various breathing problems associated with preterm infants! When understood further, VNS techniques could knock a huge chunk off infant mortality rates. Later on, the same studies could be extrapolated for adults, too. And in a way, there have been similar attempts...

Breathing In Vagus Nerve Benefits

We've discovered how the vagus nerve can trigger the brain to release self-healing (essentially, self-transforming) chemicals, but that's not the only major organ that can benefit from the vagus nerve's wonders.

Recently, VNS has also been looked into for the treatment of lung injury — specifically one induced by ventilators during hospital confinement, whose pressure could rupture the alveoli (the little grape-like air sacs in the lungs that allow oxygen to transfer to the bloodstream). These same injuries are also often accompanied by sepsis, resulting in pulmonary inflammation.

Being one of the main organs affected by the vagus nerve, the lungs benefit greatly from the vagus nerve's ability to reduce inflammation. By regulating this inflammatory response, the nerve also makes way for the healing process that results in a significantly faster recovery rate. The process, however, has only been proven effective in tandem with pharmaceutical interventions.

Of course, if the lung can benefit from its connection to the vagus nerve, then the gut — significantly more connected to the vagus nerve as a sort of second brain — should also benefit. This is proven by some research, which found that gut and lunch injuries can be treated together in a "two birds with one stone" approach. There have been some studies that show how most septic issues in lung injuries are caused by bacteria breaking through the intestinal walls and getting into the lungs. Such movement is arrested by the vagus nerve's ability to regulate the permeability of the gut. This regulation of gut permeability has a role to play as well in the prevention of other gut-related diseases, though this field still needs more study.

"Will Vagus Stimulation Work For Me?"

As the vagus nerve moves from being an object of interest to becoming an actual point of cure, people will start answering whether or not vagus nerve stimulation will be the right treatment platform for them. In the recent past, the simple answer was "we'll never know until we try." However, thanks to a recent slew of research, scientists have uncovered a possible way to assess the future effects of VNS on a person.

We've already covered the idea of Heart Rate Variability (HRV) and how it can be gleaned from one's ECG results. But the vagus nerve's primary connection is to the brain, so it's only conceivable that there are external telltale signs pointing to the vagus nerve if we observe the brain.

According to a study concluded just this May 2019. measuring the reactivity of the patient's EEG results could point to whether or not he will be responsive to VNS treatment. These EEG scans are taken during the routine preoperative stages. By observing the dynamics and activity of the EEG results of a set of patients, the researchers were able to create a predictive formula that discerns one's possible VNS response by anywhere from 80% to

90% accuracy. While the model needs to be subjected to more rigorous tests by the scientific community, this could usher in a new era for VNS treatment by letting doctors determine the people most likely to benefit from these revolutionary treatment techniques. Remember that, at least for more serious cases of depression and epilepsy where one needs to be implanted with a VNS device, there are still possible complications that may arise from the operating process despite the relative safety of the stimulations themselves. By choosing likely candidates for success from the get-go, it is possible to determine whether the chances of success are well worth the risk of going under the knife. Think of it as a skin test of a whole new level.

TAKEAWAYS:

- Future avenues of vagus nerve research open up new possibilities. In the future, it may be possible to foretell one's health status and predisposition to diseases through the vagus nerve. It might also be possible to cure erstwhile incurable conditions of the brain and nervous system. For healthy individuals, future techniques and studies may be used to improve brain performance drastically.

- It will also be possible to foretell just how effective vagus nerve treatment on a person will be, thus better assessing risks versus potential rewards.

Chapter 10: New Devices for New Techniques

"With the new day comes new strength and new thoughts." -- Eleanor Roosevelt

Back in the day, the idea of operating on a person was a horrid experience. You just need to Google for images of operations back in the 1800s to fully appreciate the horror. Stil, the idea of manipulating the human body from the inside in order to promote health was a novel concept with an amazing breadth of applications, so physicians embraced the process.

Of course, progress soon followed, and techniques have improved drastically. Nowadays, it is possible — common, even — to go under the knife in the morning and walk out of the hospital in time for lunch. New techniques merited the creation of new devices, and this is something that can be seen as well for these developments in vagus nerve stimulation. After all, the vagus nerve represents the modern equivalent of "manipulating from the inside" in order to promote health.

True to Form

One of the most common issues with current vagus nerve stimulation implants is the latter's inherent inflexibility. The electrodes that interface with the vagus nerve are rigid, whereas the nerve itself is not. The problem is also present in other neuromodulating implants, where the electrodes may rub against the nerve and cause damage during movement. There have been reports of such implants causing damage to the axons of the nerves, the part where the transmission of neural signals from one nerve fiber to another happens. Manufacturing electrodes that fit the vagus nerve precisely would also be difficult and impractical, since everyone's measure is completely different.

To get around this, a team of Chinese researchers have created a type of electrode that takes inspiration from the climbing ability of vines and some other plants. Using a type of "memory metal", which changes shape under certain conditions (usually heat or electricity), the researchers have been able to create a type of electrode that conforms to the individual shape of the person's vagus nerve. This means doctors can now create implants that do not pose the threat of mechanical damage to the person's nerves. It would still take some time before this process is refined, and mass-produced. However, this would represent a huge leap in electronic VNS.

Perhaps an advancement that would hit the market sooner would be the new microelectrodes that researchers hope can deliver better therapeutic value by fine-tuning which parts of the vagus nerve will be targeted. These microelectrodes have the potential to stimulate just a very specific part of the nerve, connected to a specific function. This is expected to reduce side effects as much as possible.

In 2018, a team of researchers have created a different use for microelectrodes. The current model of VNS using electrodes is by sticking the electrodes into the nerve itself, and delivering electronic impulses from there. This necessitates a fairly complicated operation procedure. Instead of this, the team created a type of "wraparound system" using microwires that hug the vagus nerve instead of going through it. Fixed in place then insulated, this technique achieves a small footprint and allows for good contact even during the patient's movement. Perhaps more importantly, the technique can be potentially applied on awake patients without the need for a general anesthesia. Thus, in the future, it would indeed be possible to have a microwire planted into your vagus nerve in the morning, and you can still make it to your favorite place for lunch.

Mapping the Vagus Nerve

Another challenge, directly related to VNS (especially if we're talking about microelectrodes) is the inherent complexity of the vagus nerve. While we have a rough idea of which part activates what, we still do not have enough data on the vagus nerve's internal workings.

A Stanford study back in 2018 seeks to remedy this, and in a big way. Earlier in this book, we described how cytokines help relay neural signals from one part of the vagus nerve to another. The Stanford researchers used these cytokines as a type of marker that would enable them to map the way neural signals in the vagus nerve work. This opens up a way for future researchers to map the way signals weave their way through the vagus nerve, and (coupled with a knowledge of how these signals are transmitted chemically through cytokines) to potentially intervene with these signals to drive a certain outcome.

TAKEAWAYS:
- Using futuristic shape metals, microelectrodes, and more could usher in an era of safer and more effective vagus nerve stimulation.
- In the same vein, efforts to map the transmissions of the vagus nerve can also greatly improve the effect of stimulations.

CHAPTER 11: Paying It Forward

"Who will take responsibility for raising the next generation?" -- Ruth Bader Ginsburg

Let's face it — most of the issues we have today (health-wise, at least) stem from our upbringing and our adjustment to the modern world. Everything from stress to illness is a by-product of our fast-changing world, a world that we are forced to live in before we actually come to know how to *properly* do so.

This is the same issue with many of the issues that touch the vagus nerve and its complex network. Everything from poor diet and vice, to bad posture, to shallow and hasty breathing, is an adaptation to the world — and pretty ineffective ones, too. Unless we put a stop to the factors that inhibit the proper functioning of the vagus nerve (and thus the whole body), the effects will snowball to the next generation. And this generation will have a much more difficult time as the effects of vagus nerve impairment is felt with greater force.

An essential part of growing up

Nowhere are the myriad functions of the vagus nerve more pronounced than in infancy, when the body is still developing the advanced functions that will come into full play as an adult. During infancy, the vagus nerve has been found to be associated not just with physical development, but also with socioemotional development.

In experiments, the vagus nerve of term infants were stimulated through massage therapy. The researchers have found that this produces gastric motility, which helped drive weight gain and therefore growth. Aside from massage therapy, however, the researchers have found a different way to stimulate infantile vagus nerves — close proximity to and positive interactions with their mothers. In contrast, low vagal activity has been recorded for those infants whose mothers are depressed, angry, or anxious. Infants later found out to be autistic also showed low vagus nerve stimulation even when in a synchronous activity with their mothers.

This caused the researchers to look into the vagus nerve's involvement in the emotional growth of a child. It has been found that the more active the vagus nerve is, the more mature the overall structure of the autonomic nervous system is. Furthermore, when the vagus nerve activity is compared across a sample of term and preterm infants, it has been found that those with a higher vagal activity in infancy ended up to have better social skills, mental processing abilities, and motor skills. In contrast, those with low vagal stimulation during infancy were more likely to have less competence in the aforementioned factors. These have been followed up to school age, and the results are mostly constant. What's even more surprising is that using vagus nerve activity as a predictor for these factors ended up a much more accurate measure than other birth metrics such as birth weight, family health history, and even the economic status of the child's family. The researchers went one step further and tried to measure the vagus nerve activity of infants in the 36 to 40-month gestation period (done by observing a pattern of respiration and heartbeat in the fetuses) and found that the same conclusion holds.

VNS Should Start in Youth

It's one thing to try and raise a child to understand the importance of the vagus nerve and its effects to body, and another to try and insulate him from the vagus-tearing factors that persist in the outside world. How much one tries to do either or both will depend on his parenting style. One might want to teach a child how to do "bullet time" breathing when stressed, and another might increase the child's intake of vagus nerve-friendly food.

But while what happens at home is up to the parents, what happens in hospitals should be regulated by doctors and scientific evidence. And all evidence points to the fact that the vagus nerve plays a very important role in the wellbeing of a child, so much that its assessment and stimulation should be standard process in the battery of medical tests and procedures a child undergoes.

The aforementioned study looked at the case of preterm infants and those with low vagal stimulation, and found that techniques such as kangaroo care (close contact between mother and child) and massage therapy are effective and non-intrusive means of stimulating the vagus nerve. When these interventions were done, preterm infants showed a rapid maturation of vagal activity. Other aspect of infant life were also affected. The study noted that those who received kangaroo care ended up having longer hours of quiet, peaceful sleep and better alertness during waking hours. The periods of restless, active sleep were also reduced. The same study, done in Korea, also noted that infants receiving tactile and kinesthetic massage had increased levels of vagus nerve activation compared to those who did not receive such an intervention. Upon follow up studies, the researchers found the massage group to have grown more alert, more attentive, and more organized than their peers. They also had less instances of being underweight — back in 2007, a study detailing the effect of vagus nerve stimulation in infants noted that even without consuming more calories, infants who underwent VNS had better weight gain than others.

To drive home the importance of vagus nerve stimulation as a part of child development, a correlation was also drawn by the study between speech development and vagal activity. According to records, a child that has better vagal activity is more likely to exhibit a wide array of positive emotions. This child is also more likely to vocalize earlier and more actively than his peers. They were also found to have better temperament than others.

It is also to be noted that the success of vagal stimulation on infants depends greatly on the vagal tone of the mothers as well. A mother who has a low vagal tone is very likely to pass the same to her child during face-to-face interactions. Children born of mothers who are depressed, for example, have been found to have elevated levels of cortisol — the stress hormone that activates the sympathetic nervous system as a response to perceived threats or pressure in the environment. And note that this happens at a time when the child should have no concept yet of stress! The elevated cortisol levels are also combined with a decreased level of dopamine and serotonin. Since the vagus is also responsible for innervating the facial nerve, one can easily see how an infant reflects a mother's blank facial expression.

To the Land Before Birth

Perhaps even more shocking than these findings is the fact that researchers have found a link between a mother's low vagus nerve stimulation before her child's birth, and a similarly low vagus nerve activation of the child upon birth. Specifically, those expectant mothers who have a high level of anxiety or anger during the second trimester of pregnancy appear to pass on their vagal tones to their children. This has been attributed to the tendency of infants to mimic the biochemical profiles of their mother while in development. The infants are consequently born with low serotonin and dopamine levels, and high epinephrine and cortisol levels. In effect, they are born anxious, depressed, and angry!

The idea that one could "fix" these issues after birth is also met with difficulty. According to a separate research, the vagus nerve shows the most active myelinization rates during the first nine months of life — inside the mother's womb. While the child is still unborn, the myelinization process already "bakes" preset neural pathways in his vagus nerve, therefore preconditioning himm to certain responses. If these myelinated pathways are the wrong ones, you would have a child that is already preconditioned to have low vagal activity.

The message is clear. For us adults, all these talk about vagus nerve stimulation could either give us a better shot at wellbeing, or could maintain that wellbeing. But for children, vagus nerve stimulation could literally define the rest of their lives. Sure, there are individual differences, and the vagus nerve may not be a 100% accurate system of predicting a child's development. But to argue that, we would be entering into a theory that spans a vast multitude of systems. Some of these systems can be completely out of our control, such as the social order and physical environment in which we choose to raise our children. But that does not take away the fact that the vagus nerve *is* among the many systems at play, and at least this one can be controlled.

One could continue arguing that a child's future will in fact be determined by how we choose to raise them, but consider this. Children with subpar vagus nerve activity are often found to be more difficult to handle during the formative years. In effect we have children who already have fundamental biochemical and neurological issues to begin with, and now we are faced with the added difficulty of correcting the possible issues *while* these same issues make it more difficult to do so.

Perhaps the most important thing the current generation can do right now is to become more aware of the importance of the vagus nerve, and how it relates to one's growth and progress. If that can be done, then the future generations would be less exposed to the vagus-busting trends that so dominate the world today. We all want to raise a generation that is better-equipped to handle the world's evolving problems, and we could greatly increase our chances if we could raise a vagus-friendly environment for our children.

TAKEAWAYS:
- The vagus nerve plays a critical role in the physical and emotional growth of infants, along with how successful they will be in social situations as they grow up. The higher the vagal tone, the better one's chances of growing up without deep-seated socio-emotional troubles.
- Given this fact, vagus nerve stimulation should start at infancy, and vagus nerve assessment should be a part of every infant assessment.

Conclusion

If I had told you at the start that there is one nerve in the body whose activity effectively controls our destinies, perhaps you wouldn't have believed me. In fact, it would still be hard to believe up until now, if not for the wealth of scientific resources one can find about this topic. There is a huge body of research on disparate topics, all joined together only by the fact that the vagus nerve has something to do with them.

Perhaps it's a good time to really appreciate the wonder and complexity of the human body. Many of us had been taught of the body as a sort of computer where the brain is the central processing unit, the heart is the battery, and the lungs and gut the power cords connecting us to the power supply that is food, water, and air. But the human body is instead an intricate and highly organic system, where even the mighty brain takes cues from the rest of the body. Every organ system has a hand in determining the next steps for the body, and somewhere in that great switchboard of information, the vagus nerve sits trying to sort everything out.

This book has taken you through the whole gamut of research and details on the vagus nerve. By now, you should know pretty much everything there is to know about it, from its anatomy to its myriad of functions, from harnessing it for overall health to the issues that it can address in the near future.

But if there is one piece of info that you should never forget out of all that you have read, it is this: the vagus nerve is just a part of a network, a vast network of feedback and control, of input and assessment that we have not yet completely explored and mapped. With all these information on the vagus nerve, it would be so easy to spend all your time trying to stimulate your vagus nerve to its optimal tone. Now, all that's good, but it's still just a part of the overall equation of health.

Remember that the vagus nerve does not just relay information from the brain to the rest of the body. It also actively picks up information from the rest of the body, sending it up to the brain. While one can (in the light of all the research we covered) make the assertion that a person can only be as healthy as his vagus nerve, it would be more accurate to say that the vagus nerve could only be as healthy as the organ surrounding it.

You could have a perfectly functioning active vagus nerve... but you may still develop various illnesses thanks to your lifestyle choices. You may still be a victim of one of the GBDs. Note that while vagus stimulation can ward off certain issues, the vagus nerve is more or less just a mirror reflecting your state of overall health when it comes to other illnesses. It's so easy to confuse these two concepts. Stimulating your vagus nerve can't (at least not yet) cure cancer, but this cancer can show important signs when viewed through the vagus nerve.

In short, take care of the vagus nerve as much as you need — do the "bullet time" breathing exercises (or take a deep look at the contemplative traditions if you have time), fix your diet, do a routine vagal massage, and perk up your posture. But don't neglect the rest of the body, too. When you feel that something is wrong with a different part of the body, seek ways to cure it independently of vagus stimulation — but let the stimulation continue as a means of augmenting whatever other remedy you may use.

Observing the vagus nerve up close shows us a very important lesson, too. We are exposed to the idea that what we know about the slew of diseases affecting the world might just be the tip of the iceberg. With all the in-depth research we have, we are just gradually becoming more and more aware of just how interconnected things are, and how seemingly disparate things can actually be deeply related because of an overarching factor. Who knew that a reading in the EEG could predict whether or not you are likely to suffer from depression? Who knew that stimulating something other than the brain could help the brain repair itself from stroke? Who knew that the word "gut feel" actually has scientific backing, since the gut indeed talks to the brain? Who knew that the microbial flora in one's gut could even affect how moody a person can be?

One can only imagine the surprise of the first people who discovered the wonders of the vagus nerve. Today, that wonder lives on in the people who have had the opportunity to explore the powers of this twin bundle of nerve fibers winding its way through the human body. Just do a cursory search online and you will be seeing a lot of articles hailing the vagus nerve as the body's best kept secret to health, a holy grail of cures.

But again, be careful of such labeling. The vagus nerve isn't the holy grail — the human body, as a whole, is. We haven't even mapped the entirety of the vagus nerve yet, and science is still busy trying to find the best way to tame and stimulate it. But who knows if, in the future, we find some specific part of the vagus nerve — or a different part of the body, for that matter — that will concentrate all the nerve's powers into a smaller area? And then another one before that? The search for "the secret" will always continue, but never take your eyes off the fact that the body is a holistic system, meant to function as a whole.

Just like the meditative masters of old, may the knowledge you gained about the vagus nerve serve as building blocks on which you can build something synergistic — something that really is at one with the body and everything that is around it.

Thank you

Before you go, I just wanted to say thank you for purchasing my book.

You could have picked from dozens of other books on the same topic but you took a chance and chose this one.

So, a HUGE thanks to you for getting this book and for reading all the way to the end.

Now I wanted to ask you for a small favor. **Could you please consider posting a review on the platform? Reviews are one of the easiest ways to support the work of authors.**

This feedback will help me continue to write the type of books that will help you get the results you want. So if you enjoyed it, please let me know.

www.ingramcontent.com/pod-product-compliance
Lightning Source LLC
Chambersburg PA
CBHW082027120526
44592CB00039B/2515